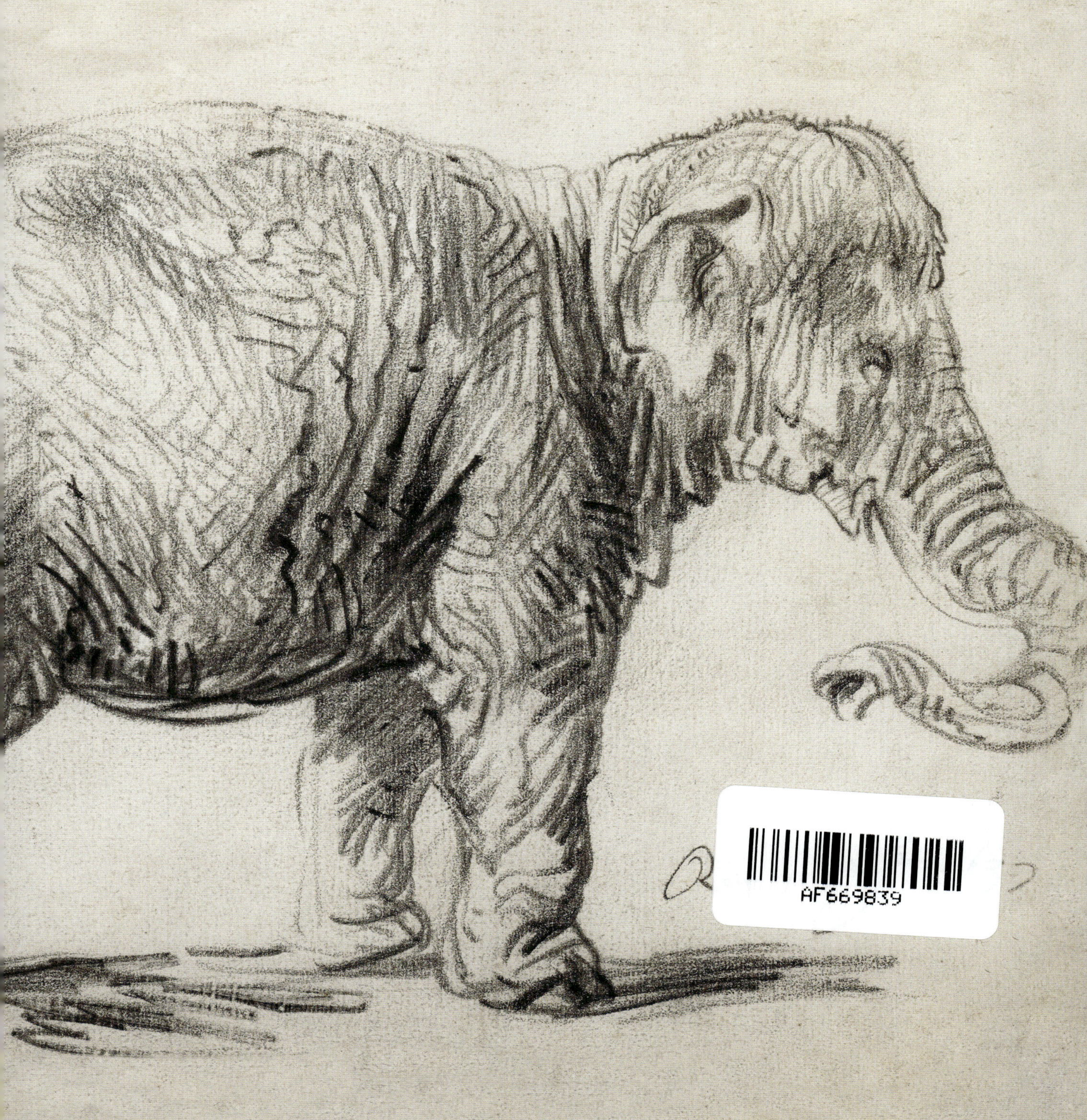

AF669839

Seymour Slive

The Drawings of Rembrandt

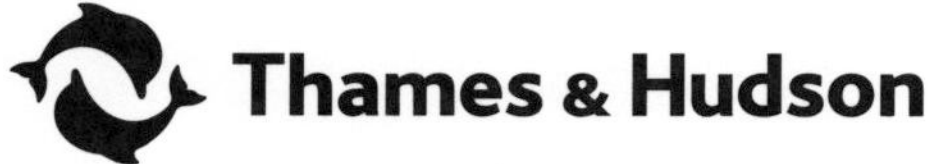

Cover image credits
Front cover: *Sheet of Drawings for "Saint John the Baptist Preaching,"* ca. 1634–35.
Kupferstichkabinett, Staatliche Museen, Berlin, inv. KdZ 5243. Photo: Bildarchiv Preussischer Kulturbesitz/Art Resource, N.Y. Photographer: Jörg P. Anders.
Back cover: *Sheet of Studies of Heads and Three Sketches of a Woman Holding an Infant*, ca. 1635.
Photo © The Barber Institute of Fine Arts, University of Birmingham/The Bridgeman Art Library.

Unless otherwise noted, the illustrations have been provided by their owners and are reproduced by their permission.

First published in the United Kingdom in 2009 by
Thames & Hudson Ltd, 181A High Holborn,
London WC1V 7QX

This paperback edition first published in 2019

© 2009 J. Paul Getty Trust

Getty Publications
1200 Getty Center Drive, Suite 500
Los Angeles, California 90049-1682
www.getty.edu

All Rights Reserved. No part of this publication may be reproduced or transmitted in any form or by any means, electronic or mechanical, including photocopy, recording or any other information storage and retrieval system, without prior permission in writing from the publisher.

British Library Cataloguing-in-Publication Data
A catalogue record for this book is available from the British Library

ISBN: 978-0-500-29535-9

Printed and bound in China

To find out about all our publications, please visit **www.thamesandhudson.com**.
There you can subscribe to our e-newsletter, browse or download our current catalogue, and buy any titles that are in print.

CONTENTS

ACKNOWLEDGMENTS

MY FIRST DEBT OF GRATITUDE is to Otto Benesch for his illustrated six-volume corpus of Rembrandt drawings, which appeared in 1954–57 and was enlarged and revised in 1973. Secondly, I am beholden in many ways to the international group of experts who have corrected and amplified his formidable effort. A roll call of their names would include most of the authors listed in the bibliography whose publications postdate Benesch's volumes. Among them, very special thanks are due to I. H. van Eeghen, Peter Schatborn, Martin Royalton-Kisch, and Christopher White. In the following pages more than a few of their finds and admirable observations are cited.

Yet again I am heavily indebted to Alice I. Davies for steadfast editorial assistance. This time it is particularly appreciated because it was given while she was working almost around the clock on a major publication of her own. To William W. Robinson and Joseph Umphres I extend deep thanks for helpful suggestions and comments on an early draft of the manuscript.

At the Getty Museum my chief debts are to John Walsh and Lee Hendrix, director emeritus and curator of drawings, respectively, for their initial and subsequent enthusiastic support of the project; to Benedicte Gilman, my editor, for her superior editorial work; and to Catherine Lorenz for the book's beautiful design. Suzanne Watson oversaw the production and made sure the color images came through to their best advantage.

S. S.

INTRODUCTION

THE MODERN LITERATURE on Rembrandt's supreme draftsmanship is vast. Most important is Otto Benesch's monumental six-volume *The Drawings of Rembrandt: A Critical and Chronological Catalogue* published in 1954–57 (enlarged and edited by Eva Benesch, his widow, in 1973). Benesch's corpus ascribes more than fourteen hundred drawings to the artist.

Although those volumes remain the foundation for the study of Rembrandt's drawings, subsequent specialists have rightly questioned a huge number of his attributions, first in scholarly reviews and then in a small avalanche of catalogues of the holdings of the world's principal drawing collections (among them Amsterdam, Berlin, Chatsworth, Dresden, Haarlem, London, Munich, New York, Paris, Rotterdam, Stockholm, Vienna) and in temporary exhibition catalogues as well as studies devoted to Rembrandt, his pupils, and his followers.

In the event, it has been dramatically and convincingly demonstrated that hundreds of drawings ascribed to the master by Benesch and other early cataloguers are, in fact, by Rembrandt's host of very gifted pupils, who worked with him during every phase of his activity; by members of his workshop; by close followers who show strong reflections of his manner though, to our knowledge, they never had his instruction; or by contemporary or later copyists.

Experts of our time have reduced to about eight hundred the number of drawings ascribed to him. That number, which includes sketches that escaped the nets of Benesch and others or that have surfaced since they published their catalogues, remains approximate because differences of opinions still exist regarding the status of a fraction of the reduced number accepted as his.

It is not difficult to understand why an incontrovertible consensus on the canon of Rembrandt's drawings remains elusive. Merely about seventy of his existing drawings are securely documented with a genuine monogram, signature, autograph inscription, or other probative evidence. If any of these proofs is missing, after establishing that a drawing was unquestionably done with materials available to Rembrandt, its authenticity can be determined only by an appraisal of congruences of its style and that of uncontested drawings, a method not immune to subjective judgments capable of generating different opinions.

About eight hundred drawings may not seem a very considerable body of work until we recall that knowledge of the draftmanship of other leading seventeenth-century Dutch artists is infinitesimal or nonexistent. For example, not a single drawing by Frans Hals, Johannes Vermeer, or Pieter de Hooch has survived, and only one sheet with sketches on both sides of it can be securely ascribed to the prolific Jan Steen.

In this volume an effort has been made to include only a selection of drawings accepted today by common consent as authentic; a few exceptions have been signaled in the notes. Drawings have been grouped into sixteen categories. As we learn from an inventory made in 1656 of Rembrandt's effects, he himself classified some of his drawings by subject or category. The inventory cites no less than twenty-four albums and books and two packets of his drawings. One book is listed as full of his drawings of nude men and women and another as containing drawings of animals done from life. Two books had sketches of figures and two copies of sculpture. His landscape drawings were in an album, a book, and a vellum book full of landscapes done from life. The most tantalizing item is simply described as: "A book bound in black leather with Rembrandt's best sketches."[1] We can only guess which drawings were in it. I can hope, however, that some are illustrated in this book.

It will be seen that occasionally the boundaries between categories offered here are porous; some drawings fit under more than one rubric. Nevertheless, this arrangement has been adopted because it helps show the artist's seemingly matchless range, development, and remarkably different ways of using his drawings material for similar subjects. It also is a reminder that at times Rembrandt fits into a pigeonhole only if some of his limbs are amputated.

NOTE

1 Strauss and van der Meulen 1979, 373, no. 1656/12, no. 236: *"Een boeck in swart leer gebonden met de beste schetsen van Rembrant."*

EDITORIAL NOTES

In the dimensions of works, height precedes width.

Following Dutch usage, patronymics have been abbreviated in the text. Those ending in *sz* or *sdr* should be read as "*zoon*" or "*dochter,*" that is, the son or daughter of. Put another way, Harmensz means Harmenszoon (the son of Harmen) and Harmensdr means Harmensdochter (the daughter of Harmen).

Illustrations whose captions do not cite an artist are all by Rembrandt, unless otherwise indicated in a note.

ABBREVIATIONS

acc. no.	accession number
Bartsch	A. Bartsch 1797, cat. no. (see bibliography)
Benesch	O. Benesch 1954–57, cat. no. (see bibliography)
Bredius	A. Bredius 1969, cat. no. (see bibliography)
ca.	circa
cat.	catalogue [number]
Corpus	Bruyn et al., vols. 1–3; Van der Wetering et al., vol. 4 (see bibliography)
ed.	editor/edited by
edn.	edition
enl.	enlarged (by)
exh.	exhibition
fol.	folio
inv.	inventory [number]
n./nn.	note/notes
no./nos.	number/numbers
p./pp.	page/pages
pub.	published by
rev.	revised/revised by
RMN	Réunion des Musées Nationaux, Paris
trans.	translator/translation/translated by
vol./vols.	volume/volumes

BIOGRAPHY OF REMBRANDT

1606	Rembrandt Harmensz van Rijn born at Leiden on 15 July, son of a miller.
1613–20	Pupil at Leiden's Latin School.
1620	Matriculates at the University of Leiden, 20 May.
ca. 1621–24	Pupil of the Leiden artist Jacob Isaacsz van Swanenburgh.
1625	Studies in Amsterdam for six months with the preeminent history painter Pieter Lastman. Returns to Leiden. Begins independent artistic activity specializing in history painting.
ca. 1631–32	Moves to Amsterdam. Starts painting commissioned portraits. Quickly establishes reputation as a leading portraitist with *The Anatomy Lesson of Dr. Tulp,* 1632.
1634	Marries Saskia van Uylenburgh, daughter of a Frisian burgomaster, in Saint Anna parish, Friesland, on 22 June.
1635–36	Son Rumbartus baptized 15 December; buried 15 February 1636.
1638	Daughter Cornelia baptized 22 July; buried 13 August.
1639	Buys a large house in Amsterdam on Saint Anthoniebreestraat (now Jodenbreestraat 4–6, home of the Museum het Rembrandthuis).
1640	Second daughter, also called Cornelia, baptized 29 July; buried 12 August.
1641	Birth of son Titus, baptized 22 September. He is the only child who survives Saskia. Around this time Geertje Dircx enters the household as housekeeper and Titus's "dry nurse."

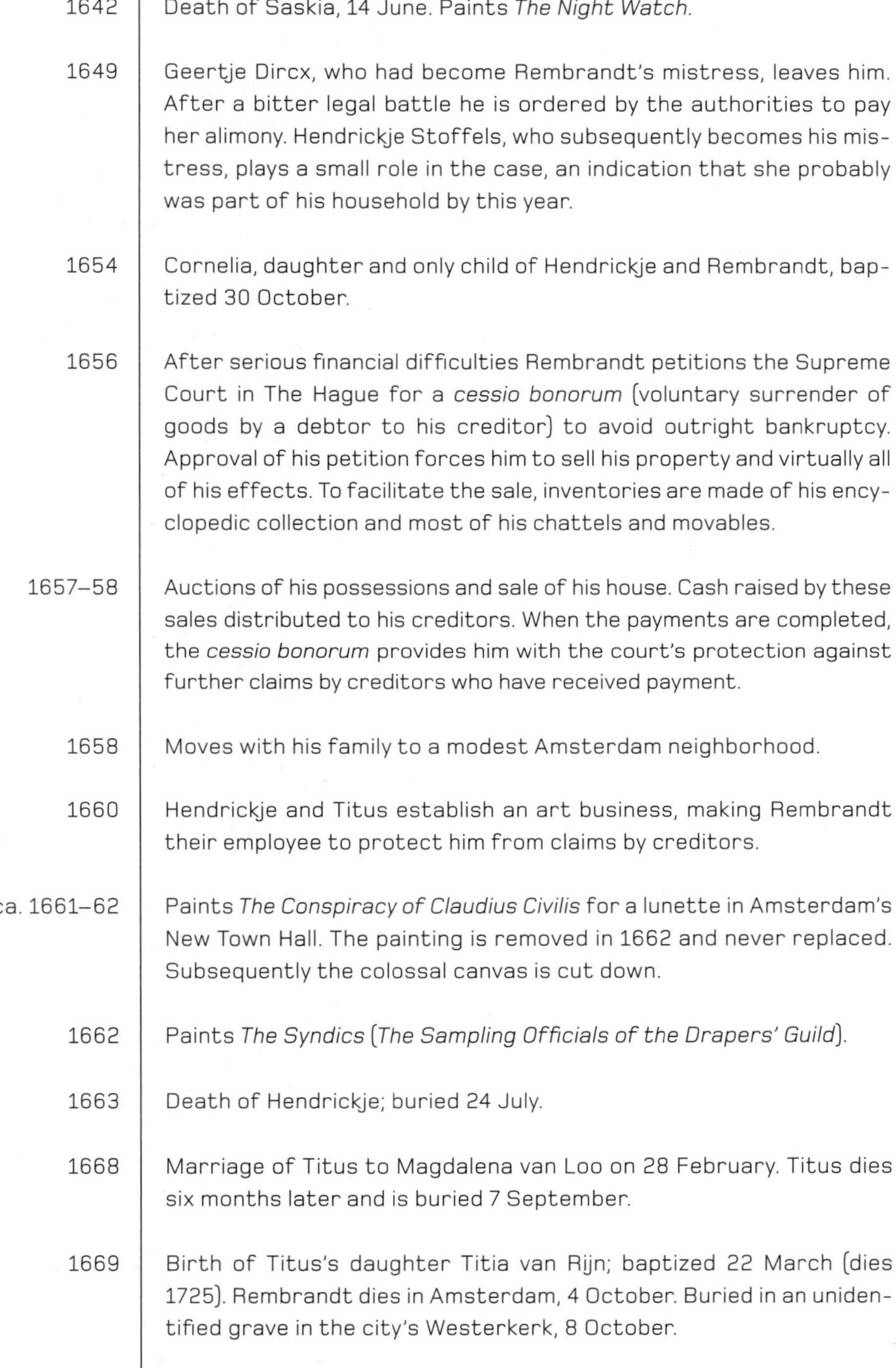

1642 Death of Saskia, 14 June. Paints *The Night Watch*.

1649 Geertje Dircx, who had become Rembrandt's mistress, leaves him. After a bitter legal battle he is ordered by the authorities to pay her alimony. Hendrickje Stoffels, who subsequently becomes his mistress, plays a small role in the case, an indication that she probably was part of his household by this year.

1654 Cornelia, daughter and only child of Hendrickje and Rembrandt, baptized 30 October.

1656 After serious financial difficulties Rembrandt petitions the Supreme Court in The Hague for a *cessio bonorum* (voluntary surrender of goods by a debtor to his creditor) to avoid outright bankruptcy. Approval of his petition forces him to sell his property and virtually all of his effects. To facilitate the sale, inventories are made of his encyclopedic collection and most of his chattels and movables.

1657–58 Auctions of his possessions and sale of his house. Cash raised by these sales distributed to his creditors. When the payments are completed, the *cessio bonorum* provides him with the court's protection against further claims by creditors who have received payment.

1658 Moves with his family to a modest Amsterdam neighborhood.

1660 Hendrickje and Titus establish an art business, making Rembrandt their employee to protect him from claims by creditors.

ca. 1661–62 Paints *The Conspiracy of Claudius Civilis* for a lunette in Amsterdam's New Town Hall. The painting is removed in 1662 and never replaced. Subsequently the colossal canvas is cut down.

1662 Paints *The Syndics* (*The Sampling Officials of the Drapers' Guild*).

1663 Death of Hendrickje; buried 24 July.

1668 Marriage of Titus to Magdalena van Loo on 28 February. Titus dies six months later and is buried 7 September.

1669 Birth of Titus's daughter Titia van Rijn; baptized 22 March (dies 1725). Rembrandt dies in Amsterdam, 4 October. Buried in an unidentified grave in the city's Westerkerk, 8 October.

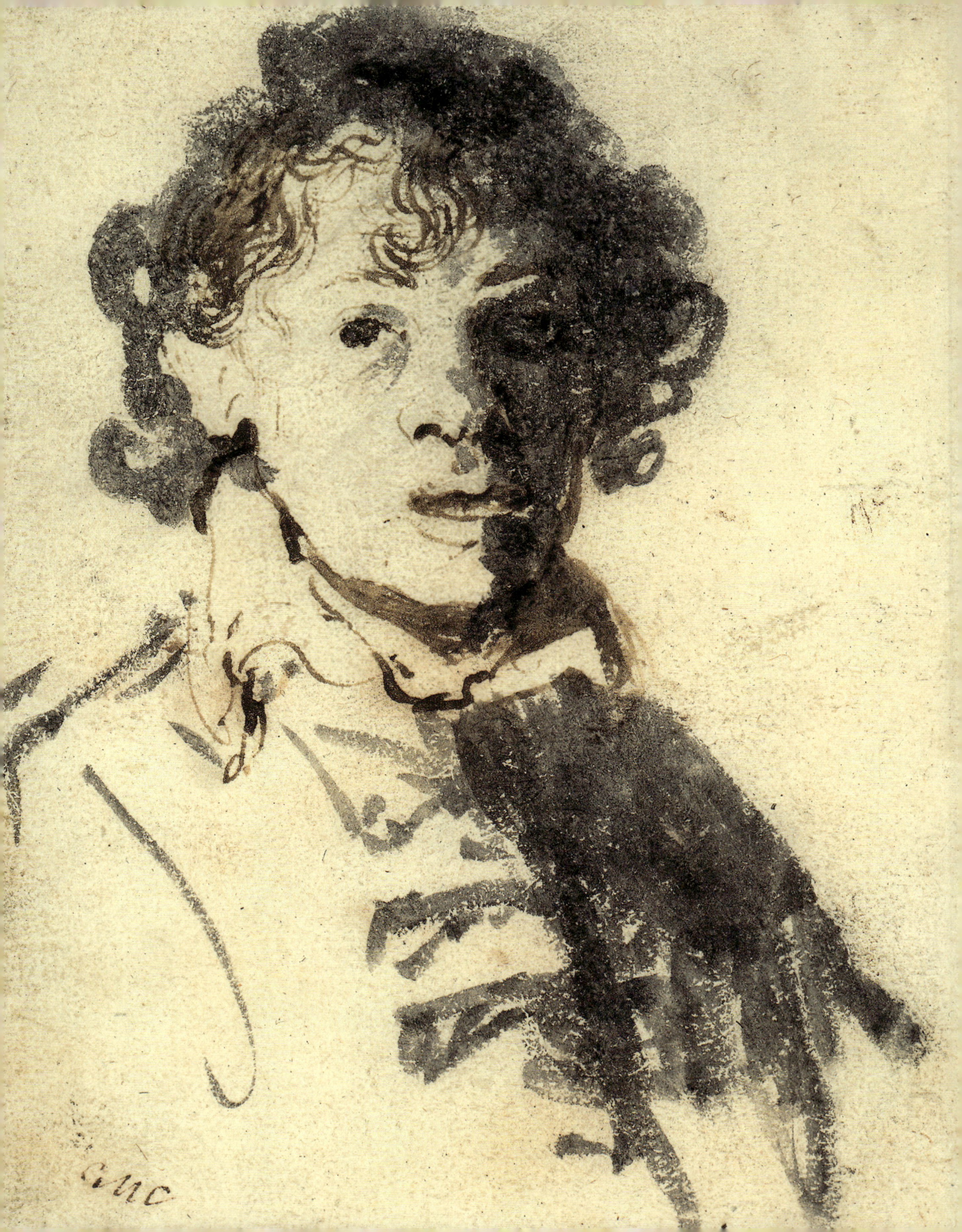

1 | Self-portraits

1 | SELF-PORTRAITS

IN 1625, WHEN EIGHTEEN- or nineteen-year-old Rembrandt's hand is first recognizable, he used himself as a model for a terrified figure witnessing *The Stoning of Saint Stephen*, a painting now in Lyons. Young Rembrandt can also be seen as a participant in historical, biblical, and genre paintings done in 1626 and 1627. The earliest existing drawn, etched, and painted self-portraits in which he portrays himself alone are datable about a year or two later. It is common knowledge that his fascination with his own face was not a passing fancy. By the time of his death in 1669 he had made at least eighty-five drawn, etched, or painted self-portraits, a number not one of his predecessors or contemporaries begins to match.

His two drawn self-portraits of about 1628–29 are at the British Museum (fig. 1.1) and the Rijksmuseum (fig. 1.2). They are virtually identical in size, and both are done in pen, ink, brush, and wash, but their effects are quite different. The London drawing impresses by the artist's intense, momentary expression that includes raised eyebrows and a view of his slightly open mouth. Contrast between light areas and those in shadow is sharp—almost certainly the sketch was done in artificial light.

By contrast, the Amsterdam drawing portrays the artist viewing himself steadily in a more even light. Unusual is the broad brushwork of the artist's mop of wild hair and the vigorous, dry brush hatching of the shadow his body casts. The drawing is closely related to Rembrandt's coarse, heavily bitten etching of 1629, a rare print that exists in only two impressions (fig. 1.3). Perhaps he wanted to simulate the drawing's effect in the print. The latter gives greater emphasis to his potato-like nose, and he wears a fashionably long lock of hair, in his day called a lovelock, cascading over his

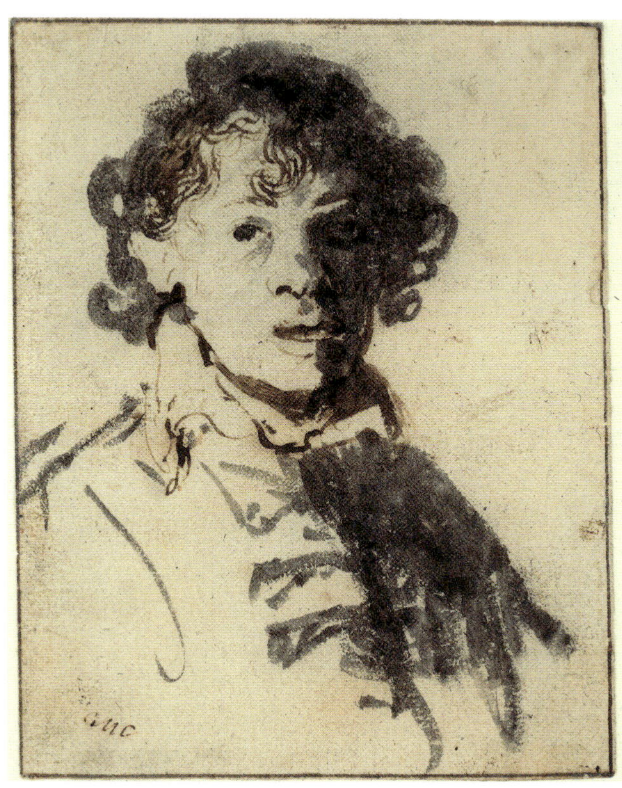

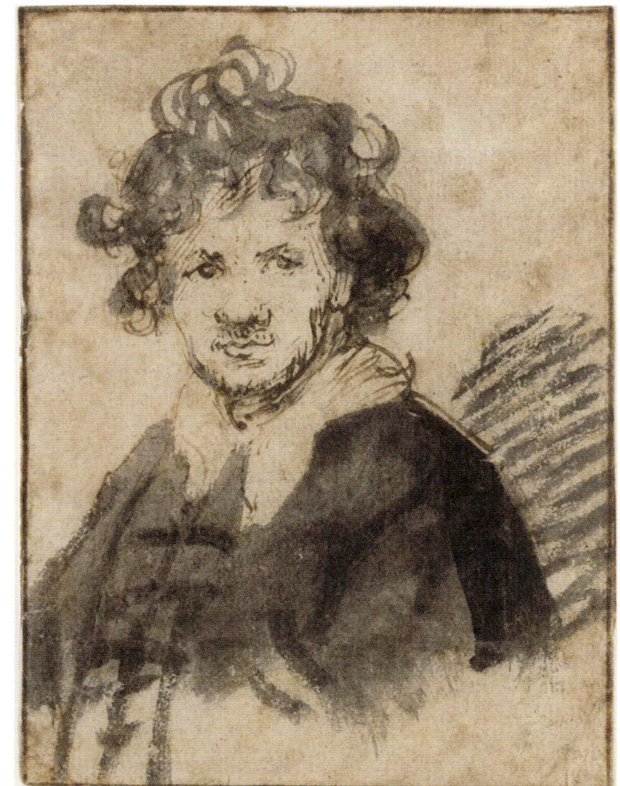

1.1 | *Self-portrait, with Mouth Open*, ca. 1628–29. Pen and brown ink, gray wash; 12.7 × 9.5 cm (5 × 3¾ in.). The British Museum, London, inv. PD Gg.2-253. Photo: Erich Lessing/Art Resource, N.Y.

1.2 | *Self-portrait*, ca. 1628–29. Pen and brown ink, gray wash, on paper; 12.7 × 9.4 cm (5 × 3¾ in.). Rijksmuseum, Amsterdam, inv. RP-T-1961.75.

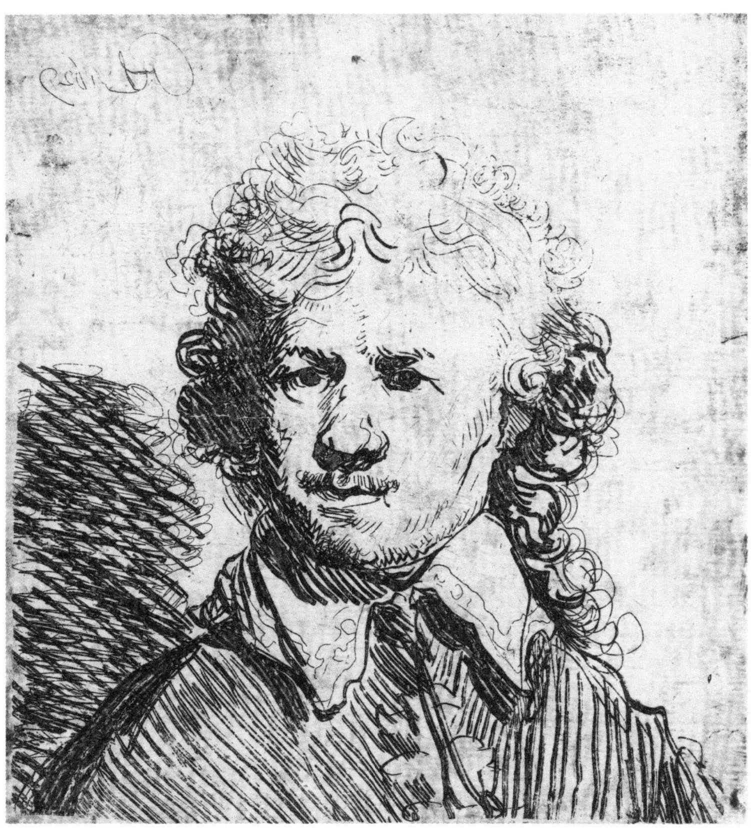

shoulder. The monogram and date on the etching are printed in reverse. For a moment he may have forgotten that what he inscribed with his etcher's needle on his copperplate would appear backwards when printed—or perhaps he didn't give a fig if what he wrote was going to be flopped.

From the beginning Rembrandt drew directly on impressions of his etchings, particularly in their early states. Notable examples of this practice are his two touched-up early impressions of *Self-portrait in a Soft Hat*, monogrammed and dated 1631. They are at the British Museum (fig. 1.4) and the Bibliothèque Nationale, Paris (fig. 1.5). Only the heads, hair, and hats of both impressions are etched; the rest—the collars and busts—is done in black chalk. In the British Museum sheet Rembrandt shows himself looking over his shoulder with his bust nearly in profile, and he has added a framing arch at the top. The Bibliothèque Nationale impression presents his bust turned more to the viewer, producing a less dramatic effect.

At first glance it may appear that these touched-up impressions are studies for two different ways to complete the etching, which in its first four states includes only

1.3 | *Self-portrait, Bareheaded, Roughly Etched*, monogrammed and dated 1629. Etching; 17.8 × 15.4 cm (7 × 6⅛ in.). Rijksmuseum, Amsterdam, inv. RP-P-OB-723.

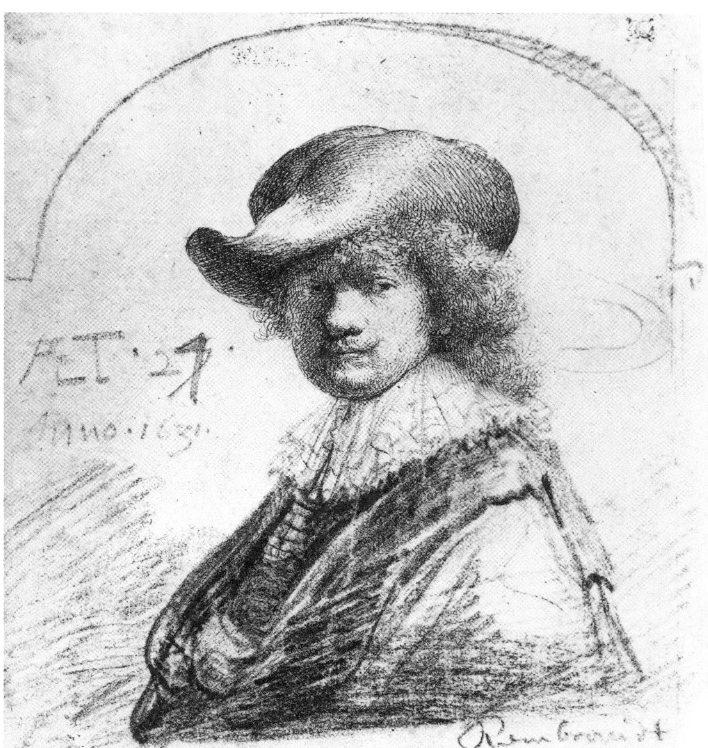

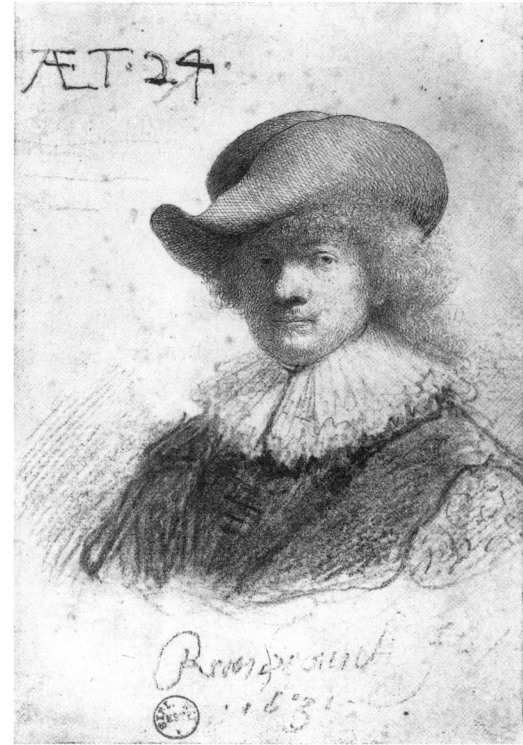

1.4 | *Self-portrait in a Soft Hat*, 1631–ca. 1634. Etching, with black chalk, pen, and brown ink; 13.3 × 12 cm (5¼ × 4¾ in.). The British Museum, London, inv. 1973.U.789. Photo © The Trustees of The British Museum. All rights reserved.

1.5 | *Self-portrait in a Soft Hat*, 1631–ca. 1634. Etching, with black chalk; 14.8 × 9.9 cm (5⅞ × 3⅞ in.). Bibliothèque nationale de France, Paris, Réserve Cb-13a.

the head, hair, and hat. By the fifth and later states (there are no less than eleven states of it) Rembrandt completely abandoned the idea of making a bust self-portrait; instead, he portrays himself as a smartly dressed burgher seen almost three-quarters length with his cloak draped over his akimbo right arm (fig. 1.6).

There is, however, better reason to conclude that both drawn-on impressions were made a couple years after the artist decided upon the final form of the etching. Recent investigation has established that the paper used for an impression of its ninth state bears a countermark that strongly suggests the impression was pulled in or very soon after 1631.[1] If this hypothesis is correct, the early Paris and London impressions (second and fourth states, respectively) must have been pulled by 1631 or very soon afterward.

Further indication that the drawn-on impressions are postscripts to, not preliminary studies for, the 1631 self-portrait are their inscriptions. Both are genuinely signed "Rembrandt" (the form of signature he employed only from 1633) and dated 1633 in the same black chalk the artist used for drawing the collars and busts. He also is responsible for giving his age as "24" and then changing it to "27," an

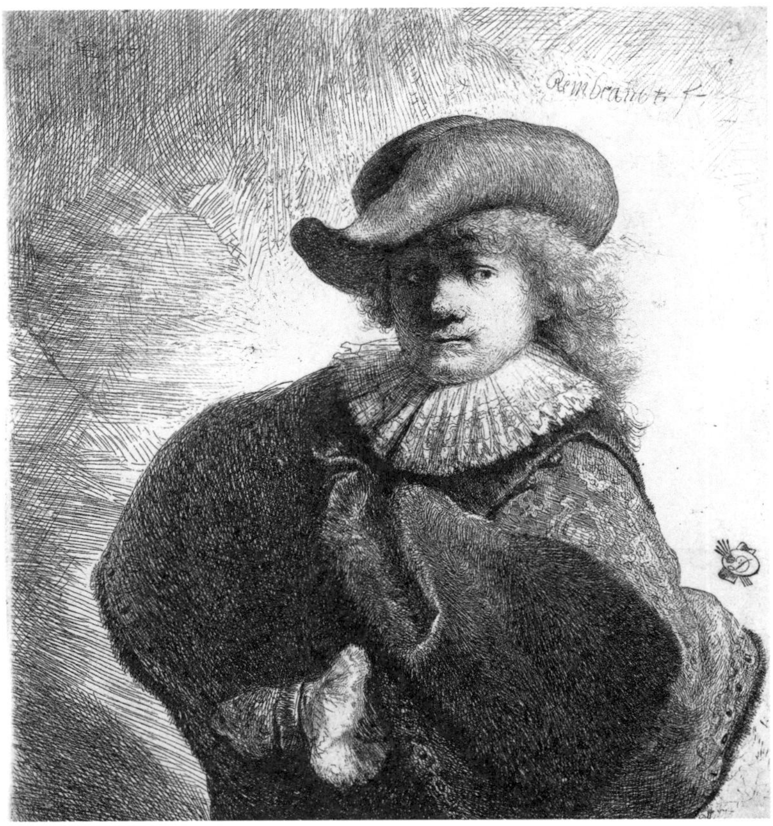

amendment that dates the touched-up impressions to 1633 or 1634.

The serious, almost pained expression Rembrandt gives himself in his pen-and-wash *Self-portrait* in Berlin[2] (fig. 1.7), datable about 1636, is akin to the one he offers in his familiar etched *Self-portrait with Saskia* of 1636 (fig. 1.8). The Berlin drawing is more intimate, however. Rembrandt is hatless, and his open shirt reveals his bare chest, a feature that gives a foretaste of Goya's open shirt in his intense painted *Self-portrait* now at the Prado, done in 1815 when he was about seventy.

Equally serious is the face Rembrandt shows in his red-chalk *Self-portrait Wearing a Cap* at the National Gallery of Art, Washington, D.C. (fig. 1.9). As in a few other early self-portraits, a long lovelock hangs down one shoulder. His carefully drawn beret has a small visor that shades his eyes.

A similar beret with a visor is seen in an untraceable painted self-portrait in which he depicted himself holding a sketchbook, a quill pen, and an ink pot. Jacob Gole's mezzotint gives a good idea of the original, the artist's only

1.6 | *Self-portrait in a Soft Hat and Patterned Cloak*, signed; datable 1631–ca. 1633. Etching; 14.8 × 13 cm (5⅞ × 5⅛ in.). The Pierpont Morgan Library, New York, inv. RvR 8. Photo © The Pierpont Morgan Library, New York.

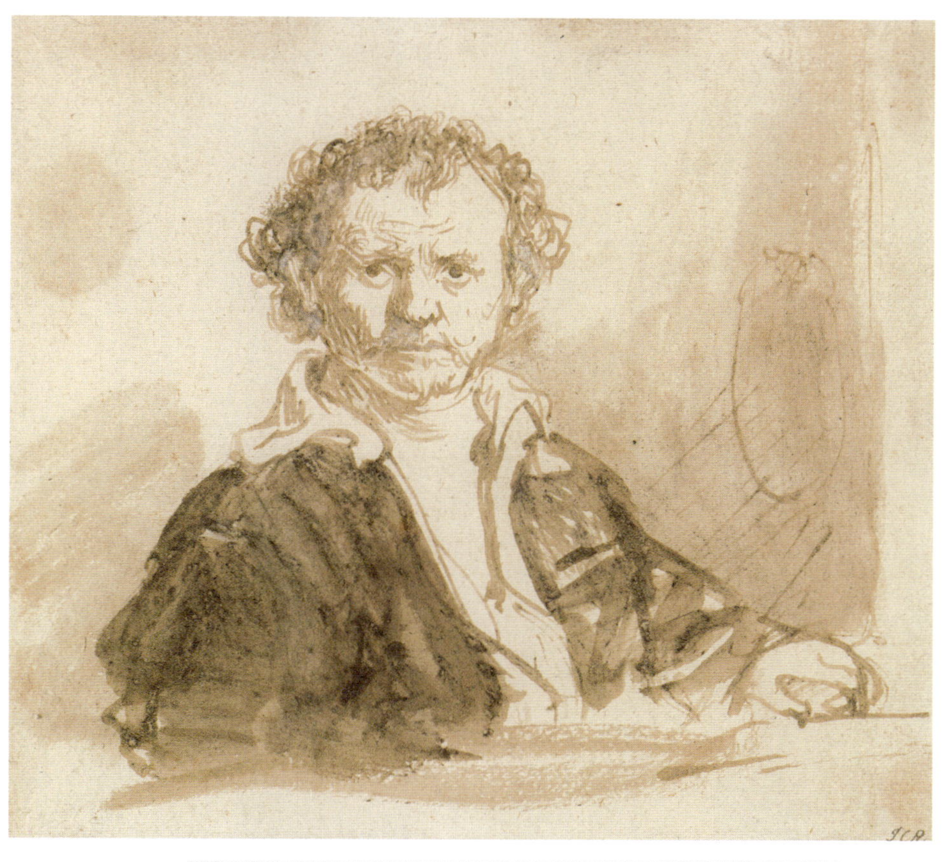

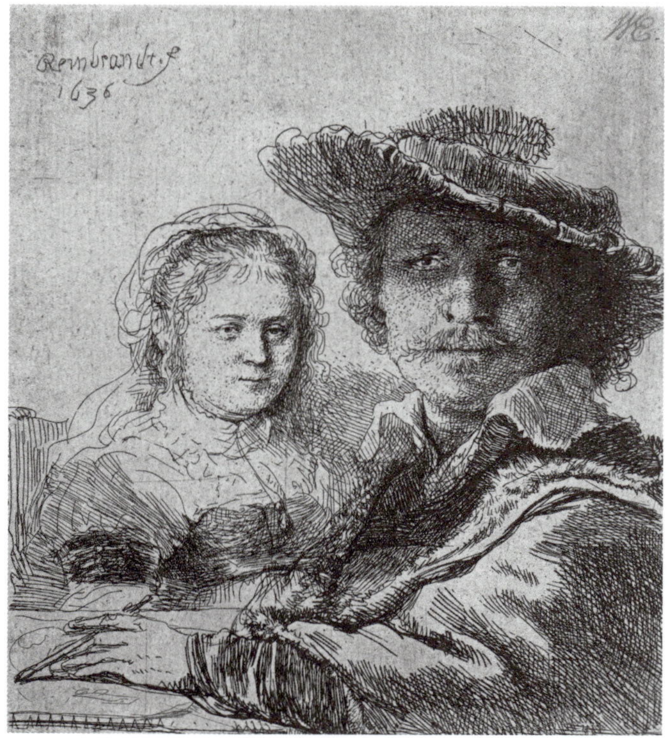

1.7 | *Self-portrait in an Open Shirt*, ca. 1636. Pen and brown ink, brown wash, corrected with white, a few later touches in pen and black ink; 12.6 × 13.7 cm (5 × 5⅜ in.). Kupferstichkabinett, Staatliche Museen, Berlin, inv. KdZ 1553. Photo: Bildarchiv Preussischer Kulturbesitz/Art Resource, N.Y. Photographer: Jörg P. Anders.

1.8 | *Self-portrait with Saskia*, third state, signed and dated 1636. Etching; 10.4 × 9.5 cm (4⅛ × 3¾ in.). The Pierpont Morgan Library, New York, inv. (P)1949.5. Photo © The Pierpont Morgan Library, New York. Photographer: Joseph Zehavi, 2005.

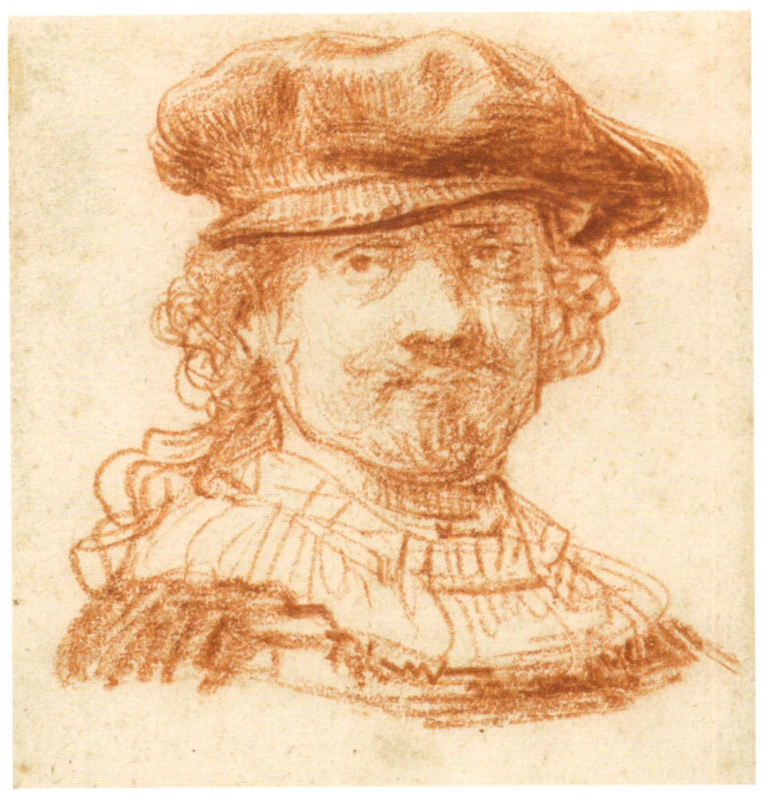

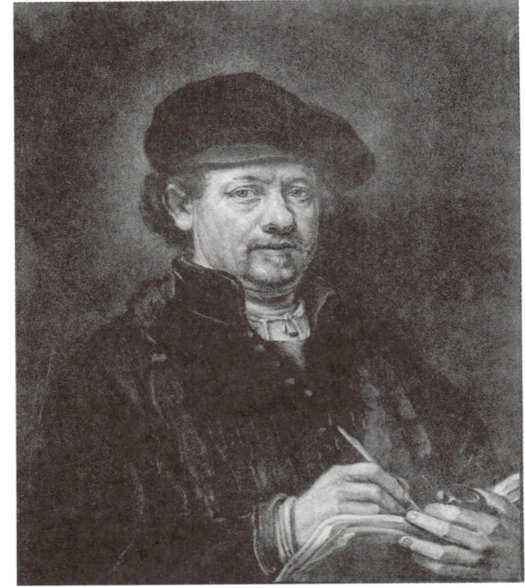

painted self-portrait that shows him as a draftsman holding a sketchbook and ink pot in his left hand and a quill pen in his right (fig. 1.10).[3] As known from masterworks of his painterly achievement in both youthful and fully mature self-portraits, Rembrandt had no inhibitions whatsoever about painting himself as a working artist at his easel with palette, brushes, and maulstick.

The imposing full-length, pen-and-wash *Self-portrait* of about 1650 at the Museum het Rembrandthuis shows the stocky artist frontally with his hands on his hips and his legs apart[4] (fig. 1.11). The drawing is presently attached to cardboard. A strip of paper has been pasted beneath the drawing with an inscription by an unidentified seventeenth-century hand: *"drawn by Rembrandt van Rhijn after his own image / as he used to dress in his studio."*[5] His working clothes include a long plain coat tied at the waist with a sash. Its slit, full sleeves are elbow length; they would not easily drag on the artist's laid palette. His undergarment has long, close-fitting sleeves and a collar. He wears a narrow-rimmed cylindrical hat. As for his footwear it is hard to tell if he showed himself wearing shoes or slippers.

1.9 | *Self-portrait Wearing a Cap* (recto), ca. 1636–38. Red chalk; 12.9 × 11.9 cm (5⅛ × 4¾ in.). National Gallery of Art, Rosenwald Collection, Washington, D.C., inv. 1943.3.7048. Photo courtesy of the Board of Trustees, National Gallery of Art.

1.10 | Jacob Gole (Dutch, 1660–1737), after Rembrandt, *Self-portrait with a Sketchbook* (untraceable). Mezzotint.

1.11 | *Self-portrait, Full-length*, ca. 1650. Pen and brown ink; 20.3 × 13.4 cm (8 × 5¼ in.). Museum het Rembrandthuis, Amsterdam, inv. 246. Photo: The Rembrandt House Museum, Amsterdam.

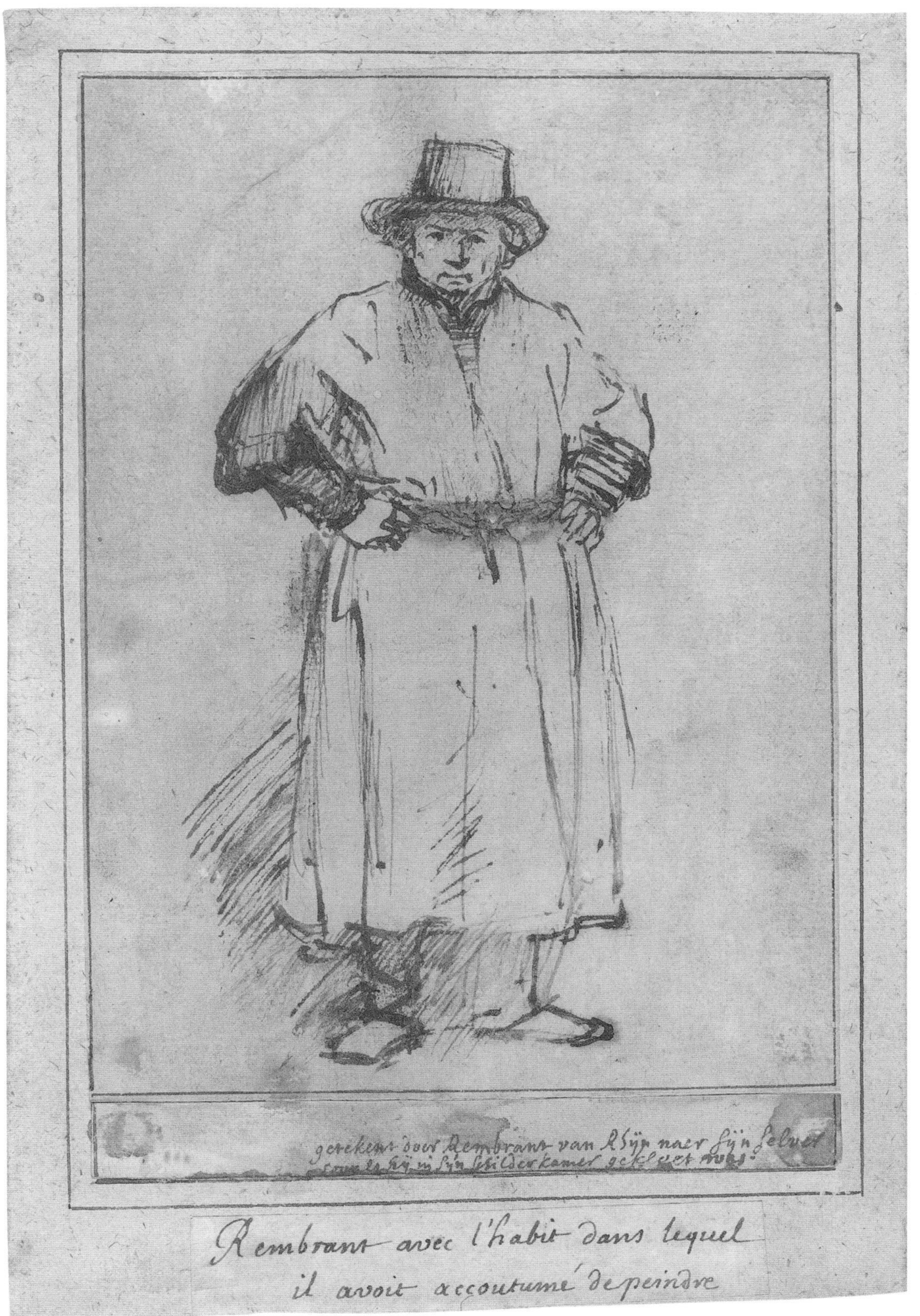
Rembrant avec l'habit dans lequel
il avoit accoutumé de peindre

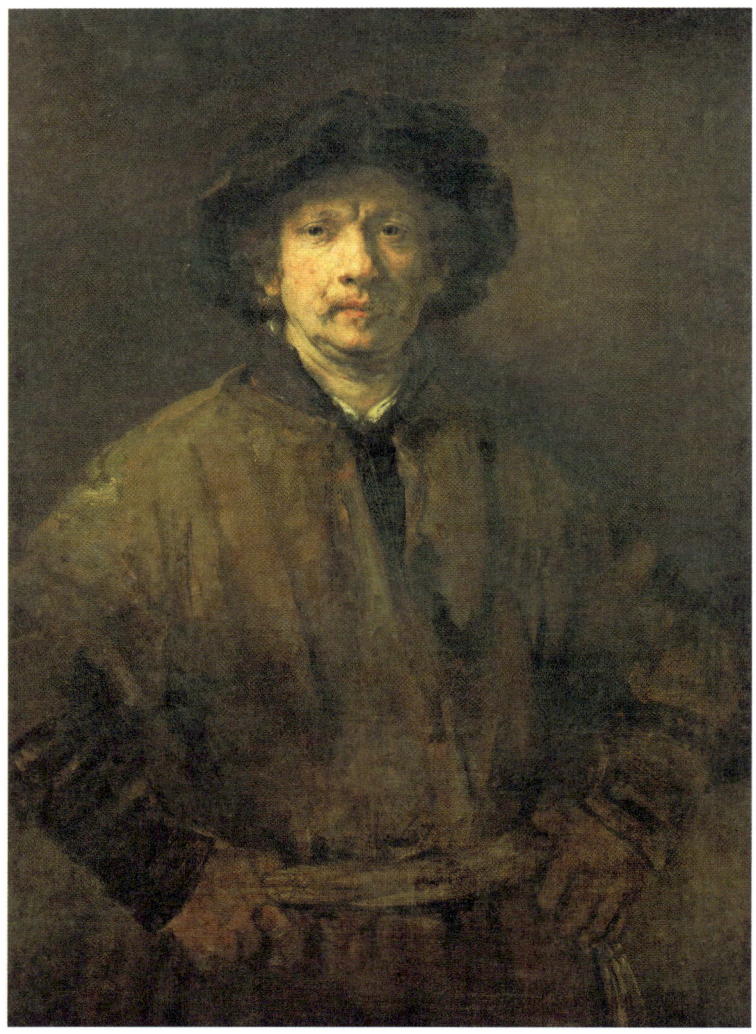

The confident pose and defiant look are strikingly similar to the way the artist is seen in his life-size, three-quarters length painted *Self-portrait,* dated 1652, at the Kunsthistorisches Museum, Vienna (fig. 1.12). Apart from the headgear—in the Vienna *Self-portrait* he wears a large beret—the costumes are remarkably similar. Rembrandt may have found inspiration in the drawing when he worked on the painting.

In view of the close connection of the expression and gaze of the artist in his small *Self-portrait* at the Albertina (fig. 1.13) with his life-size painted *Self-portrait at the Easel,* dated 1660, at the Louvre (fig. 1.14), it too may be classified as a preliminary study for a painting. Special care was lavished upon the sketch's execution. After covering the paper with brown wash, he made the drawing with a reed pen.

1.12 | *Self-portrait*, signed and dated 1652. Oil on canvas; 112 × 81.5 cm (44 1/8 × 32 1/8 in.). Kunsthistorisches Museum, Vienna, inv. 411. Photo: Erich Lessing/Art Resource, N.Y.

Parts of the background, face, and hair were then touched with gray wash. A few traces of white paint can be spotted. White paint was also added to the cap. During his last years Rembrandt seemed to favor a white cloth cap when working. He not only wears one in his Louvre *Self-portrait at the Easel*[6] but it appears again in his *Self-portrait Holding Brushes and a Palette* (London, Kenwood House). In each work he shapes the cap differently. He was as creative with plain white cloth caps as he was with berets of sundry shapes, sizes, and materials. If memory serves, it was Kenneth Clark who said that if Rembrandt had not been Holland's greatest artist, he would have been its greatest milliner.

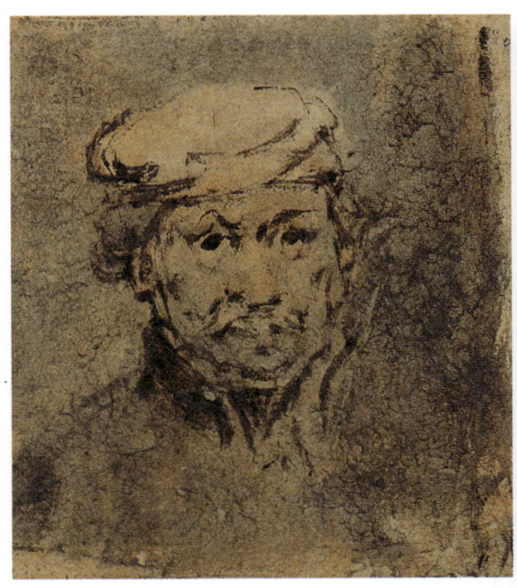

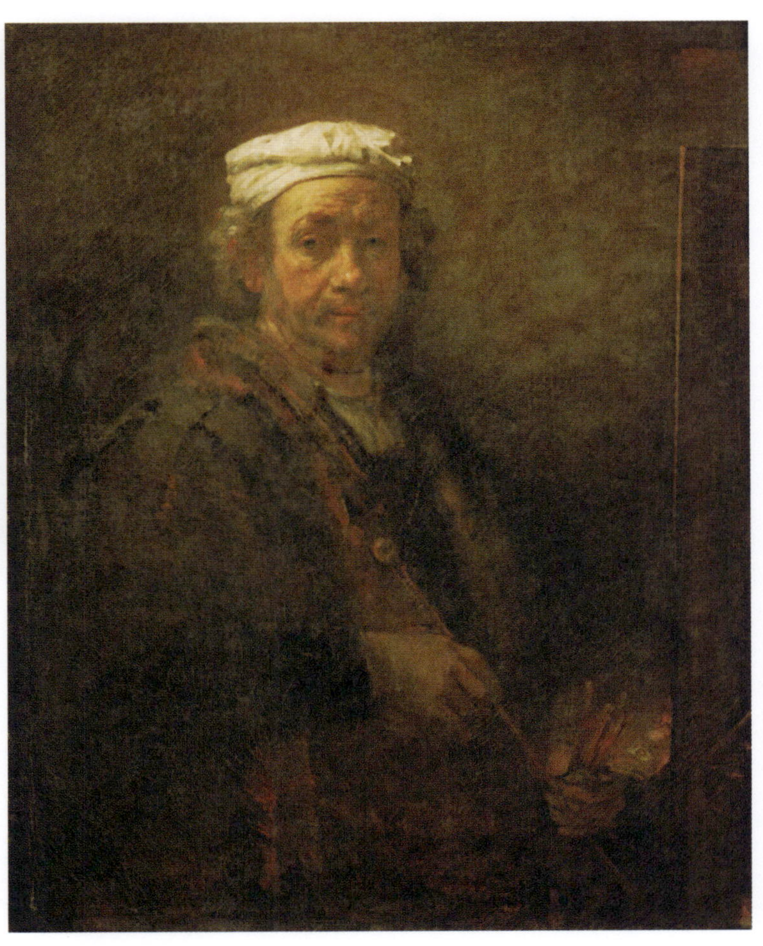

1.13 | *Self-portrait* (detail), ca. 1660. Pen and brown ink, brown, gray, and white wash, touches of white and gray paint on paper prepared with brown wash; 8.2 × 7.3 cm (3¼ × 2⅞ in.). Graphische Sammlung Albertina, Vienna, inv. 25.449. Photo © The Albertina Museum, Vienna.

1.14 | *Self-portrait at the Easel*, signed and dated 1660. Oil on canvas; 110.9 × 90.6 cm (43⅝ × 35⅝ in.). Musée du Louvre, Paris, inv. 1747. Photo: Erich Lessing/Art Resource, N.Y.

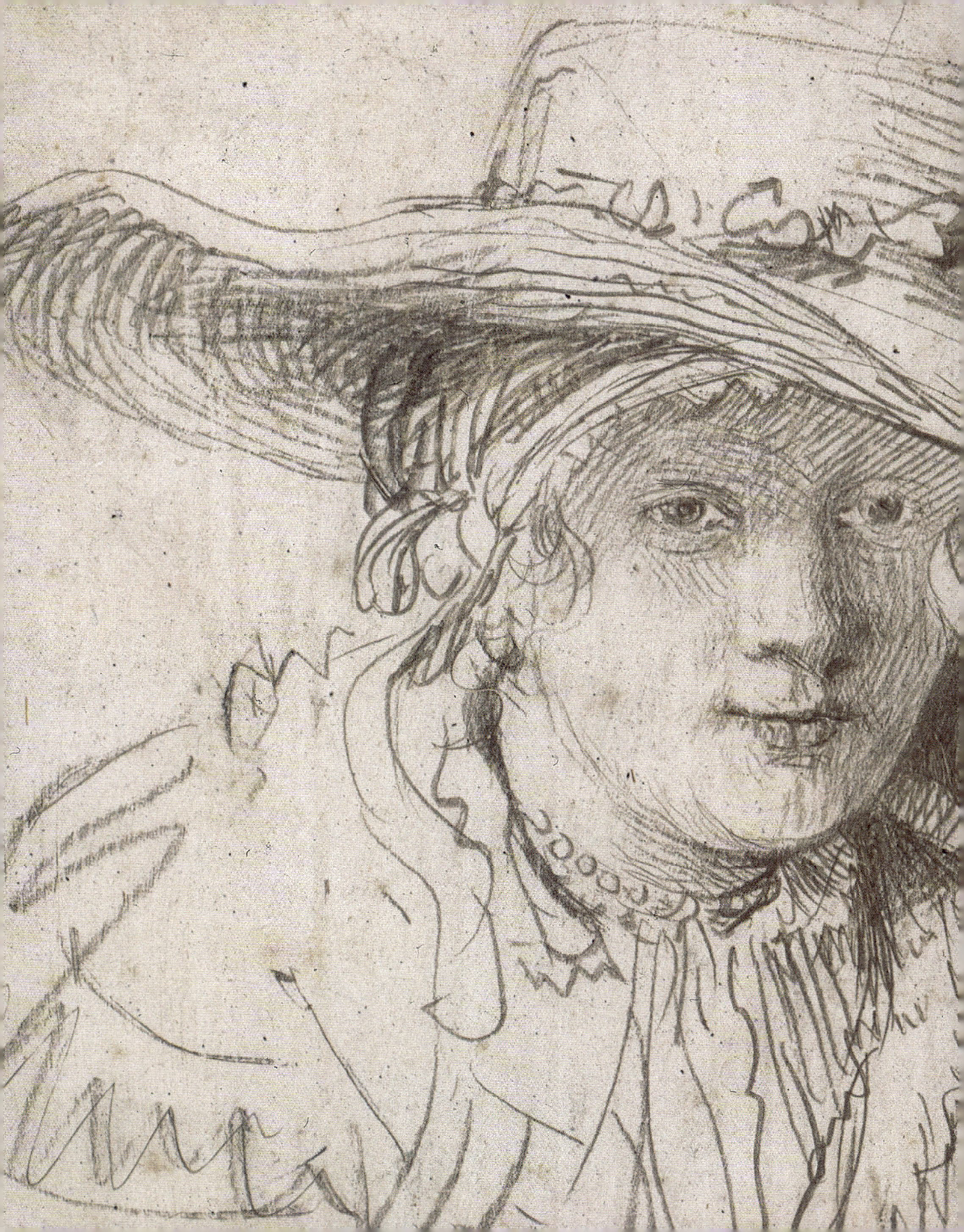

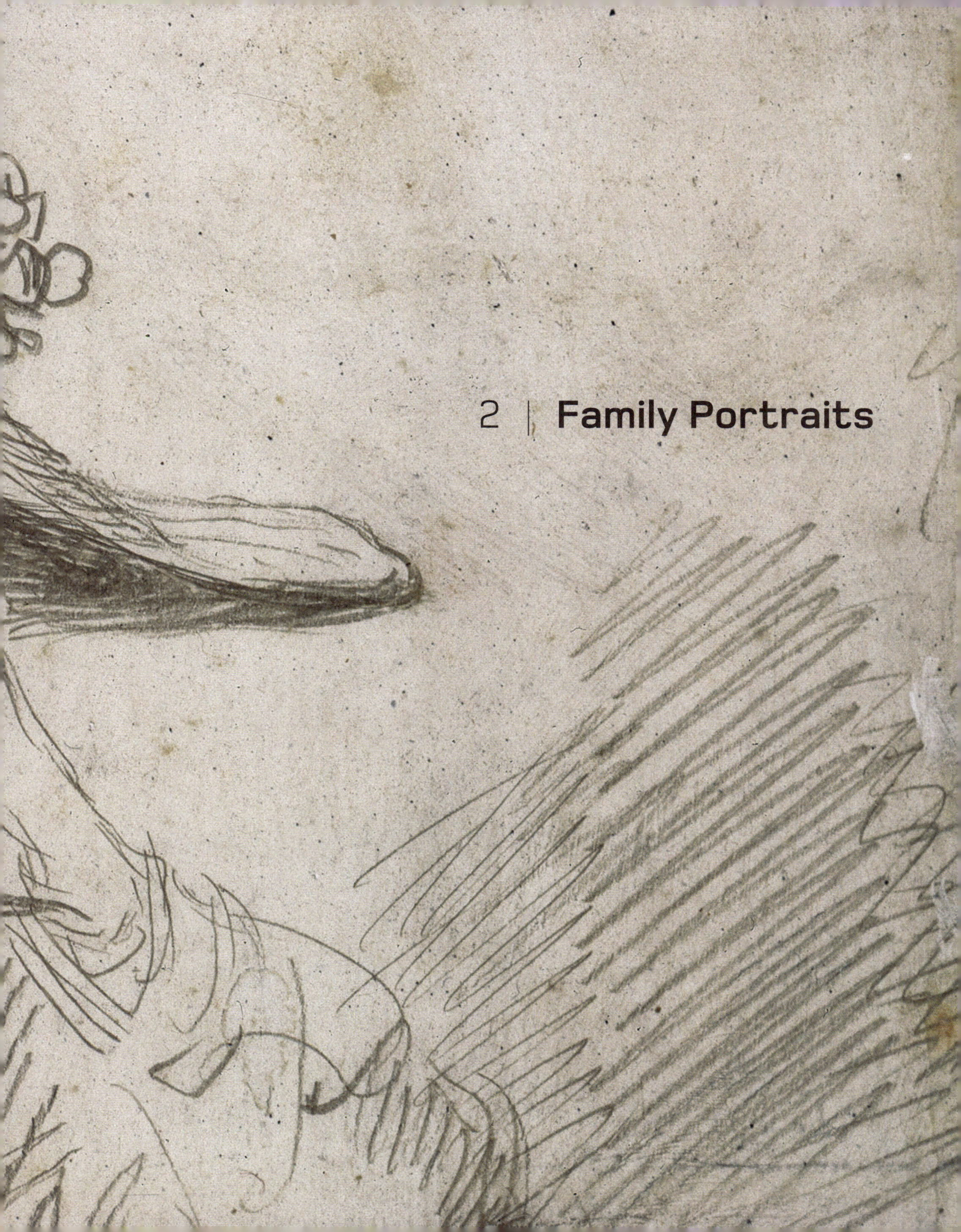

2 | Family Portraits

2 | FAMILY PORTRAITS

A CAUTIONARY TALE that centers upon Rembrandt's sympathetic pen-and-brush sketch of a boy at Stockholm is a helpful starting point for a discussion of his portrait drawings of members of his family (fig. 2.1). The story begins early in the twentieth century when the tradition that began soon after the artist's death of attaching fanciful family names to people portrayed by Rembrandt was still very much in vogue. At that time the Stockholm drawing was dubbed a portrait of Rumbartus, Saskia and Rembrandt's firstborn child, who was baptized 15 December 1635. The identification seemed reasonable. Judging from the sketch's style, it is datable about 1637–38. The boy in the sketch appears to be two or three years old, an age that fits with a birth year of 1635. The fit was so convincing that other Rembrandt drawings of infants and young children datable about 1636–41 were subsequently identified as Rumbartus. One specialist labeled no fewer than fifteen portraits by Rembrandt in this fashion, most notably including the baby in the arms of a young woman swiftly descending a staircase in a beautiful drawing at The Pierpont Morgan Library (see fig. 7.9).[7]

The notion that Rumbartus is portrayed in these works is appealing, but in 1956 it became evident that it was patently wrong. That year a document was published establishing that Rumbartus lived only about two months—he was buried on 15 February 1636.[8] The children previously identified as Rumbartus are obviously more than two months old.

There is a sheet at Rotterdam, however, that may include sketches of Rumbartus as well as four pen studies of Saskia (fig. 2.2). The second sketch from the top shows a slightly drawn infant's head next to his mother's; the bottom sketch depicts an infant tenderly cradled in his mother's

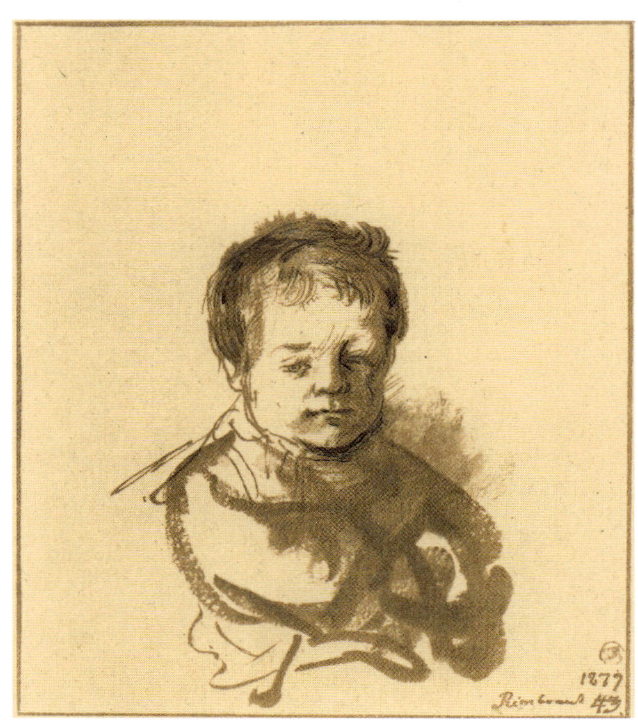

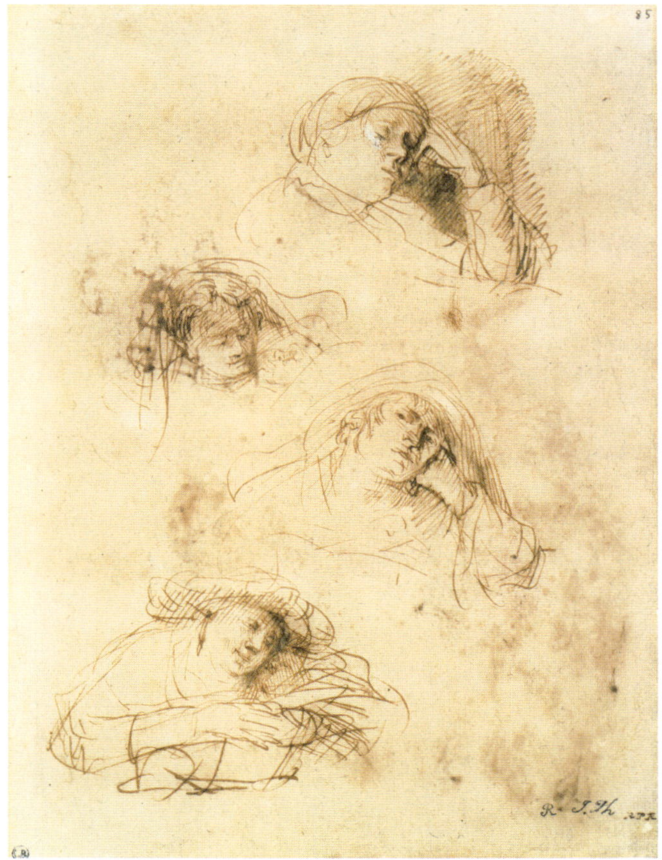

2.1 | *Portrait of a Boy*, ca. 1637–38. Pen and brown ink, brown wash, on paper prepared with pale yellowish-brown wash; 12.6 × 10.7 cm (5 × $4\frac{1}{4}$ in.). Nationalmuseum, Stockholm, inv. 2080/1863. Photo © The National Museum of Fine Arts.

2.2 | *Four Sketches of Saskia* (recto), ca. 1635–36. Pen and brown ink, gray wash, corrected with white; 20 × 15 cm ($7\frac{7}{8}$ × $5\frac{7}{8}$ in.). Museum Boijmans Van Beuningen, Rotterdam, inv. R83 recto (Koenigs Collection).

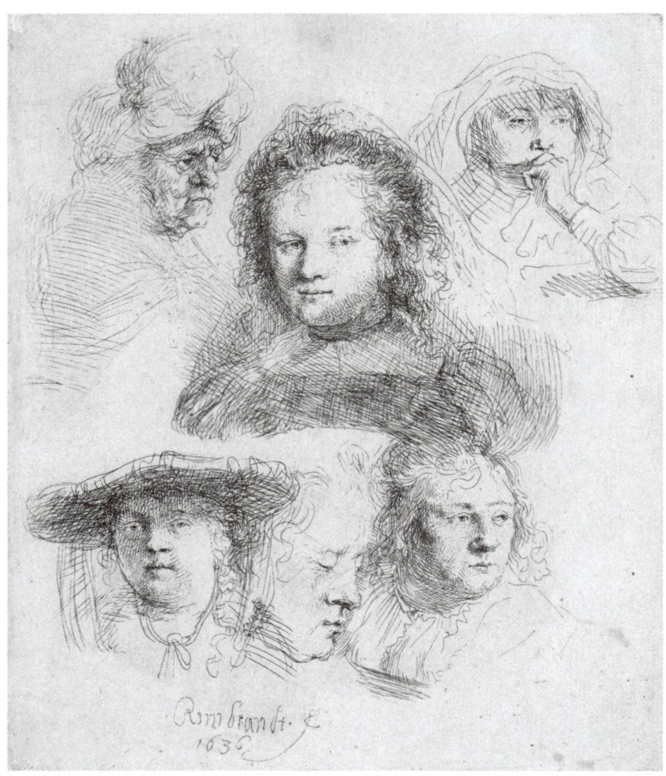

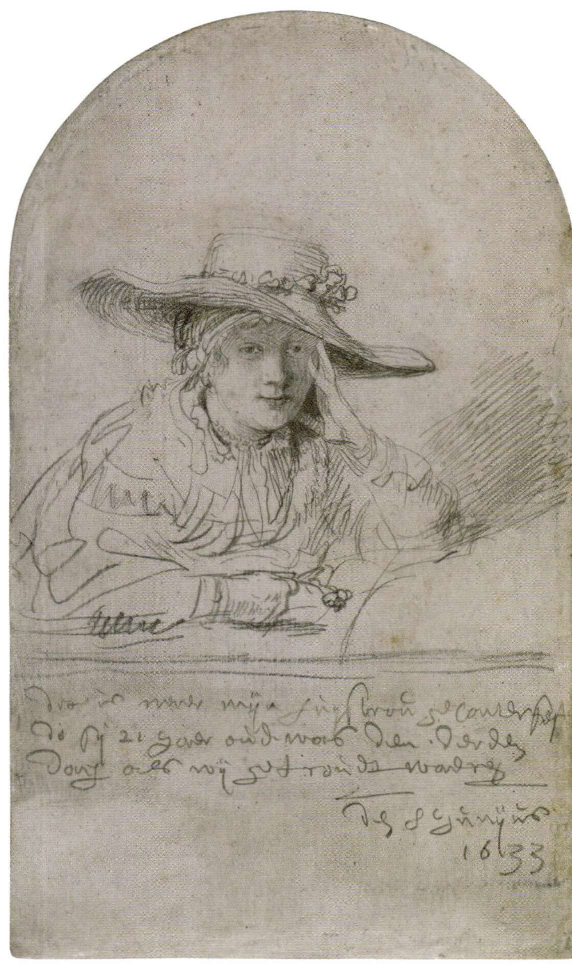

arms. Similarities between the woman depicted in the drawing and an etching, dated 1636, that includes studies of Saskia's head (fig. 2.3) supports the identification of the woman in the drawing as Rumbartus's mother.

Rembrandt's exquisite silverpoint on prepared vellum of *Saskia van Uylenburgh* at Berlin is by far his most tender drawing of a woman (fig. 2.4). Made upon the occasion of his betrothal to Saskia, it is inscribed in the artist's hand: "*this is drawn after my fiancée, when she was 21 years old, the third day of our betrothal, the 8th of June 1633.*"[9] Since the Berlin portrayal of Saskia is the only securely documented likeness of her, it sets the standard for all other proposed portraits of the woman who became his wife on 22 June 1634.

A pen-and-wash drawing of Saskia's older sister Titia van Uylenburgh seen wearing her pince-nez in a strong light engrossed in sewing is at Stockholm (fig. 2.5). Rembrandt

2.3 | *Studies of the Head of Saskia and Others*, signed and dated 1636. Etching; 15 × 12.6 cm (5⅞ × 5 in.). Rijksmuseum, Amsterdam, inv. RP-P-OB-767.

2.4 | *Saskia van Uylenburgh*, 1633. Silverpoint on vellum prepared with white pigment; 18.5 × 10.6 cm (7¼ × 4⅛ in.), arched top. Kupferstichkabinett, Staatliche Museen, Berlin, inv. KdZ 1152. Photo: Bildarchiv Preussischer Kulturbesitz/Art Resource, N.Y. Photographer: Jörg P. Anders.

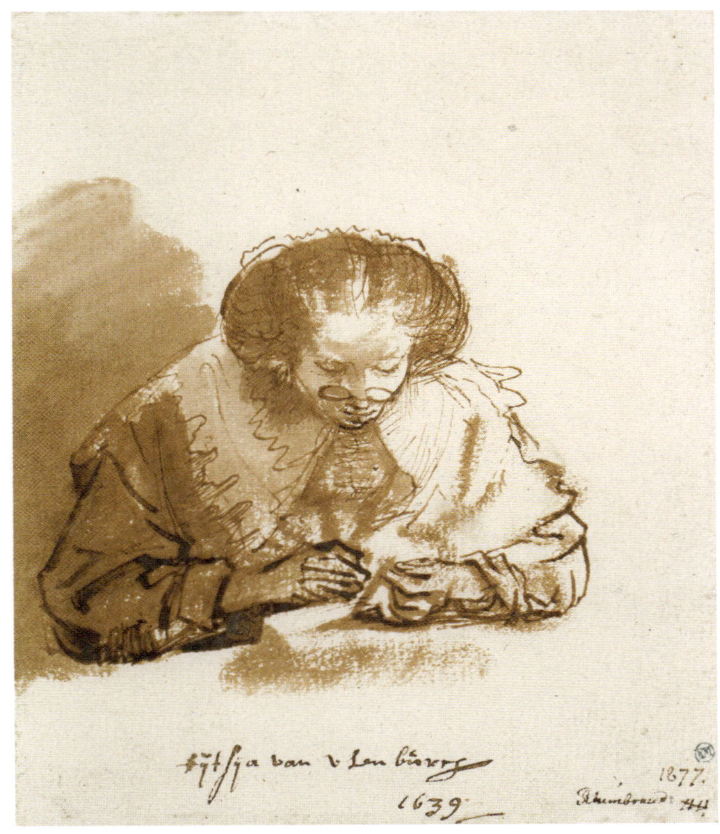

inscribed his sister-in-law's name and the year 1639 at the bottom of the sheet. Titia and her husband were godparents of Saskia and Rembrandt's first three children. We have heard Rumbartus, the first child, lived about two months. The second and third children, born in 1638 and 1640, respectively, each lived only about two weeks—the infant mortality rate in seventeenth-century Holland was frightfully high. Titia died on 15 June 1641. Titus—Saskia and Rembrandt's fourth child and the only one to survive to young manhood—was born fourteen weeks later and was probably named after her.

After Saskia's death in 1642 two women figured in Rembrandt's life. Both became his mistresses. The first was Geertje Dircx, who entered Rembrandt's household in the early 1640s as a "dry nurse" caring for young Titus and as a housekeeper. The arrangement, which lasted for less than a decade, ended badly. In 1649 she complained to the authorities that the artist had slept with her and subsequently broke his promise to marry her. Rembrandt was ordered to pay her debts and alimony. Later, after she was imprisoned in Gouda's house of correction, it seems he made an effort to extend

2.5 | *Titia van Uylenburgh*, 1639. Pen and brown ink, brown wash; 14 × 14.6 cm (5½ × 5¾ in.). Nationalmuseum, Stockholm, inv. 2078/1863. Photo © The National Museum of Fine Arts.

her confinement. The sordid end of the relationship does not enhance what is known about the artist's character. It has been proposed that Geertje served as a model for two drawings; however, as we shall see (pp. 70–73 and figs. 6.8, 6.9), their identification is not certain.

On the basis of circumstantial evidence a few magnificent paintings and some equally fine drawings have been identified as portrayals of Hendrickje Stoffels, the second woman to enter Rembrandt's household. However, it should be stressed that there is no documented portrait of her in any medium.

Most likely Hendrickje began to work for the artist by 1649 when Geertje sued him for breach of promise to marry her. The following years were not easy.

In July 1654 the consistory of the Reformed Church of Amsterdam ordered Hendrickje to do penitence and banned her from communion for living with Rembrandt like a whore (the artist was not summoned by the consistory because he was not a member of the church). Three months later their daughter Cornelia was born out of wedlock. Hendrickje remained faithful to Rembrandt during the troubled years of his maturity. In 1656, after he had petitioned the authorities and been granted a *cessio bonorum* (a less degrading procedure than outright bankruptcy), he had to relinquish to his creditors his great Amsterdam house; his wondrous collection of works of art; natural curiosities; various categories of his own drawings, etchings, and paintings; as well as most of his chattels and movables. It is to these serious financial difficulties that we owe the 1656 inventory of his effects that were sold at public auctions in 1657–58. After his house was sold in 1658, he moved to rented quarters in a modest Amsterdam neighborhood with Hendrickje, Cornelia, and Titus.

Hendrickje and Titus devised a clever scheme in 1660 to protect from unpaid creditors the new assets Rembrandt acquired from his work. They established an art business and made the artist their employee. Additionally, they contracted to give him room and board and exempted him from housekeeping expenses and rent. He, in turn, agreed to aid the partners and promote their business. The partnership was not long-lived. Hendrickje died in 1663.

The proposal that Rembrandt's poignant drawing at the Louvre of a young man holding a flower (fig. 2.6) portrays Titus is not contradicted by works traditionally identified as portraits of the artist's son. Its summary touch, pronounced

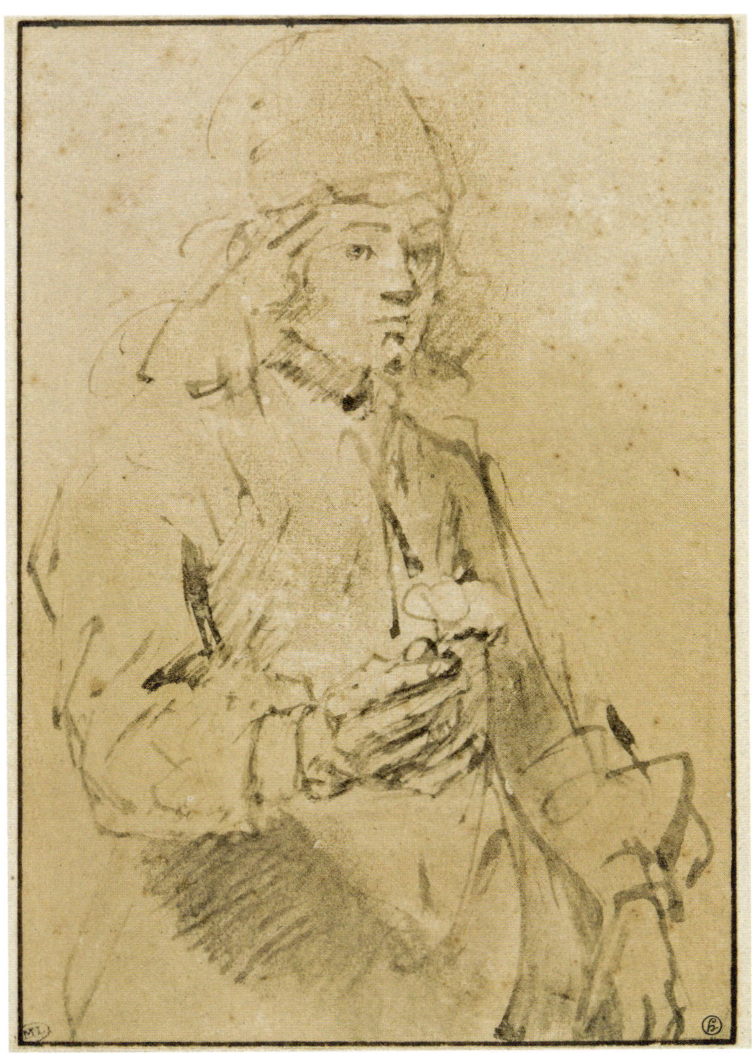

2.6 | *Young Man Holding a Flower* (*Titus van Rijn?*), ca. 1658–60. Pen and brown ink, brown wash; 17.5 × 11.8 cm (6⅞ × 4⅝ in.). Musée du Louvre, Paris, inv. 22917. Photo © RMN—Grand Palais/Art Resource, N.Y. Photographer: Gérard Blot.

hatching, and transparent shadows are characteristic of Rembrandt's style of the late 1650s. It has been suggested that the high hat, clothing, and pose of offering a flower were inspired by late fifteenth-century Netherlandish portraits.[10] In the latter, a carnation or pink, held by a sitter, can be an allusion to marriage. If the Louvre drawing is indeed a portrait of Titus, the flower cannot refer to his marriage, which occurred in 1668 (he died and was buried in the same year); the portrait is datable about a decade earlier.

Portraits of Rembrandt's mother, father, and siblings are even scarcer than those of his nuclear family. His mother, Cornelia (also called Neeltgen) Willemsdr van Zuytbrouck, had at least ten children. If Rembrandt made drawings or etchings of any of them, not a single one has been identified. As for

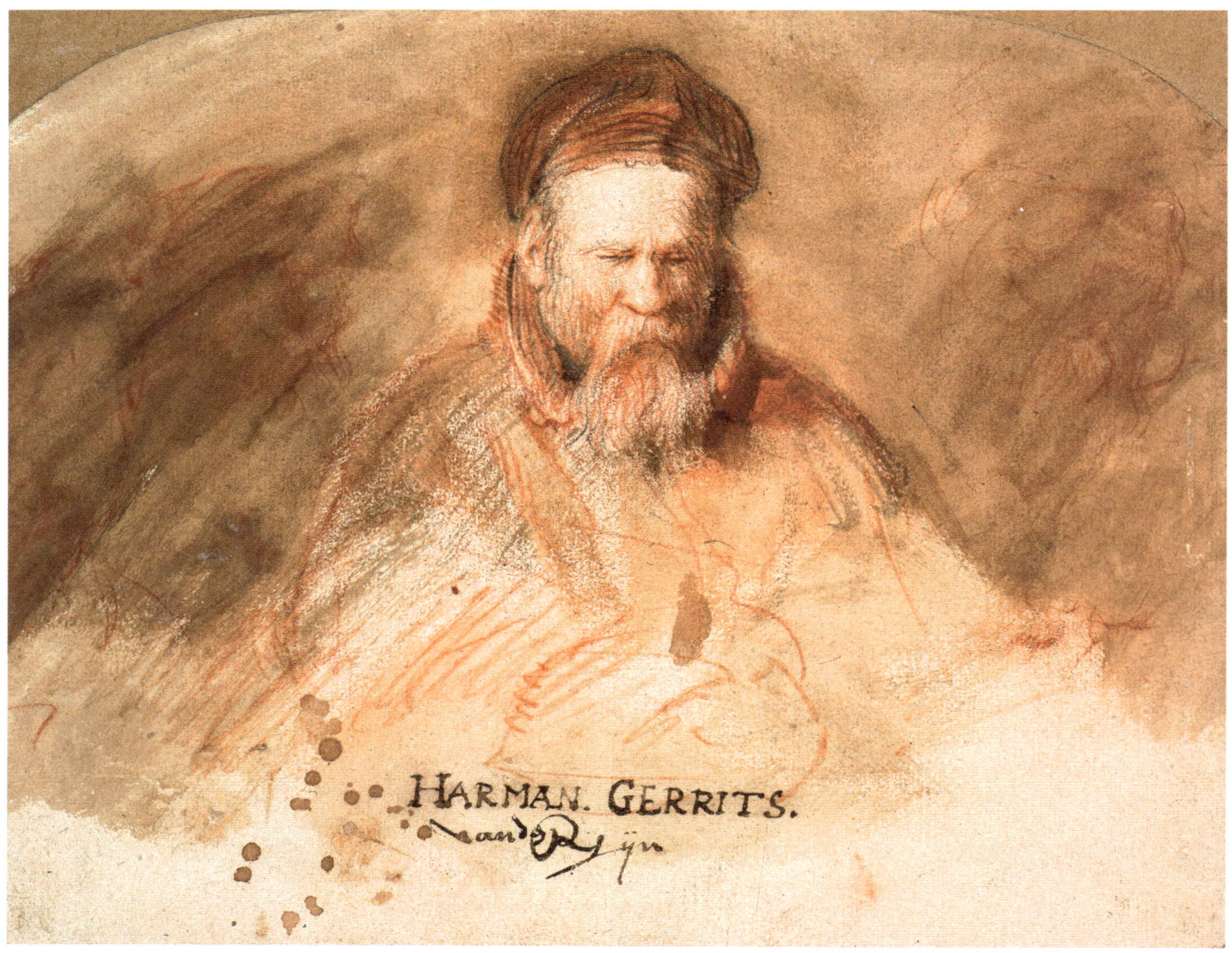

the small group of authentic Rembrandt paintings that upon occasion have been classified as portraits of his sister Elysabeth, not a scrap of evidence supports this identification, and of all the paintings that have been optimistically called portraits of his brother Adriaen, not one is by his hand.

Rembrandt's drawing of his father, Harmen Gerritsz van Rijn, can be identified, but, it is necessary to add, with some qualification, for questions have been raised about the reliability of its inscription, which serves as the basis of its identification (fig. 2.7). There is, however, general agreement that the drawing is datable about 1630, the year of Harmen's death. If the inscription is trustworthy—I side with those who endorse the view that it is—it is the artist's only existing portrayal of him.

Only one drawing of Rembrandt's mother is known. It is a rapid sketch for a work in progress that consists of only a

2.7 | *Portrait of an Old Man (Rembrandt's Father)* (recto), ca. 1630. Red and black chalk, on paper prepared with brown wash; 19 × 24 cm (7½ × 9½ in.). The Ashmolean Museum, University of Oxford, acc. no. WA1855.11, cat. no. PI 182. Photo © The Ashmolean Museum, University of Oxford.

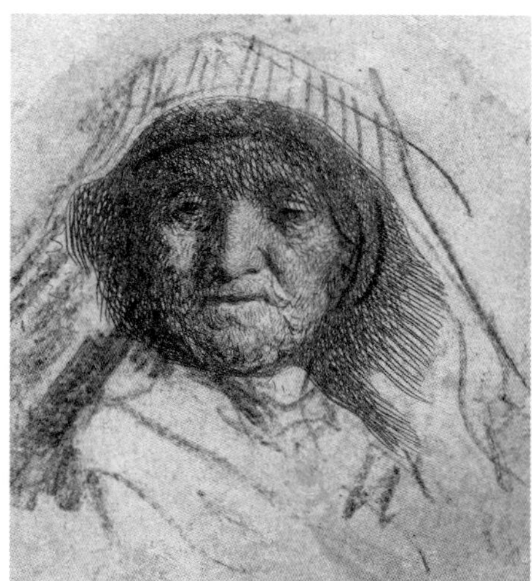

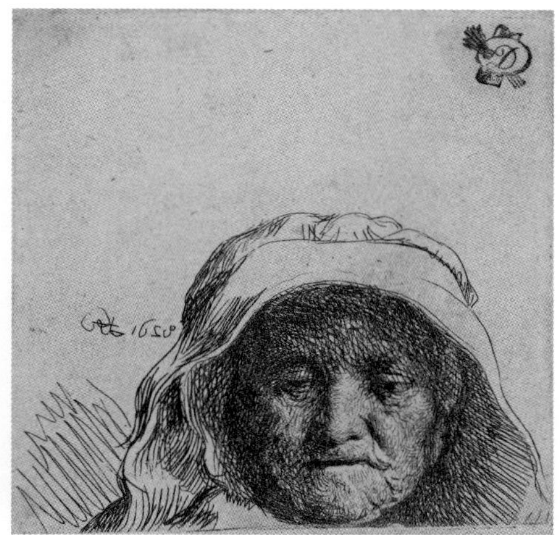

few meaningful black-chalk strokes of a hood and bust on the first state of the artist's 1628 etching of his mother's head (fig. 2.8). In the second and final state of the early print he obviously had second thoughts about the way he would complete the work. In the end he cropped his mother's head below her chin (fig. 2.9). Why? Perhaps the biting of the plate partially failed when he etched her bust, and he salvaged what he could by cutting off the lower part of the plate. In any event, the youthful artist's monogram and date on the etching's second state indicate he considered the small portrait of his mother with her head resting on the bottom edge of a print a worthy effort. Not many will quarrel with his judgment.

2.8 | *Portrait of Rembrandt's Mother*, ca. 1628. Etching, with black chalk; 6.5 × 5.8 cm (2½ × 2¼ in.). Rijksmuseum, Amsterdam, inv. RP-P-OB-747.

2.9 | *Portrait of Rembrandt's Mother*, monogrammed and dated 1628. Etching; 6.4 × 6.4 cm (2⅜ × 2⅜ in.). The British Museum, London, 1973,U.737. Photo © The Trustees of The British Museum/Art Resource, N.Y.

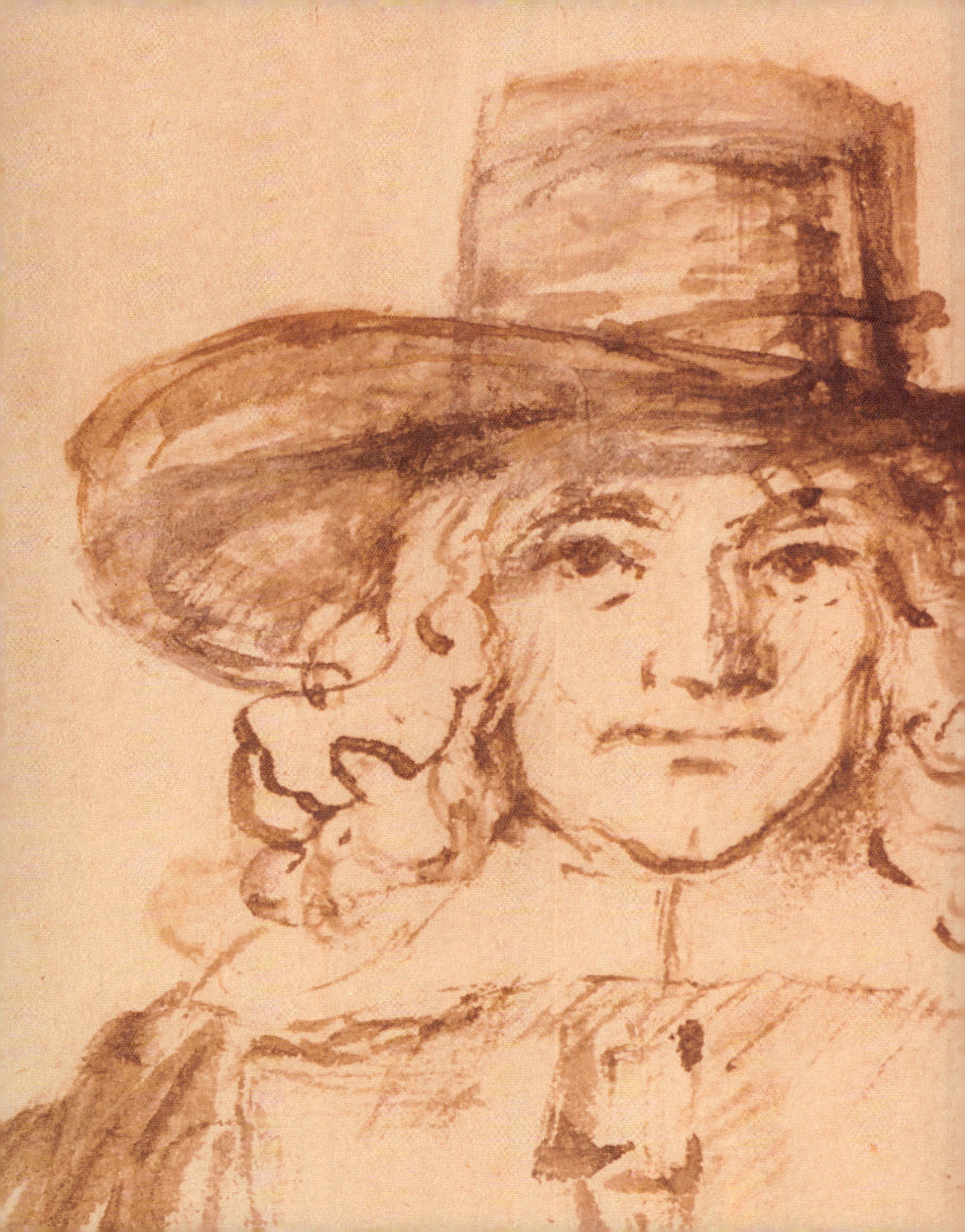

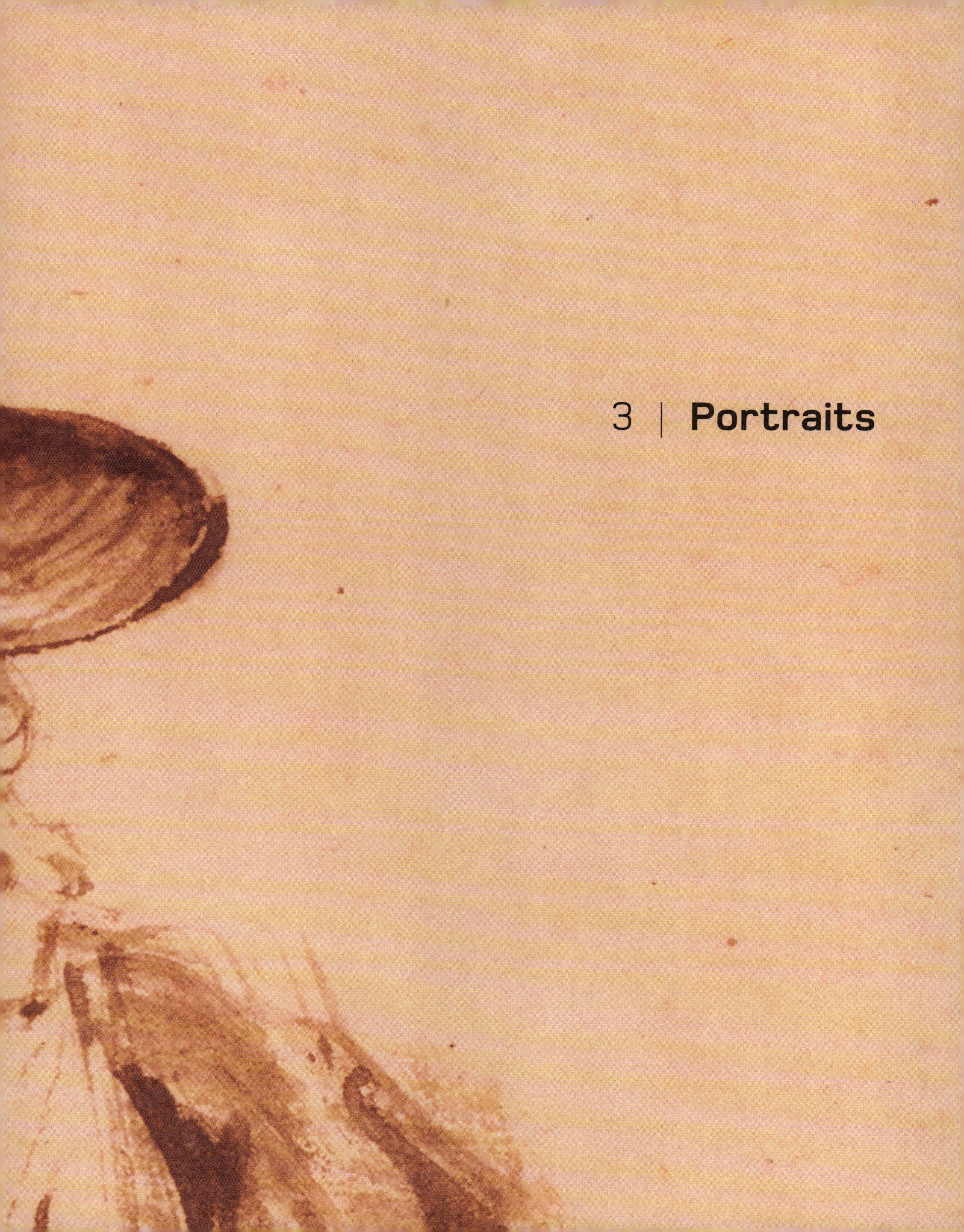

3 | Portraits

3 | **PORTRAITS**

3.1 | *Portrait of a Man in an Armchair* (*Willem Jansz van der Pluym?*), signed and dated 1634. Black and red chalk, brown ink, and gray brown wash on vellum prepared with white ground; 37.3 × 27.2 cm (14⅝ × 10¾ in.). Harvard Art Museum, Fogg Art Museum, Private collection, TL37860. Photo © President and Fellows of Harvard College. Photographer: Allan Macintyre.

FROM THE TIME REMBRANDT set himself up as an independent artist at Leiden in 1625 until he left his native city to settle in Amsterdam in 1631 or 1632, he did not to our knowledge paint a single commissioned portrait. To be sure, he made a few *tronies,* the Dutch name normally given to picturesque paintings of old people, men and women in fancy dress, or physiognomic studies, but not likenesses made to order. *Tronies* were a sideline. Young Rembrandt had a higher ambition. He did not want to make a mark as a mere face painter. He dedicated himself to what was considered until well into the nineteenth century a more noble calling: depiction of biblical, historical, and mythological subjects—the category known as history painting.

Immediately after his move to Amsterdam there was a dramatic shift. He did not abandon history painting or *tronies,* but he began to accept dozens of portrait commissions. By the end of the 1630s he had acquired a reputation as the most fashionable portraitist in Holland's leading metropolis.

Today we know almost a hundred bespoke painted portraits by his hand, made between 1631 and his death in 1669. His *Man in an Armchair* (fig. 3.1), highly worked up in red and black chalk, and brown ink and gray brown wash, on vellum prepared with a white ground, is his only portrait drawing that qualifies as a completed independent work. This conclusion is supported by its unmatched degree of finish and its prominent authentic inscription: *Rembrandt. f. 1634.* Its large size and unusual vellum support also speak for its special character; the artist's only other portrait on vellum is his betrothal portrait of Saskia (see fig. 2.4) done a year earlier. The drawing's fictive window frame, which suggests we are

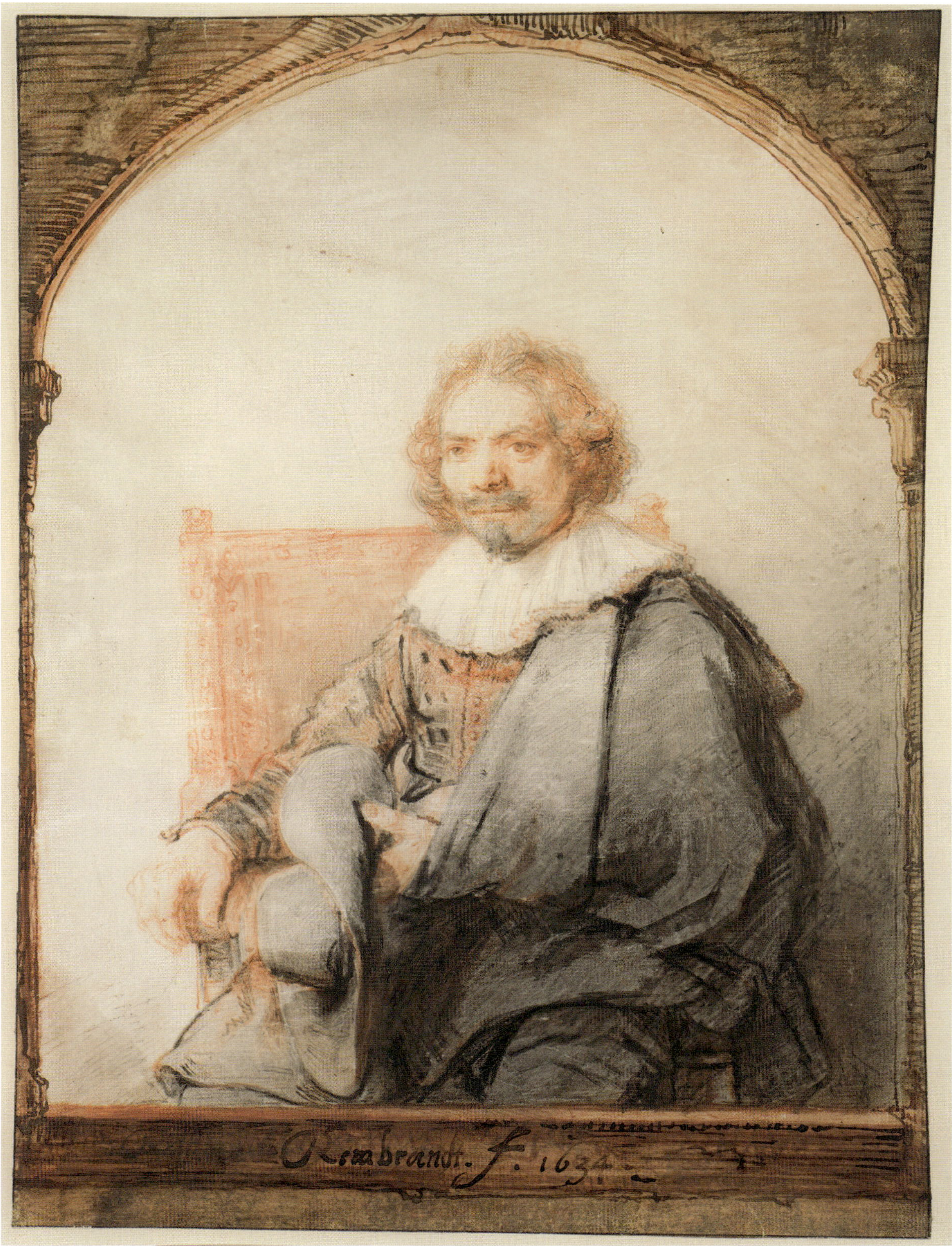
Rembrandt. f. 1634

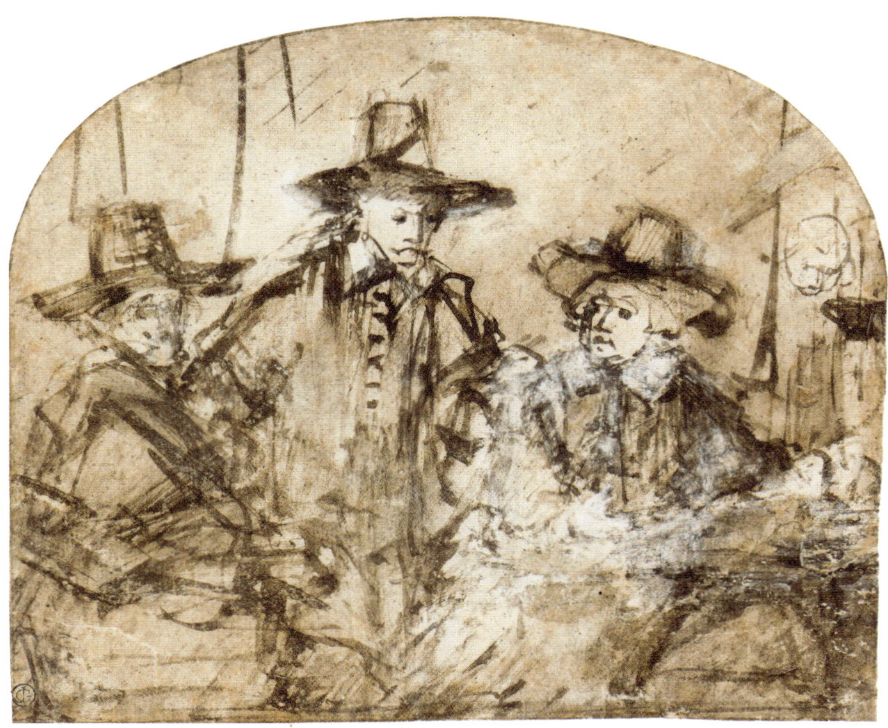

looking at the serious sitter from another room, is a device the artist used in other painted and etched portraits.

Rembrandt's model may tentatively be identified as Willem Jansz van der Pluym, a prosperous Amsterdam plumber and slater, who was distantly related to the artist. In a will Van der Pluym drew up in 1675 he cites a "drawing of himself done by Rembrandt van Rijn hanging in the entrance hall" of his house. There is no question that this stunning drawing was suitable for mounting in a home, and the will may refer to it; but the bald reference is not sufficient to clinch the identification.[11]

Rembrandt's painted portraits range from bread-and-butter pendants of burghers and their wives exquisitely portrayed in their Sunday best to summits of his achievement. Among the latter is his portrait of *Jan Six,* which with Velázquez's portrait of *Pope Innocent X* are arguably the greatest portraits painted in Europe during the seventeenth century. Rembrandt's portraits come in all sizes and represent virtually all types. There is even a life-size equestrian portrait of *Frederik Rihel* (London, National Gallery).

Preliminary and preparatory drawings for this large body of work tell another story. They are exceedingly rare. Their rarity, however, is not as extraordinary as may seem at first blush. The usual practice of Dutch portraitists of Rem-

3.2 | *Preliminary Study for "The Syndics,"* ca. 1662. Reed pen and brown ink, brown wash, heightened and corrected with white; 17.3 × 20.5 cm (6¾ × 8⅛ in.), with round top. Kupferstichkabinett, Staatliche Museen, Berlin, inv. KdZ 5270. Photo: Bildarchiv Preussischer Kulturbesitz/Art Resource, N.Y. Photographer: Jörg P. Anders.

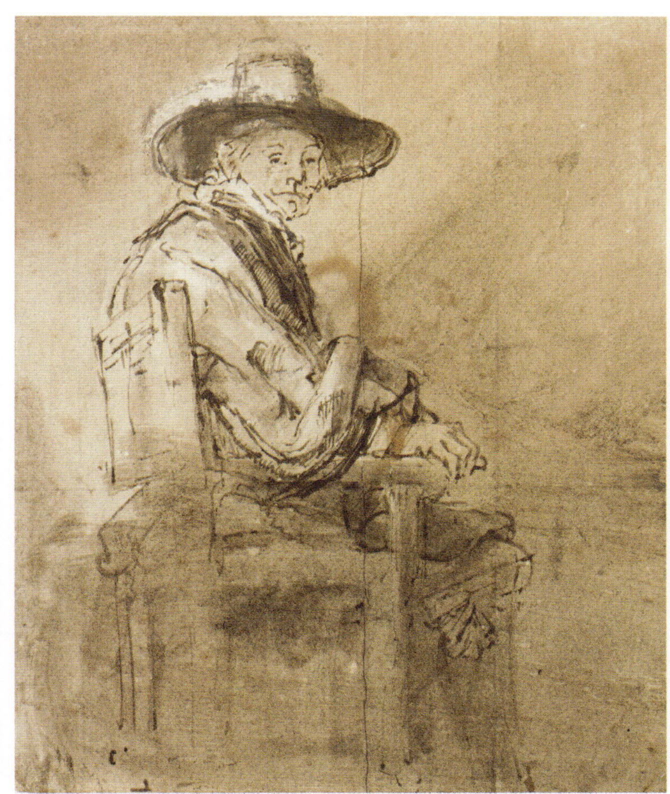

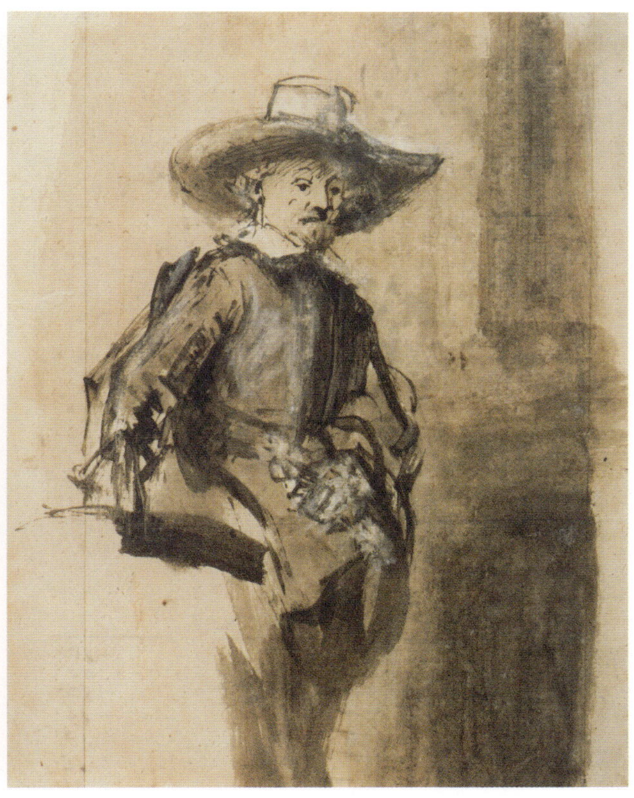

3.3 | *Preparatory Study for a Seated Syndic* (*Jacob van Loon*), ca. 1662. Pen and brown ink, brown wash, touches of white; 19.5 × 16 cm (7⅝ × 6¼ in.). Rijksmuseum, Amsterdam, inv. RP-T-1896-A-3172.

3.4 | *Preparatory Study for a Standing Syndic* (*Volckert Jansz*), ca. 1662. Pen and brown ink, brown wash, heightened and corrected with white, on cashbook paper; 22.5 × 17.5 cm (8⅞ × 6⅞ in.). Museum Boijmans Van Beuningen, Rotterdam, inv. R133 (Koenigs Collection).

brandt's day was to paint their sitter's likeness directly on canvas or wooden panel without making a preliminary drawing for their patron's inspection and approval or for use as a guide during subsequent work. There is no reason to believe that Rembrandt did not normally follow this practice.

On the other hand, the existence of three preliminary drawings in different collections (figs. 3.2, 3.3, 3.4) for his superb final group portrait known as *The Syndics* (fig. 3.5) indicates that this was not invariably the case. The Berlin drawing (see fig. 3.2), in less-than-good condition and with a rounded top that is probably not original, is the fragment of a very quick reed pen-and-wash compositional study for the group portrait. Part of a hat that can be seen to the right of the three figures indicates that the sheet was once larger. The study was made before Rembrandt decided to show the second syndic bending slightly as he stands. The haunting drawings of a single syndic in Amsterdam (see fig. 3.3) and Rotterdam (see fig. 3.4) were likewise done before a decision had been made about the painting's final form. Notable are the different chairs given to the seated syndic in the Amsterdam drawing and in the painting as well as the changes in his cos-

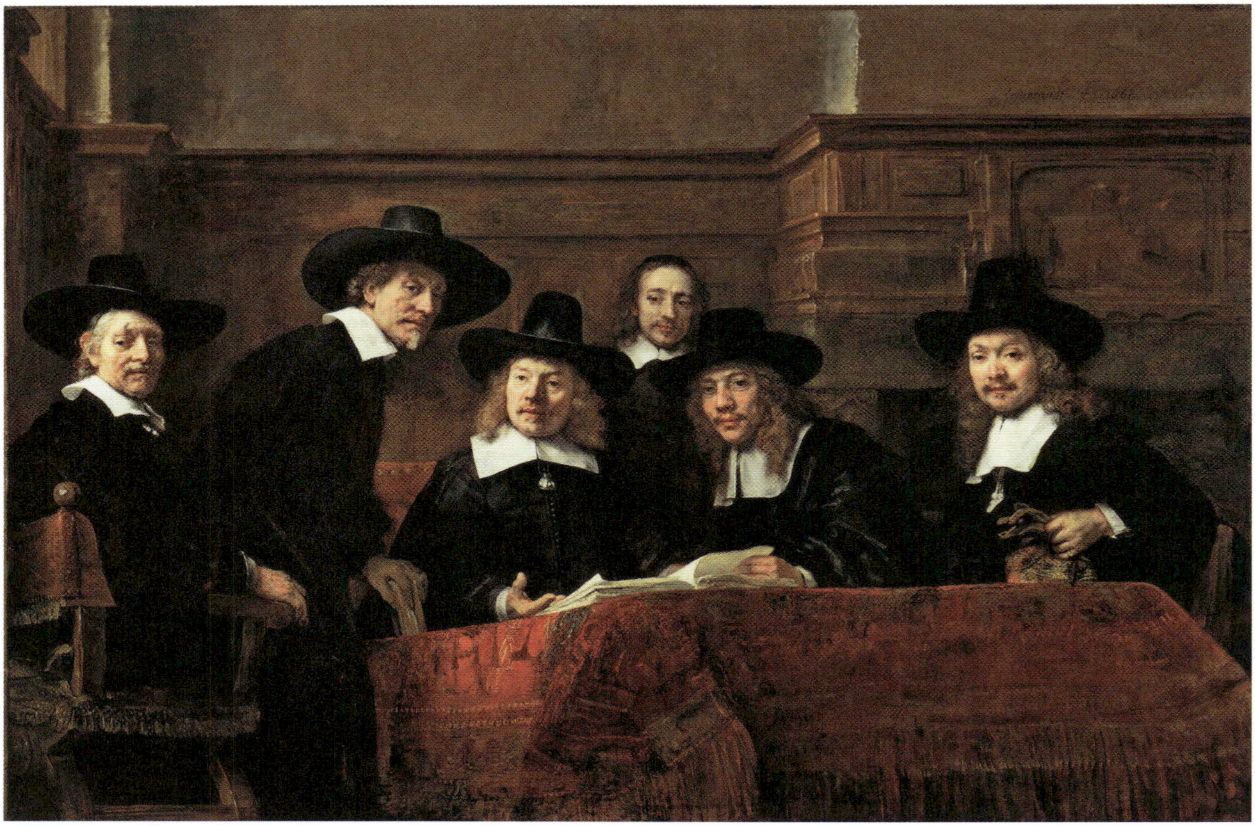

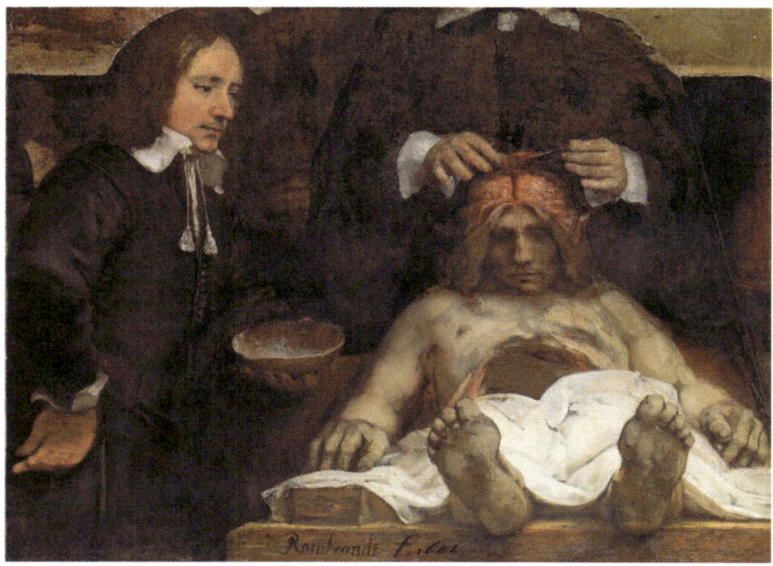

tume. Even more striking is the shift in the standing syndic's posture from the Rotterdam sheet. There he stands erect, while in the painting he appears to be rising from his chair.

An X-radiograph montage of *The Syndics* reveals that Rembrandt continued to make radical alterations to his composition as it evolved on his canvas.[12] Only after he painted the second syndic standing straight did he change his pose to a momentary one. X-radiographs of the seated syndic to the right of the rising one transforms him into a trinity. He was altered three times; his head appears in three different positions, and his outstretched hand has three thumbs. In the battlefield of light and dark passages on the right side of the montage it is possible to distinguish the original appearance of the hatless servant who was subsequently shifted and given a serene place near the center. What the naked eye sees of the large group portrait's perfection is obviously the result of a formidable struggle, first on paper and then on canvas.

The search for drawings related to the artist's three other frequently discussed group portraits has been disappointing. Not a single sketch has been found that can be linked in any way to the surgeons or cadaver depicted in *The Anatomy Lesson of Dr. Nicolaes Tulp* of 1632. If Rembrandt made preliminary drawings seeking the best way to represent Dr. Tulp's right hand pulling on the cadaver's flexor muscles while repeating with his left hand how these muscles make fingers curl—and it is hard to imagine he did not—they have disappeared.

3.5 | *The Syndics*, signed and dated 1662. Oil on canvas; 191.5 × 279 cm (75⅜ × 9 ft. 1⅞ in.). Amsterdam Historisch Museum, on loan to the Rijksmuseum, Amsterdam, inv. SK-C-85.

3.6 | *The Anatomy Lesson of Dr. Joan Deyman*, signed and dated 1656. Oil on canvas (fragment); 100 × 134 cm (39⅜ × 52¾ in.) (originally ca. 245 × 300 cm [96½ × 118 in.]). Amsterdam Historisch Museum, inv. SA 7394, on loan to the Rijksmuseum, Amsterdam, inv. SK-C-85.

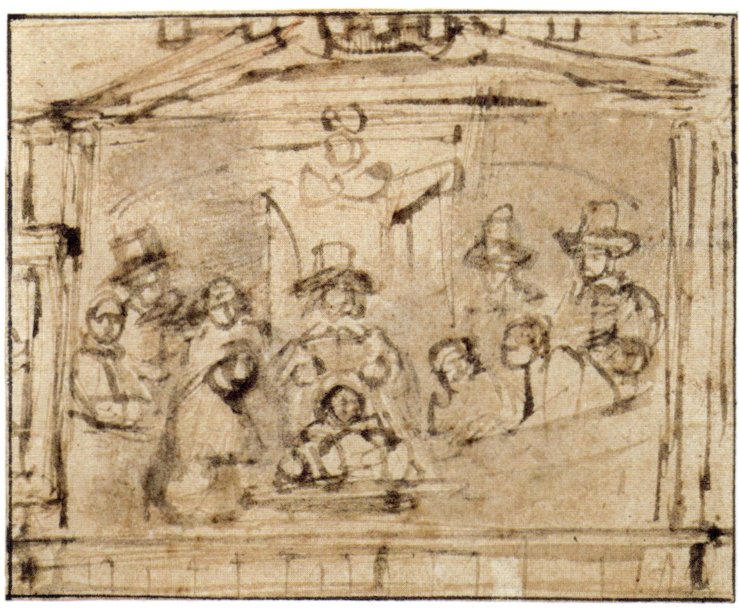

3.7 | *Sketch of the "Anatomy Lesson of Dr. Joan Deyman" Mounted in the Surgeons' Guildhall*, ca. 1656. Pen and brush and brown ink, red chalk, on paper; 10.9 × 13.1 cm (4¼ × 5⅛ in.). Amsterdam Historisch Museum, inv. TA 7395, on loan to the Rijksmuseum, Amsterdam, inv. SK-C-1192 (R).

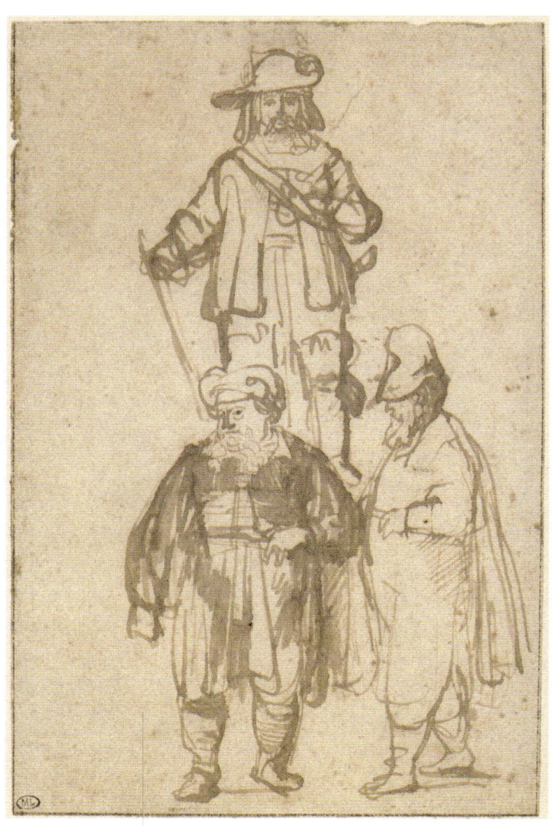

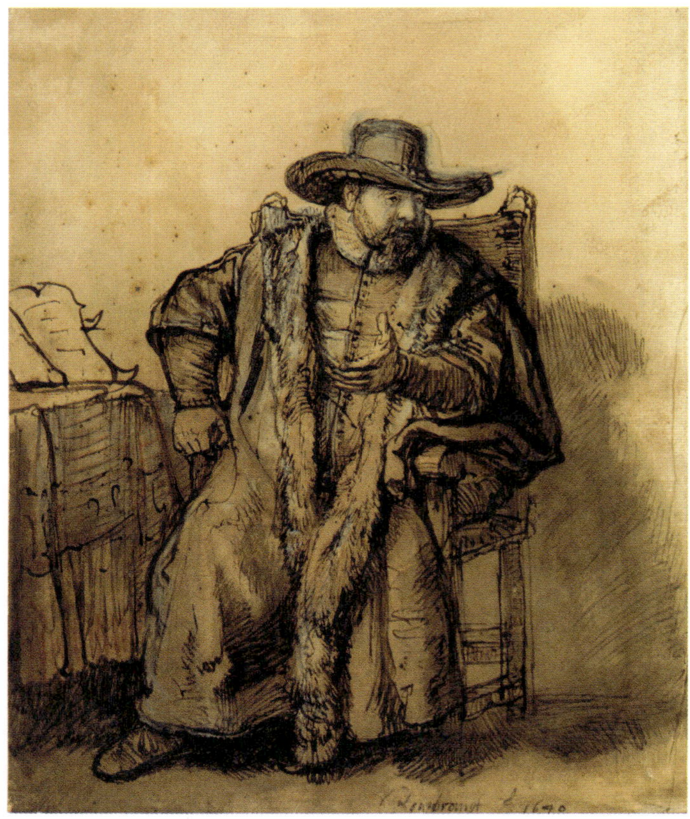

In 1656 Rembrandt painted *The Anatomy Lesson of Dr. Joan Deyman*. A fire all but destroyed the painting in 1723. The fragment that remains is exhibited at the Rijksmuseum (fig. 3.6). The single drawing related to it (fig. 3.7), an autograph small diagrammatic reed pen-and-wash sketch, shows the way the artist intended the framed, life-size group portrait to look on a wall in the Amsterdam surgeons' guildhall.[13] He indicates that an open window seen at the left in the sketch would not obstruct the painting; the beams that support the ceiling are shown by small rectangles at the top. Though today we have only the sketch and the painting fragment showing the dramatically foreshortened cadaver, the body and hands of Dr. Deyman operating on his brain, and an assistant holding the top of his skull, it is still possible to get an idea of the powerful effect the portrait must have had before the disastrous fire.

The Night Watch, Rembrandt's most famous painting, brilliantly transforms traditional Dutch civic-guard portraiture into an unprecedented, highly animated, unified composition. None of the master's group portraits seems to have been in greater need of both preliminary sketches to help plot its

3.8 | *Sketch of an Officer and Two Standing Figures*, ca. 1640–42. Pen and brown ink; 21.2 × 13.4 cm (8⅜ × 5¼ in.). Musée du Louvre, Paris, inv. RF29031. Photo © RMN—Grand Palais/Art Resource, N.Y. Photographer: Michèle Bellot.

3.9 | *Cornelis Claesz Anslo* (1592–1646), signed and dated 1640. Pen and brown ink, brown and gray wash, red chalk, heightened with white; 24.6 × 20.1 cm (9⅝ × 7⅞ in.). Musée du Louvre, Paris, Collection Edmond de Rothschild, inv. 192DR. Photo © RMN—Grand Palais/Art Resource, N.Y.

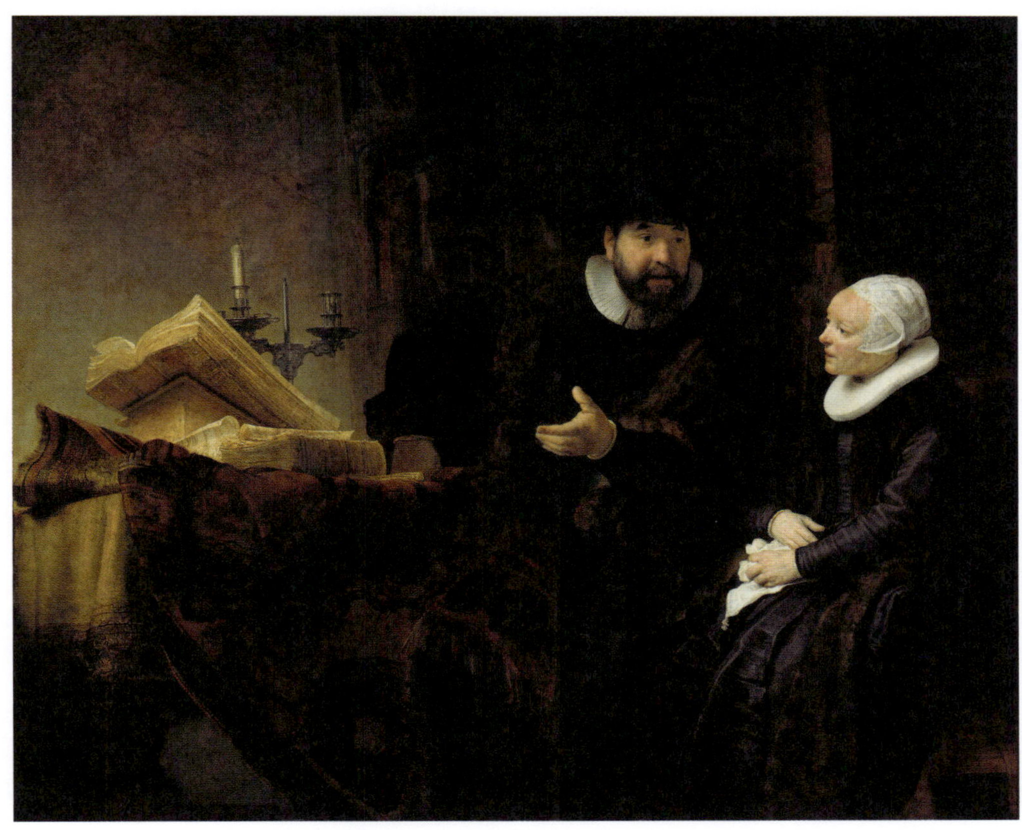

3.10 | *Double Portrait of the Mennonite Preacher Cornelis Claesz Anslo and His Wife Aeltje Gerritsdr Schouten*, signed and dated 1641. Oil on canvas; 176 × 210 cm (69¼ × 82⅝ in.), upper corners rounded. Gemäldegalerie, Staatliche Museen, Berlin, inv. 3981. Photo: Bildarchiv Preussischer Kulturbesitz/Art Resource, N.Y. Photographer: Jörg P. Anders.

complex spatial design and preparatory drawings for its colossal cast of thirty-one characters. (Before the painting was cropped in about 1715, it had thirty-four.) However, neither compositional studies nor preparatory studies for the figures exist. Merely the top figure in a study sheet at the Louvre has been related to the work (fig. 3.8). There are no others. The figure in the Louvre's drawing bears a vague resemblance to Captain Frans Banning Cocq, the principal officer of the civic guard group, but there is no suggestion whatsoever of the way he strides forward in the finished painting. No one would be astonished if some readers dismiss the proposed connection between the sketch and the captain as too slight to be valid.[14]

Rembrandt made two fully signed drawings of the Mennonite preacher and cloth merchant Cornelis Claesz Anslo in 1640. The one at the Louvre (fig. 3.9), in pen, red chalk, and brown and gray wash, shows Anslo full-length, seated near a table with his arm stretched forward, as if stressing a point as he speaks. It served as a preliminary drawing for his 1641 life-size, double portrait of Anslo with his wife, Aeltje Gerritsdr Schouten, who listens attentively to his words (fig. 3.10).

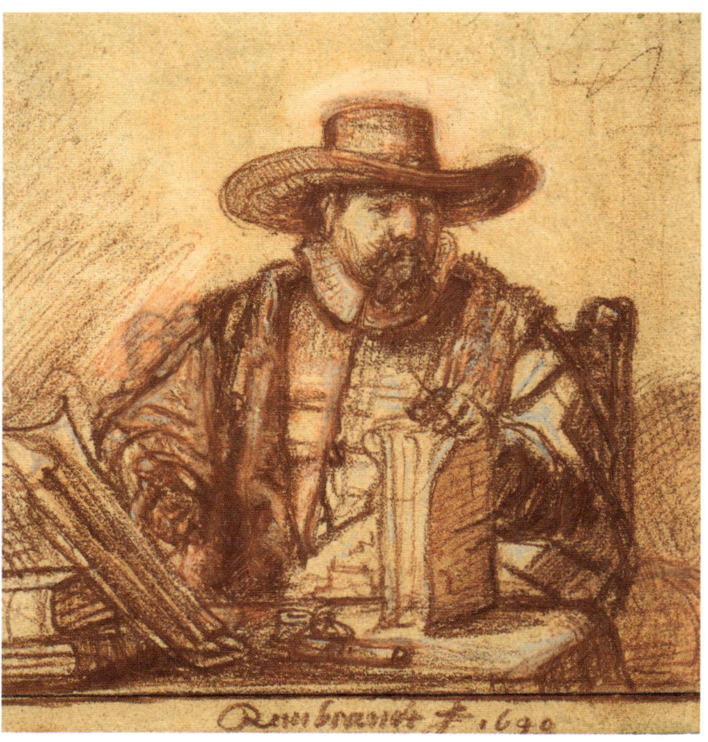

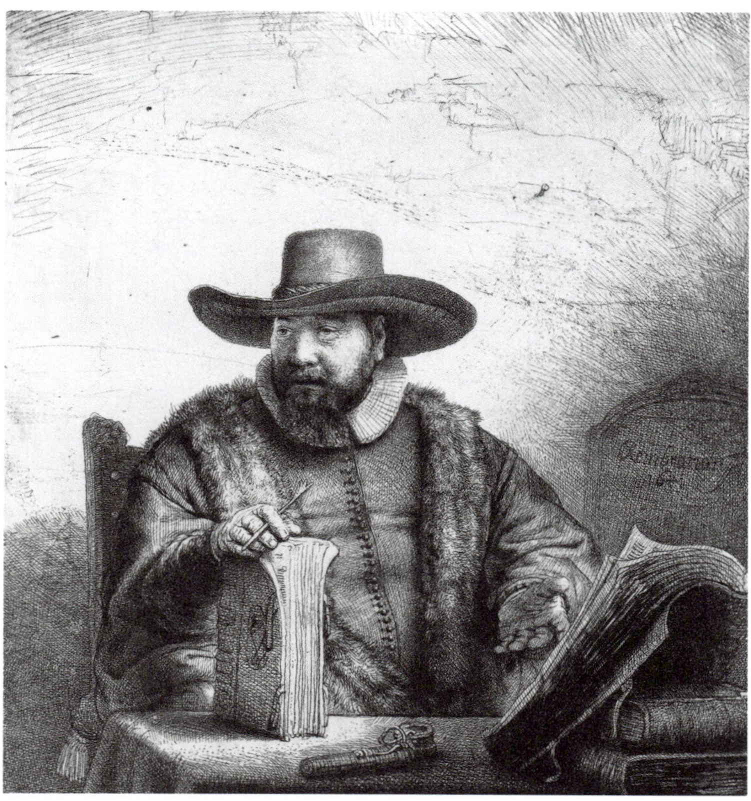

3.11 | *Cornelis Claesz Anslo*, signed and dated 1640. Red chalk, heightened with white, some red wash, outlines indented for transfer; 15.7 × 14.4 cm (6⅛ × 5⅝ in.). The British Museum, London, inv. 1848,0911.138. Photo © The Trustees of The British Museum/Art Resource, N.Y.

3.12 | *Cornelis Claesz Anslo, Preacher*, signed and dated 1641. Etching and drypoint; 18.8 × 15.8 cm (7⅜ × 6¼ in.). The Pierpont Morgan Library, New York, inv. RvR 365. Photographer: David A. Loggie.

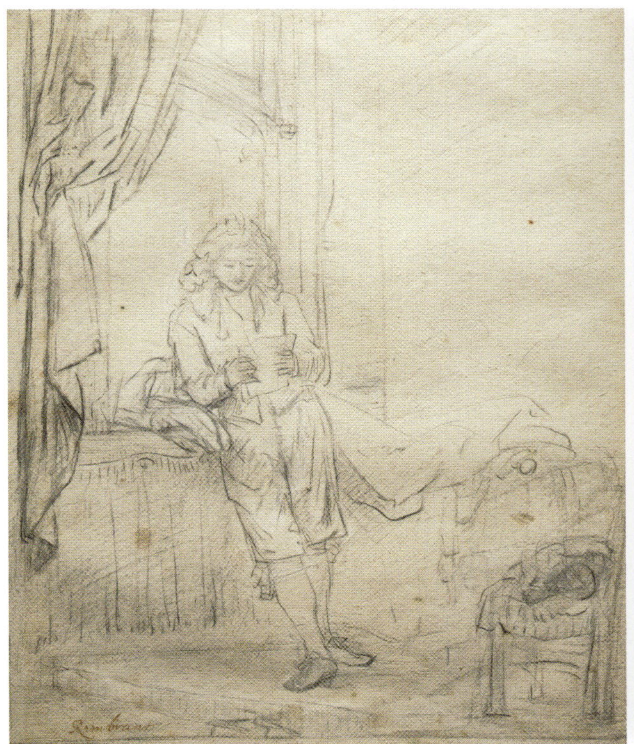

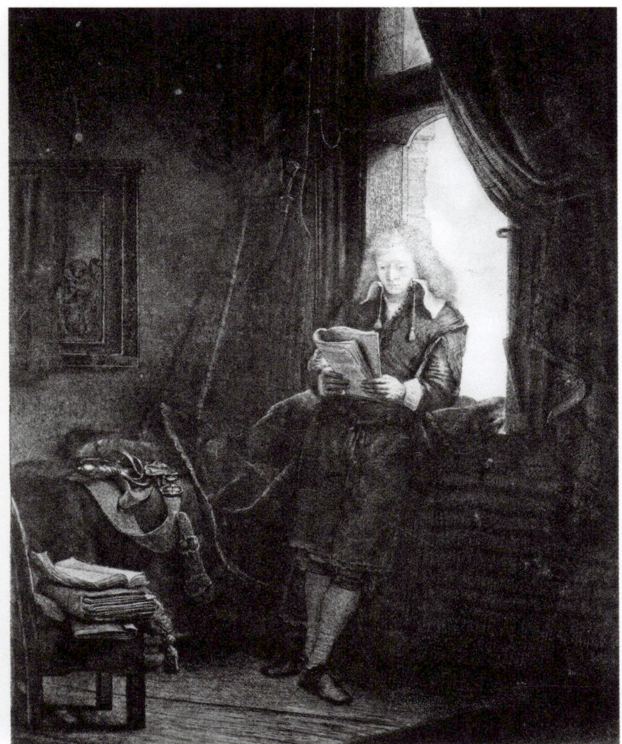

Rembrandt's other 1640 drawing of Anslo, done in red chalk with touches of red wash, is at the British Museum (fig. 3.11). It is a working drawing (in reverse) for his etching of the preacher seen half-length, seated behind a table with books, dated 1641 (fig. 3.12). The drawing has been indented with a stylus for transfer to the copperplate. Again Anslo is seen gesturing as if speaking. For some of the artist's clients a speaking likeness was clearly more than a figure of speech.

Another portrait drawing indented for transfer to a copperplate is the black-chalk preparatory sketch (in reverse) Rembrandt made for his etching of his wealthy patron and friend Jan Six in his study (fig. 3.13). The rich, atmospheric etching is dated 1647 (fig. 3.14). Two other preliminary drawings for the print are also known. One is a quick, difficult-to-decipher black-chalk, half-length study (in reverse) of Six reading (fig. 3.15), almost as depicted in the print; it is on the verso of a sketch of a group of beggars. The second study shows Six in a more relaxed mood (fig. 3.16). Here he is not engrossed in reading, but at ease leaning on the sill of an open window. His hound is jumping up his thigh, begging for attention. If Rembrandt had resolved the furious changes he made with broad reed pen and washes in the drawing and

3.13 | *Jan Six*, 1647. Black chalk, outlines indented for transfer; 24.5 × 19.1 cm (9⅝ × 7½ in.). Collectie Six, Amsterdam, collection no. CS 00204.

3.14 | *Jan Six*, signed and dated 1647. Etching, drypoint and burin; 24.5 × 19.1 cm (9⅝ × 7½ in.). Photo: Foto Marburg/Art Resource, N.Y.

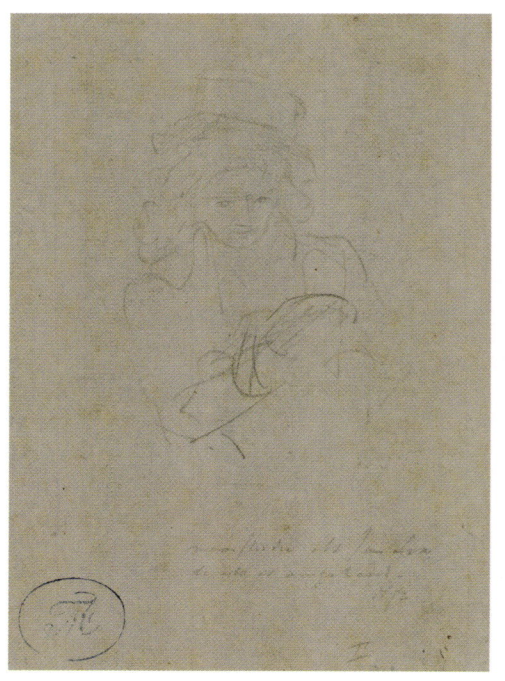

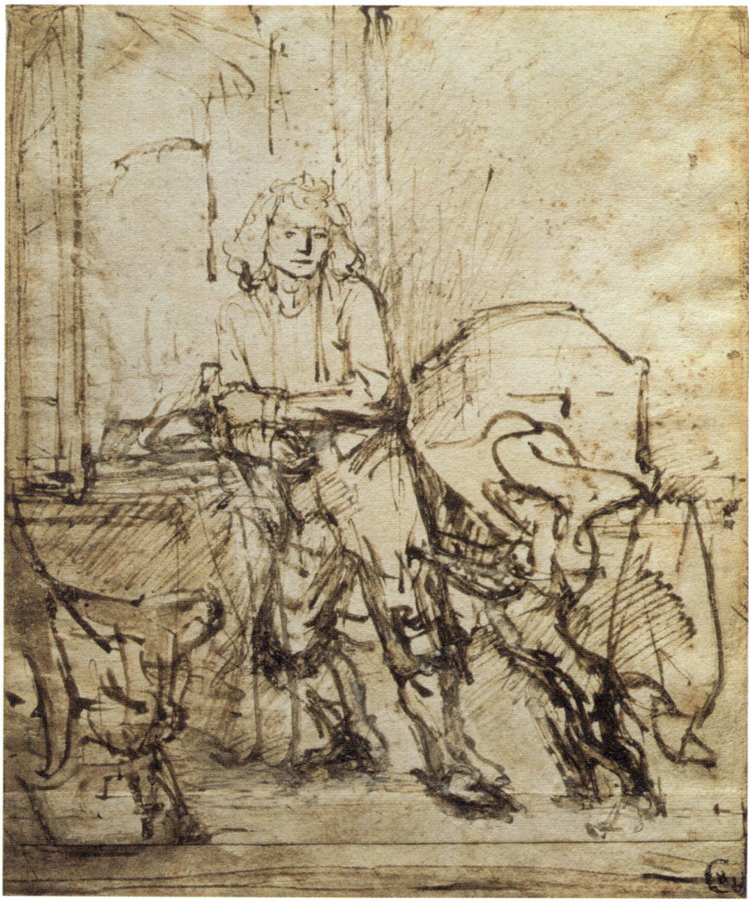

translated it into an etching or painting, the finished work would have qualified as one of the most informal portraits done in seventeenth-century Holland. We do not know if Six rejected the scheme or if Rembrandt himself decided it was inappropriate for a finished portrayal of his friend.

We do know that Rembrandt and Jan Six continued to have contact. In 1648, a year after Rembrandt completed his etched portrait, Six published his play *Medea;* the artist etched a fine frontispiece for the volume. As we shall see, in 1652 he contributed two drawings to a friendship album (see pp. 189–90) his patron owned. Six loaned him a thousand guilders in 1653, and in the following year Rembrandt painted his stellar three-quarters length portrait of Six (Six collection, Amsterdam). He also owned other pictures by the master: *Half-length Profile Portrait of Saskia,* now at Kassel, and his grisaille (a monochromatic painting in shades of gray) of *Saint John the Baptist Preaching* at Berlin. And there is good reason to believe Rem-

3.15 | *Jan Six* (detail of verso), ca. 1647. Black chalk, 13.1 × 9.6 cm (5⅛ × 3¾ in.). Amsterdam Historisch Museum, inv. A10268.

3.16 | *Jan Six*, ca. 1647. Pen and brown ink, brown wash, corrected with white; 22 × 17.7 cm (8⅝ × 7 in.). Collectie Six, Amsterdam, collection no. 00203.

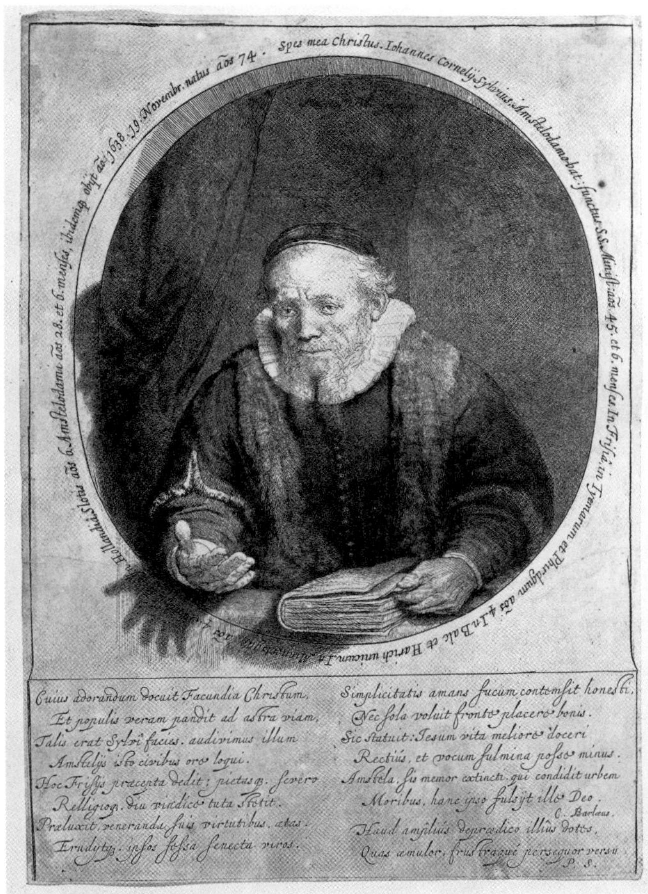

3.17 | *Jan Cornelisz Sylvius*, signed and dated 1646. Etching and drypoint; 27.8 × 18.8 cm (11 × 7³⁄₈ in.). Private collection.

brandt made a drawing of a frame designed for the latter work when it was in Six's collection in the mid-1650s (see fig. 16.5).

The artist's posthumous portrait of the Dutch Reformed minister Jan Cornelisz Sylvius, dated 1646 (fig. 3.17), is the only other etched portrait for which drawings survive. The artist knew Sylvius well: He was Saskia's cousin. In 1633, the year Rembrandt etched his first portrait of the minister (Bartsch no. 266), the artist was granted permission to marry Saskia. Two years later Sylvius witnessed the baptism of the couple's firstborn child, and in 1638, the year of Sylvius's death, he baptized their secondborn.

Who or what prompted Rembrandt to etch Sylvius's portrait eight years after his subject's death remains a mystery. The etching includes more text (none of it in the artist's hand) than any of his other prints. The minister's thumbnail biography is found inscribed around its fictive oval frame, and below it are two Latin eulogies by different authors.

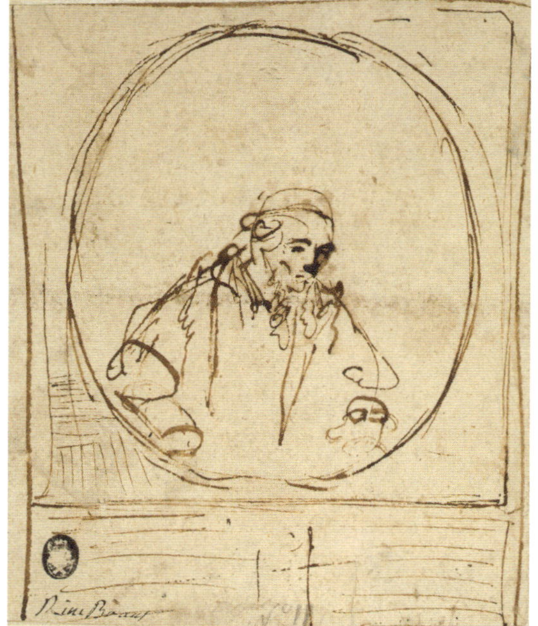

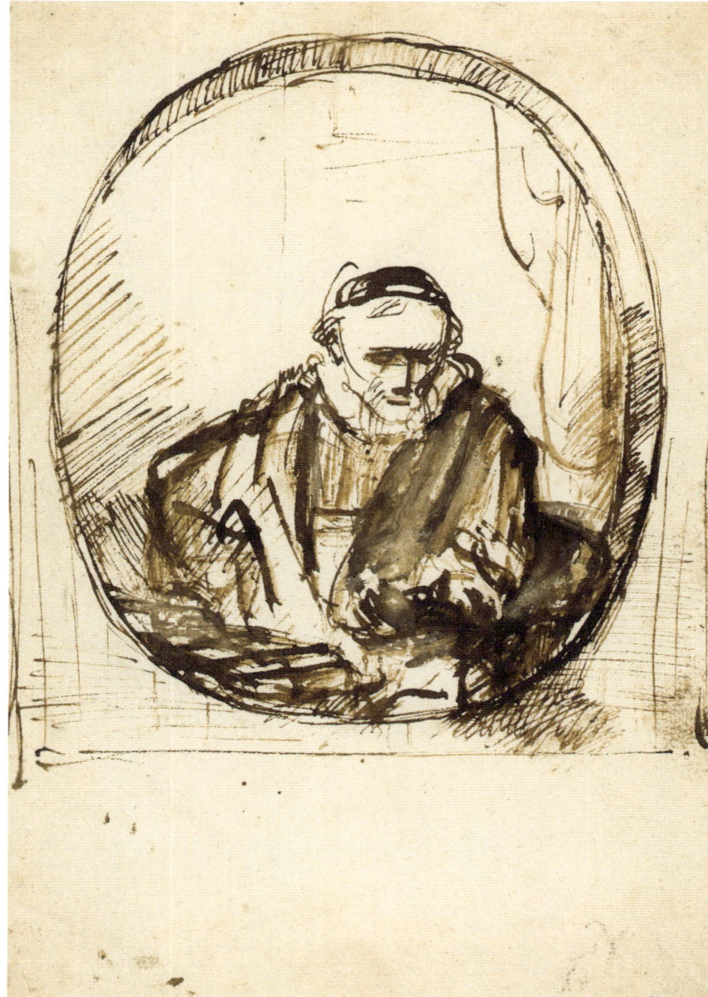

The surviving preliminary studies were sketched (in reverse) after a decision had been made to place Sylvius behind an oval opening and the eulogies below it. The Stockholm sheet is a hasty layout sketch, almost certainly the result of no more than a minute or two of work (fig. 3.18). Probably Rembrandt sketched similar fugitive studies for other prints and paintings that have disappeared because neither he nor his contemporaries believed they were worth saving. Survival of the Stockholm sheet can be called a happy accident that occurred before collectors learned to treasure every scrap, as if it were a holy relic, if it has marks on it recognizable as Rembrandt's. In the Stockholm sketch they are found in the shorthand scribbles and looping strokes that define Sylvius. The British Museum's vigorous sketch includes the minister's hand thrust forward beyond the fictive frame as well as the

3.18 | *Jan Cornelisz Sylvius*, ca. 1646. Pen and brown ink; 14.3 × 11.3 cm (5⅝ × 4½ in.). Nationalmuseum, Stockholm, inv. 137/1973. Photo © The National Museum of Fine Arts.

3.19 | *Jan Cornelisz Sylvius*, ca. 1646. Pen and brown ink, with brown wash, heightened with white; 28.3 × 19.4 cm (11¼ × 7⅝ in.). The British Museum, London, inv. 1874,0808.2272. Photo © The Trustees of The British Museum/Art Resource, N.Y.

shadows his hand and body cast (fig. 3.19). These elements are developed further in the etching, which also includes the shadow cast by the open folio, surely a Bible, projecting beyond the oval opening.

Until recently Rembrandt's pen-and-wash drawing of Maria Trip at the British Museum (fig. 3.20) had been classified as a modello for a client's approval or a preliminary drawing for his exquisite painted portrait of her, dated 1639, now on loan at the Rijksmuseum (fig. 3.21). However, X-radiographs of the painting conclusively demonstrate it is neither. They reveal that originally a balustrade ran across the picture's entire lower edge and that the sitter's left hand rested upon it. Then Rembrandt changed his mind. The drawing shows the principal change: The banister rail has been considerably shortened, as now seen in the painting. The drawing as well as a technical examination of the painting's canvas support also

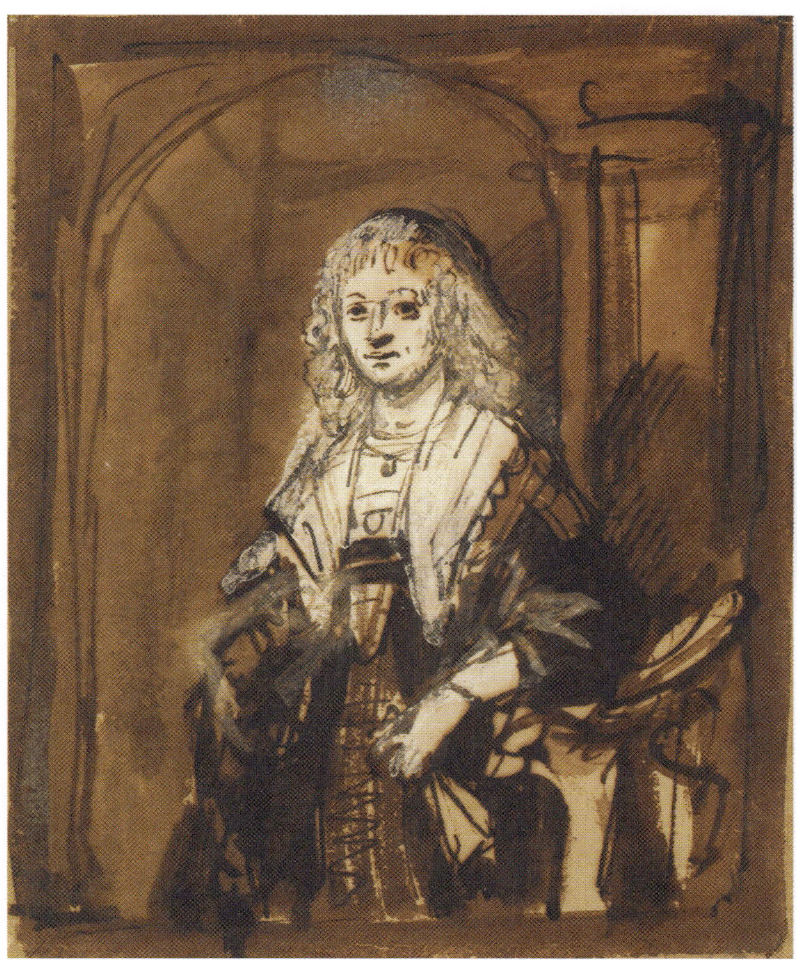

3.20 | *Maria Trip* (1619–1683), ca. 1639. Pen and brown iron-gall ink, brown wash, heightened with white; 16 × 12.9 cm (6¼ × 5⅛ in.). The British Museum, London, inv. 1891-7-13-9. Photo © The Trustees of The British Museum/Art Resource, N.Y.

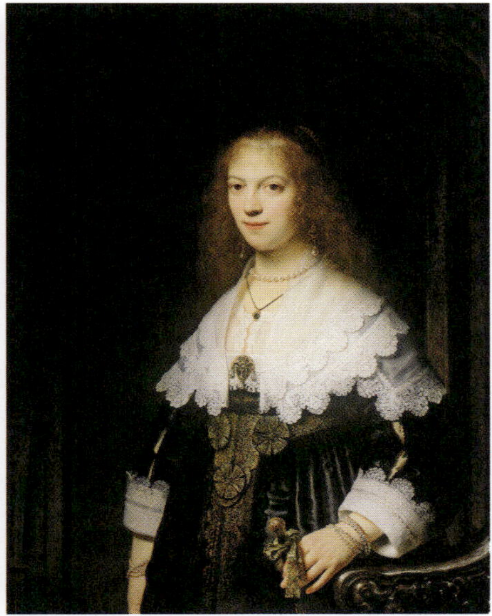

3.21 | *Maria Trip*, signed and dated 1639. Oil on panel; 107 × 82 cm (42⅛ × 32¼ in.). Rijksmuseum, Amsterdam, inv. SK-C-597 (on loan from the Van Weede Family Foundation).

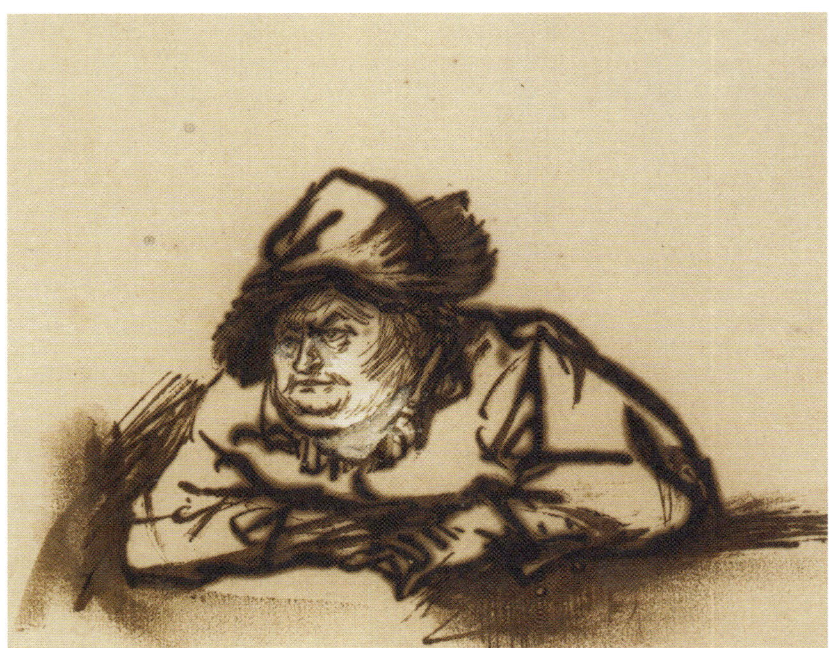

indicate that the picture was once considerably larger. Additionally, comparison of the drawing with the present portrait shows other significant differences; Maria Trip's lace collar has become more elaborate and much larger, it has become a virtual shawl draped over her shoulders; her gown has acquired huge lace cuffs and rosettes; and she holds a fan. In short, the British Museum drawing is an intermediate working study, executed to help implement changes in the portrait after it was well under way and before what we now enjoy on the picture's surface.[15]

The quill-pen lines of the drawing of Maria Trip are done in brown iron-gall ink, a medium composed of an extract of ground nut galls (usually from oak trees) mixed with iron sulphate and bound with gum arabic, which Rembrandt favored in the mid- and late 1630s. Another portrait in the same medium, executed about the same time as his portrayal of Trip, is of the tavern keeper and famous Amsterdam actor Willem Bartolsz Ruyter[16] (fig. 3.22). In this portrait the deleterious effect of iron-gall ink is obvious: it has the propensity to oxidize and eat into paper. Its tendency is evident even in the fine quill-pen lines that define Ruyter's stout face and prominent dewlap but much more so in the vigorous pen strokes that have bitten into the paper and are now flanked by radiant browns, which in some passages appear to be areas of wash. The soft brown shadows at Ruyter's sides and below his

3.22 | *Willem Bartolsz Ruyter*, ca. 1639. Pen and brown iron-gall ink, heightened with white gouache, on paper prepared with yellowish-brown wash; 13.9 × 17.4 cm (5½ × 6⅞ in.). Rijksmuseum, Amsterdam, inv. RP-T-1996-6.

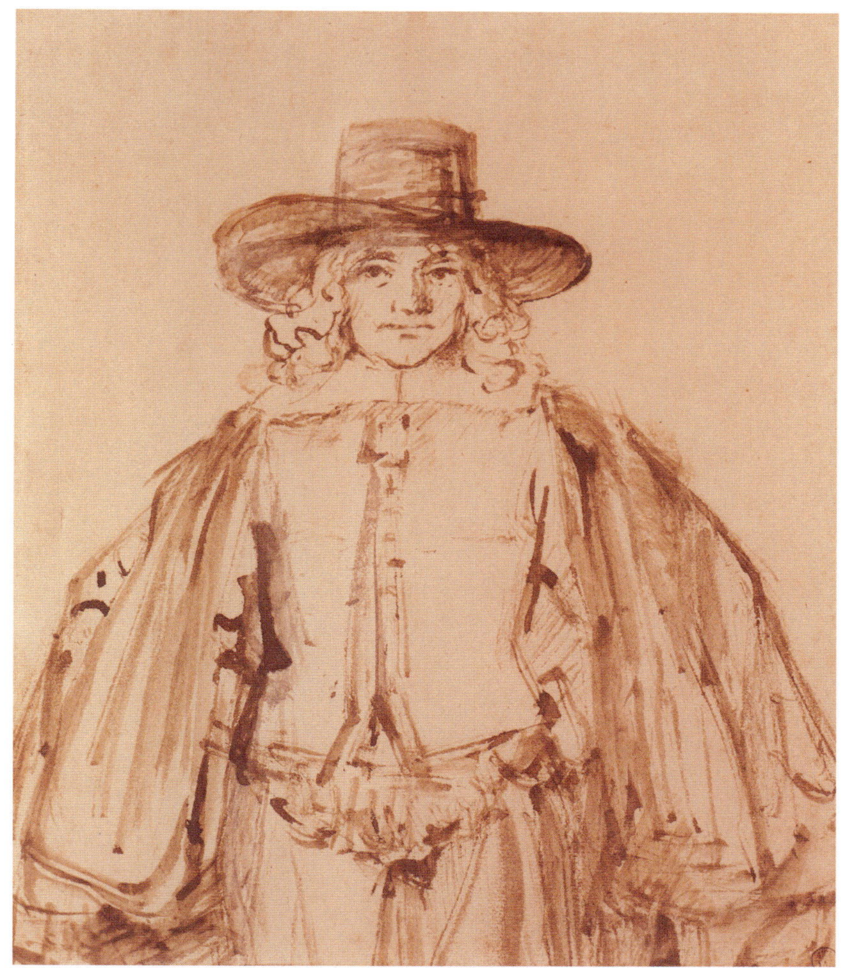

arms were deftly created by ink lightly and swiftly smudged by the artist's fingers. Rembrandt also made drawings of Ruyter in the role of Bishop Gozewijn in Joost van den Vondel's play "Gijsbrecht van Amstel" in Amsterdam's new theater, which opened in the late 1630s. Vondel's play is little known today outside the Netherlands, but it is fair to say it appealed to some seventeenth-century Dutch theatergoers the way "Hamlet" attracts modern audiences.

The imposing three-quarters length *Portrait of a Man,* datable ca. 1655–60 (fig. 3.23), has been variously called Jan Six and Rembrandt's son Titus, but neither identification is justifiable. The handsome young man remains anonymous. His portrait was vigorously executed with a broad reed pen, an instrument for which the artist had a predilection in his maturity, as we have already seen in his small, late *Self-portrait* at the Albertina (see fig. 1.13), studies for *The Syndics* (see figs. 3.2, 3.3, 3.4),

3.23 | *Portrait of a Man*, ca. 1655–60. Reed pen and brown ink; 23.2 × 19.4 cm (9⅛ × 7⅝ in.). Collectie Six, Amsterdam, collection no. 00216.

and the sketch related to the *Anatomy Lesson of Dr. Joan Deyman* (see fig. 3.7). The changes and revisions made in the size of the man's broad-brimmed, cylindrical hat give glimpses of the artist searching for forms he considers just.

Most likely the bold strokes below the man's waistcoat indicate a series of ribbon loops, or gallants, which were worn as an apron-like skirt at the waist; it was a French creation called a *tablier de galants*.[17] A clearer depiction of the fashionable accessory is seen in Frans Hals's outstanding life-size three-quarters length *Portrait of a Man*, datable ca. 1650–52 (fig. 3.24); his *tablier de galants* is comprised of lilac, gray-green, and rose ribbons. It is no accident that both Rembrandt and Hals gave their patrons frontal poses. After mid-century both artists often sought quieter and more stately effects.

3.24 | Frans Hals (Dutch, ca. 1582–1666), *Portrait of a Man*, early 1650s. Oil on canvas; 110.5 × 86.4 cm (43½ × 34 in.). The Metropolitan Museum of Art, New York, Marquand Collection, Gift of Henry G. Marquand, 1890, inv. 91.26.9. Image © The Metropolitan Museum of Art.

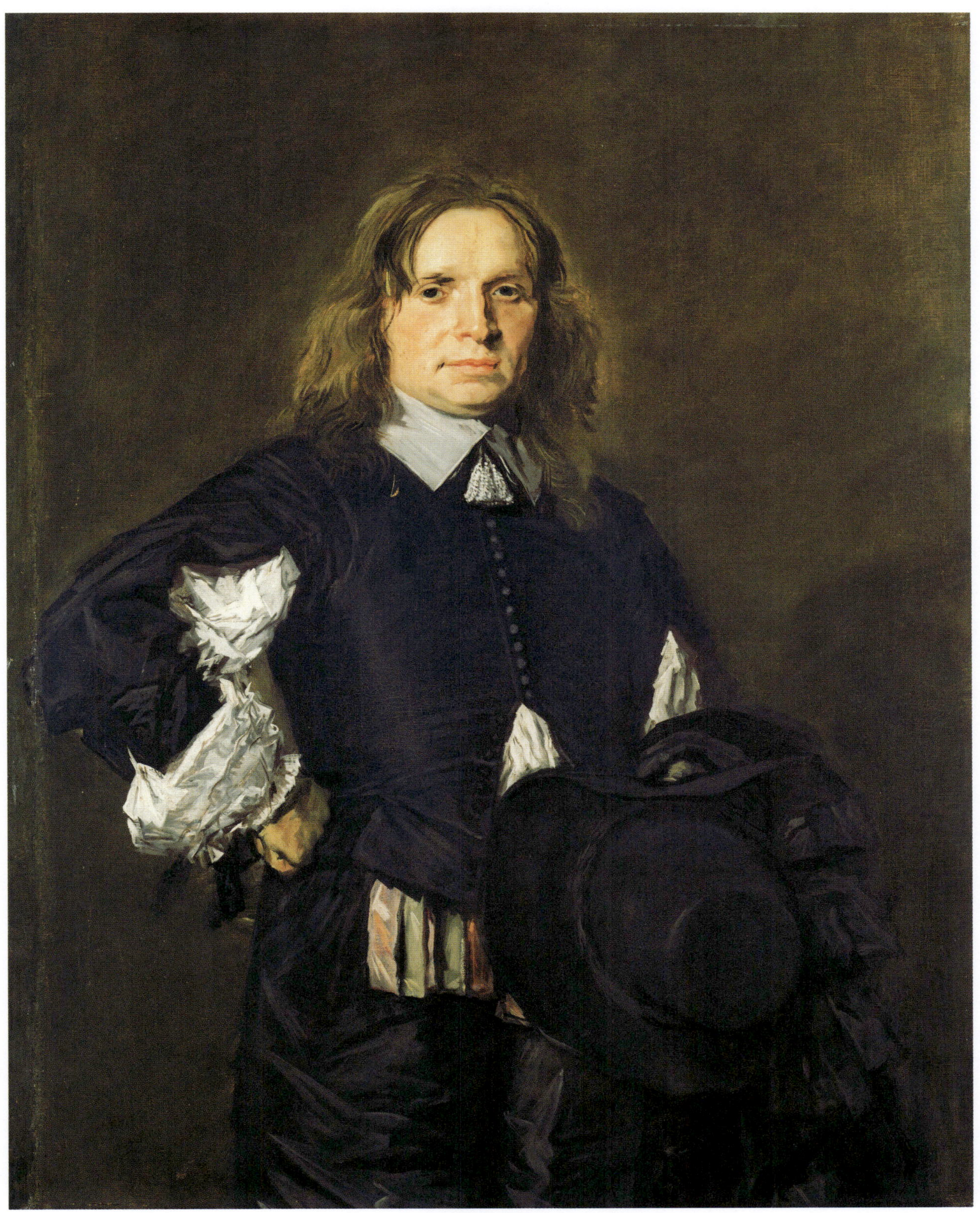

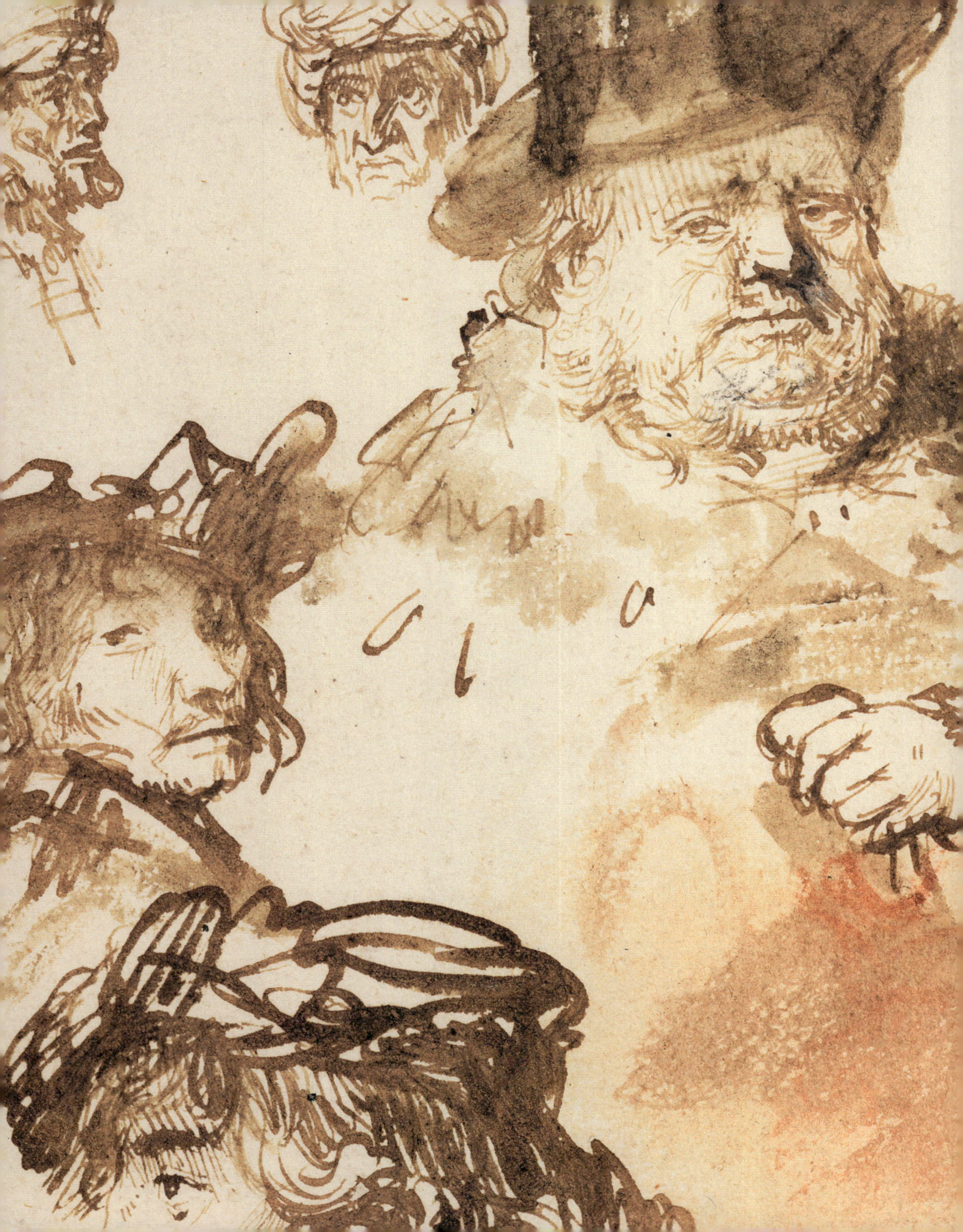

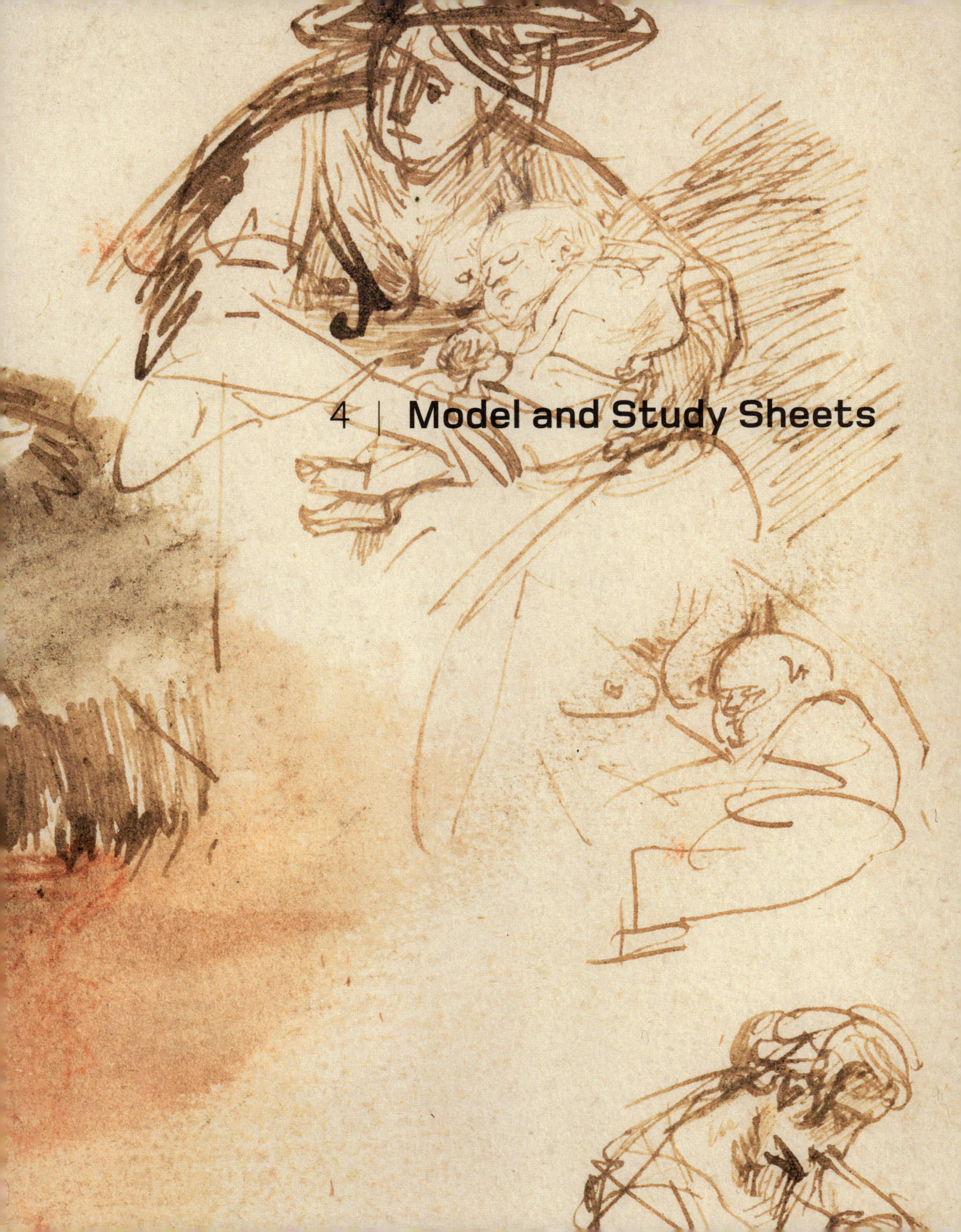

4 | Model and Study Sheets

REMBRANDT CONTINUED THE OLD TRADITION of drawing various motifs on a single sheet for his own use or as models for his many pupils. These sheets must have appealed also to some contemporary collectors. If not, it is difficult to understand why he made etchings of the same type (for examples, see figs. 4.1 and 2.3); etchings, of course, allowed for wider circulation in the art market than unique drawings. Dealers occasionally cut up some of the sheets to earn more money by selling bits of them as individual drawings, a practice that accounts for a number of small drawings of heads and figures by the master in public and private collections. In Berlin there is a precious collage of various expressive heads, figures, and what appears to be a goose's head and neck on seven small pieces of paper that were pasted upon a new sheet after they were cut (fig. 4.2). When the drawings were attached to their present support is unknown, but since the collage's provenance can be traced back to Sir Thomas Lawrence, whose drawing collection was unrivaled in his time, it must have been assembled before his death in 1830.

The artist's finest model sheet is now in The Barber Institute of Fine Arts, Birmingham (fig. 4.3). At its top is the bust and hand of a very fat grizzly man wearing an outer garment with a fur collar and a plumed hat. Below him are two sketches of a handsome man's head seen in different positions. Tucked in the upper left corner are two small studies (one is incomplete) of turbaned men. A quick drawing of a leaning man wearing a fur-trimmed hat is at the bottom of the sheet; he is done primarily in red chalk—all the other studies are in pen or pen and wash. On the right, three sketches are executed with energetic strokes of the pen or gossamer-fine lines: a seated, bare-breasted woman holding

4.1 | *Sheet of Studies with a Woman Lying in Bed*, ca. 1639. Etching; 13.5 × 15.1 cm (5¼ × 6 in.). The British Museum, London, inv. 1973,U.904. Photo © The Trustees of The British Museum. All rights reserved.

4.2 | *Seven Studies of Heads and Figures*, ca. 1635–38. Pen and brown ink; pasted to their present support by an anonymous later hand; 17.5 × 18.4 cm (6⅞ × 7¼ in.). Kupferstichkabinett, Staatliche Museen, Berlin, inv. KdZ 2315. Photo: Bildarchiv Preussischer Kulturbesitz/Art Resource, N.Y. Photographer: Jörg P. Anders.

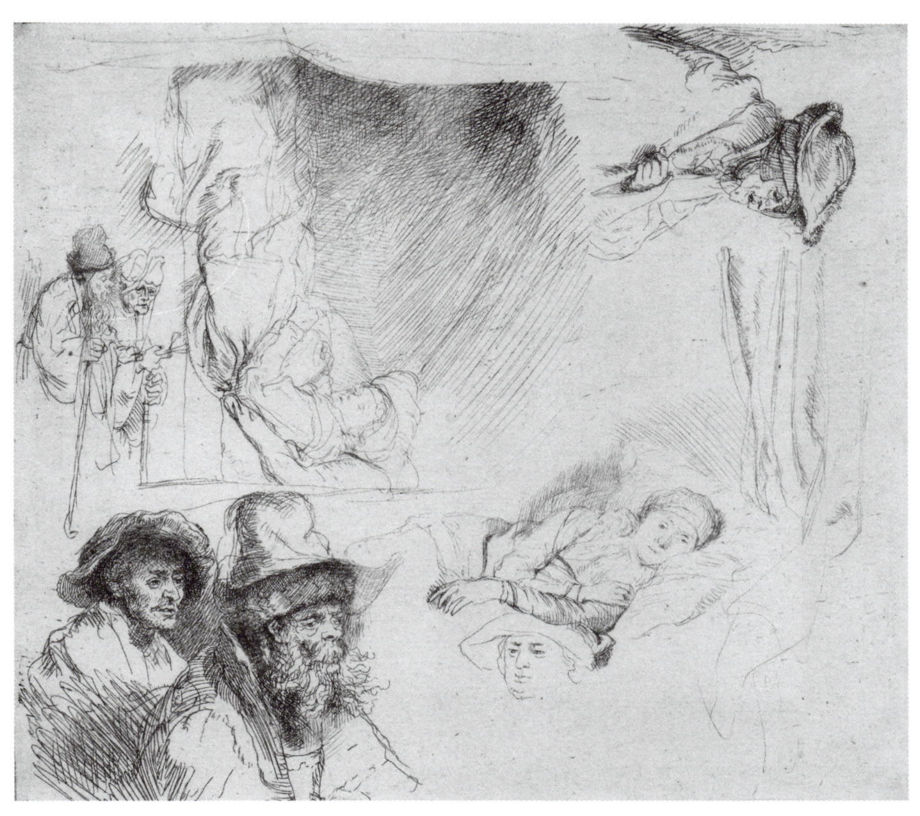

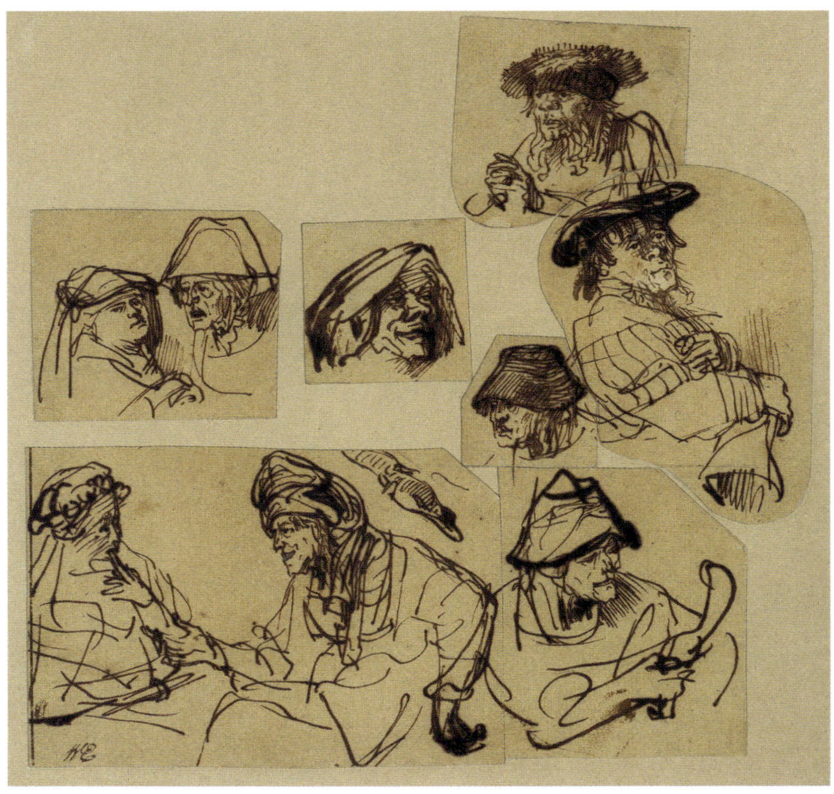

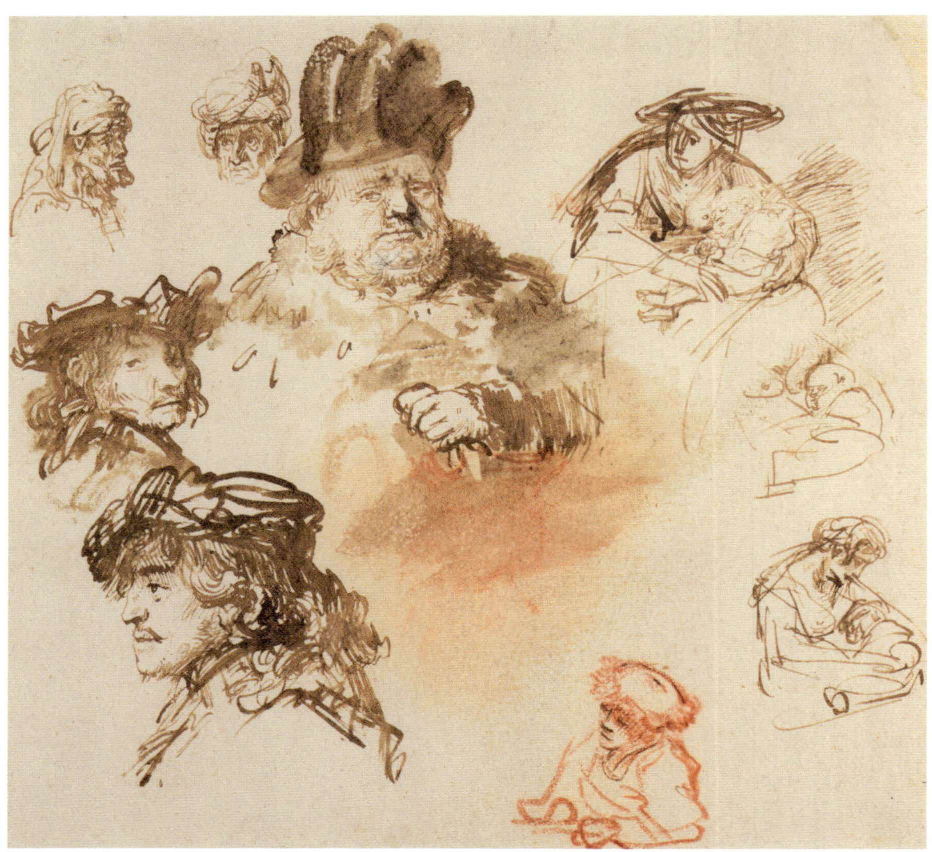

4.3 | *Sheet of Studies of Heads and Three Sketches of a Woman Holding an Infant*, ca. 1635. Pen and brown ink, brown wash, red chalk; 22 × 23 cm (8⅝ × 9 in.). Photo © The Barber Institute of Fine Arts, University of Birmingham/The Bridgeman Art Library.

a sleeping baby; another sleeping baby seen against a woman's bare breasts; and yet another study of an infant sleeping in a bare-breasted woman's arms.

The silverpoint drawing in Rotterdam of four heads and a half-length figure of a woman on prepared vellum is on a smaller scale (fig. 4.4). On its verso is a rapid silverpoint drawing of two cottages of a special type (see fig. 12.1). Rembrandt may have put the delicate double-sided drawing created with precious and unusual materials into the hands of an exceptionally gifted and trustworthy pupil to study or copy, but it is very unlikely that he gave it frequent use as instructional material.

More personal is the study sheet at The Pierpont Morgan Library that includes the beginning of a self-portrait (fig. 4.5). The unusual three-quarters view of the artist does not come as a surprise. Rembrandt did not find it necessary to portray his face from a mirror.[18] He knew it well enough to be able to do it from memory, and it would not be astonishing to learn that, if he doodled, among the motifs he doodled was his own face.

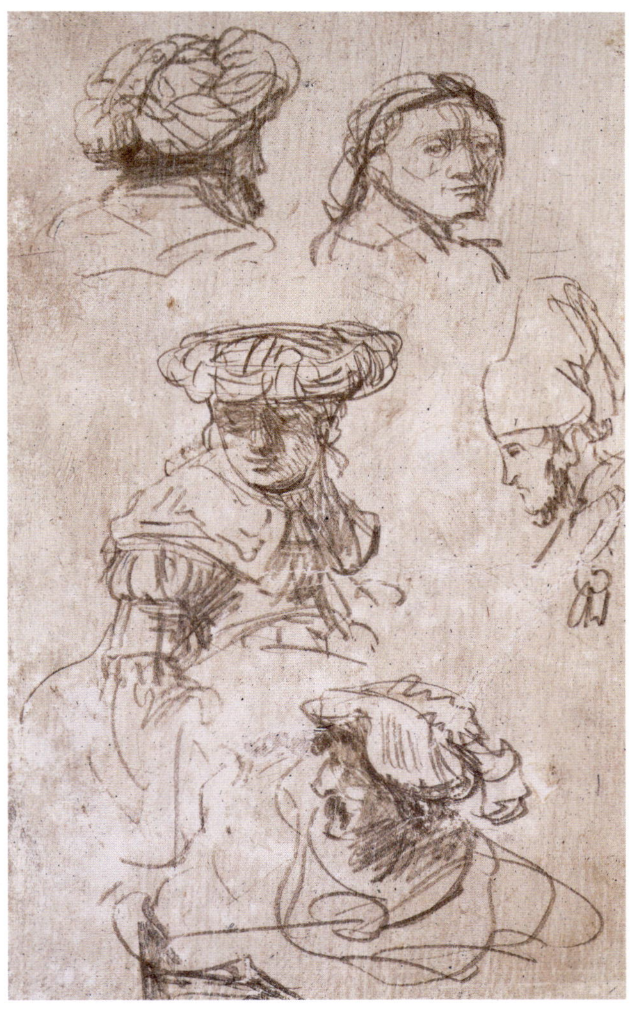

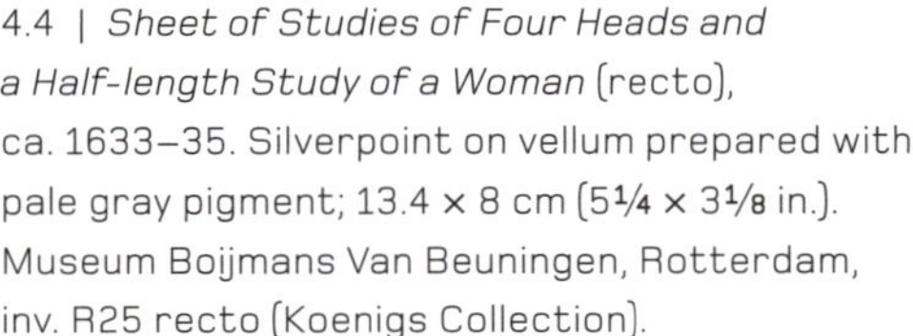

4.4 | *Sheet of Studies of Four Heads and a Half-length Study of a Woman* (recto), ca. 1633–35. Silverpoint on vellum prepared with pale gray pigment; 13.4 × 8 cm (5¼ × 3⅛ in.). Museum Boijmans Van Beuningen, Rotterdam, inv. R25 recto (Koenigs Collection).

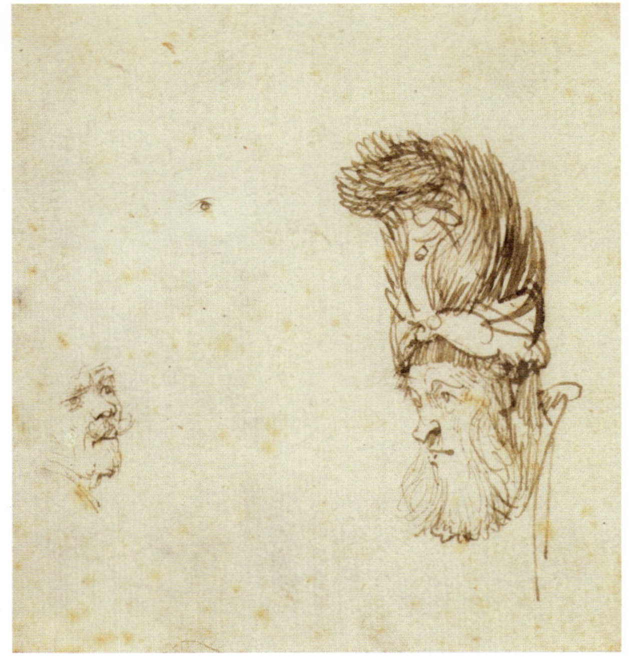

4.5 | *Head of a Man in a High Fur Hat; Self-portrait*, ca. 1634–35. Pen and brown ink, on paper prepared with light brown wash; 10.5 × 9.6 cm (4⅛ × 3¾ in.). The Pierpont Morgan Library, New York, inv. I, 174a. Photo © The Pierpont Morgan Library, New York.

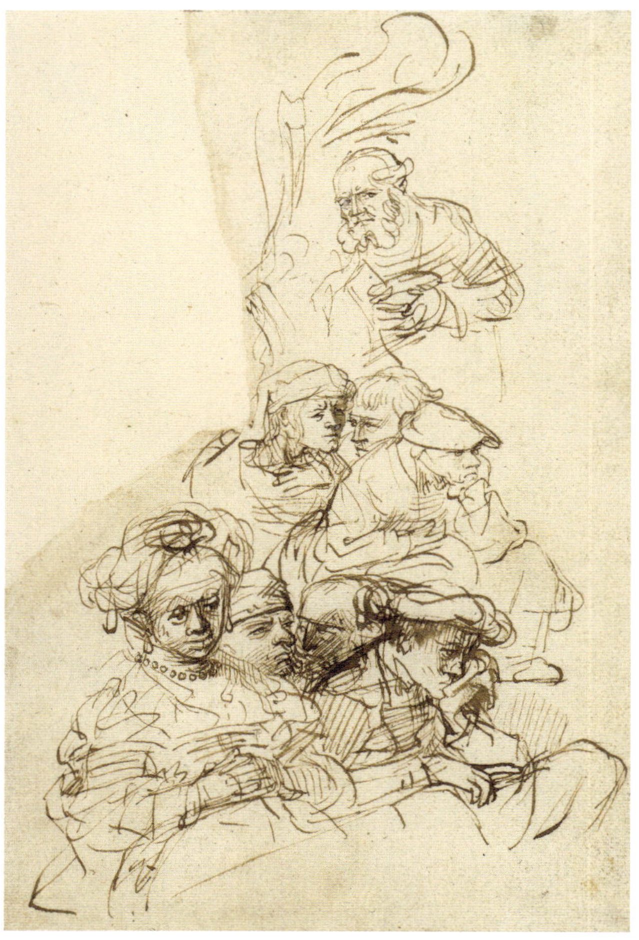

4.6 | *Sheet of Drawings for "Saint John the Baptist Preaching,"* ca. 1634–35. Pen and a bit of brush in brown ink; 19 × 12.5 cm (7½ × 4⅞ in.), large repair on the left. Kupferstichkabinett, Staatliche Museen, Berlin, inv. KdZ 5243. Photo: Bildarchiv Preussischer Kulturbesitz/Art Resource, N.Y. Photographer: Jörg P. Anders.

The Morgan sheet's bearded man with an elaborate high fur cap is related to the central figure in the group of three Pharisees (or Sadducees) in the center foreground of Rembrandt's grisaille of *Saint John the Baptist Preaching*, of about 1634–35, at Berlin. That remarkable picture includes almost one hundred figures, some attentively listening, others ignoring the words of the painting's protagonist. Another model drawing mostly related to the listening figures in that painting is likewise at Berlin (fig. 4.6). We can only speculate whether the Morgan drawing is a fragment of a larger model sheet that included other studies. However, it is possible to observe that above and to the left of its center is a tiny sketch of an eye. Perhaps it was the beginning of the drawing of a head that was abandoned for a reason that now escapes us.

Berlin's drawing collection is rich in Rembrandt model sheets. In addition to the seven-piece collage and the study

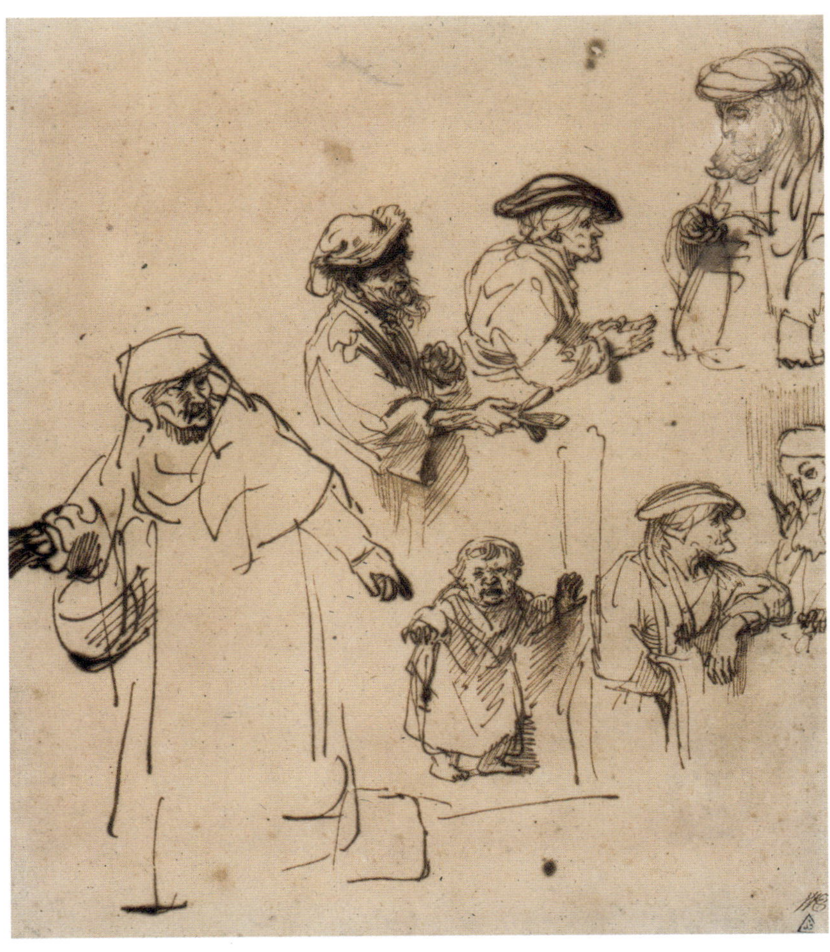

4.7 | *Sheet of Studies of an Old Woman, a Crying Child, and Five Half-length Figures*, ca. 1635–38. Pen and iron-gall ink, wash, heightened with white; 21.8 × 18.5 cm (8½ × 7¼ in.). Kupferstichkabinett, Staatliche Museen, Berlin, inv. KdZ 2316. Photo: Bildarchiv Preussischer Kulturbesitz/Art Resource, N.Y. Photographer: Jörg P. Anders.

connected with figures in *Saint John the Baptist Preaching* mentioned above, there is yet another related to the same painting (Benesch no. 141) and a splendid sheet with three genre scenes (fig. 4.7). The fragmentary character of the figures on the right side of this drawing indicates that it must have been cut down on that side. Despite the loss, the *mise-en-page* of the three unrelated scenes remains impressive. So is the characterization of the figures portrayed. Rembrandt had a penchant in the 1630s for depicting crying toddlers (see also figs. 7.10, 14.8). This one stands precariously balanced on his tiny feet, and it is virtually certain it will take more than coaxing to make him join the old woman beckoning to him. At the bottom right a crone listens to a smiling man. In the upper part of the sheet is a touching scene of two beggars—one with a leper's clapper—receiving alms from a turbaned, elderly man. The fine drawing of the hands of these figures is as expressive as their faces.

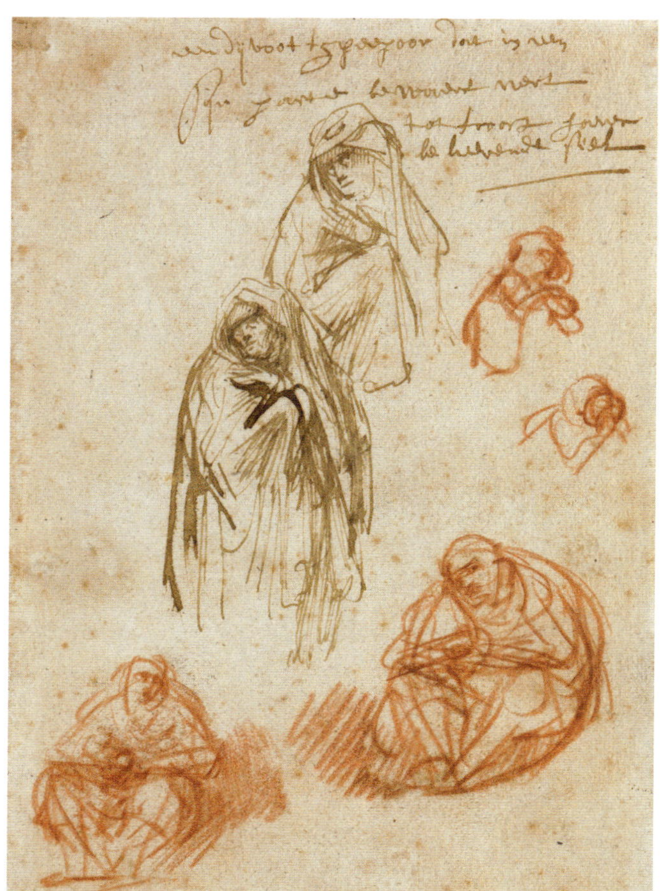

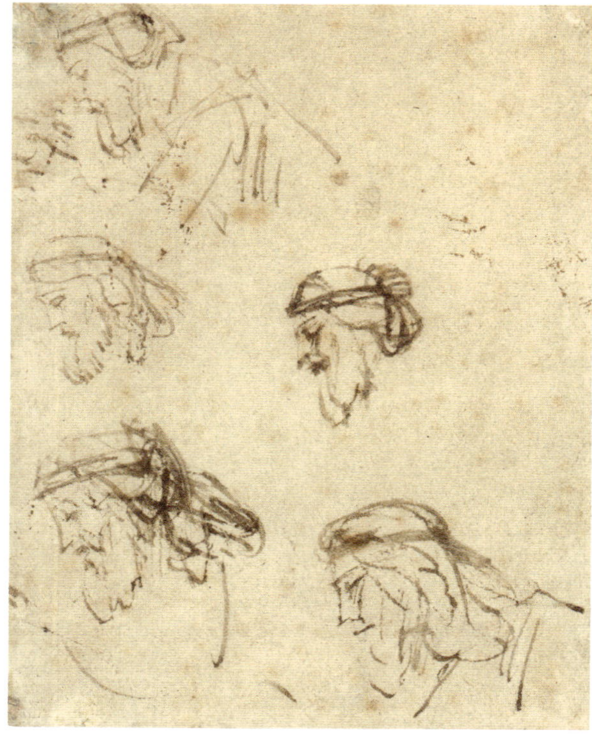

A study sheet in Amsterdam (fig. 4.8) is linked to motifs in the artist's *Entombment*, one in the series of five Passion pictures painted for Frederik Henry of Nassau, Prince of Orange, stadholder (viceroy) of five provinces of the Netherlands; the series is now in the Alte Pinakothek, Munich. Two paintings of the commission, *The Elevation* and *Descent from the Cross*, were completed by 1633. Thanks to a letter Rembrandt sent to Constantijn Huygens, the prince's secretary—who was the very first critic to express an appreciation for Rembrandt's work, and who was most probably responsible for procuring the choice commission for him—we know he was working on the *Entombment*, *Resurrection*, and *Ascension* in 1636. The *Ascension* was completed in the same year. From another letter written by Rembrandt it is clear Huygens must have complained late in 1638 or early in 1639 that it was scandalous that the *Entombment* and *Resurrection* were not yet finished, and that it was high time for Rembrandt to get on with the job.

4.8 | *Sheet of Sketches of Lamenting Marys*, ca. 1635–36. Pen and brown ink, red chalk, on paper; 20.1 × 14.3 cm ($7\frac{7}{8} \times 5\frac{5}{8}$ in.). Rijksmuseum, Amsterdam, inv. RP-T-1947-213.

4.9 | *Sheet of Five Studies of the Head of an Old Man*, ca. 1655–60. Pen and brown ink on paper; 13.4 × 10.4 cm ($5\frac{1}{4} \times 4\frac{1}{8}$ in.). Rijksmuseum, Amsterdam, inv. RP-T-1930-16.

Rembrandt's letter to Huygens written on 12 January 1639 gives his reason for the delay and includes a passage on what he tried to achieve: "...for in these two pictures the greatest and most natural emotion has been observed, which is also the principal reason they have been so long in the making."[19] The brief phrase "the greatest and most natural emotion" is a precious one. It is the only known remark by the artist himself about the intent of his work.

In the Amsterdam drawing the grief-stricken woman wrapped in a cloak that completely covers her except for her tilted head and the hand on her bosom is drawn in pen twice. Below her are two hasty red-chalk drawings of a seated figure. There are congruences between these figures and the depictions of Mary, mother of Christ, and Mary, mother of Saint James, both seated at Christ's feet in Rembrandt's painting of the *Entombment*. The other small, red-chalk scribbles on the sheet are indecipherable. At the top of the drawing the artist wrote that Christ shall be preserved in Mary's heart as a blessed treasure to comfort her soul, filled with emotion.[20] Although Rembrandt's inscription resonates with his declaration to Huygens that he was preoccupied with expressing emotion when he painted the *Entombment* and *Resurrection* for Frederik Henry, it is difficult to pinpoint its precise connection with the figures in the drawing.

Rembrandt continued to draw model and study sheets until his last years. A fine one in Amsterdam, in pen, shows five profile heads of an old bearded man (fig. 4.9), datable to the artist's full maturity. Differences between the heads and headdresses are slight, but they exist: Rembrandt seemed incapable of repeating himself. It is hard to determine which head was drawn first, for the sheet is a fragment of a larger one. It is evident, however, that he was dissatisfied with his first effort. Therefore, he drew the head again, then again, and again, and yet again, searching for a satisfactory portrayal of the expressive head he had in mind.

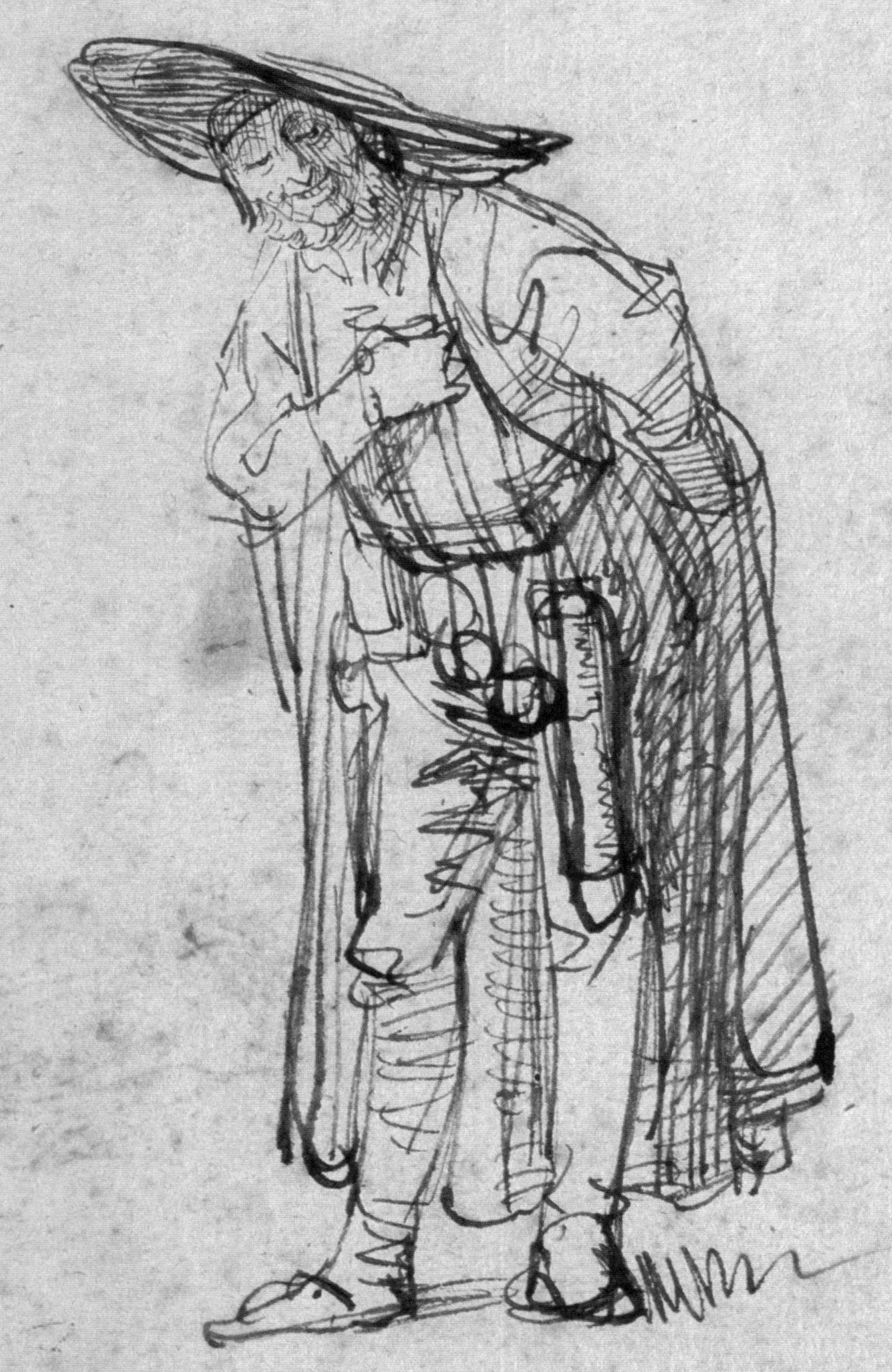

5 | **Figure Drawings**

5 | FIGURE DRAWINGS

AFTER ATTENDING LEIDEN'S LATIN SCHOOL, Rembrandt enrolled in the University of Leiden in 1620, when he had almost reached the age of fourteen. He soon became a drop-out because, as his earliest biographer put it in an account published in 1641, his natural inclination was for painting and drawing.[21] Then, we are told, he was apprenticed to the Leiden artist Jacob van Swanenburgh for three years. Rembrandt's work there showed such great promise that his father, in order to ensure his best advantage, sent him to Amsterdam to study with the celebrated history painter Pieter Lastman with whom he worked for six months. In 1625 Rembrandt returned to Leiden where he set himself up as an independent artist.

Not one of his student works has been identified, but it is not hard to imagine what the teenager's life was like when he was with his teachers. From late medieval times until art academies began to appear in the Netherlands after the middle of the seventeenth century apprentice painters were bound to their masters. Apart from sundry workshop and domestic chores, they learned how to grind pigments, set a palette, stretch a canvas and then lay a ground on it or on a wooden panel, make and use drawing materials, and, not least, how to draw and then to paint.

According to a long-established tradition, drawing lessons consisted first of copying model-sheet motifs; then copying prints, drawings, casts, sculpture; and, finally, live models. The deep impression Pieter Lastman's life-drawing instruction made upon Rembrandt can be seen in his early studies done from models. For example, his *Old Man Seated with a Book*, datable about 1627–28, now at Berlin, shows an unmistakable debt to his most influential teacher (fig. 5.1). This is seen in the work's large scale, the high finish of every part of the drawing, the expert use of red and black chalk, and the pale yellow wash that was laid on the paper before the sketch was begun, a practice that was a feature of Lastman's drawings.[22] The drawing was used, with some changes, for one of the principal figures in *Two Old Men Disputing* of 1628, now at the National Gallery of Victoria, Melbourne (fig. 5.2).

Dresden's black-chalk drawing of an *Old Man with Arms Outstretched* was almost certainly sketched from life (fig. 5.3). Like Berlin's *Old Man Seated with a Book*, done a year or two earlier, this one is on a large sheet. But here the similarity ends. The Dresden drawing is a study of expressive movement and gesture executed with furious, speedy chalk strokes. Intense light obscures forms on the right. There was no need to render the old man's features or his feet. It was the tilt of his virtually bald head and upper torso and his outstretched hands that were important. A spot of shadow on the left sets the figure in space. When the drawing is juxtaposed to the Berlin sheet, the latter acquires something of the character of a meticulous study for a still life that includes yards of drapery.

Dresden's drawing was used as a preliminary study for Peter (in reverse) in Rembrandt's large etching of *Peter and John at the Temple Gate*, datable about 1629 (fig. 5.4). The etching was not a success. Many of the etched lines were too heavily bitten, and streaks on the print suggest that passages of the etching ground likely deteriorated during the biting. Its deficiencies probably explain why only four impressions of the print are known.

During the artist's last year in Leiden a favorite model was the bearded old man who posed for the chalk drawing now in a private collection (fig. 5.5). Seven other drawings of him are known. All are in red chalk, and some, like this one, have touches of black chalk and are on paper that has been prepared with a pale yellow wash. The present drawing is monogrammed and dated 1631, and so is one in Haarlem that shows the same model full-length, seated in the same folding chair, but turned to the right. Yet another, in the National Gallery of Art, Washington, D.C., is dated 1630. The entire group is characterized by a vivid play of rich tones and strong light softened by fluid transitions.

The model appears in several of the artist's paintings and etchings, particularly those that include patriarchs and saints. The present sheet served as a preliminary study for the figure of Jacob in Rembrandt's grisaille in Amsterdam of

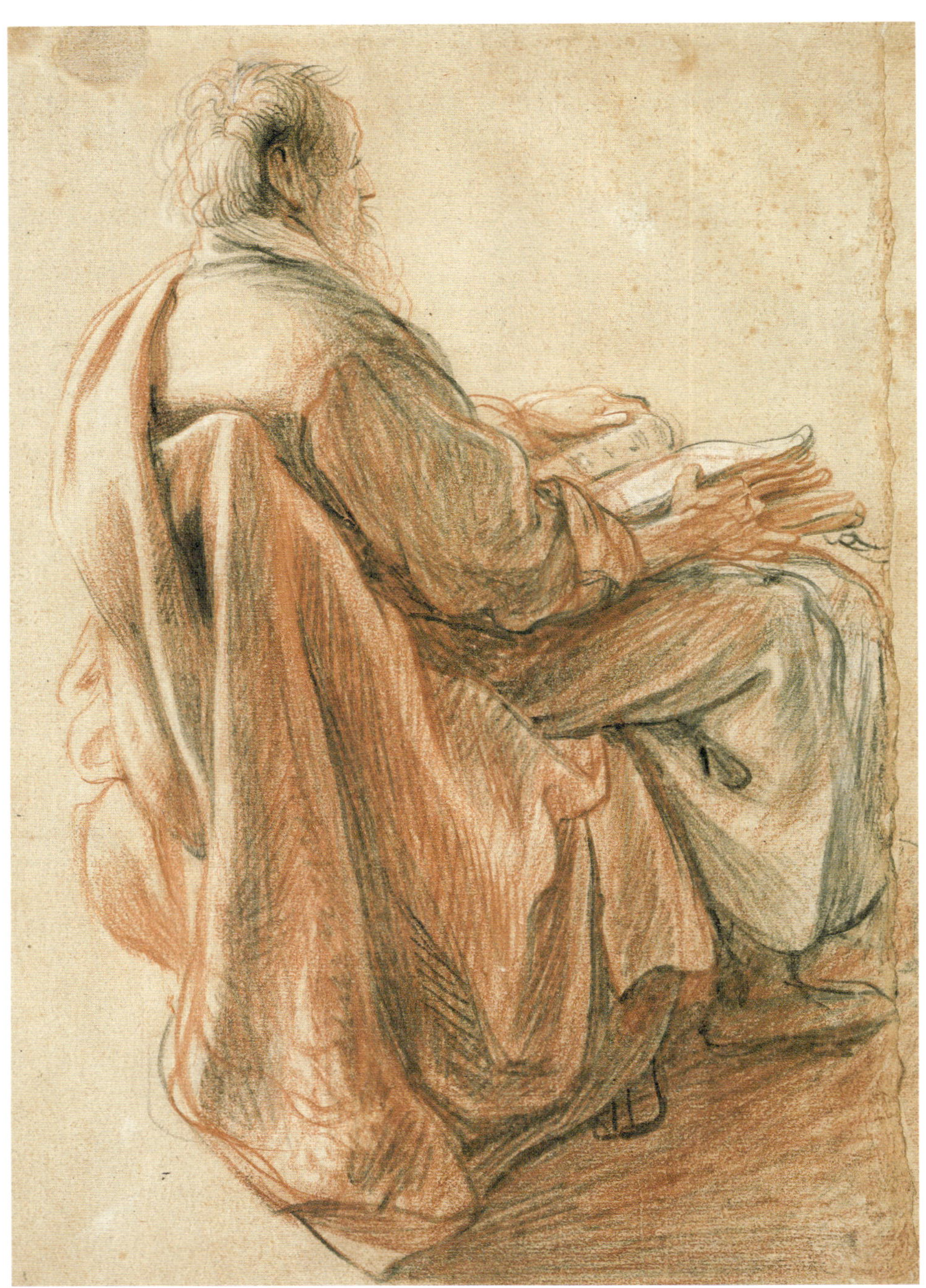

5.1 | *Old Man Seated with a Book*, ca. 1627–28. Black and red chalk, pencil, on paper prepared with pale yellow wash; 29.5 × 21 cm (11⅝ × 8¼ in.). Kupferstichkabinett, Staatliche Museen, Berlin, inv. KdZ 5284. Photo: Bildarchiv Preussischer Kulturbesitz/Art Resource, N.Y.

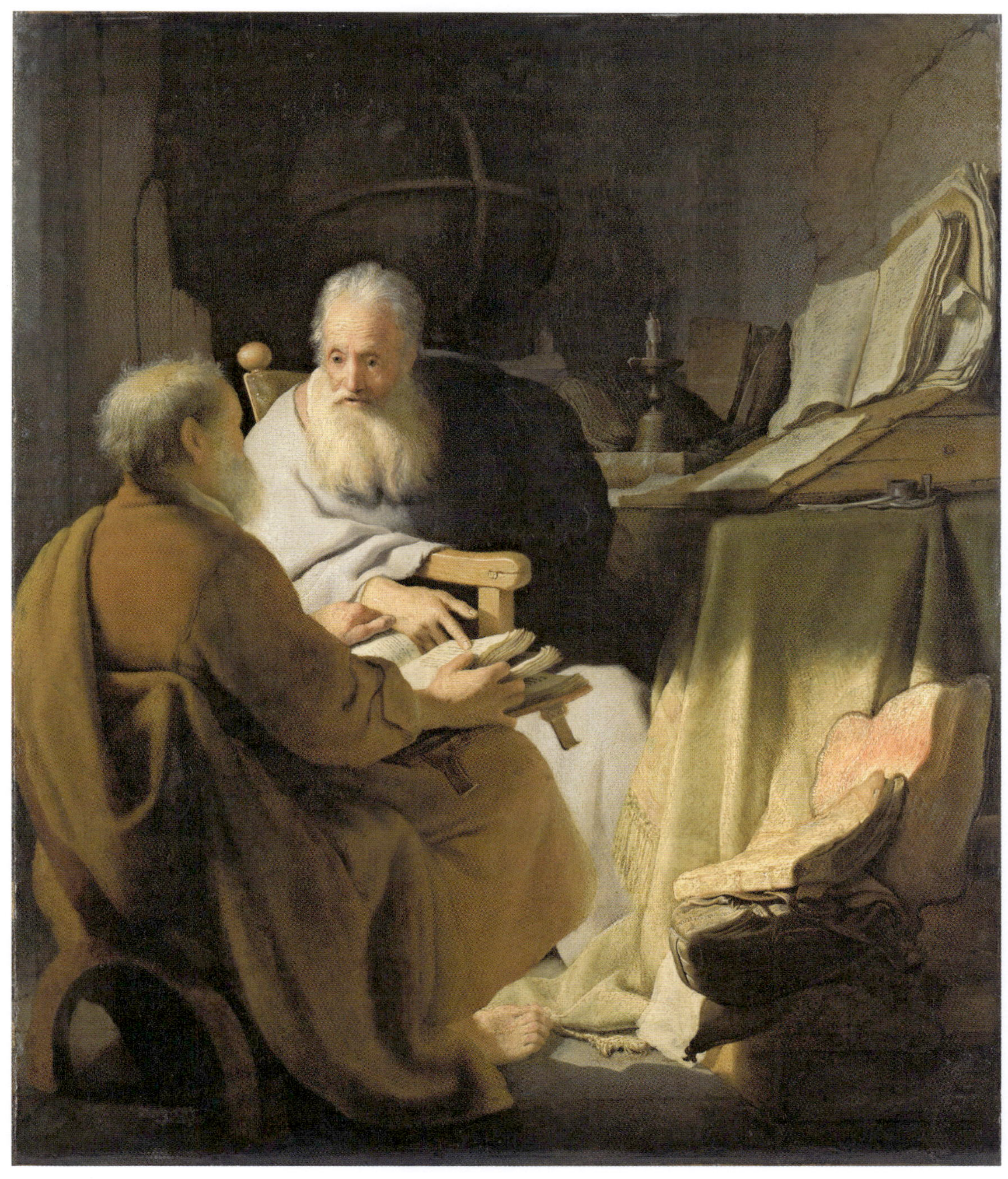

5.2 | *Two Old Men Disputing*, monogrammed and dated 1628. Oil on panel; 72.4 × 59.7 cm (28½ × 23½ in.). National Gallery of Victoria, Melbourne, Felton Bequest, 1936 (349/4).

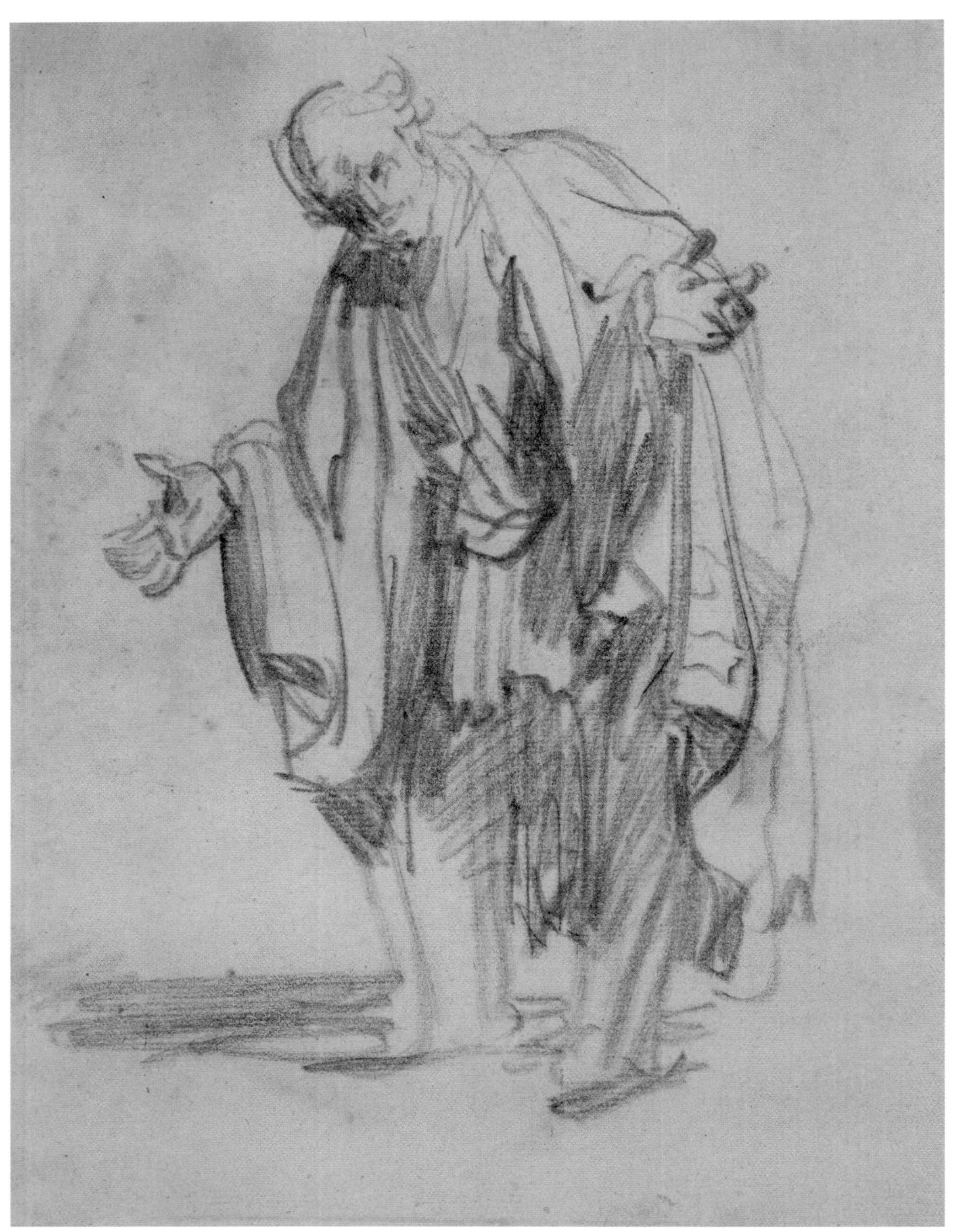

5.3 | *Old Man with Arms Outstretched*, ca. 1628–29. Black chalk; 25.4 × 19 cm (10 × 7½ in.). Kupferstich-Kabinett, Staatliche Kunstsammlungen Dresden, inv. C1971-26. Photo: Bildarchiv Preussischer Kulturbesitz/ Art Resource, N.Y. Photographer: Ursula-Maria Hoffmann.

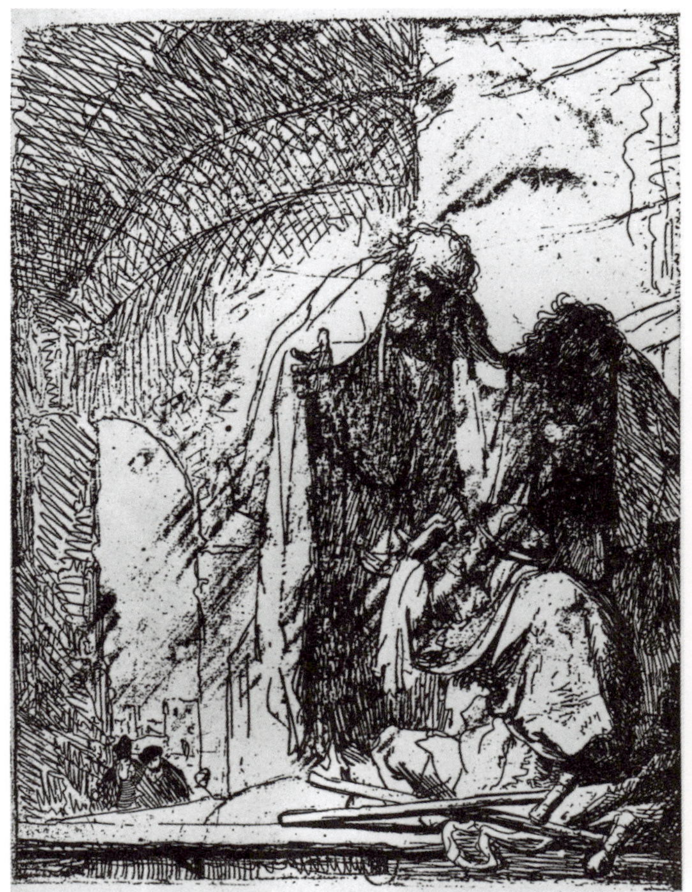

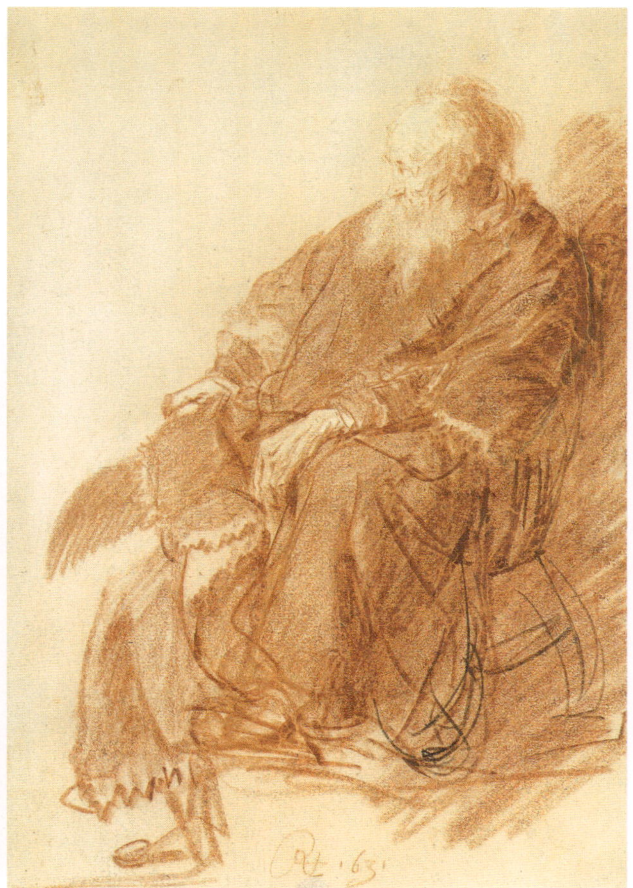

Joseph Telling His Dreams (fig. 5.6), datable about 1633, and once again as Jacob (in reverse) in his 1638 etching of the same subject (fig. 5.7). The fact that a drawing securely monogrammed and dated 1631 was unmistakably used for works done about 1633 and again in 1638 indicates that the artist kept some drawings on file for later use or inspiration. Rembrandt also probably incorporated a drawing of a curled-up sleeping dog (similar to the one in fig. 10.6) into his grisaille of *Joseph Telling His Dreams* of about 1633, where it appears in the lower right corner.

Three Studies of a Bearded Old Man (fig. 5.8) at Fondation Custodia, Paris, have generally been accepted as studies for one of the two pilgrims who met Christ after the resurrection but did not recognize him. The pilgrims accompanied him to Emmaus where, only after he broke bread with them, did they recognized that he was Christ. The best interpretation of the drawing is that it shows three possible reactions of one of the pilgrims to the revelation. The portrait-like character

5.4 | *Peter and John at the Temple Gate*, ca. 1629. Etching; 22.1 × 16.9 cm (8⅝ × 6⅝ in.). Graphische Sammlung Albertina, Vienna. Photo © The Albertina Museum, Vienna.

5.5 | *Bearded Old Man Seated in an Armchair*, monogrammed and dated 1631. Red and black chalk, on paper prepared with pale yellow wash; 22.9 × 15.9 cm (9 × 6¼ in.). Private collection.

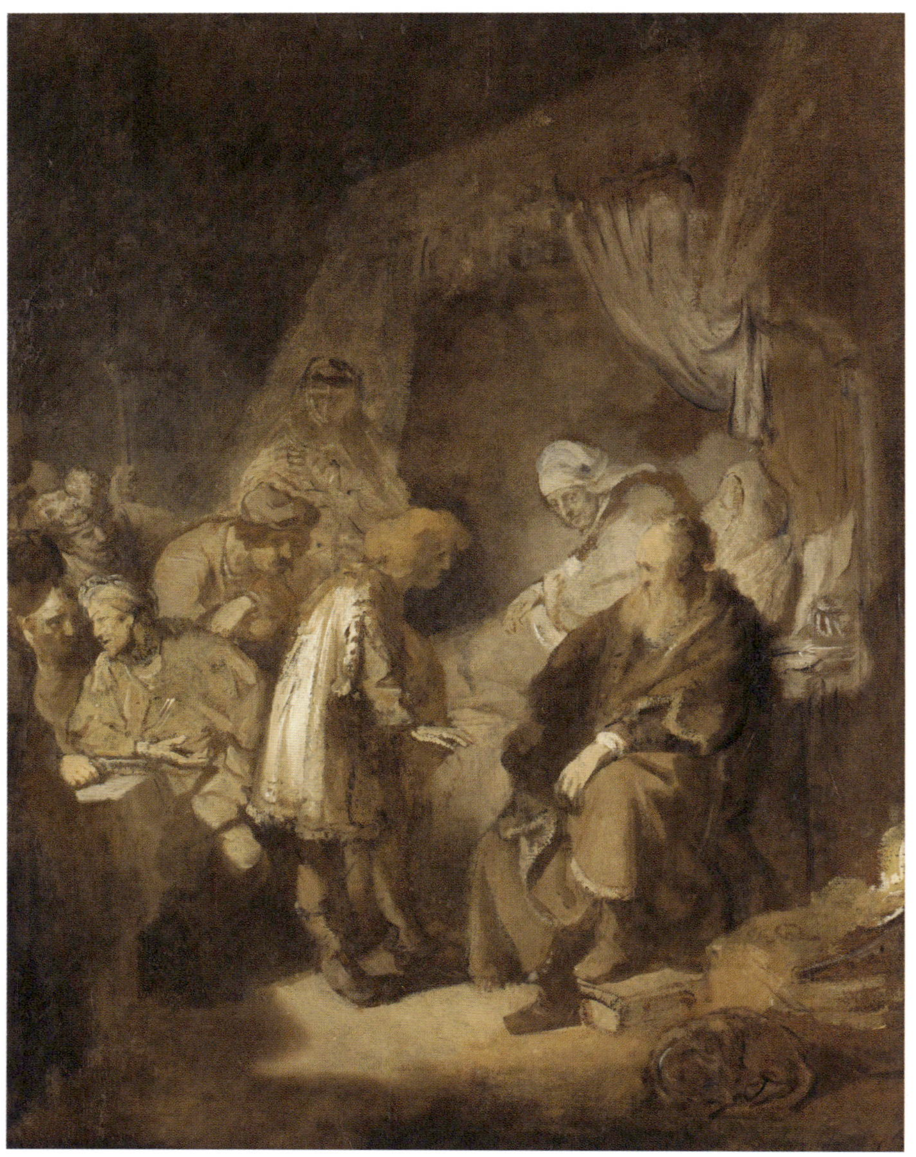

of the drawings supports the notion they were done from life. However, it would be rash to assert categorically that Rembrandt did not invent their expressions and gestures, for the exceptional power of his imagination is as marked as the exceptional power of his observation. The drawing is datable about 1635. Not one of the studies on the sheet is incorporated into the artist's subsequent representations of the Supper at Emmaus in other media. Despite the examples cited above, more often than not Rembrandt found no need to thumb through his stock of drawings searching for bits and pieces to use for works in hand.

5.6 | *Joseph Telling His Dreams*, signed; ca. 1633. Oil (grisaille) on paper on cardboard; 51 × 39 cm (20⅛ × 15⅜ in.). Rijksmuseum, Amsterdam, inv. SK-A-3477.

It has been reasonably suggested that the Fondation Custodia drawing is among Rembrandt's first model sheets that include motifs for his students to copy.[23] If this is the case, the drawing also served his students as a paradigm of their master's economic touch, evident not only in the figures but also in the virtually nonexistent table. Hardly a line indicates a table in the upper two sketches, and no line suggests one in the lower sketch, yet there is no question that Rembrandt has given three convincing views of a man at a table.

The pen drawing in the Groningen museum, of a man bowing with one arm on his breast and the other behind his back and wearing a sly smile, represents an actor in the role of Pantalone (fig. 5.9). It belongs to a series of drawings of actors made in the 1630s. Pantalone was a stock figure in the repertoire of commedia dell'arte players. He assumed the role of a miserly, lecherous merchant—it is not accidental that Rembrandt used heavy strokes of his pen to emphasize the long baton (or flute case?) and two balls that hang from the cord around the actor's waist. Most other parts of the drawing are done with very fine lines, particularly Pantalone's face. Sharp eyes will see that Rembrandt's delicate pen even drew the teeth that the actor's ingratiating smile reveals.

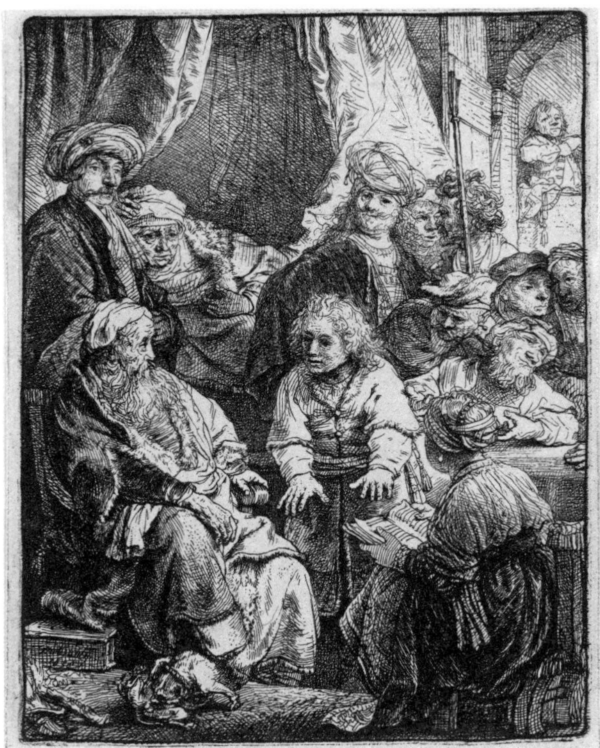

5.7 | *Joseph Telling His Dreams*, signed and dated 1638. Etching, second state; 11 × 8.3 cm (4 3/8 × 3 1/4 in.). Kupferstichkabinett, Staatliche Museen, Berlin, inv. 9-1879. Photo: Bildarchiv Preussischer Kulturbesitz/Art Resource, N.Y. Photographer: Jörg P. Anders.

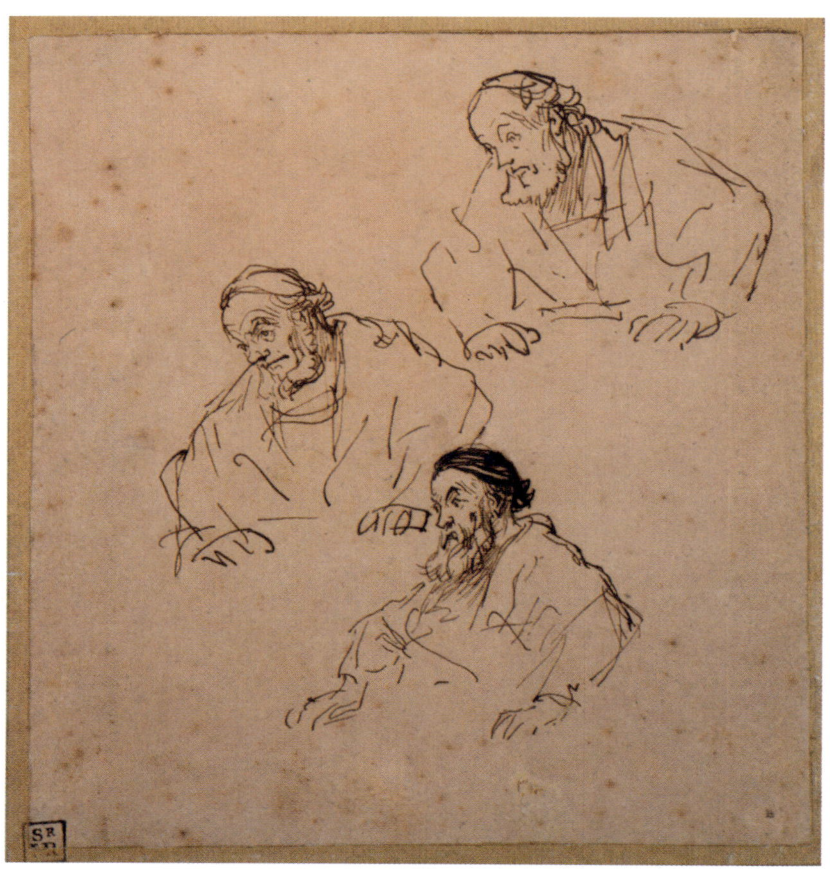

5.8 | *Three Studies of a Bearded Old Man*, ca. 1633–35. Pen and brown ink; 17.4 × 16 cm (6⅞ × 6¼ in.). Fondation Custodia, Collection Frits Lugt, Paris, inv. 1922.

Pantalone's stance may have been inspired by knowledge of Jacques Callot's etching of the character made in Florence in about 1618,[24] but Rembrandt did not plagiarize the French artist's print. Callot offers a side view of the player's head and figure; Rembrandt's Pantalone confronts us head-on.

Seated Old Man with a Stick, at Dresden, exemplifies the artist's mature figure drawings (fig. 5.10). The half-length is done with a coarse reed pen. Only a few abbreviated touches delineate the sympathetic old man's tilted head and full beard. His large beret and outstretched arm holding a stick are indicated by broad, economic hatching. A few strong impetuous strokes complete the rest of the figure and the armchair.

On its verso the drawing is dated 1650. Although the date is not in the artist's hand, it is a reasonable one. Early specialists made understandable attempts to find a connection between the drawing and various Rembrandt paintings of contemplative old bearded men done around the middle of the century. Their attempts failed. All was not lost, however. The search for a related painting has a successful ending.

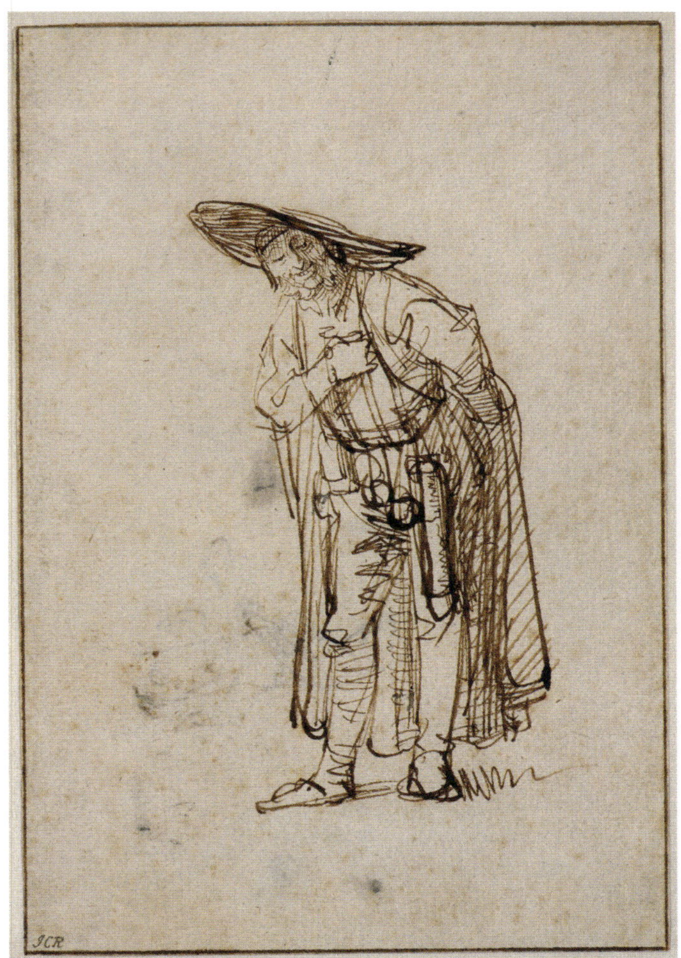

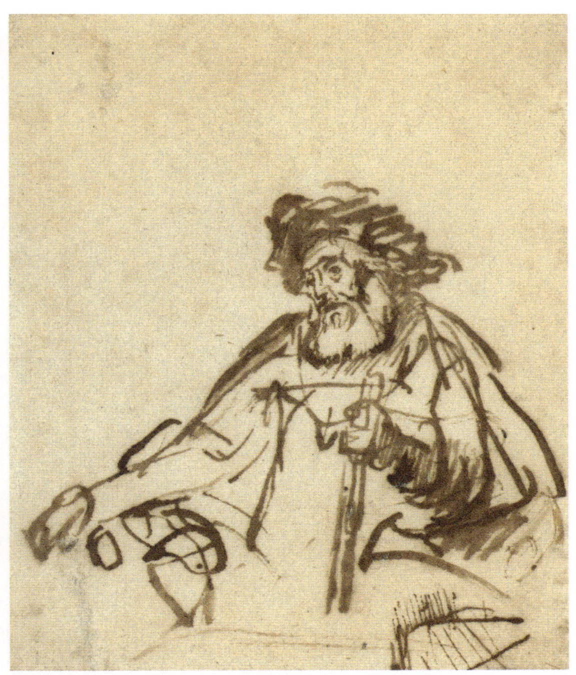

5.9 | *Pantalone* (recto), ca. 1635. Pen and brown ink; 19.3 × 13 cm (7⅝ × 5⅛ in.). Collection Groninger Museum (on loan from "Gemeente Groningen," Collection Hofstede de Groot), Groningen, inv. 1931-187. Photographer: John Stoel.

5.10 | *Seated Old Man with a Stick*, ca. 1650. Pen and brown ink; 13 × 11 cm (5⅛ × 4⅜ in.). Kupferstich-Kabinett, Staatliche Kunstsammlungen Dresden, inv. C1980-495. Photo: Bildarchiv Preussischer Kulturbesitz/Art Resource, N.Y. Photographer: Herbert Boswank.

It occurred in 1973 with the publication of an X-radiograph of Rembrandt's dramatic painting of *Joseph Accused by Potiphar's Wife*, dated 1655, at Berlin.[25] The X-radiograph clearly reveals that the biblical scene is painted on a canvas that already had another painting on it. The underpainting is a half-length portrait of a seated old bearded man wearing a large beret, which unmistakably corresponds to the figure in the Dresden sketch.

Firm ascription of the underpainting is impossible because attributions cannot be made on the basis of X-radiographs, but it has the look of a picture by a talented pupil or follower. Its existence establishes that the drawing must have been made by 1655. Both the drawing and the underpainting anticipate the solemn series of half-lengths of old men, apostles, and saints Rembrandt and his followers painted during the years of his full maturity.

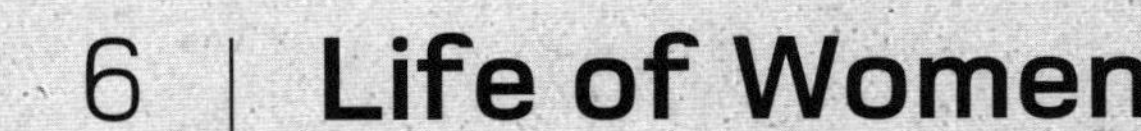

6 | Life of Women

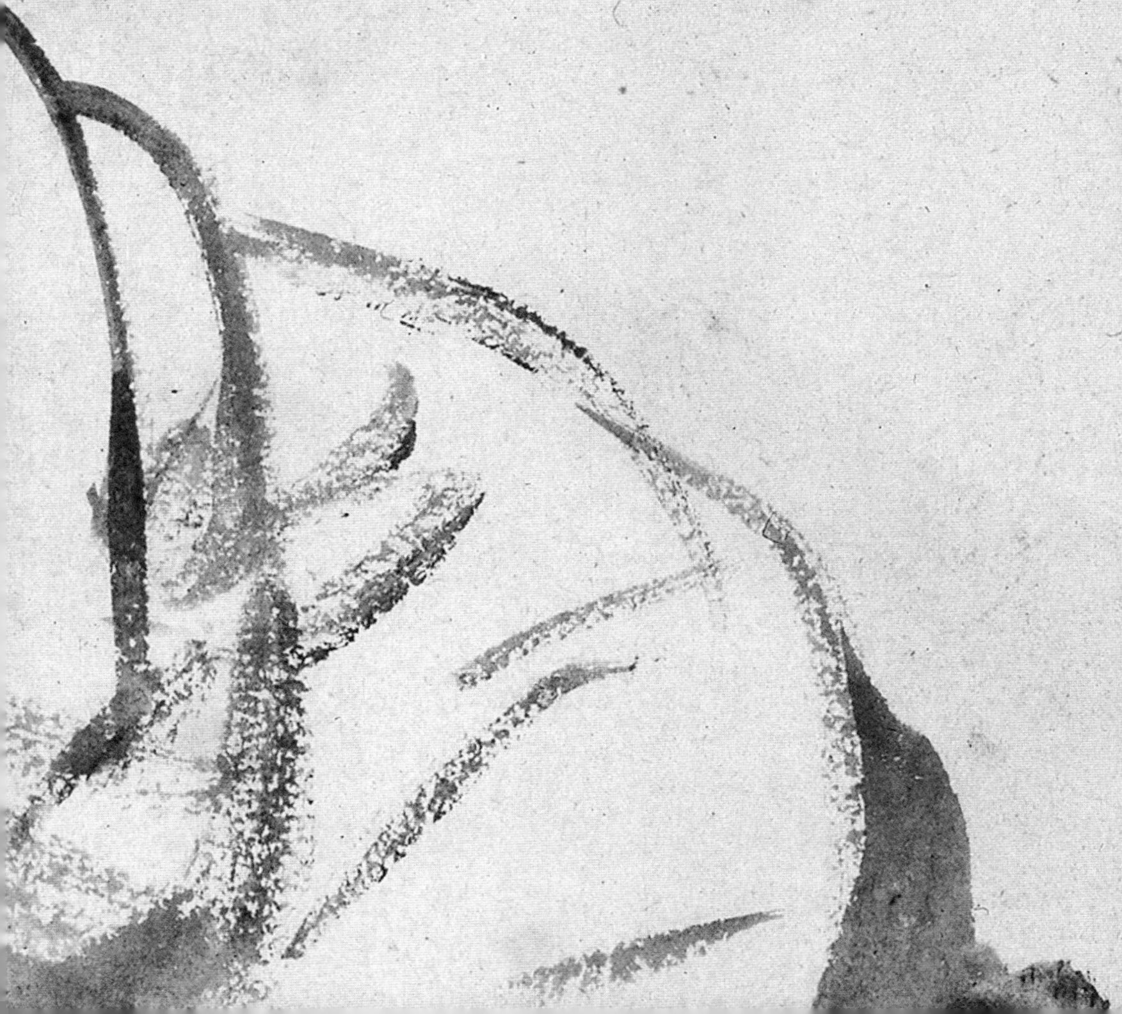

6 | LIFE OF WOMEN

WHEN WE CONSIDER REMBRANDT'S MARRIAGE to Saskia and, after her death, his life with Geertje Dircx and then with Hendrickje Stoffels, it is fair to say he was the kind of man who had a need for a woman in his household. His work as a draftsman offers ample evidence that he also liked to scrutinize and record the domestic activities of women. His sketches of women with children, which have been recognized as a special category since his own time, are the subject of chapter 7.

Determining whether one of Rembrandt's drawings was done from life, from memory, or from imagination is not an easy task, but there can be little doubt that his quick pen sketches at The Pierpont Morgan Library of Saskia sleeping (fig. 6.1) and at the Metropolitan Museum of a chubby young woman reading (fig. 6.2) were life studies. There are slight, yet marked variations in the two sketches of Saskia asleep. In the lower one Saskia's head is deep in a pillow, her nightcap is more pronounced, and her mouth is slightly open. I recall the prominent connoisseur Jakob Rosenberg saying that in the Morgan sketches we seem to hear Rembrandt's wife breathe. The two sketches of a plump young woman reading a very small book, which show much greater variation in the pose than those of Saskia asleep, are equally vivid and direct.

We know that Rembrandt had no inhibitions whatsoever depicting female nudes (see chapter 9), but it is noteworthy that, unlike some earlier and later artists, he never portrayed women at their toilet stark naked or partially dressed. Pace some of his critics, he could display an exquisite sense of decorum. Witness his intimate, small sketch at Fondation Custodia of a woman having her heavy hair combed (fig. 6.3) or the Albertina's beautiful drawing of an older woman braiding the hair of a seated young woman with her

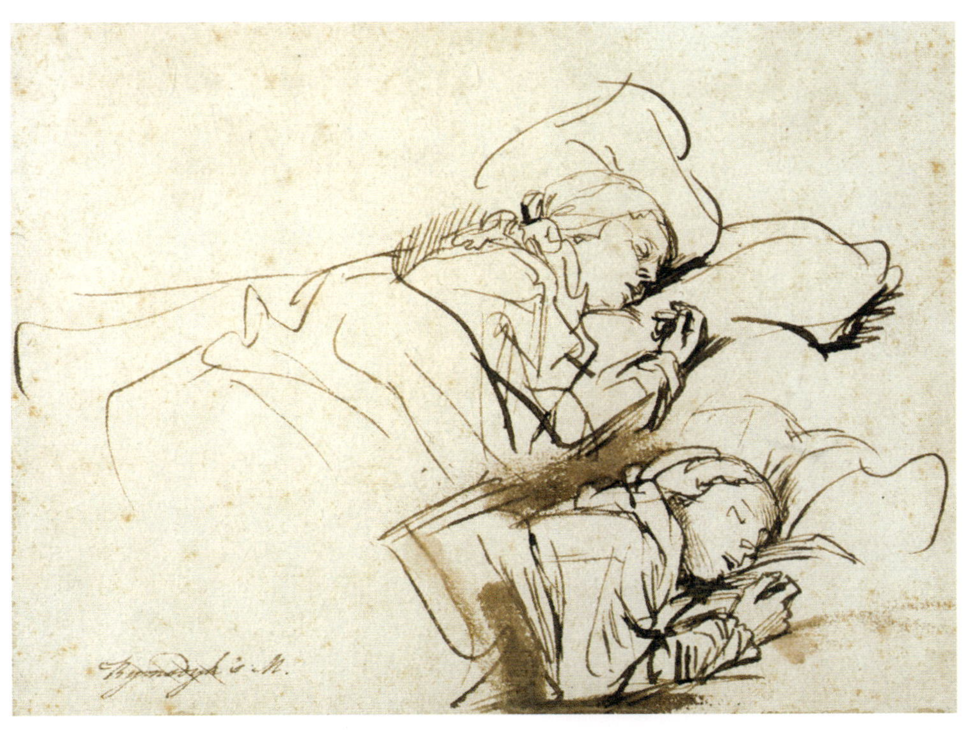

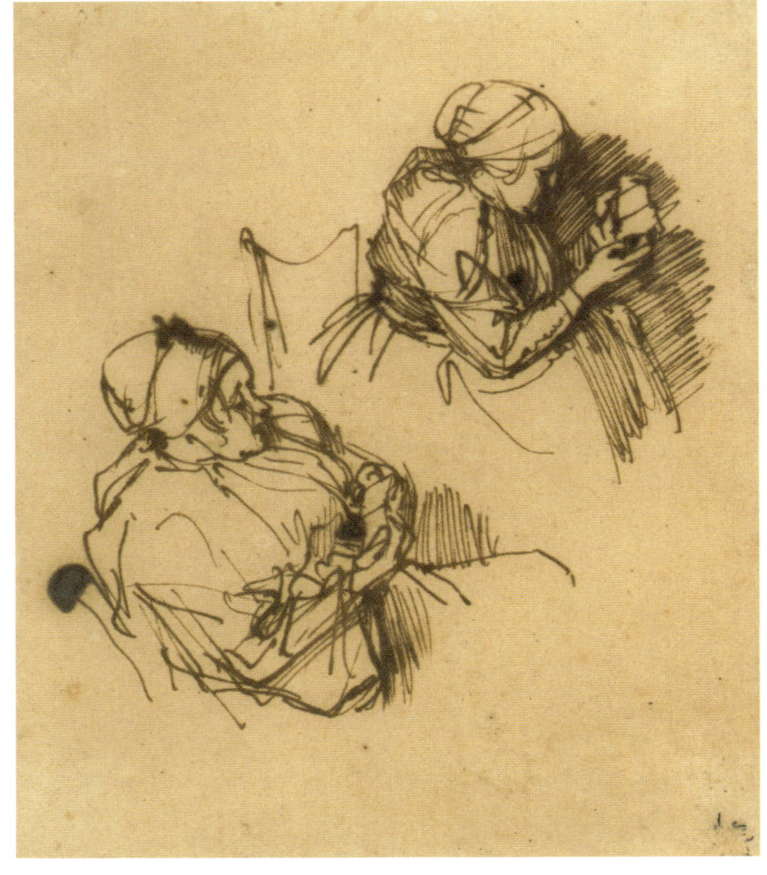

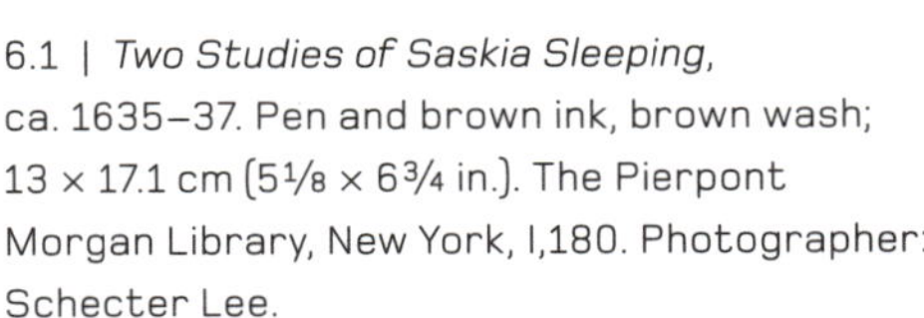

6.1 | *Two Studies of Saskia Sleeping*, ca. 1635–37. Pen and brown ink, brown wash; 13 × 17.1 cm (5⅛ × 6¾ in.). The Pierpont Morgan Library, New York, I,180. Photographer: Schecter Lee.

6.2 | *Two Sketches of a Woman Reading*, ca. 1635–40. Pen and brown ink; 17.3 × 15 cm (6¾ × 5⅞ in.). The Metropolitan Museum of Art, New York, Bequest of Mrs. H. O. Havermeyer, 1929, inv. 29.100.932. Photo copyright © The Metropolitan Museum of Art/Art Resource, N.Y.

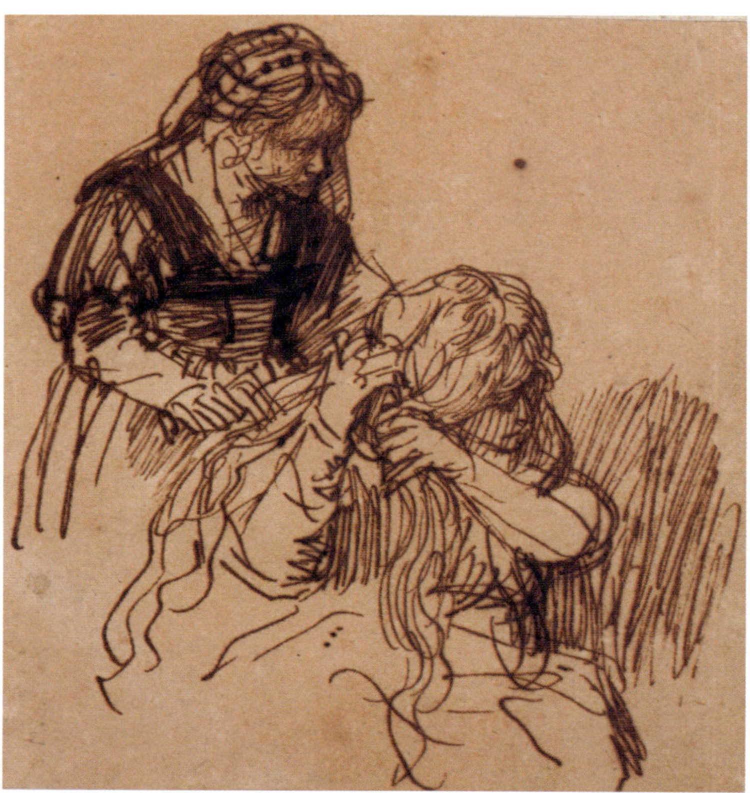

hands in her lap holding a finished braid (fig. 6.4). The braiding woman concentrates upon her task as intently as Vermeer's *Lacemaker* studies the bobbins and pins on her lace cushion.

A theme that Rembrandt as well as many of his contemporaries favored is a woman at a window. The one at Rotterdam of Saskia leaning on a windowsill looking directly at us is one of the earliest and most attractive (fig. 6.5). The full sunlight that bathes her, the window frame, and the wall hardly penetrates the dark interior. Saskia's features could scarcely have been depicted with greater economy. Rembrandt portrayed his young wife in informal attire. She is wearing a linen nightcap with a separate strip bound around her forehead and a night rail is draped over her shoulders. Night rails were used also in bed or while dressing. The young woman having her hair braided in the Albertina's drawing wears one.[26]

Light likewise plays a key role in the drawing of about 1650, at the Louvre, of a mature woman looking out of a window (fig. 6.6) and in a drawing done a few years later, now at Stockholm, of a young woman at a window basking in the sun with her eyes closed (fig. 6.7). The Louvre's sheet is principally

6.3 | *Woman Having Her Hair Combed*, ca. 1635–38. Pen and brown ink, on paper prepared with light brown wash; 10.7 × 9.8 cm (4¼ × 3⅞ in.). Fondation Custodia, Collection Frits Lugt, Paris, inv. 805.

6.4 | *Young Woman Having Her Hair Braided*, ca. 1635–38. Pen and brown ink, brown and gray wash; 23.8 × 18.4 cm (9⅜ × 7¼ in.). Graphische Sammlung Albertina, Vienna, inv. 8825. Photo: Nimatallah/Art Resource, N.Y.

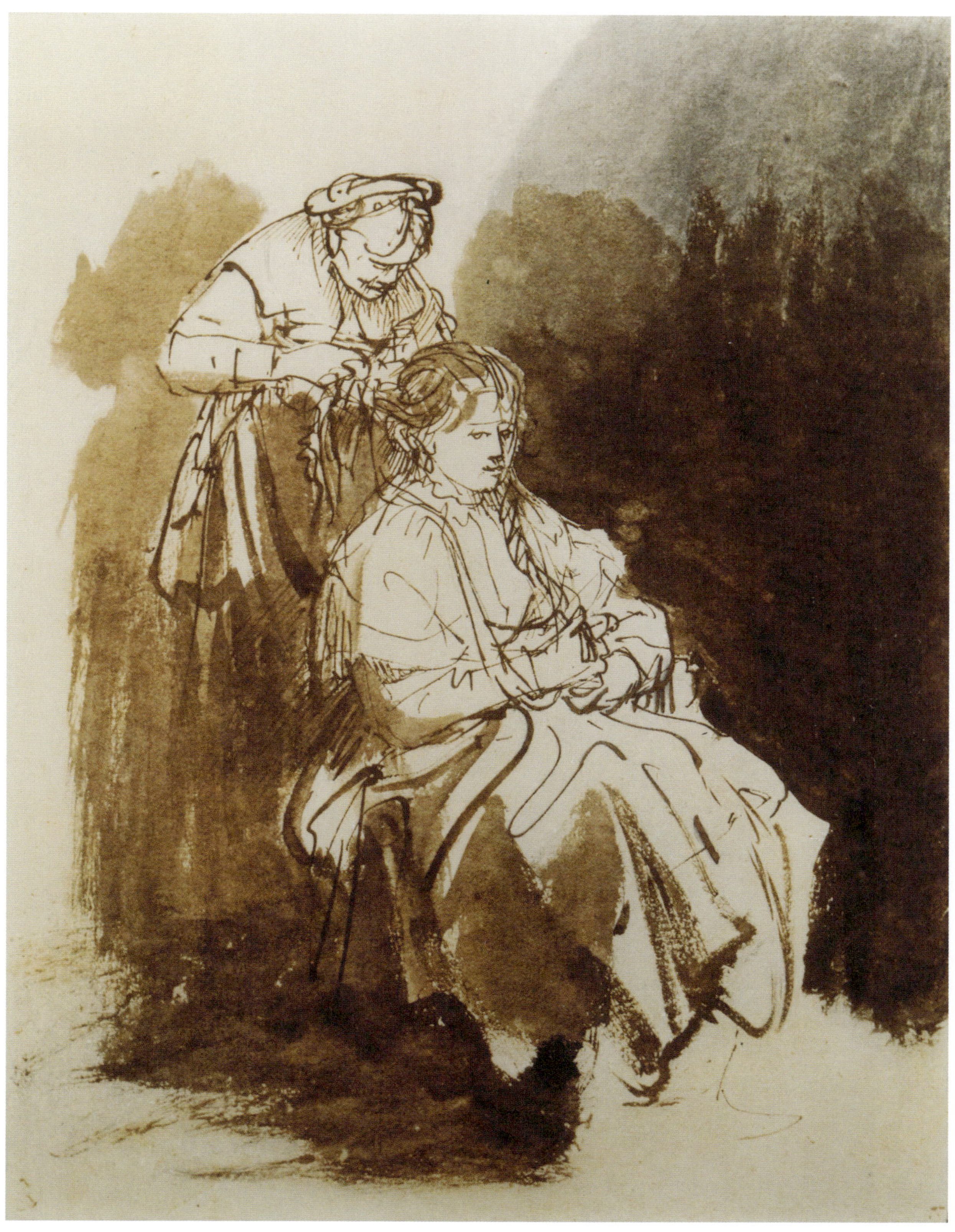

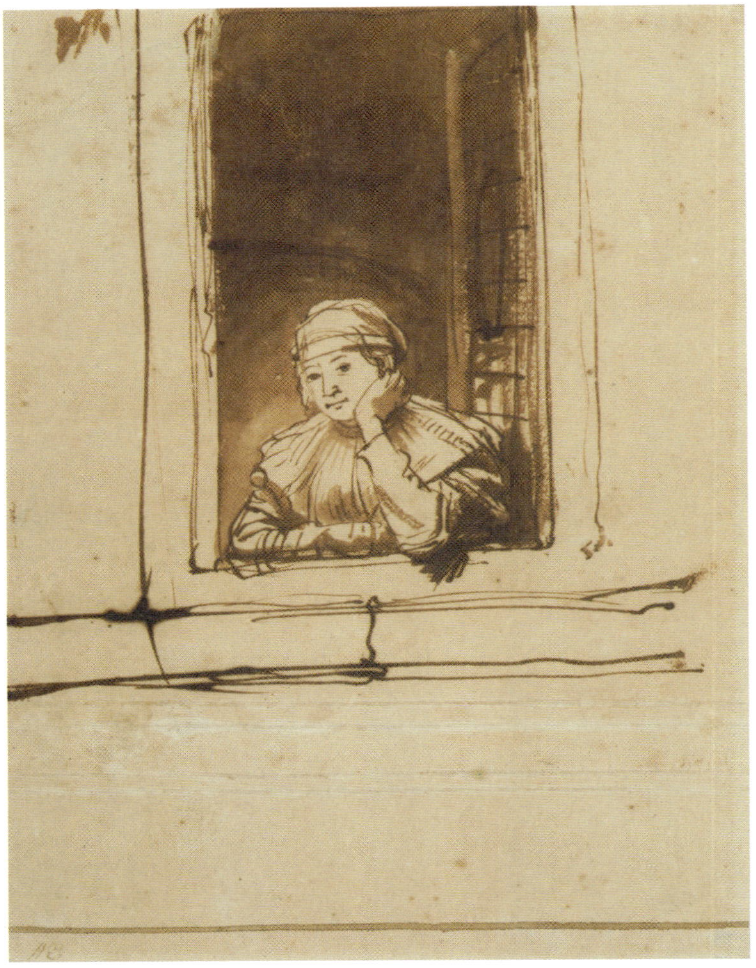

executed in wash. The white of the paper and the delicate gradations of wash suggest outdoor and interior ambient light and atmosphere. In contrast, the luminous darks of the woman's figure and amorphous shadows around her glow. The Stockholm sketch is executed with economic, firm strokes of a broad reed pen, brown wash, and touches of white opaque watercolor. The portions of the drawing's paper support that Rembrandt left untouched are equally important. They convey something of the heat of the sun warming the young woman's body and soul.

There are two drawings of a woman wearing a North Holland costume. One, at the British Museum, shows her from the front (fig. 6.8). The other, at the Teyler Museum, Haarlem, depicts her from the rear in the same pose and in the same costume (fig. 6.9); the suggestion that the summarily sketched figure in the background may very well be another

6.5 | *Saskia at an Open Window*, ca. 1637–39. Pen and brown ink, brown wash, on tinted paper; 23.6 × 17.8 cm (9¼ × 7 in.). Museum Boijmans Van Beuningen, Rotterdam, inv. R131 (Koenigs Collection).

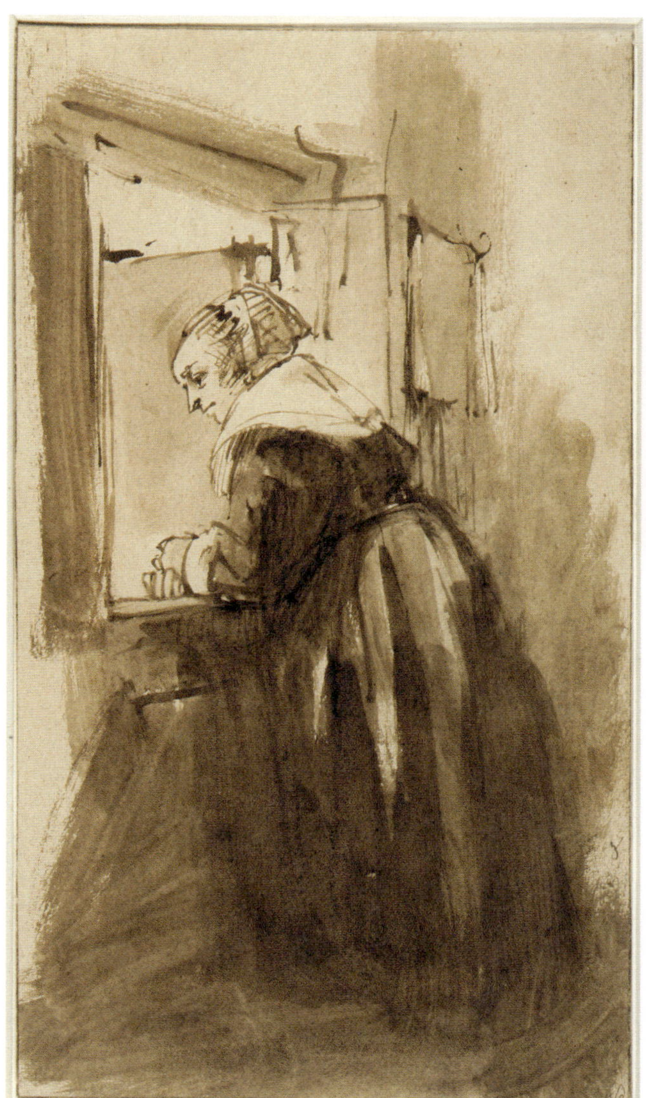

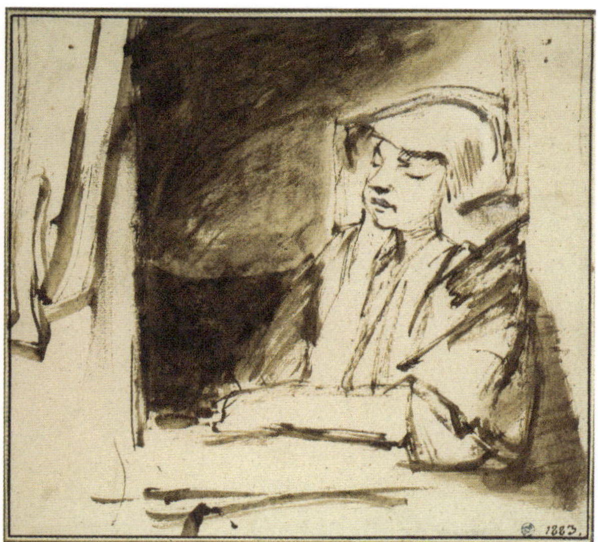

6.6 | *Woman Looking out of a Window*, ca. 1650. Pen and brown ink, brown wash; 29.5 × 16.4 cm (11⅝ × 6½ in.). Musée du Louvre, Paris, Collection Edmond de Rothshchild, inv. RF191DR. Photo © RMN—Grand Palais/Art Resource, N.Y. Photographer: Gérard Blot.

6.7 | *Woman Asleep at a Window*, ca. 1655. Pen and brown ink, brown wash, corrected with white opaque watercolor; 16.3 × 17.5 cm (6⅜ × 6⅞ in.). Nationalmuseum, Stockholm, inv. 2084/1863. Photo © The National Museum of Fine Arts.

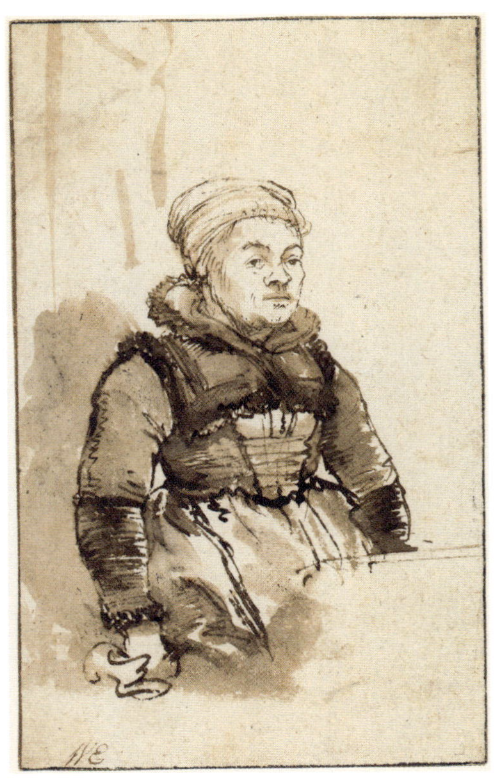

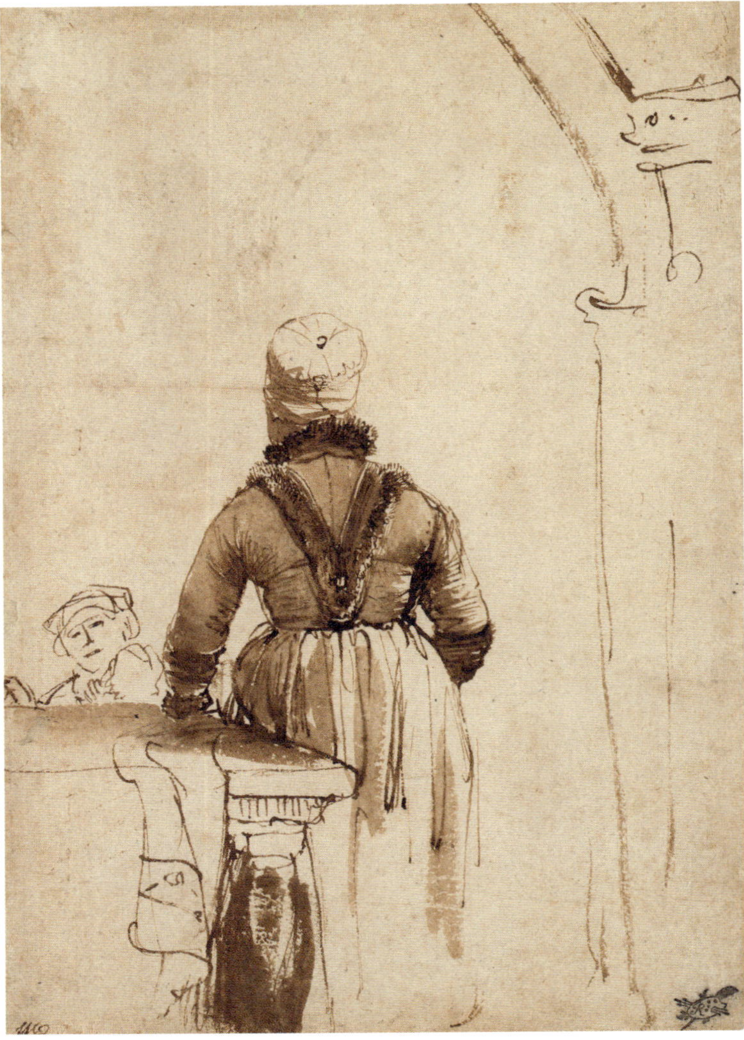

artist (a Rembrandt pupil?) drawing the model from the front is a bright one.[27] The verso of the Haarlem drawing is inscribed in red chalk by a later hand: "*the wet nurse / of Titus son / of Rembrandt.*"[28] This inscription has led to the assumption the woman is Geertje Dircx. We have heard she entered the artist's household shortly before or soon after Saskia's death in 1642, and that in 1649 she sued Rembrandt for breach of promise. The distinctive tightly laced bodice of her dress and fur collar and V-shaped fur marking the back lend support to the identification of the woman as Geertje, for her costume is characteristic of those worn in North Holland; Geertje was born in Edam, a city in the region.

It is necessary to add that the identification as Geertje is not a closed case. In the draft of an agreement

6.8 | *Woman in a North Holland Costume (Geertje Dircx?)*, early 1640s. Pen and brown ink, brown wash; 13 × 7.8 cm (5⅛ × 3⅛ in.). The British Museum, London, inv. 1895,0915.1270. Photo © The Trustees of The British Museum/Art Resource, N.Y.

6.9 | *Woman in a North Holland Costume, Seen from Behind (Geertje Dircx?)*, early 1640s. Pen and brown ink, brown wash; 22.2 × 15.4 cm (8¾ × 6 in.). Teyler Museum, Haarlem, inv. O* 51.

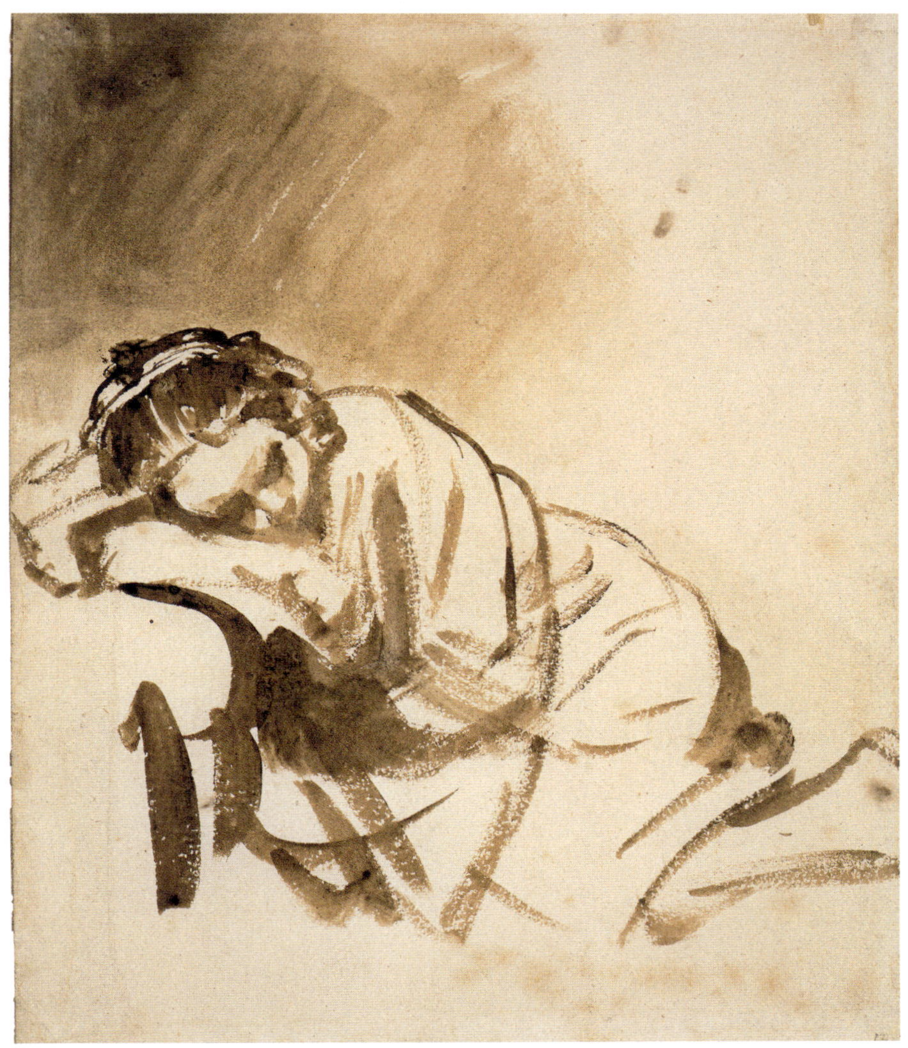

drawn up in October 1649 to settle the bitter breach-of-promise suit Geertje pressed against Rembrandt, she is specifically described as Titus's "dry nurse,"[29] not his "wet nurse." Thus, if the inscription on the verso of the Haarlem drawing is correct, the model cannot be Geertje. In any event, there can be no question regarding the artist's interest in capturing her likeness and his fascination with details of her costume, particularly the fur on the back of her bodice.

A Young Woman Sleeping at the British Museum is universally recognized as one of the master's finest drawings (fig. 6.10). With powerful strokes and peerless economy his swift brush suggests his model's form and the atmosphere that envelops her. The drawing is entirely done in brush, an exceedingly rare technique for Rembrandt (for a landscape

6.10 | *A Young Woman Sleeping*, ca. 1655. Brown wash, some white gouache; 24.6 × 20.3 cm (9⅝ × 8 in.). The British Museum, London, inv. PD1895,0915.1279. Photo © The Trustees of The British Museum/Art Resource, N.Y.

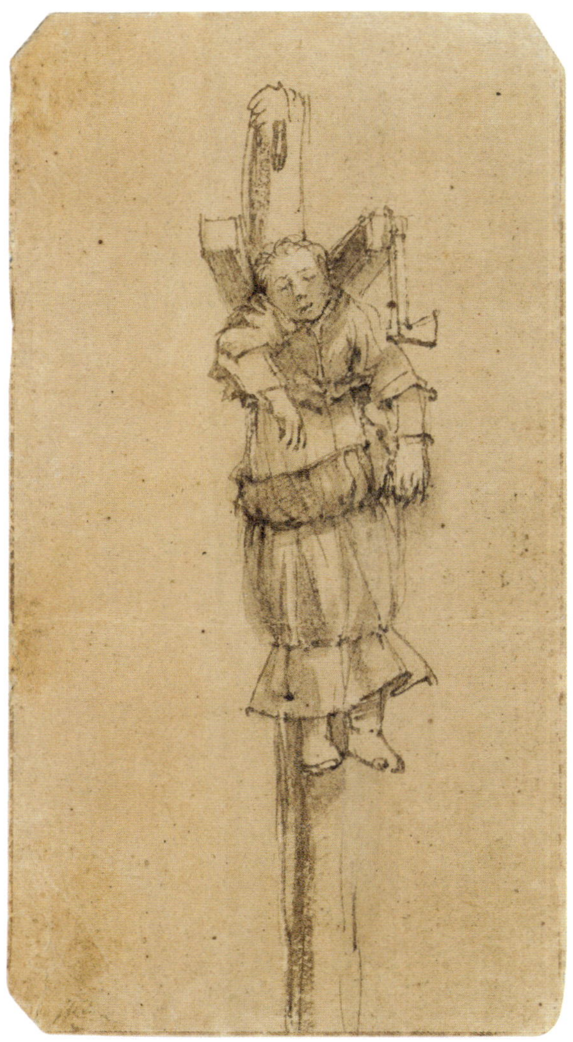

also entirely in brush, see fig. 11.19). Looking at the broad liquid brushstrokes in the lower part of the sheet with Western twenty-first-century eyes, it is hard not to think, at least for a moment, of the finest works one knows by Chinese and Japanese calligraphers or by superior abstract expressionists that give the impression of absolute spontaneity but that are, of course, completely controlled.

The sleeping woman has been identified, with more or less certainty, as Hendrickje Stoffels who entered the artist's household in the late 1640s. As mentioned earlier, no documented portrait of Hendrickje is known. Therefore, the argument that the young woman is Hendrickje is not strong, and it becomes weaker when we see that the facial features of the sleeping figure are obscured by soft shadows. Sup-

6.11 | *Elsje Christiaens Hanging on a Gibbet*, 1664. Pen and brown ink, brush and brown wash; 17.1 × 9.1 cm (6¾ × 3½ in.). The Metropolitan Museum of Art, New York, H. O. Havermeyer Collection, Bequest of Mrs. H. O. Havermeyer, 1929, inv. 29.100.937. Image © The Metropolitan Museum of Art.

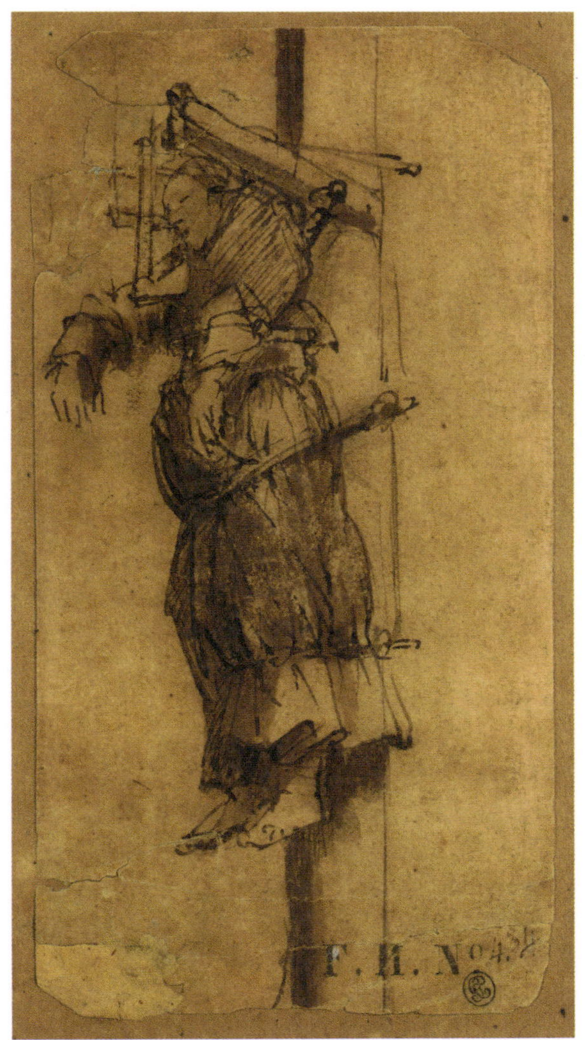

port for her identity rests primarily on similarities that can be found between the shape of her round face and thick, dark hair and other portraits traditionally called portrayals of Hendrickje. Another factor cannot be ignored. It is the desire, despite odds, to affirm that the miraculous drawing portrays the woman who gave birth to Rembrandt's daughter Cornelia, and who was the mature master's companion during the last two decades of her life (she died in 1663).

6.12 | *Elsje Christiaens Hanging on a Gibbet*, 1664. Pen and brown ink, brush and grayish brown wash on heavy brownish paper; 15.8 × 8.0 cm (6¼ × 3⅛ in.). The Metropolitan Museum of Art, New York, The Robert Lehman Collection, inv. 1975.1.803. Photo copyright © The Metropolitan Museum of Art/Art Resource, N.Y.

This discussion of the artist's drawings of the life of women closes with two gruesome depictions of a dead young woman hanging on a gibbet, both at the Metropolitan Museum (figs. 6.11, 6.12). There is no need to debate her name. Thanks to the research of the indefatigable Amsterdam archivist I. H. van Eeghen, we know that she was eighteen-year-old Elsje

Christiaens from Jutland, Denmark, who came to Amsterdam in April 1664 to find work as a servant.[30] On the 27th of that month her landlady beat her with a broomstick because she failed to pay her rent. Elsje, in turn, grabbed an axe that was at hand. In the fight that followed, the landlady fell down the stairs to her death. Elsje fled but was quickly apprehended. She was sentenced on May 1st to be secured to a stake on a scaffold and choked until she died (a regular form of execution at the time) and then receive blows on her head with the same axe with which she had attacked her landlady. The court had more to say. After her death she was to be displayed on Volewijk, an island in the River IJ just north of Amsterdam, the guilty axe placed by her head, her body left to rot. The gallows field on Volewijk, seen by domestic and foreign sailors entering Amsterdam's harbor, was intended to deter crime. A drawing of it by Anthonie van Borssum, a follower of Rembrandt, includes Elsje and her axe on a gibbet in the lower right and other dead criminals serving as food for carrion birds (fig. 6.13).

Rembrandt's drawings of Elsje are highly exceptional in his oeuvre. They and his drawing of the ruins of Amsterdam's Old Town Hall, dated by the artist 9 July 1652, a few days after it was gutted by fire (see fig. 12.7), are his only known drawings of sensational contemporary events. There must have been much ado in Amsterdam when word of Elsje's execution spread. Twenty-one years had passed since a woman had received such a severe sentence. Both of Rembrandt's drawings are executed in pen and brown wash. In the one in which Elsje is seen frontally, her face has a childlike quality, not that of a convicted criminal. In the other, which is in less-than-good condition and has some wash added by another hand, Rembrandt gives equal attention to the limp, lifeless figure and to the straps, bolts, blocks, and timber stakes to which she has been secured.[31]

6.13 | Anthonie van Borssum (Dutch, ca. 1630–1677), *View of the Gallows Field at Volewijk Outside of Amsterdam*, 1664. Pen and brown ink, watercolor, on paper; 20.5 × 31.8 cm (8⅛ × 12½ in.). Rijksmuseum, Amsterdam, inv. RP-T-1954-182.

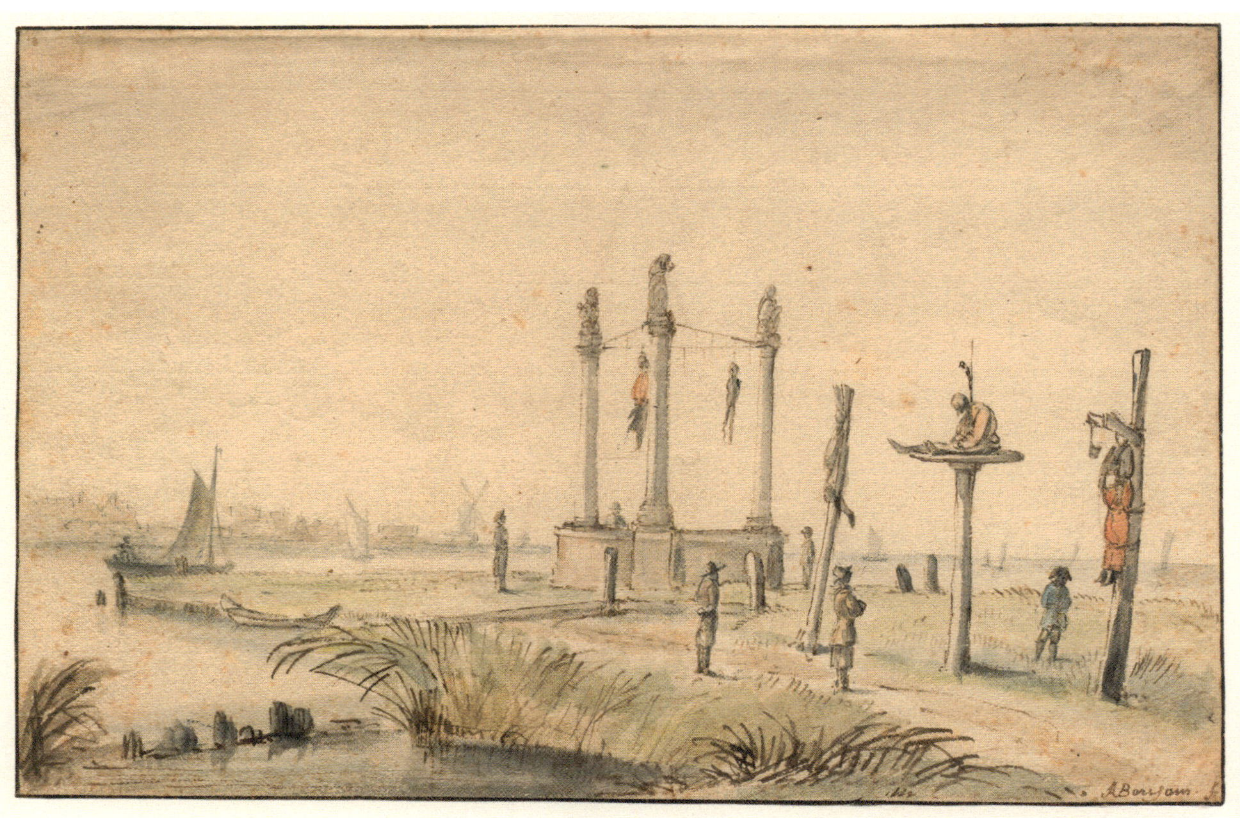

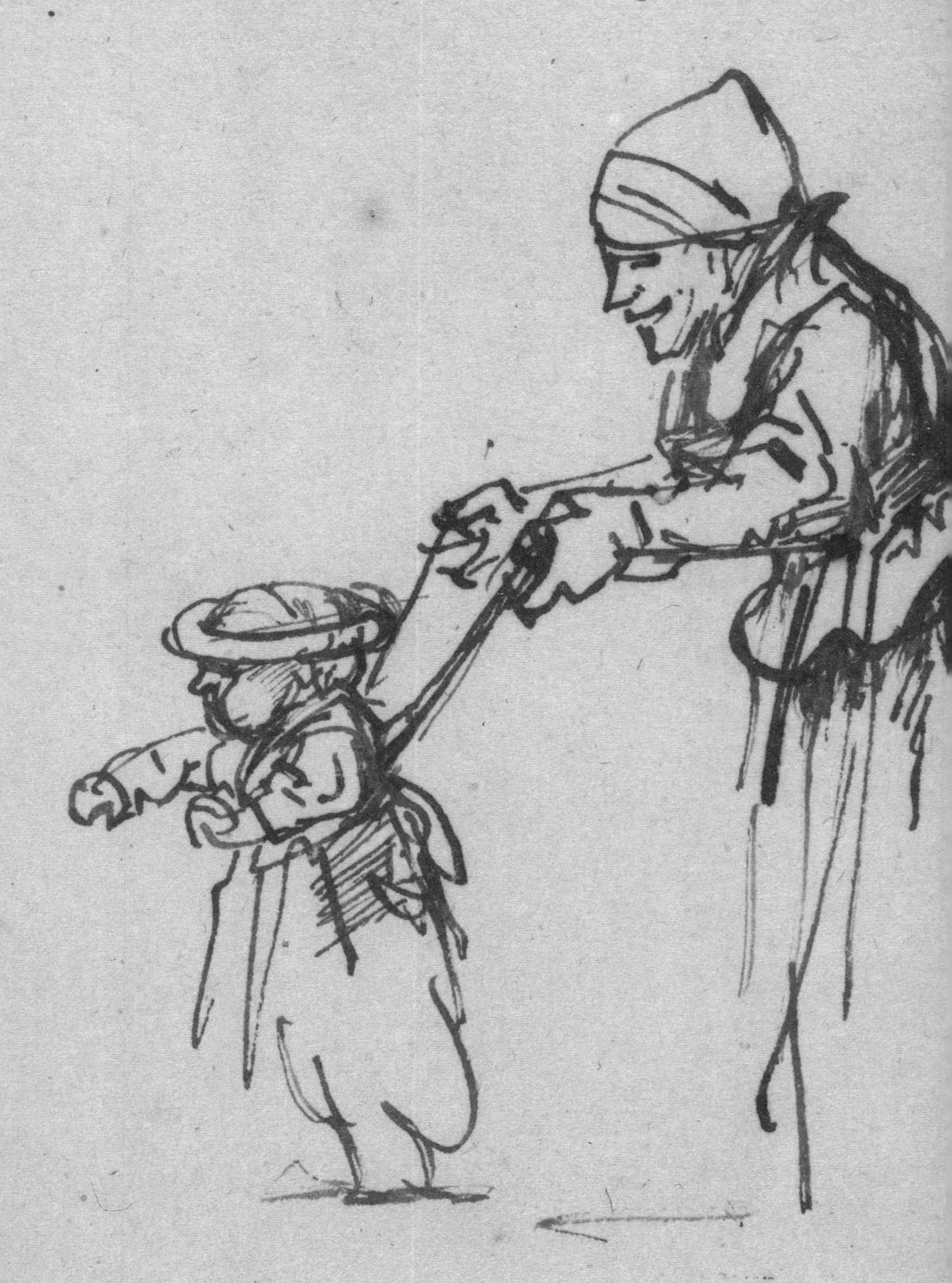

7 | Life of Women and Children

JAN VAN DE CAPPELLE, the seventeenth-century Dutch marine painter of mirror-smooth waters surmounted by majestic clouds, did not devote all of his energy to art. He also helped manage and then inherited his father's profitable dye works. At his death in 1679 he was worth a fortune of more than 90,000 guilders, owned substantial holdings in real estate and a pleasure yacht, as well as an awesome art collection, known from a posthumous inventory of 1680, of almost two hundred paintings and more than seven thousand drawings. Rembrandt was well represented with seven paintings, including an untraceable portrait of Van de Cappelle, and by the breathtaking number of about five hundred drawings in five portfolios.

Van de Cappelle was most probably a very active bidder when Rembrandt's effects were put on the auction block in 1657–58. In addition to the Rembrandt paintings, his posthumous inventory itemizes two portfolios with a total of 277 landscape drawings by the artist. Van de Cappelle was following Rembrandt's lead. It will be recalled that Rembrandt's 1656 inventory tells us he kept his own landscapes in two special albums and a vellum book. Van de Cappelle had another portfolio with forty-eight sketches by Rembrandt and Pynas (Jan and/or his brother Jacob; both artists, despite reasonable objections to the nonsensical label, are often called "Pre-Rembrandtists").

Van de Cappelle also had large holdings of two categories of Rembrandt drawings that are not mentioned by name in the artist's 1656 inventory. Nevertheless, there can be little doubt that at least some of them belonged to Rembrandt until they were auctioned off to satisfy his creditors. They are listed as: "A ditto [portfolio] with 56 history draw-

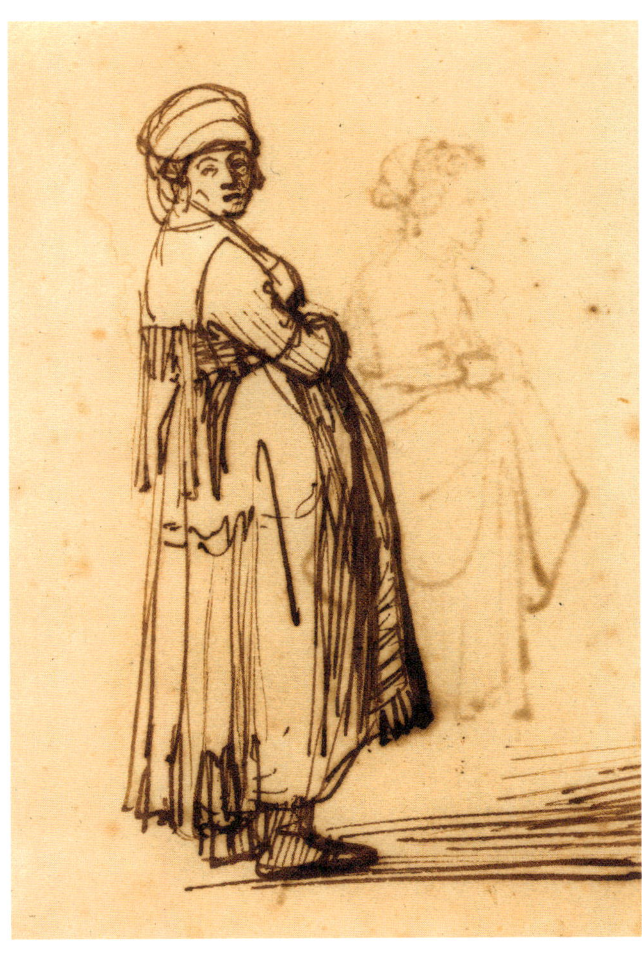

7.1 | *Pregnant Woman Standing* (recto), ca. 1639. Pen and brown iron-gall ink, on paper prepared with brown wash; 16.5 × 11.1 cm (6½ × 4⅜ in.). The British Museum, London, inv. 1910,0212.184. Photo © The Trustees of The British Museum. All rights reserved.

ings by Rembrandt" and "A ditto [portfolio] with 135 drawings of the life of women with children by Rembrandt."[32] Neither category astonishes. After all, during the course of his career the artist sketched more histories, that is, scenes from the Old and New Testaments, lives of saints, classical mythology, and history, than any other subject. As for the drawings depicting the life of women with children, Van de Cappelle's huge collection of them indicates he found them as intriguing as we do.

Rembrandt's remarkable pen drawing of a standing pregnant woman at the British Museum (fig. 7.1) would not have been out of place in Van de Cappelle's portfolio. She is most certainly heavy with child. With a few lines the artist caught the momentary expression of a woman who has difficulty looking over her shoulder because of her rigid back buttressing her enormous belly. The drawing is done in iron-gall ink, which has bitten slightly into its paper support prepared

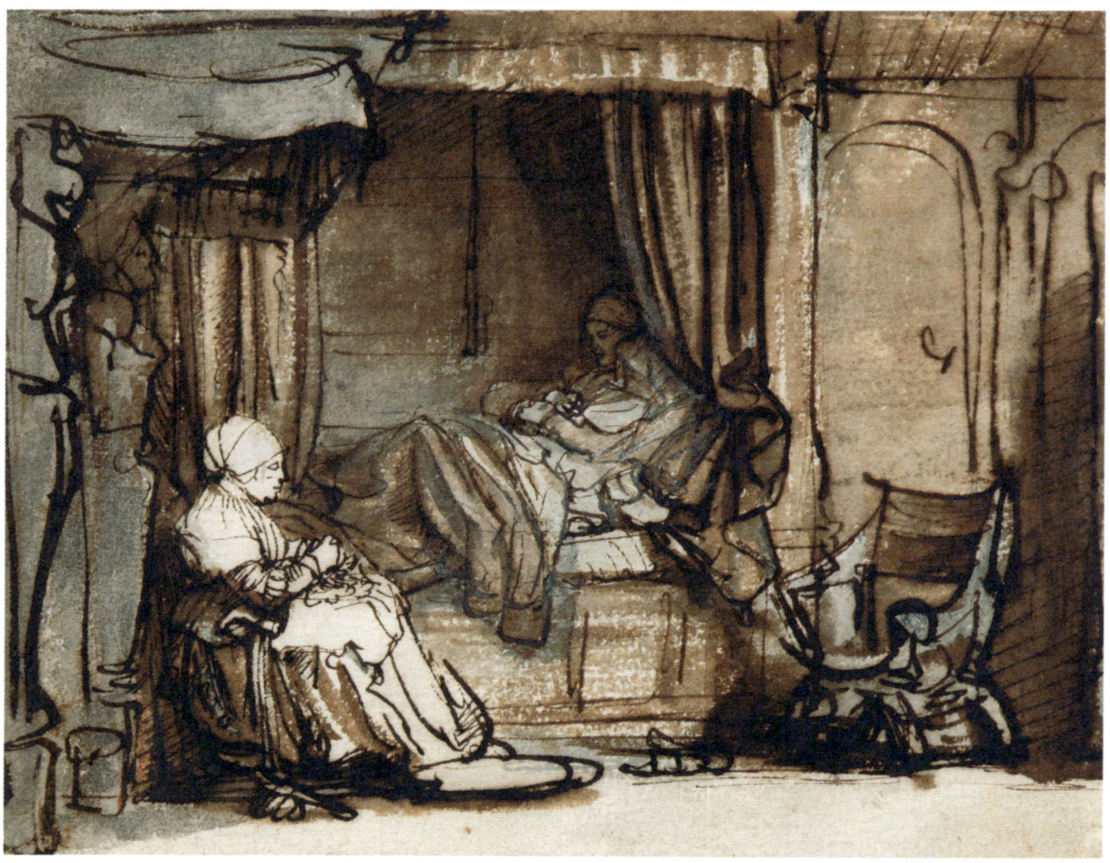

with a light brown wash. Some of the lines of a pen sketch of a standing young woman on the verso, also in gall ink, are visible on the recto of the sheet.

A highly worked up drawing of an interior with a woman lying in bed and a seated attendant winding lace, at Fondation Custodia, Paris (fig. 7.2), is the artist's most elaborate treatment of a confined woman, a subject he often depicted from about 1635 until 1641. As we have heard, these were the years in which Saskia gave birth to four children, three of whom died in infancy. Two drawings of the group, which concentrate on the woman in bed, but not an interior, are also illustrated. One shows a woman sitting up (fig. 7.3); the other depicts its subject ill and frightened (fig. 7.4).

The woman in these and similar sketches is often identified as Saskia either soon before or after she gave birth. This may be the case. Indeed, it has been argued with good reason, on the basis of the date of about 1639–41 that can be assigned to the Fondation Custodia drawing, that it shows a room in the large house Rembrandt bought in January 1639 on

7.2 | *Interior with a Woman (probably Saskia) in Bed*, ca. 1639–41. Pen and brown ink, gray and brown wash, touches of white, touches of red and black chalk; 14.2 × 17.7 cm (5 5/8 × 7 in.). Fondation Custodia, Collection Frits Lugt, Paris, inv. 266.

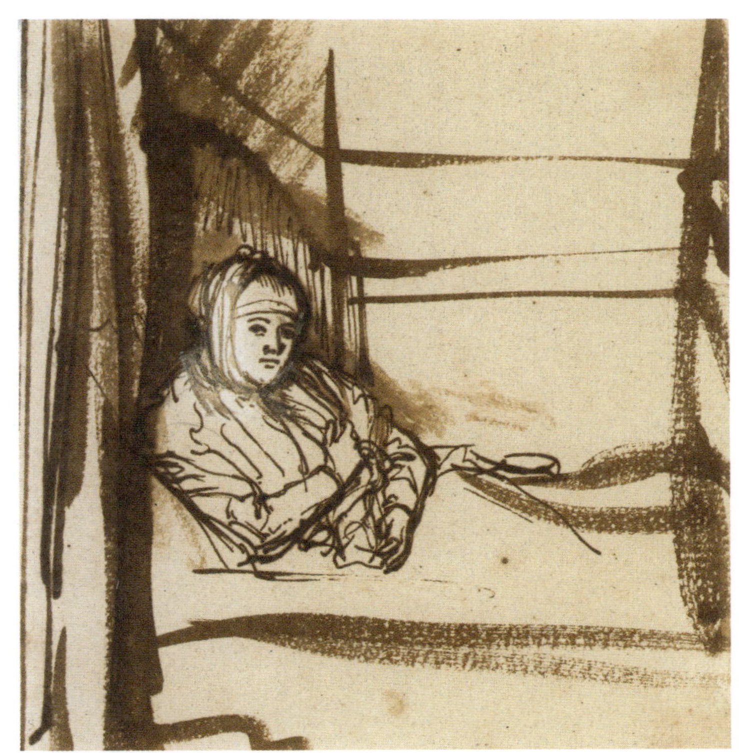

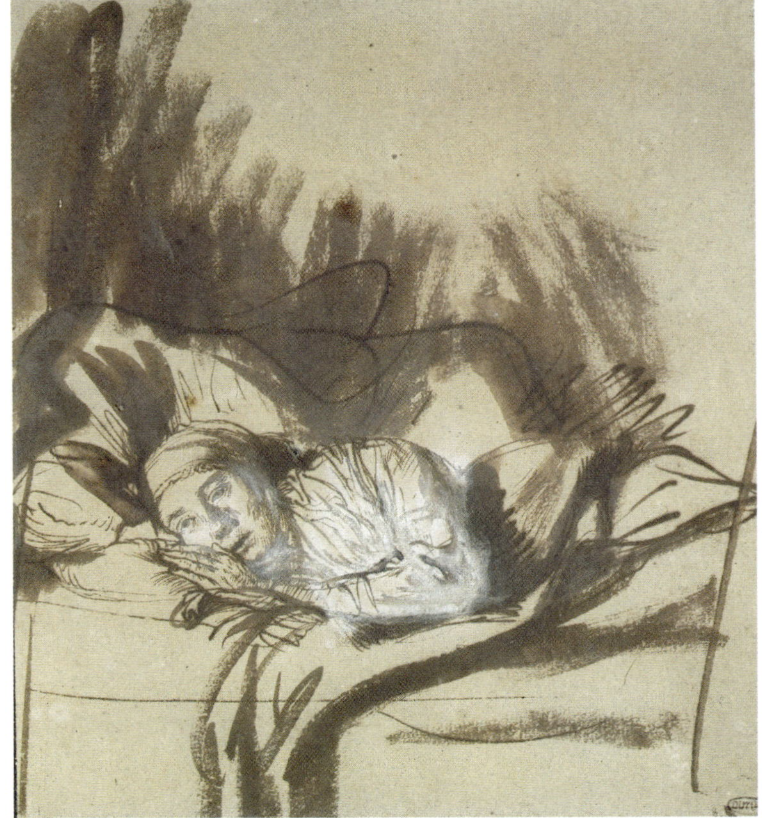

7.3 | *Woman (Saskia) Seated in Bed*, ca. 1635–36. Pen and brown ink, brown wash, corrected with white, on paper prepared with light brown wash; 15 × 13.8 cm (5⅞ × 5⅜ in.). Kupferstich-Kabinett, Staatliche Kunstsammlungen Dresden, inv. C1326. Photo: Bildarchiv Preussischer Kulturbesitz/Art Resource, N.Y. Photographer: Herbert Boswank.

7.4 | *Woman Lying in Bed (Saskia Sick)*, ca. 1635–36. Pencil and brown ink, brown wash, touches of white; 16.3 × 14.5 cm (6⅜ × 5¾ in.). Petit Palais, Collection Dutuit, Musée des Beaux-Arts de la Ville de Paris, inv. DDut 01011. Photo © RMN—Grand Palais/Art Resource, N.Y. Photographer: Agence Bulloz.

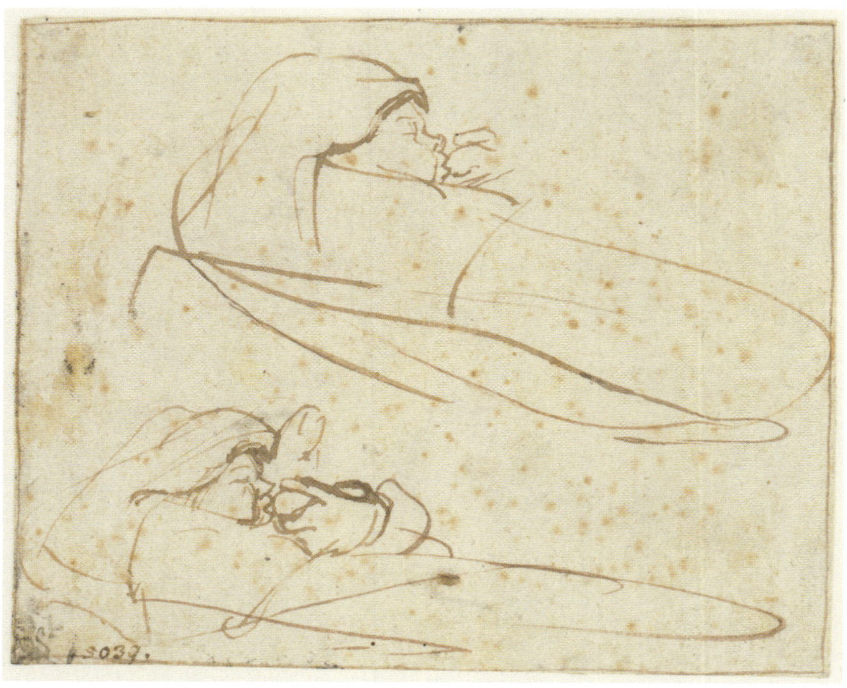

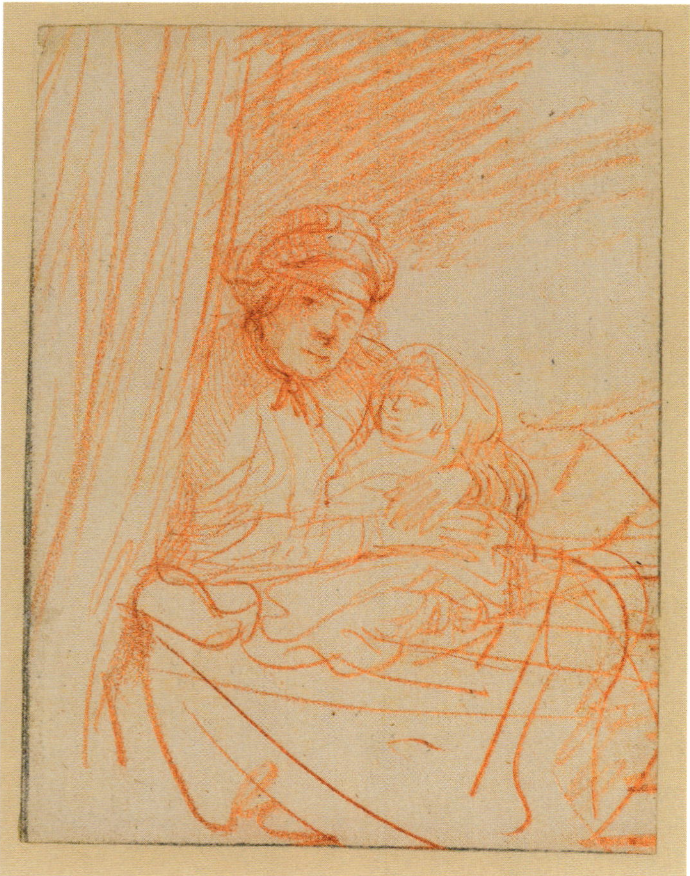

7.5 | *Two Sketches of an Infant in Swaddling Clothes Fed from a Bottle*, ca. 1635. Pen and brown ink; 10.4 × 12.6 cm (4⅛ × 5 in.). Staatliche Graphische Sammlung, Munich, inv. 1656 Z. Photo © Engelbert Seehuber.

7.6 | *Woman Sitting up in Bed with a Baby*, ca. 1635. Red chalk; 14 × 10.6 cm (5½ × 4⅛ in.). The Courtauld Gallery, Seilern Collection, London, inv. D.1978.PG.183. Photo © The Samuel Courtauld Trust, The Courtauld Gallery, London.

a street that is now named Jodenbreestraat (today it is the Museum het Rembrandthuis).[33] In that house Saskia gave birth to Cornelia, her third child, who was baptized 29 July 1640 and buried 12 August in the same year. Titus, her fourth child, was baptized 22 September 1641. Saskia, presumably the woman in deep shadow in the box bed, died in 1642. The intense daylight that bathes the seated figure and the extensive use of gray as well as brown wash in the drawing are both unusual.

Two successive moments in the feeding of an infant from a bottle are captured in a swift pen sketch at Munich (fig. 7.5). In the upper sketch there is only a suggestion of fingers holding the bottle, while the baby's swaddling clothes are indicated by just a couple of decisive lines. In the lower sketch, the hand holding the bottle is given as much emphasis as the infant's head.[34] Swaddling clothes are worn also by the infant held by a woman sitting up in bed in a delicate red-chalk sketch at the Courtauld Gallery, London (fig. 7.6). The drawing has been called Saskia with Rumbartus, her firstborn, in her arms. The identification is moot, a fact that does not diminish the sketch's charm.

The artist's ceaseless interest in life and the world around him comes out strikingly in his drawing of two women teaching a child to walk. In the red-chalk drawing at the British Museum (fig. 7.7) he makes a clear distinction between the old woman who can only follow the toddler in a slow, bent attitude, and the other woman, whose posture expresses

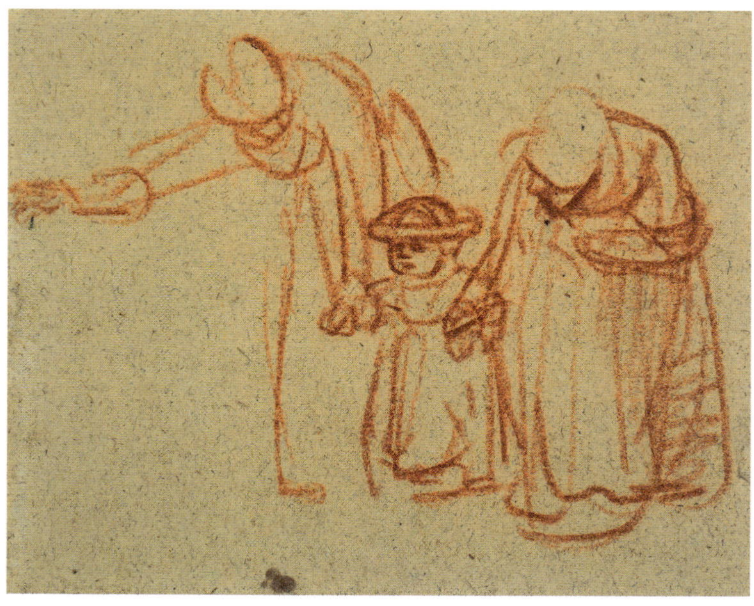

7.7 | *Two Women Teaching a Child to Walk*, ca. 1635–37. Red chalk; 10.5 × 12.8 cm (4⅛ × 5 in.). The British Museum, London, inv. PD1910,0212.187. Photo © The Trustees of The British Museum/Art Resource, N.Y.

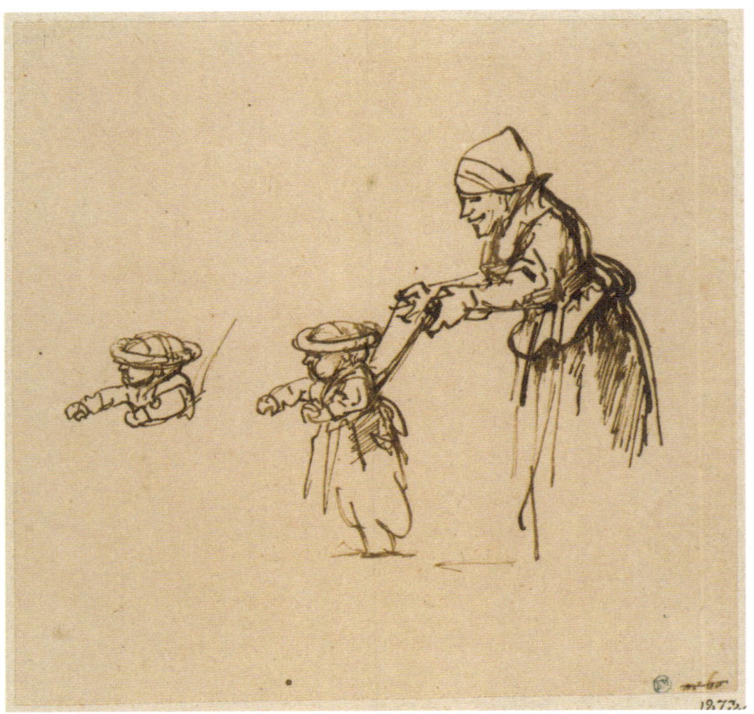

youthfulness and elasticity. Powerful lines are combined with accents on vital points, such as the attention of the two women and the anxious expression of the baby wearing a well-padded hat that will protect his little head if there is a fall. About a decade later, in an equally quick sketch, now in Stockholm (fig. 7.8), this time in pen, Rembrandt concentrates on the pleasure a mature woman takes in seeing a baby secured to lead strings take its first or second steps.

In an uncanny way the Morgan Library's dazzling pen-and-wash drawing of a young woman rushing down a spiral staircase as she clutches a heavy young child to her bosom (fig. 7.9) brings to mind Eadweard Muybridge's pioneer sequence of photographs made in the 1880s that capture the rapid movement of models by the use of multiple cameras. The drawing's chiaroscuro effect, created by broad areas of transparent wash, is bold. Strong, summary strokes define the figures, while the child's head and its unruly hair and what we can see of the young woman's profile are done with a very fine pen. It is obvious that the woman's cap is a second thought.

More anecdotal than the Morgan sheet is Berlin's drawing of a young woman using all her strength to control a child throwing a tantrum (fig. 7.10). On one side, behind the young woman, an old woman admonishes the child some may

7.8 | *Woman Teaching a Child to Walk*, ca. 1640–45. Pen and brown ink; 16 × 16.5 cm (6¼ × 6½ in.). Nationalmuseum, Stockholm, inv. 2074/1863. Photo © The National Museum of Fine Arts.

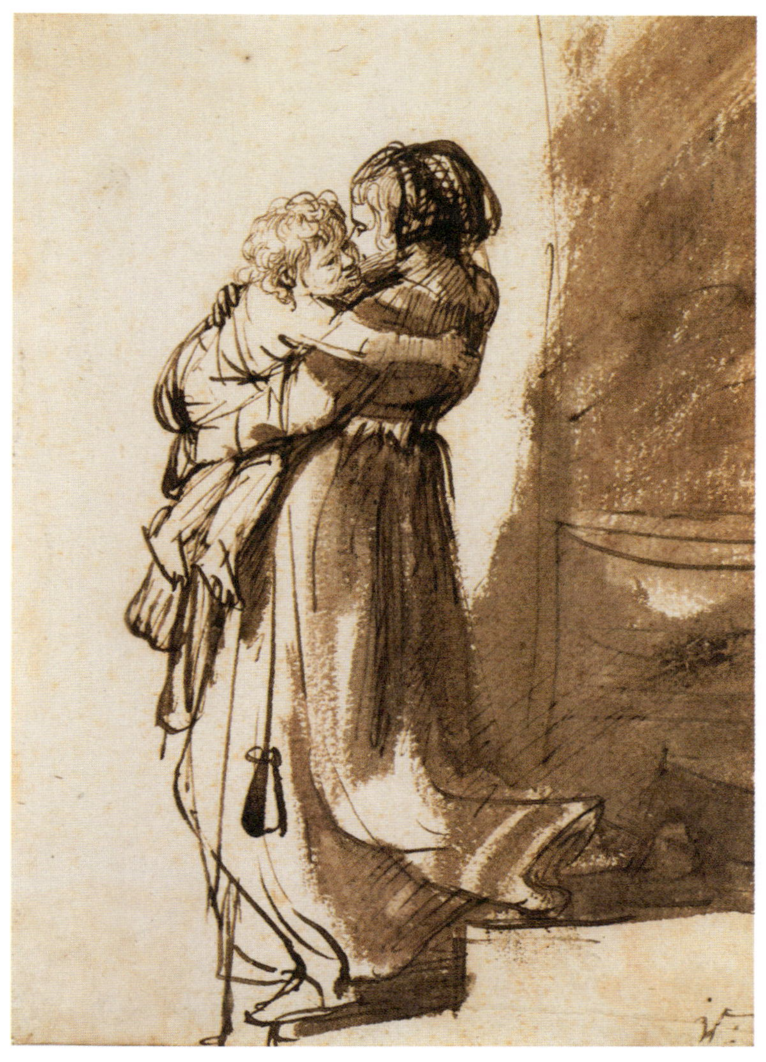

7.9 | *Woman Carrying a Child Downstairs*, ca. 1635. Pen and brown ink, brown wash; 18.7 × 13.2 cm (7³⁄₈ × 5¼ in.). The Pierpont Morgan Library, New York, inv. I,191. Photographer: Schechter Lee.

call naughty, others may characterize as a brat. On the other side, two children in a doorway are exhibiting schadenfreude. The bad boy's gown raised above his navel, his flayed limbs, and his shoe in mid-air as well as the sketchy character of the drawing's background enhance the impression that we have been given the record of a dramatic instantaneous moment in the group's life. The intellectual effort Rembrandt put into the drawing is evident after examination of the young woman's posture, the tilt of her head, her determined expression, and the position of her arms and hands. It is also significant that the artist placed the howling child's head in the drawing's optical center. Rembrandt found other roles for him. He plays a major part in the preparatory drawing (see fig. 14.8) for the picture at Dresden of the *Rape of Ganymede*, dated

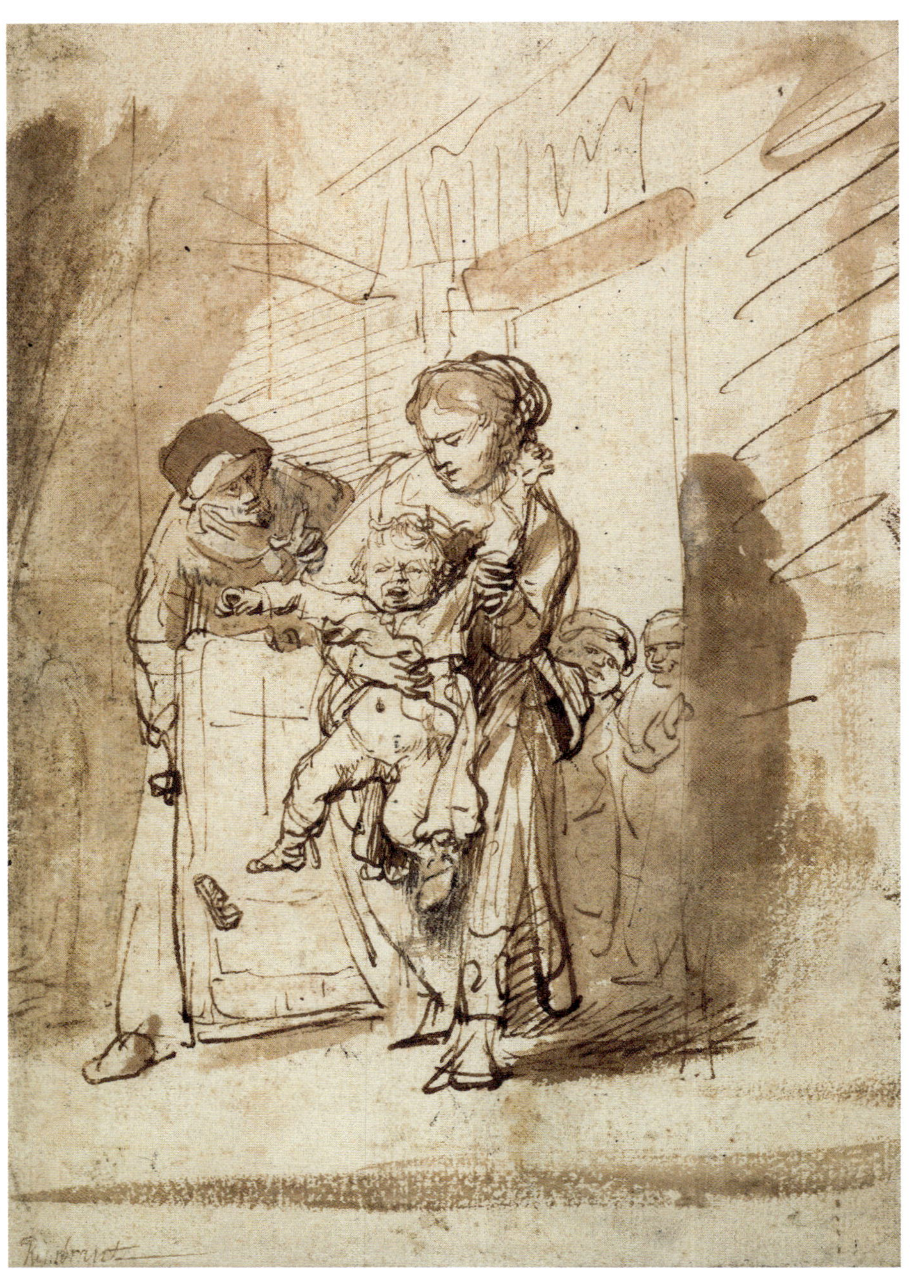

7.10 | *The Naughty Boy*, ca. 1635. Pen and brown ink, brown wash, traces of white; 20.6 × 14.3 cm (8⅛ × 5⅝ in.). Kupferstichkabinett, Staatliche Museen, Berlin, inv. KdZ 3771. Photo: Bildarchiv Preussischer Kulturbesitz/Art Resource, N.Y. Photographer: Jörg P. Anders.

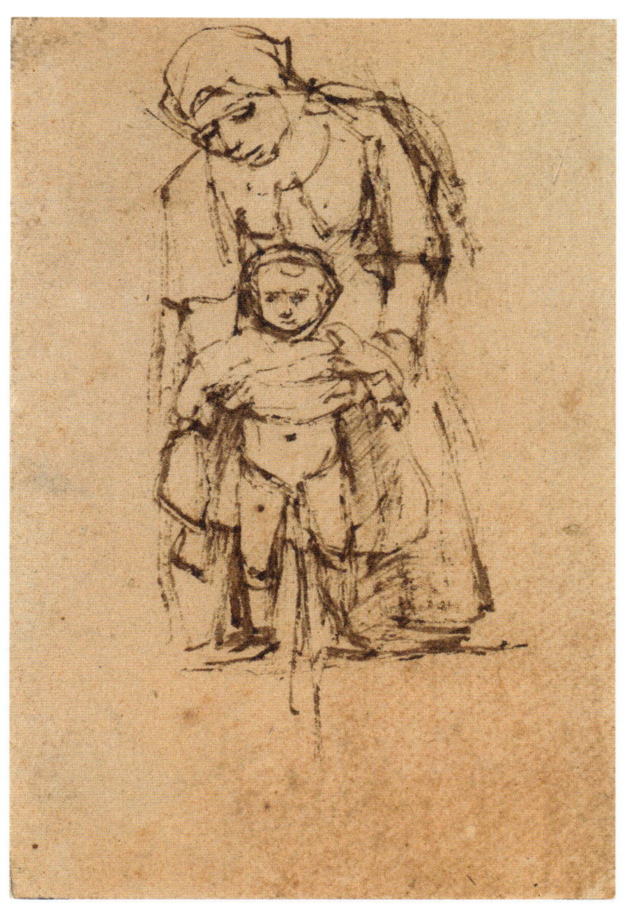

7.11 | *Woman with a Pissing Boy*, ca. 1657–60. Reed pen and brown ink, on paper prepared with a light brown wash; 13.3 × 9 cm (5¼ × 3½ in.). Kupferstich-Kabinett, Staatliche Kunstsammlungen Dresden, inv. C1896-34. Photo: Bildarchiv Preussischer Kulturbesitz/Art Resource, N.Y. Photographer: Herbert Boswank.

1635 (see fig. 14.9). He makes an appropriate appearance as a chained weeping Eros at the head of Danaë's bed in Rembrandt's painting of her visit by Jupiter as a shower of gold at the Hermitage, Saint Petersburg. And we have seen he is also a conspicuous player in a study sheet at Berlin (see fig. 4.7).

During the decades that followed Saskia's death Rembrandt made fewer drawings showing the life of women and children. A small but notable one datable to the late 1650s, or even a bit later, of a woman holding up a little boy's gown as he pisses (into a canal?) is at Dresden (fig. 7.11). The firmly built figures, seen frontally, are drawn with a few strokes of a broad reed pen. In some passages the pen was loaded with ink; in others it was virtually dry. A variation on the theme is in an Amsterdam drawing that includes a sketch of a horse's head unrelated to the figures (Benesch no. 1140A). Both drawings are on paper that has been washed with a light brown tone. The close similarity of their style and paper bolsters the suggestion that they originally belonged to the same sheet.

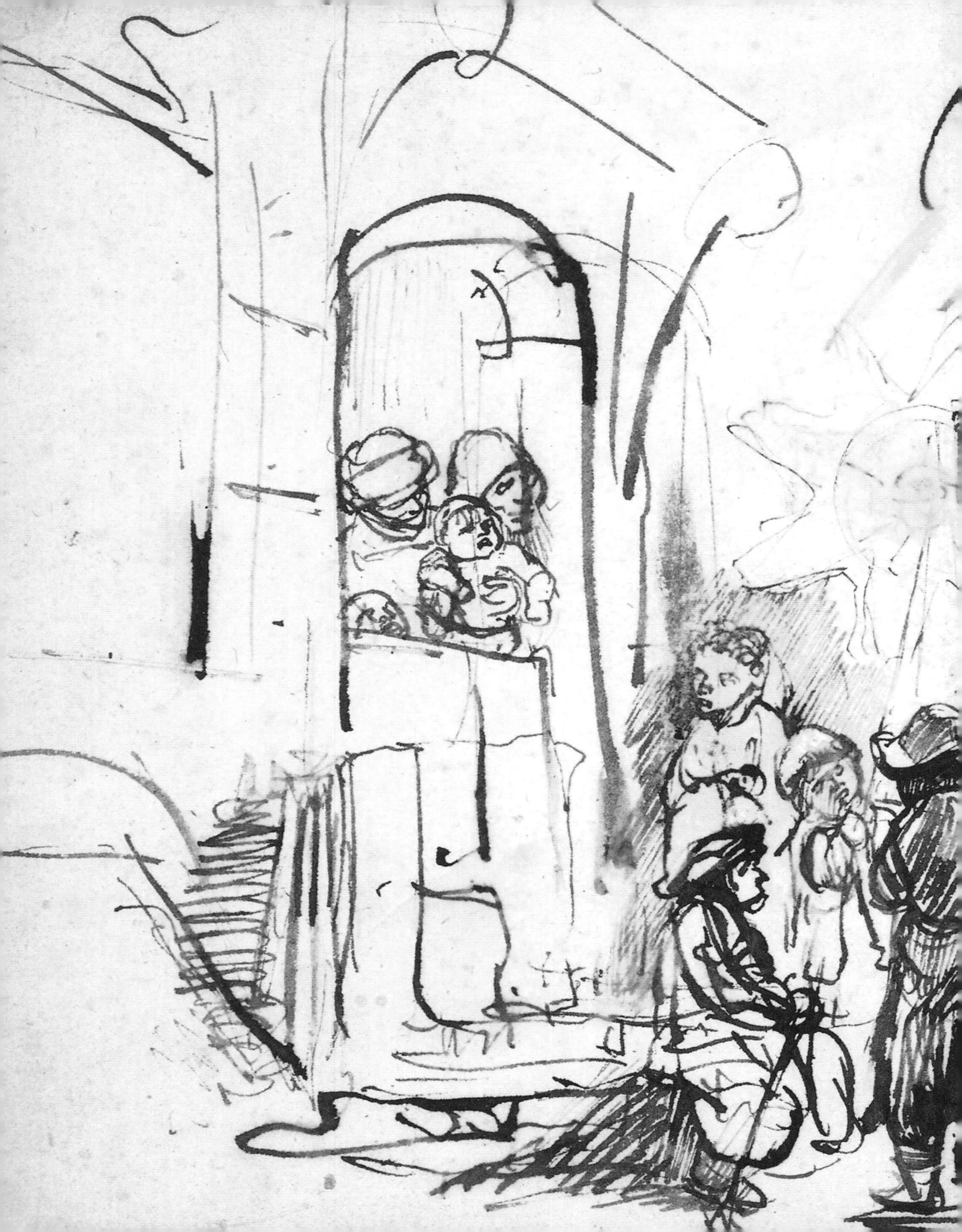

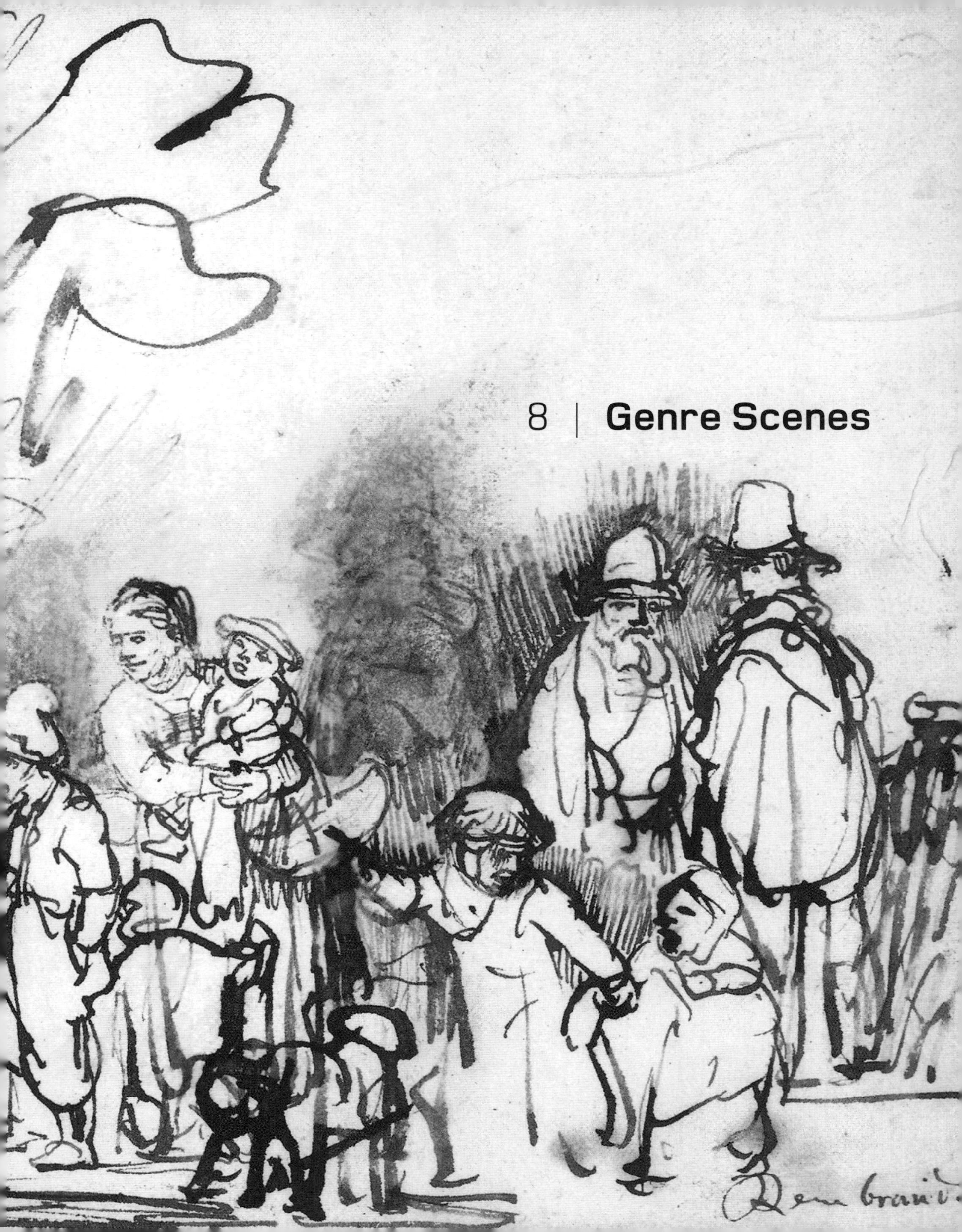

8 | Genre Scenes

8 | GENRE SCENES

EUROPEAN ARTISTS had represented scenes of everyday life since Renaissance times, but during the fifteenth and sixteenth centuries such works were seldom done for their own sake. They were made as parts of cycles of the seasons or months, or to point out a moral, convey an allegorical idea, or illustrate a proverb or a passage from the Bible. This hardy tradition was still alive and well during the seventeenth century. However, during that century an important group of artists broke with it when they depicted anonymous people doing ordinary things just for the sake of showing their actions in their milieu. And during the course of the century the Netherlands produced more and better artists representing scenes of daily life, with or without messages, than any other nation. Rembrandt was one of these artists.

To be sure, he did not paint many genre pictures. He favored etching and especially drawing for the themes. In fact, it is arguable that numerous drawings categorized in earlier chapters as scenes of the life of women with and without children should be classified as genre scenes. A justification for making them discrete categories is that they form coherent groups. Moreover, we have seen that the Amsterdam artist and avid collector Jan van de Cappelle set a sensible precedent in Rembrandt's own time for this arrangement by keeping his vast holding of the artist's drawings of women with children apart from his other sketches by the master.

Neither Van de Cappelle nor any of his contemporaries would have used the term "genre." When seventeenth-century Dutchmen wanted to refer to a picture of daily life, they merely described it; for example, *een koeckebacker* (a pancake baker), *een beeldeken* or *moderne beelden* (a picture with figures or modern figures), *een bordeeltjen* (a bordello), and so on. Dutchmen of the period had no generic name for the branch of art their countrymen developed as a specialty. In this instance, as in so many concerning Dutch art, in the beginning was the picture, not the word.

Rembrandt's *Pancake Baker* at Amsterdam is a superb example of the artist's genius for capturing the momentary drama of a modest street scene with a few strokes of the pen (fig. 8.1). The emphasis is on the young boy with an eye on pancakes being prepared by the old woman seated on a low chair. He digs deep into his pocket for a coin to make a purchase, one leg bent and its foot raised to facilitate his search. A toddler kneels near the woman's low stove. In the context of the encounter of the old vendor, her young customer, and the little witness, the hasty lines in the background on the right can be read as a fighting pair of boys. Without the foreground scene, the scribbles would be meaningless—or perhaps they could be used as material for a type of Rorschach test based on ink lines rather than ink blots.

Scribbles and scrawls are not rare in Rembrandt's drawings. They can be read variously as lightning-swift shorthand for figures, parts of a composition, or areas that are in shadow. In the midst of the scribbles and scrawls there are always a few fine passages where we recognize the hand of the artist. These are its good parts, and a sensible rule of

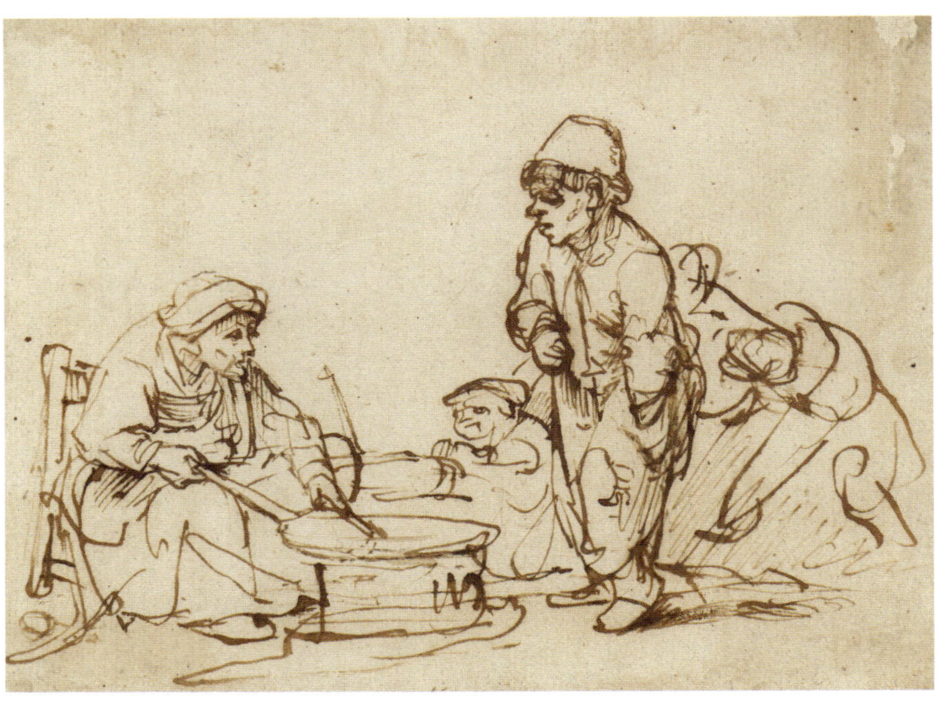

8.1 | *The Pancake Baker*, 1633–37. Pen and brown ink, on paper; 10.8 × 14.4 cm (4¼ × 5⅝ in.). Rijksmuseum, Amsterdam, inv. RP-T-1891-A-2424.

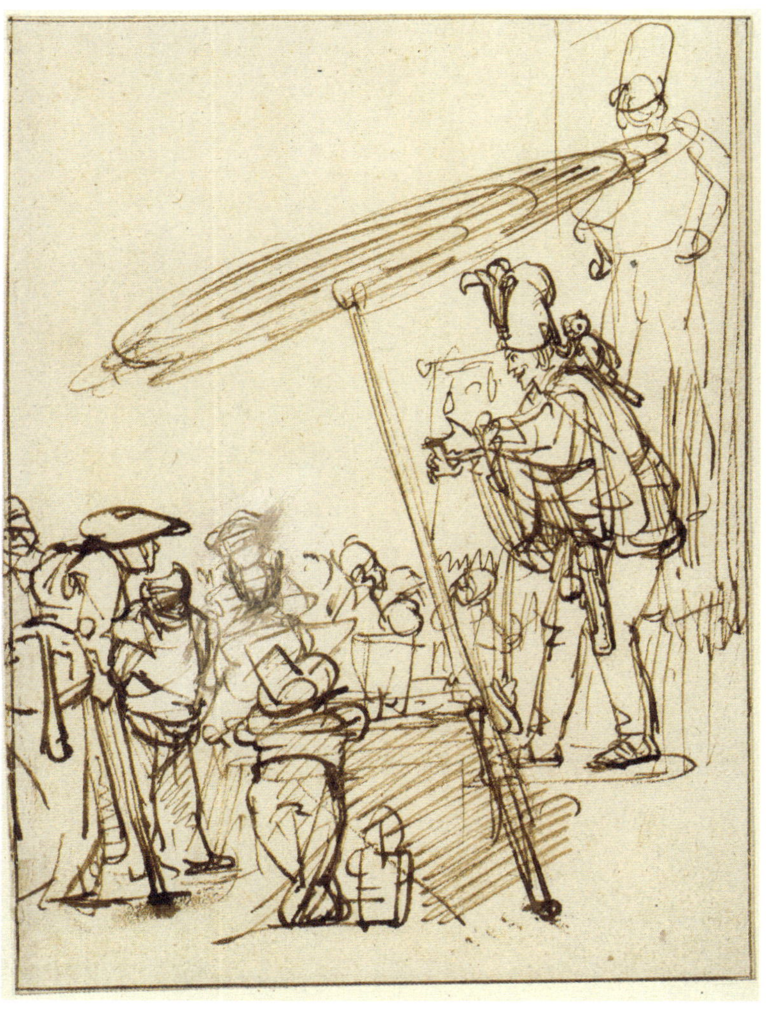

thumb in assessing a drawing is to judge it first from its good rather than its less good parts. The rule is easy to remember, for it is the one used when judging friends.

A case in point is Berlin's quack standing on a platform hawking his wares to a crowd (fig. 8.2). Part of the crowd is difficult to decipher but not so the quack's smiling face, his hands as he ticks off points on his fingers, the owl on his shoulder, his high feathered hat, and bits of his costume. The ball and long baton hanging from his waist recall accessories worn by Pantalone (see fig. 5.9). The quickly drawn umbrella shading the quack and his patrons and his schematic banner also make perfect sense.

The close-up of a man intently concentrating on sharpening a quill pen by candlelight captures the very moment a knife slices into a quill's shank (fig. 8.3). The drawing has a distinctly

8.2 | *Quack Addressing a Crowd at a Fair*, ca. 1637. Pen and brown ink, corrected with white; 20 × 14.7 cm (7⅞ × 5¾ in.). Kupferstichkabinett, Staatliche Museen, Berlin, inv. KdZ5268. Photo: Bildarchiv Preussischer Kulturbesitz/Art Resource, N.Y. Photographer: Jörg P. Anders.

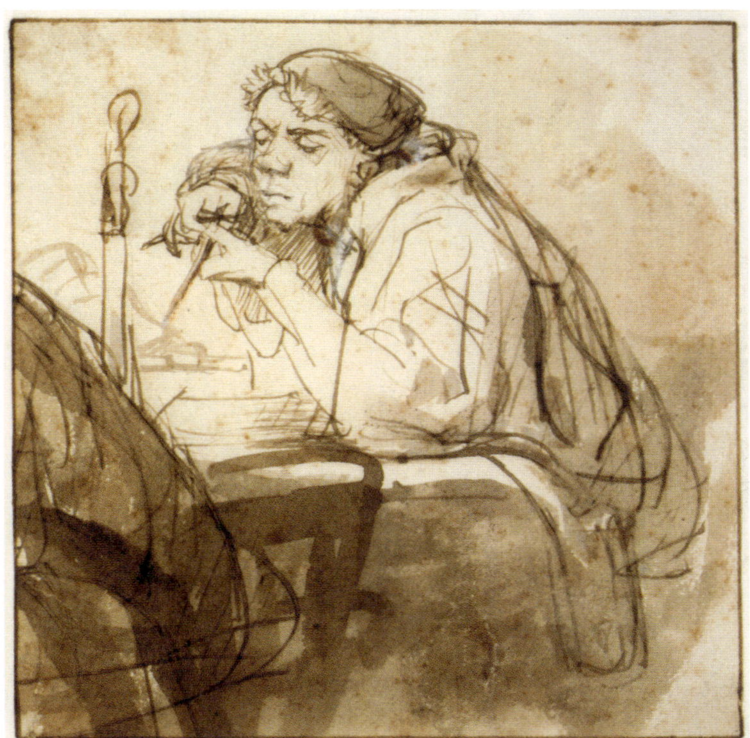

8.3 | *Man Sharpening a Quill by Candlelight*, ca. 1635. Pen and brown ink, brown wash, some red chalk, corrected with white, on handmade paper; 12.5 × 12.3 cm (4⅞ × 4⅞ in.). Klassik Stiftung Weimar, Bestand Museen, KK 5492.

portrait-like character. Perhaps it was inspired by Rembrandt's glimpse of a similar scene when one of his own students was drawing at night. But I doubt the drawing was done from life. Is it conceivable that Rembrandt had a model freeze a pose for him with his shoulders hunched, his head thrust forward, his eyes lowered, one arm resting on a table and the other in midair until he finished his sketch? Probably not.

Young and more often old men (never women) sharpening quill pens were depicted by a few other Dutch artists, among them Rembrandt's very first pupil, Gerrit Dou, and his followers. It has been suggested these works allude to the importance of constant practice, which both Renaissance and Baroque theorists agreed was as necessary as natural talent for success in the arts. Quills also appear in contemporary emblem books as illustrations for mottos such as: "Uncut, I am worthless." But there is no reason to assume Rembrandt attached a notion of this type to his quill cutter.

There is, however, at least one genre scene that has a probable connection with emblem literature. It is the hasty black-chalk sketch at Munich of a crowded horse-drawn cart with its driver cracking his whip as he crosses a bridge (fig. 8.4). Traditionally it was interpreted as no more than the

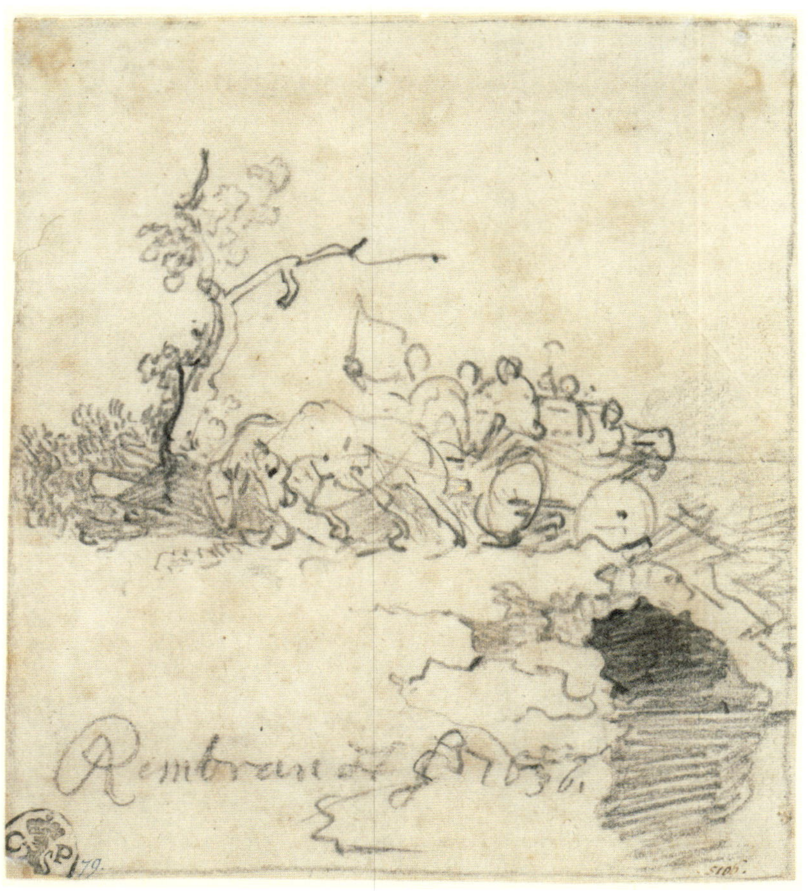

depiction of a party on an outing, but it has been reasonably argued that it possibly has another level of meaning. Probably the drawing refers to the Dutch custom of a couple kissing when crossing a bridge. Since bridges are very common in the Netherlands, there could be quite a bit of kissing by a couple following the custom while en route. Jacob Cats, author of numerous best-selling moralizing books in Rembrandt's day, published an emblem in one of his volumes with the motto: "An old driver enjoys hearing the crack of the whip." The emblem's illustration (fig. 8.5) depicts an elderly man waving to us; in the middle ground is a horse-drawn cart crowded with couples and the driver of the cart cracking his whip. The text of the emblem tells us that when the old driver hears the crack of a whip, he recalls the wild oats he sowed in his youth.

The character of the Munich sketch suggests that it may have been a page in an *album amicorum* (for two drawings by the artist still in their original albums, see figs. 14.12, 15.27). The sheet's conspicuous signature and date of 1636, which

8.4 | *Party in a Horse-drawn Cart on a Bridge*, ca. 1636. Black chalk, brown wash; 16.3 × 14.2 cm (6⅜ × 5⅝ in.). Staatliche Graphische Sammlung, Munich, inv. 1401 Z.

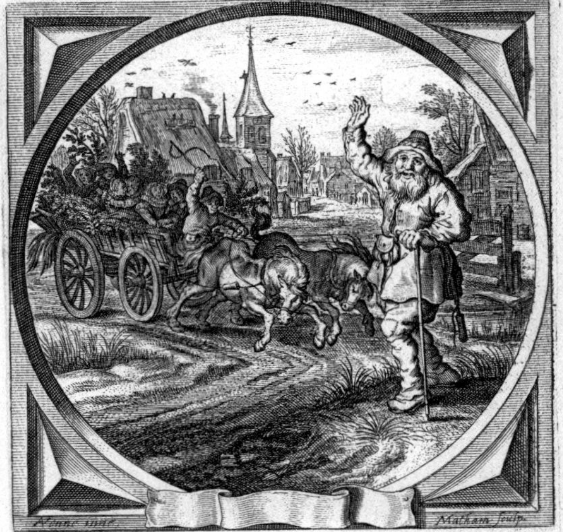
XLII. 139

Een oudt voer-man hoort geerne 'tgeklap van de ſweep.

Siet Gijs den ouden knecht die hoort de peerden trappẽ,
Die hoort de wagen gaen, die hoort de ſwepen klappẽ,
Dies ſpringt ſijn hert om hoogh, en dat vã enckel vreugt,
Om dat hy wort gewaer den handel ſijner jeugt;
Nu wou de ſtramme gaſt wel rijden aender heyden,
En met een ſnellen keer den wagen omme-leyden,
Hy wenſcht te mogen zijn daer Kees met Aefjen ſpeult,
En daermen uytter borſt op alle bruggen heult:

Sss 2 Maer

8.5 | Adriaen Jacobsz Matham (Dutch, ca. 1599–1660), "Een oudt voer-man hoort geerne 'tgeklap van de sweep." Engraving from Jacob Cats (1577–1660), *Spiegel van den voorleden, en jegenwoordigen tijdt*, part 3 (The Hague, 1632), 139, emblem no. 42. Research Library, The Getty Research Institute, Los Angeles, California, 93-B10224.

are not in the artist's hand, may have been added when it was removed from its album.[35] Although the sketch's inscription is not autograph, there is no reason to doubt its accuracy.

One of Berlin's rich collection of study sheets includes sketches of a feisty woman about to hit a soldier in the face with her fist because he is taking unwanted liberties, an amorous couple engaging in activities that need no gloss, and a fragmentary couple at the top of the drawing indicating it has been cut there (fig. 8.6). On the other side of the sheet is a quick sketch by Rembrandt of a radically different subject: *The Lamentation for Christ at the Foot of the Cross*.

Berlin's study of couples has been linked with the Prodigal Son wasting his substance with harlots, a story that is part of the parable (Luke 15:12–23) that tells of the young man who took his inheritance, left home, and then spent all he had on women and drink. Destitute, he was forced to eat what he could find in pig troughs. Finally, he repented and returned home to his father, who forgave him.

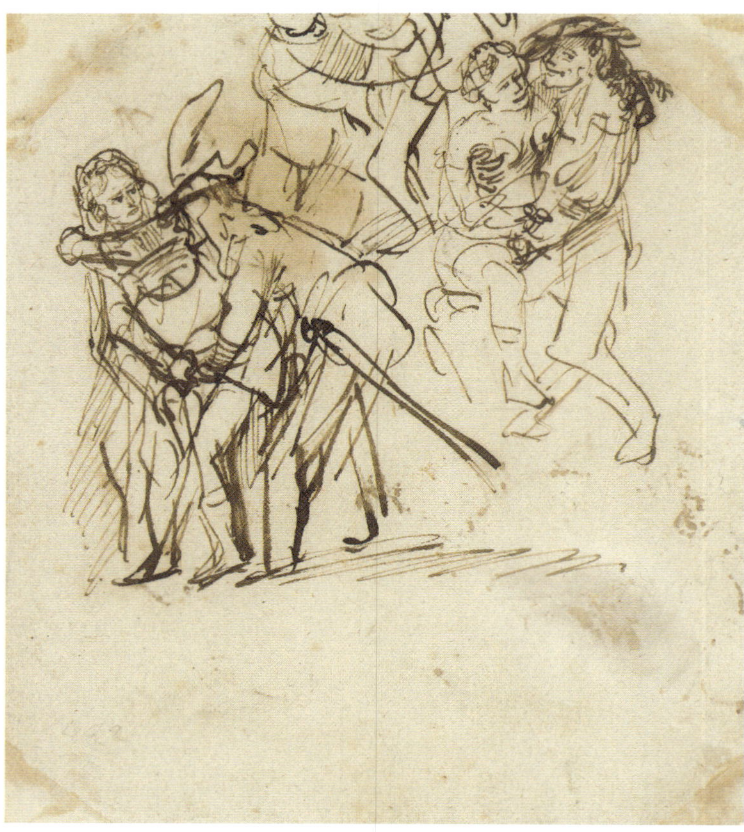

8.6 | *Sketches of Three Couples of Soldiers and Women* (verso), ca. 1635. Pen and brown wash; 17.1 × 15.4 cm (6¾ × 6⅛ in.). Kupferstichkabinett, Staatliche Museen, Berlin, inv. KdZ2312. Photo: Bildarchiv Preussischer Kulturbesitz/Art Resource, N.Y.

8.7 | *The Prodigal Son with Loose Women*, ca. 1635. Pen and brown ink, brown wash; 17.7 × 21 cm (7 × 8¼ in.). Städel Museum, Frankfurt am Main, inv. 16335. Photo © Ursula Edelmann, Frankfurt am Main. Photographer: Ursula Edelmann.

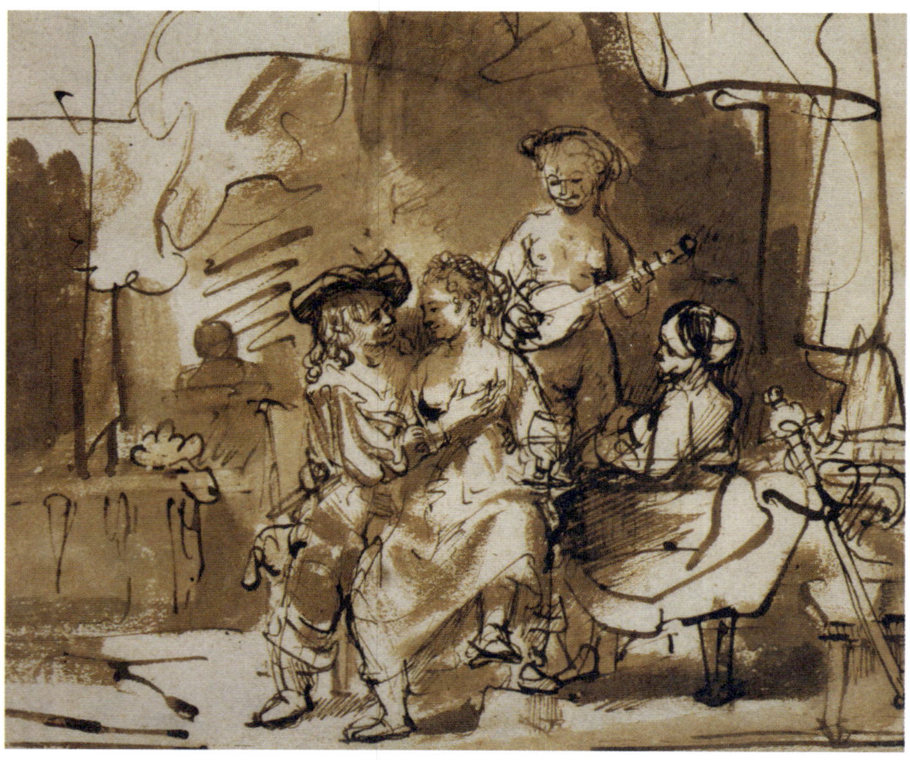

Neither the fighting nor the loving couple would be out of place in a depiction of the Prodigal Son with loose women, but we can only speculate whether Rembrandt had that episode in mind when he made his sketches. However, his pen-and-wash drawing in Frankfurt of a young man cupping the breast of a woman seated on his lap, with two naked women watching the scene, clearly represents the Prodigal Son in a brothel squandering part of his inheritance (fig. 8.7). In it Rembrandt followed a hoary tradition. Scenes of the Prodigal Son as a contemporary spendthrift in the company of women in the setting of a brothel or tavern have been represented hundreds of times by Netherlandish artists since the early sixteenth century.

Rembrandt followed the well-established tradition again in his famous *Self-Portrait with Saskia on His Lap*, a life-size painting, at Dresden (fig. 8.8), which was formerly interpreted as the artist and his young wife celebrating their unrestrained way of living during the early years of their marriage. But it has been shown convincingly that the double portrait is yet another Prodigal Son picture.[36] The conspicuous tally board hanging on the left establishes that the scene takes place in a tavern, not a home. This scoreboard, on which the drinks a customer consumed were marked, alludes to the Prodigal's wasted patrimony. The peacock pie probably refers to *Superbia* (Pride), one of the seven deadly sins. Additional strong support for interpreting the picture as the Prodigal in a tavern is offered by X-radiographs, which reveal that Rembrandt originally painted a standing young woman playing a lute directly behind the couple but later painted her out.[37] An idea of his original intention for the painted-out figure is seen in his vigorous drawing at Frankfurt in which a standing nude women is playing a lute (see fig. 8.7). Why Rembrandt showed himself and his wife as prodigals is not easy to determine. Perhaps he laughingly turned toward us with his exceedingly tall wineglass raised high to imply that we too are prodigals in need of grace and forgiveness.

Frankfurt's pen drawing of two butchers at work (fig. 8.9) is an unusual subject for Rembrandt. His depictions of tradesmen are scarce, but, as the sketch shows, when he tackles the subject, he matches—or surpasses—the efforts of other Dutch artists who specialized in such scenes. The drawing bursts with powerful energy. A crouching butcher, huge meat axe in hand, is using all his strength to split a pig's carcass. Another butcher, with one knife in his mouth and

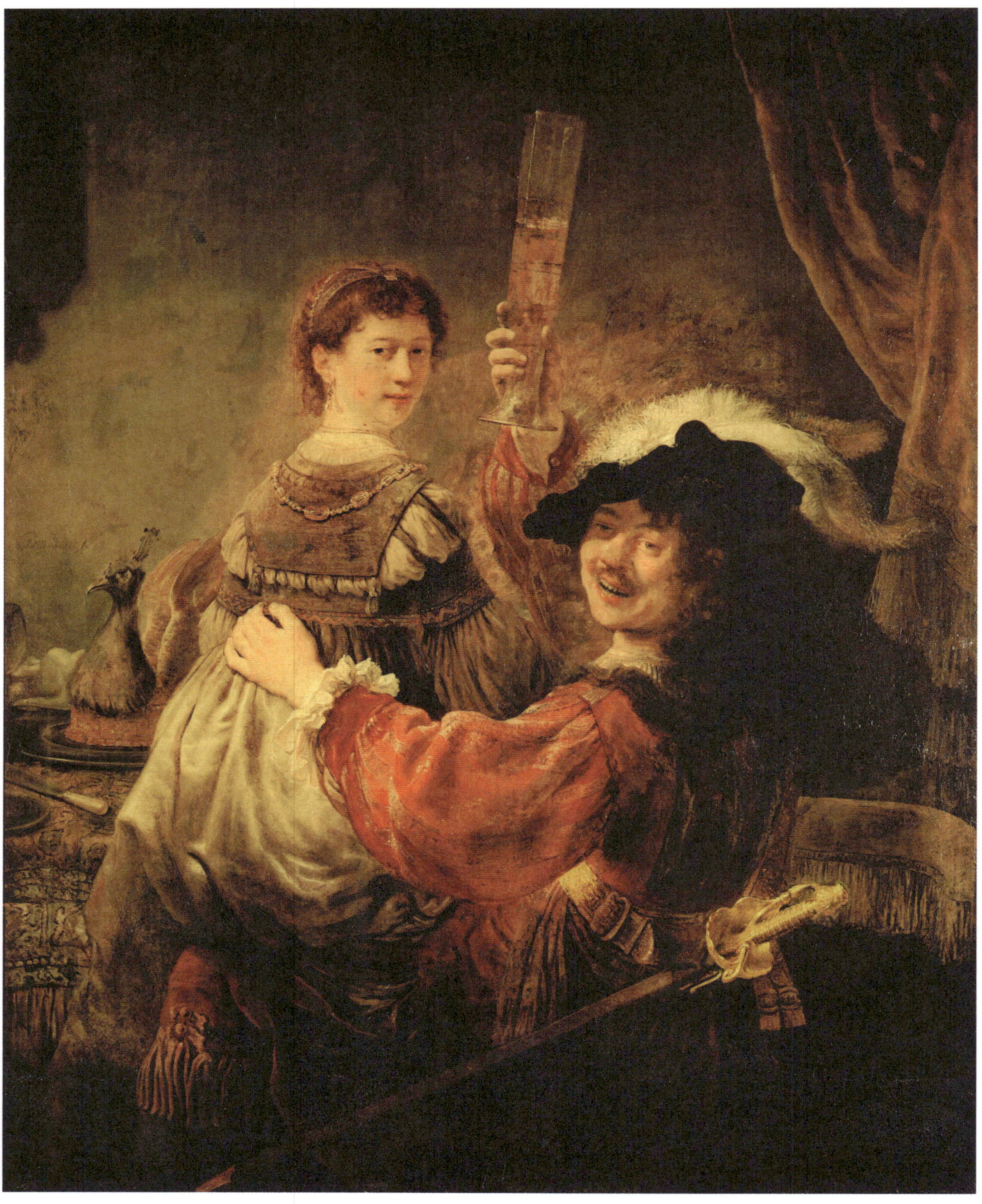

another in his hand, is flaying the carcass of a pig held against his shoulder. With little change the latter could be a participant in a picture of the rape of the Sabine women. An inscription in Rembrandt's hand, upper left, reads: "*Its skin is still attached, but it is dangling.*"[38]

Rembrandt made drawings of aspects of the daily life of men with children as well as women with children. Among the most appealing is the British Museum sheet of studies of an old man with a child (fig. 8.10). In the more finished sketch the child stands on the man's lap tugging at his skullcap. In another quick study the child has triumphantly removed the cap. Two hasty unfinished sketches of the figures are also on the sheet.

A more ambitious work, also at the British Museum, is *The Star of the Kings* (fig. 8.11). Its crowd of more and less attentive children accompanied by a mother holding a baby stand before the open half-door of a house. They are celebrating the popular Dutch custom for children on the evening of the Feast of Epiphany of carrying a lantern in the shape of a star (the "Star of the Kings") from house to house begging for alms. Almost magical is the economic way Rembrandt shows that the event is a night scene. The back of the boy holding the brilliantly lit star is heavily shadowed while others in the crowd are in bright light and behind them various shades of transparent brown wash, some of it over finely hatched lines, create a

8.8 | *Self-portrait with Saskia on His Lap (The Prodigal Son in a Tavern)*, ca. 1635. Oil on canvas; 161 × 131 cm (63⅜ × 51⅝ in.). Gemäldegalerie Alte Meister, Staatliche Kunstsammlungen Dresden, cat. no. 1559. Photo: Erich Lessing/Art Resource, N.Y.

8.9 | *Two Butchers at Work*, ca. 1635. Pen and brown ink; 14.9 × 20 cm (5⅞ × 7⅞ in.). Städel Museum, Frankfurt am Main, inv. 3626. Photo © Ursula Edelmann, Frankfurt am Main. Photographer: Ursula Edelmann.

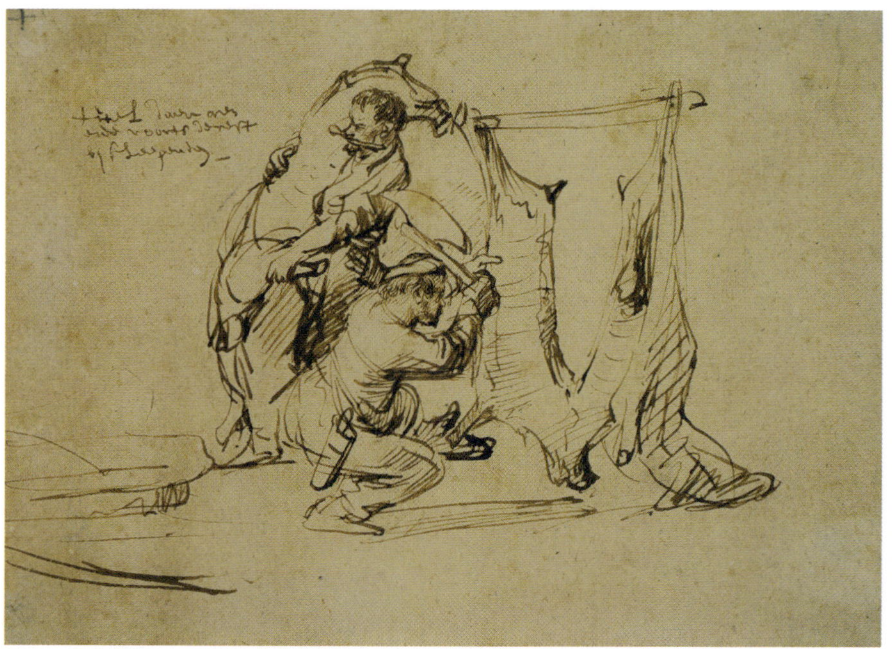

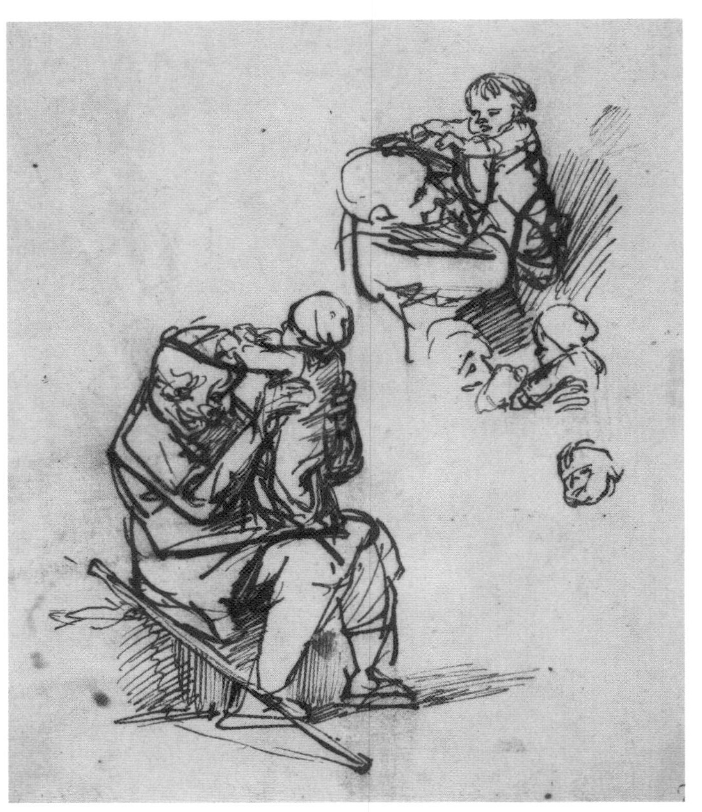

8.10 | *Sketches of an Old Man with a Child*, ca. 1640. Pen and brown ink, touches of brown wash, on paper prepared with pale brown wash; 18.9 × 15.7 cm ($7\frac{3}{8} \times 6\frac{1}{8}$ in.). The British Museum, London, inv. 1910,0212.185. Photo © The Trustees of The British Museum/Art Resource, N.Y.

8.11 | *The Star of the Kings*, signed, ca. 1645. Pen and brown ink, brown wash; 20.4 × 32.3 cm ($8 \times 12\frac{3}{4}$ in.). The British Museum, London, inv. PD1910,0212.189. Photo © The Trustees of The British Museum/Art Resource, N.Y.

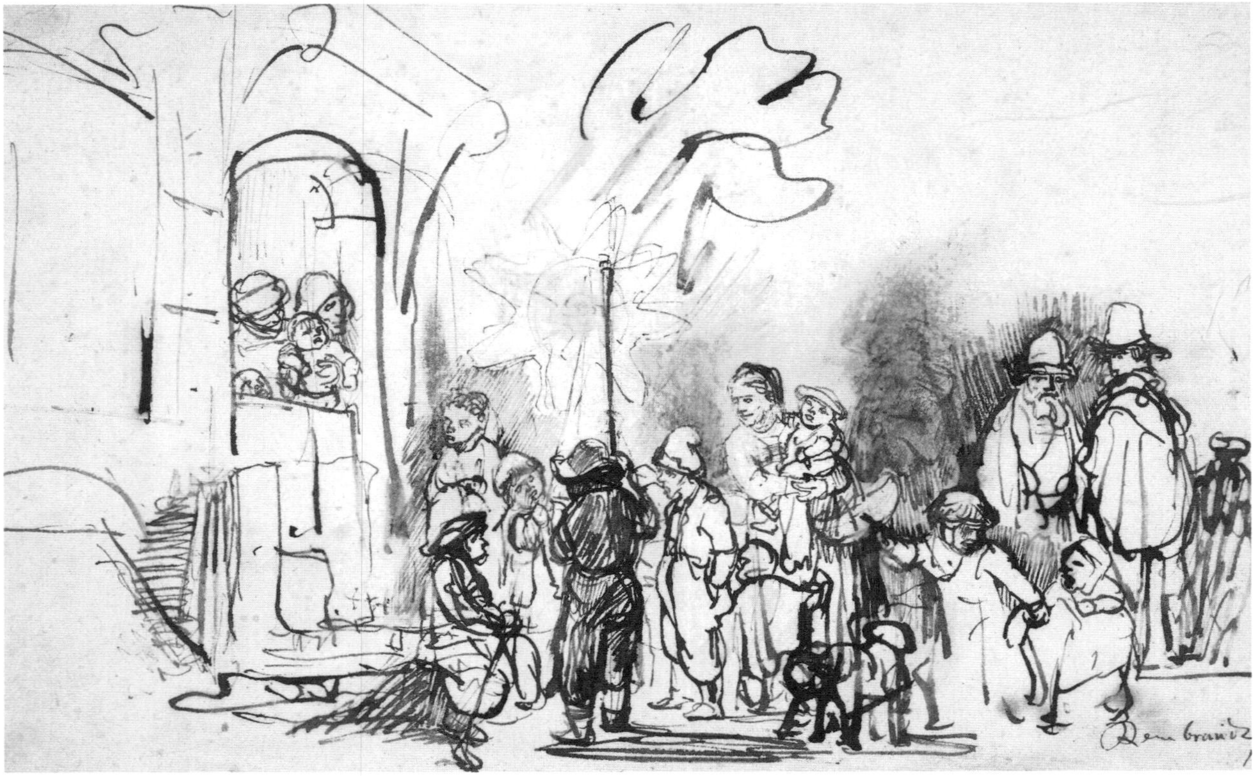

nocturnal effect. The artist must have been satisfied with his effort. It is one of the rare genre drawings that bears an original signature that proclaims he made it: "*Rembrandt f.*"

The site of a genre scene in a sketch at the Louvre, datable about 1650, showing a young draftsman at a table, can be determined thanks to the view visible through the open window of the River IJ as seen from one of the taverns in the bend of the Diemerdijk, which stretched eastward from Amsterdam (fig. 8.12). Across the water is the village of Schellingwoude. Rembrandt made landscape drawings at the same site (see pp. 137–38 and fig. 11.11). A boy standing outside looks through the window to watch the youth draw. It has been proposed that the draftsman is Jan Six and that Rembrandt made his sketch when staying with his friend at the latter's country house in the area. This nice story must be rejected. Six did not own a property in the area until after Rembrandt's death.

In the Louvre drawing wash is used generously to suggest gradations of light and shadow. All appears effortless, until we notice the artist had a bit of a struggle depicting the perspective of the right side of the table. He corrected his first attempt by painting over it with white opaque watercolor, a practice not uncommon in his drawings. In this instance, the white he used has virtually disappeared. It failed to pass the test of time. No matter. A view of the correction offers a precious glimpse of the mature master's mind at work.

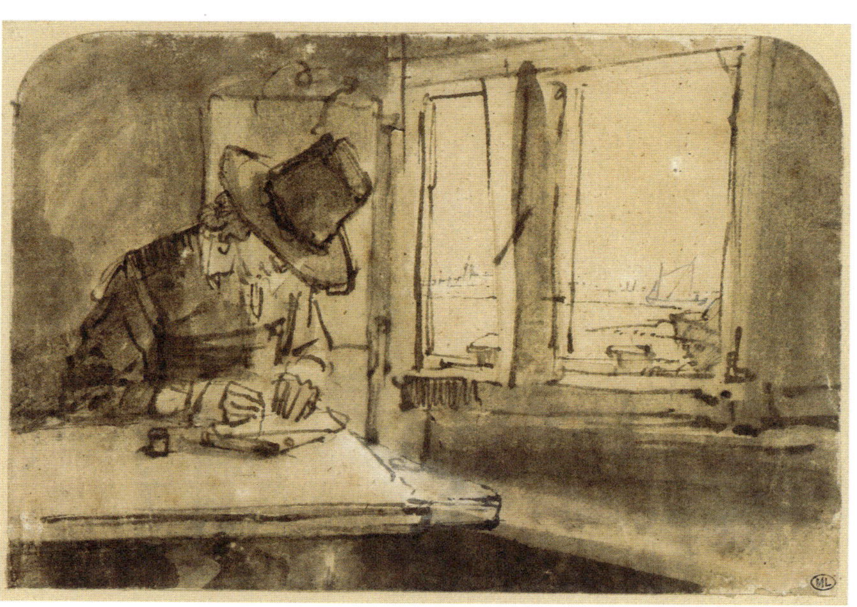

8.12 | *Interior of an Inn with a Draftsman at a Window and a View over the River IJ*, ca. 1649–50. Pen and brown ink, brown wash, corrected with white opaque watercolor; 13.5 × 19.7 cm (5¼ × 7¾ in.). Musée du Louvre, Paris, inv. RF11476. Photo © RMN—Grand Palais/Art Resource, N.Y. Photographer: Jean-Gilles Berizzi.

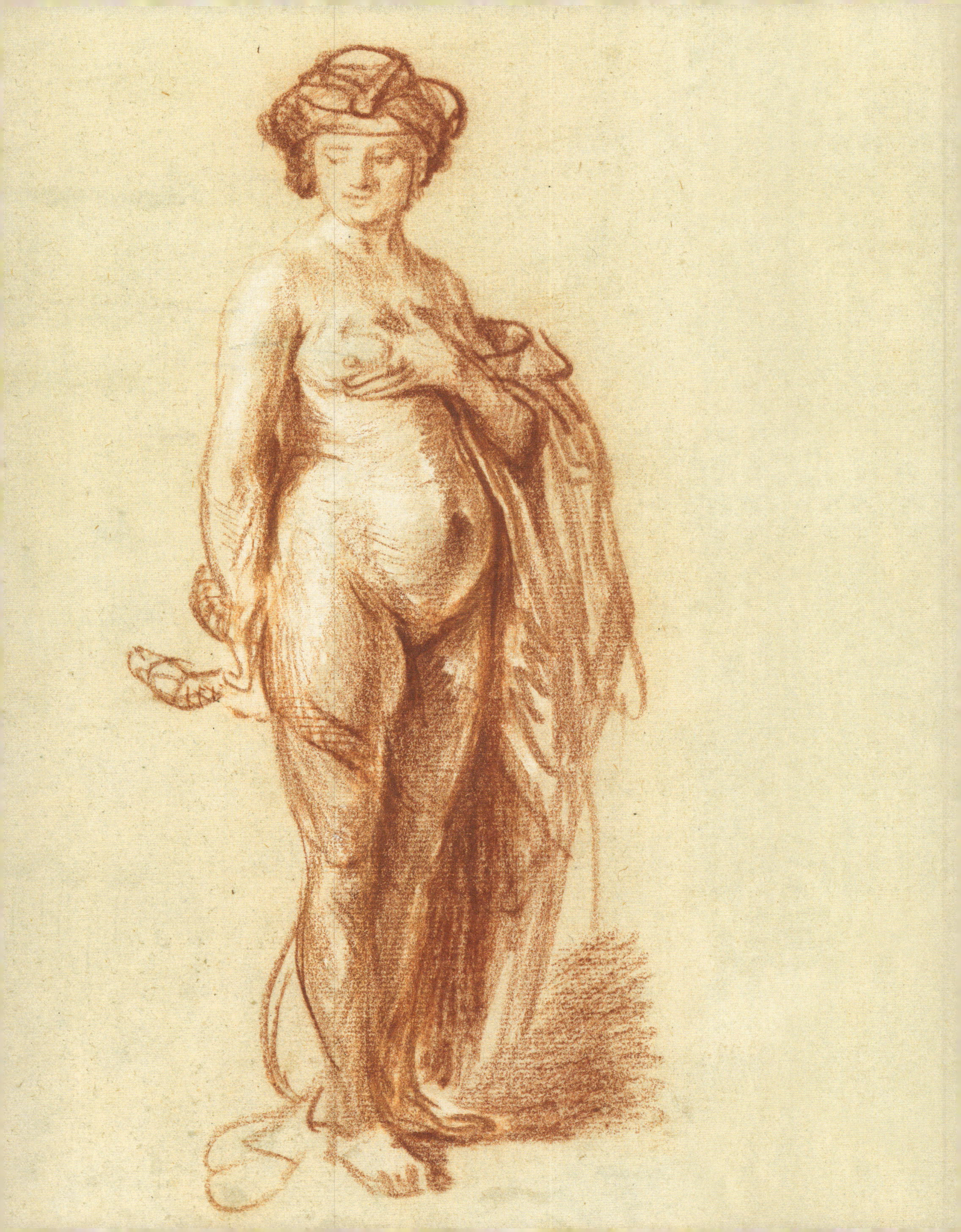

9 | **Nudes**

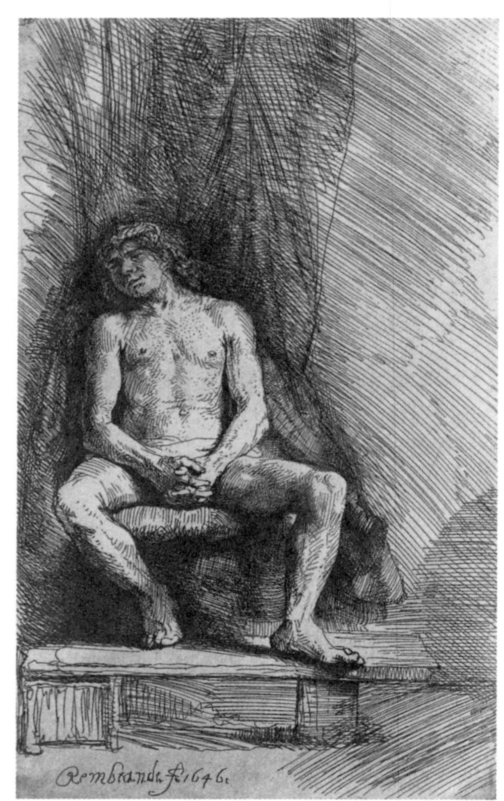

9.1 | *Nude Man Seated before a Curtain*, signed and dated 1631. Etching; 16.4 × 9.6 cm (6½ × 3¾ in.). Private collection.

AN ITEM IN THE INVENTORY of Rembrandt's effects compiled in 1656 after he declared himself insolvent lists "A book, full of drawings by Rembrandt of men and women; they being naked."[39] If the reference is taken literally, we must conclude that all of the artist's drawings of male nudes that were in the book have disappeared. Today, only drawings of nude males attributable to Rembrandt's students or followers are known. Rembrandt's three etchings of male models posing, as they still do in life classes (figs. 9.1, 9.2, 9.3), bolsters the contention that he must have made some drawings, but the fact remains that not a single one by his hand exists.

But perhaps the inventory reference should not be taken literally. Possibly Rembrandt filed student drawings he believed worth keeping in books and albums that contained his own efforts. He may have believed he had a proprietary right to Rembrandtesque sketches by his pupils. If so, he was reckless with the truth when he told the compiler of his inventory that a book or album was full of his drawings instead of declaring they were works by him and his students.

It is helpful to recall that concern about the correct attribution of works of art is not a modern phenomenon. Attributions were much discussed in Rembrandt's day. A sample of the controversies that occurred is offered by a case regarding the authenticity of a beach scene alleged to be an original by the prominent marine painter Jan Porcellis (1584–1632) that was brought before an Amsterdam notary in 1661, just five years after Rembrandt's insolvency inventory was compiled.[40] Four artists were asked to give their opinions about the Porcellis attribution. Meindert Hobbema (1638–1709) signed the document as one of the witnesses. As for the four artists: little-known Barent Kleeneknecht (seventeenth

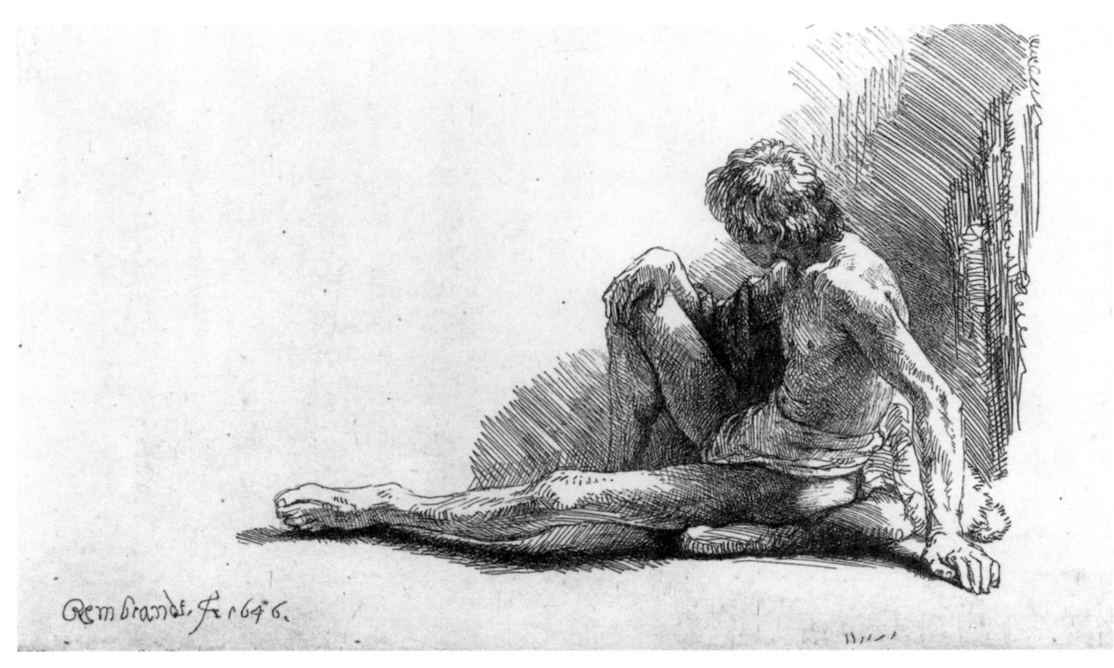

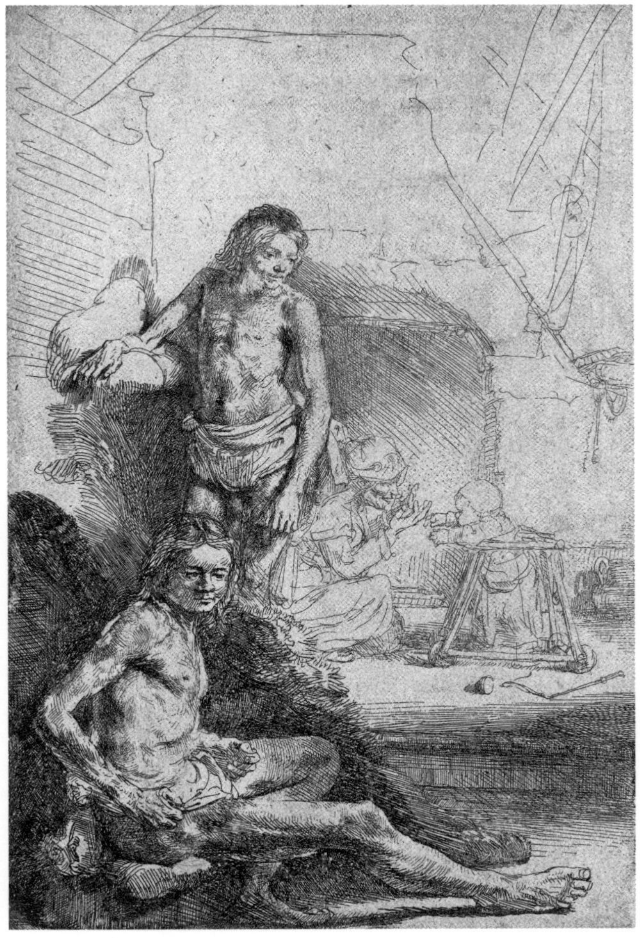

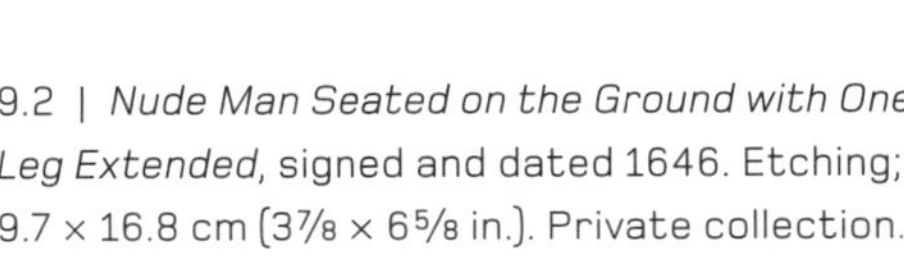
9.2 | *Nude Man Seated on the Ground with One Leg Extended*, signed and dated 1646. Etching; 9.7 × 16.8 cm (3⅞ × 6⅝ in.). Private collection.

9.3 | *Nude Man Seated and Another Standing, with a Woman and Baby in the Background*, ca. 1646. Etching, first state; 19.4 × 12.8 cm (7⅝ × 5 in.). Kupferstichkabinett, Staatliche Museen, Berlin, inv. 171-1898. Photo: Bildarchiv Preussischer Kulturbesitz/Art Resource, N.Y. Photographer: Jörg P. Anders.

century) testified that probably almost the entire picture was painted by Hendrick van Anthonissen (ca. 1605–before 1660), a pupil of Porcellis; Allart van Everdingen (1621–1675) declared that Porcellis, at most, had done something to the beach scene's cliffs; Willem Kalf (1619–1693) maintained it had nothing whatsoever to do with Porcellis's paintings; and Jacob van Ruisdael (1628/29–1682) declared that Porcellis had perhaps begun it, but in its present condition it must not be sold as his work.

Though the alleged Porcellis was obviously not borderline, there was no agreement regarding an alternative attribution. To people of our day who attempt to determine authorship of Dutch works done centuries ago, the case is humbling. What are our chances of finding definitive attributions for marginal works if four expert witnesses, who had knowledge of the art scene of their time that we can never match, failed to find one? However, a measure of comfort can be found in the affair. It is consoling to learn that experts of the period shared our frequent inability to give firm names to substandard works.

There is no question regarding the authenticity of Rembrandt's black-chalk-and-wash drawing of *Diana at the Bath* at the British Museum (fig. 9.4), which is indented for transfer to the etching ground of a copperplate. It served as the preparatory study (in reverse) for the artist's monogrammed etching of the same subject (fig. 9.5). Both works are datable about 1631. The drawing—the artist's earliest known sketch of a nude—appears to have been done from life. The model is seen in full light and looks directly at us. Much more attention has been given to the model's shape than to Diana's quickly sketched quiver and bow, which seem afterthoughts. No attempt has been made to minimize her slightly distended belly. In the etching that part of her anatomy has grown larger, and her back and foremost arm have become a bit lumpy.

When the etched Diana is juxtaposed to the woman depicted in the artist's etching of a *Naked Woman Seated on a Mound*, also datable about 1631 (fig. 9.6), the realistic elements of the print of Diana's body appear negligible. Merely a couple of years after Rembrandt's death critics who held that artists should idealize figures and strive to attain the beautiful forms achieved by classical and Italian Renaissance masters attacked Rembrandt as a heretic of art for producing works such as *Naked Woman Seated on a Mound*. The tenor

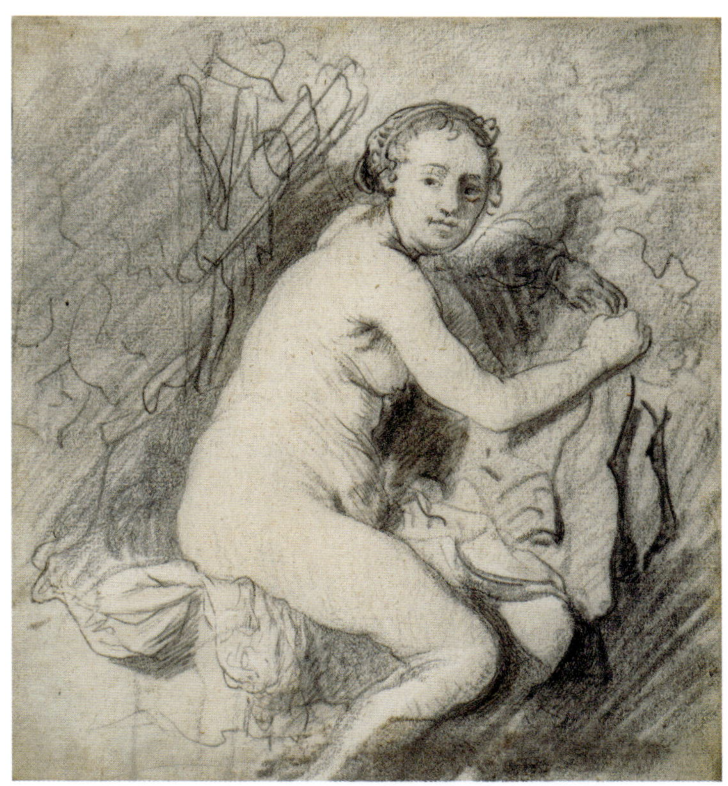

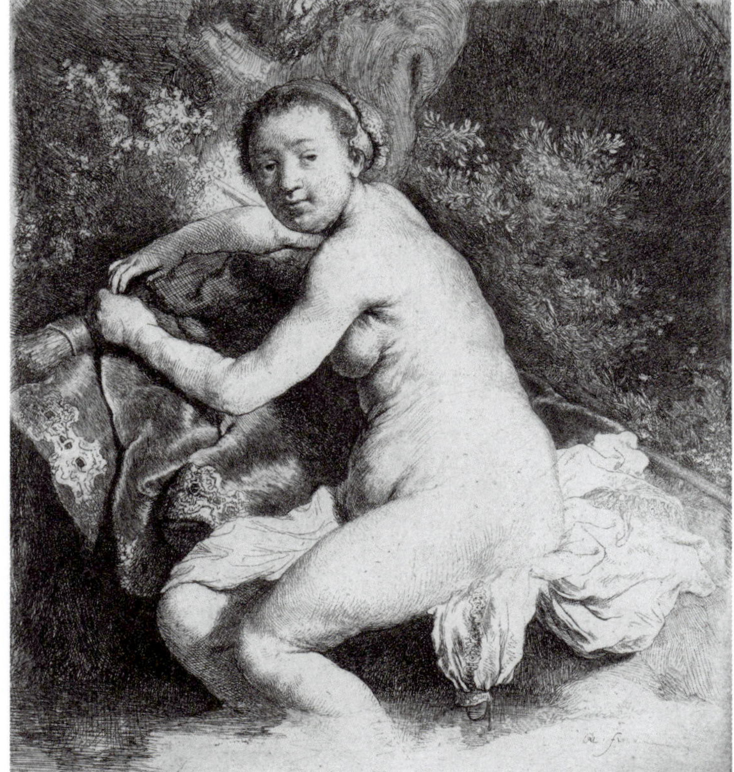

9.4 | *Diana at the Bath*, ca. 1631. Black chalk, brown wash, outlines indented for transfer; 18.1 × 16.4 cm (7 1/8 × 6 1/2 in.). The British Museum, London, inv. 1895,0915.1266. Photo © The Trustees of The British Museum/Art Resource, N.Y.

9.5 | *Diana at the Bath*, monogrammed, ca. 1631. Etching; 17.7 × 15.8 cm (7 × 6 1/4 in.). Rijksmuseum, Amsterdam, inv. RP-P-1962-70.

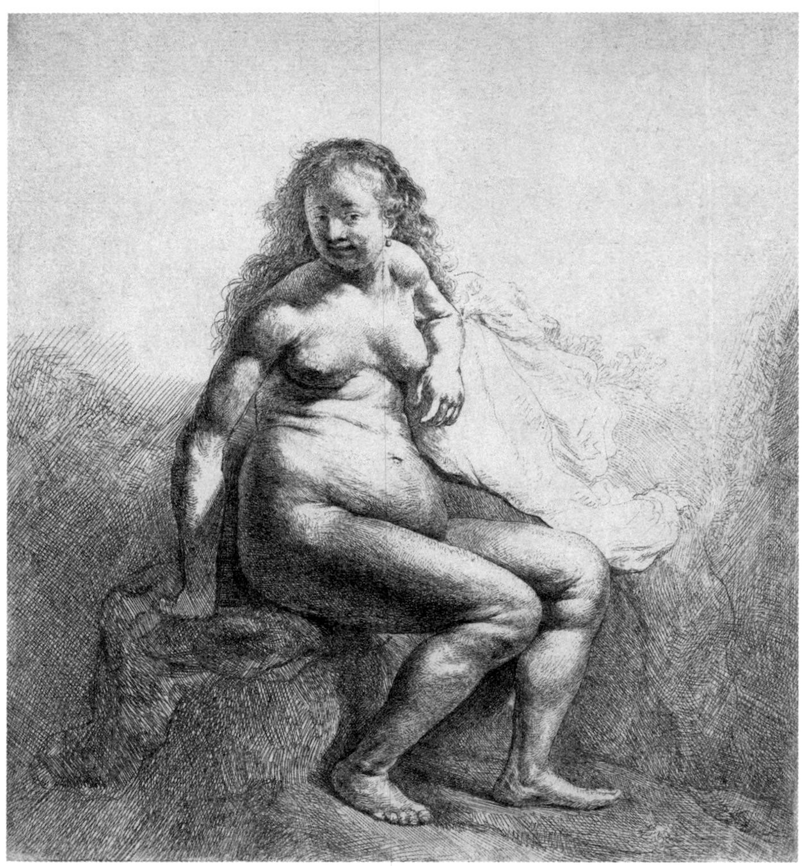

of their criticism is found in a frequently cited poem published in 1681 by the Dutch poet Andries Pels (1631–1681):

> When he would paint a naked woman, as sometimes happened, he chose no Greek Venus as his model, but rather a washerwoman or a peat-treader from a barn, naming his error truth to Nature, and everything else idle decoration. Flabby breasts, ill-shaped hands, yes even the marks of corset lacings on the stomach and the garters around the legs must all be followed if nature is to get her due. This is his nature, which would stand no rules, no principles of proportion in the human body.[41]

Rembrandt's drawing of a full-length *Nude Woman with a Snake* of about 1637 (fig. 9.7) was acquired by the Getty Museum in 1981. It is the first drawing the museum accessioned for what is now a broad, strong collection of master drawings. The work is another that would have been faulted by critics who deplored the artist's disregard of classical

9.6 | *Naked Woman Seated on a Mound*, monogrammed, 1629–33. Etching; 17.7 × 16 cm (7 × 6¼ in.). Rijksmuseum, Amsterdam, inv. RP-P-1961-1108.

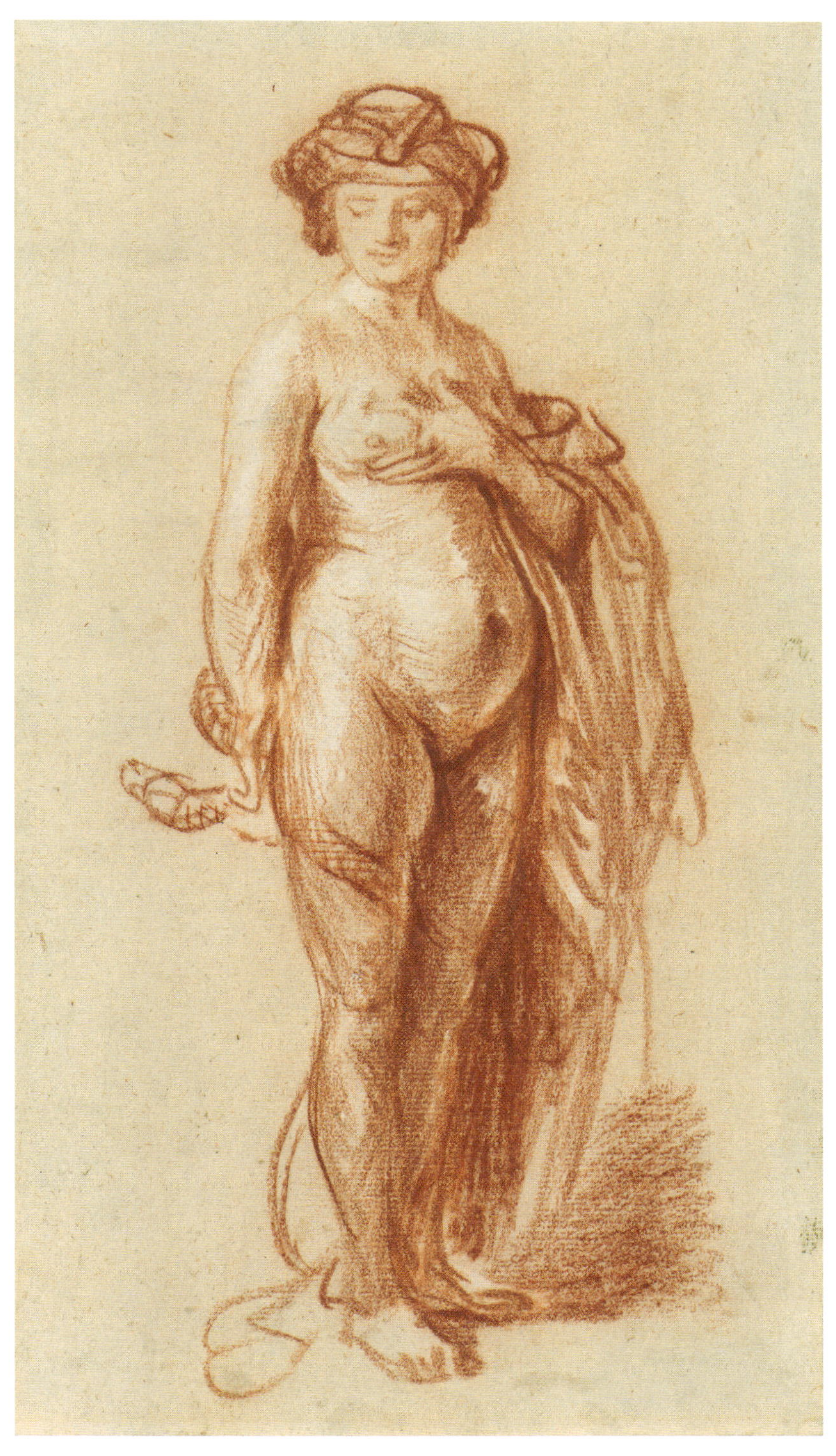

9.7 | *Nude Woman with a Snake*, ca. 1637. Red and white chalk and white opaque watercolor; 24.7 × 13.7 cm (9¾ × 5⅜ in.). J. Paul Getty Museum, Los Angeles, acc. no. 81.GB.27.

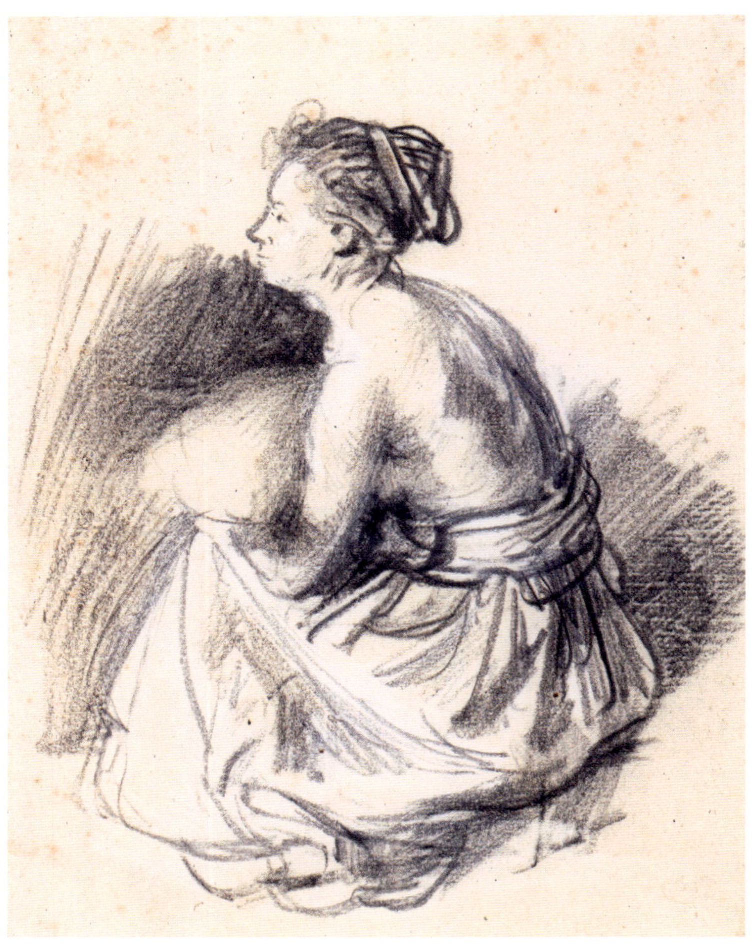

rules of proportion. The criticism would not lessen by one iota the pleasure we receive from the superb use of the full range of red chalk's tones to suggest the intense light and strong shadow that model the figure in the exceptionally well-preserved drawing. For the deepest reds Rembrandt wetted his chalk (probably with his tongue), and in the lightest areas he applied white opaque watercolor over which, in some passages, he added ever-so-light touches of red chalk to achieve a luminous effect.

The snake and the nude's emphasis on one of her breasts have been variously interpreted. She has been called a representation of Hygieia, the Greek goddess of health, whose attribute is a snake; Eve with a snake that symbolizes, in this instance, Satan; or Cleopatra, who chose to die by being bitten on her breast by an asp when she learned of Mark Anthony's suicide after his defeat in battle. The Cleopatra interpretation seems most likely.

9.8 | *Seated Woman, Naked to the Waist* (recto), ca. 1637. Black chalk, heightened with white chalk; 19.9 × 15.3 cm (7⅞ × 6 in.). Museum Boijmans Van Beuningen, Rotterdam, inv. R81 recto (Koenigs Collection).

There can be little doubt that there is a close connection between the Getty nude's figure and the artist's etching of Eve as a vixen in his extraordinary etching *The Fall of Man* (also known as *Adam and Eve*) of 1638 (see fig. 15.8). Presumably the same model inspired both figures. Rembrandt's Adam, who admonishes Eve not to bite her apple, is equally remarkable. For him, Rembrandt seems to have used a close relative of *Pithecanthropus erectus* for a model rather than a Greek Apollo.

Rotterdam's black- and white-chalk drawing of a woman naked to the waist seated on a low dais with hands resting on her lap under a pillow (fig. 9.8) is a life study of a model. From what we can see, her proportions would not distress a critic with a classical bias. The sketch is datable around 1637, about the same time as the Getty nude. On the verso is a cursory black-chalk study of the same model, still half-naked but standing. In the principal sketch the black chalk lines, especially in the head and skirt, are strong and decisive. White chalk has been used to soften contours and areas of shadow as well as to suggest the play of light.

The iron-gall ink-and-wash sketch at the British Museum of a seated artist in a studio drawing from a nude model (fig. 9.9) had been accepted as a preparatory study (in reverse) for Rembrandt's unfinished etching of the composition (fig. 9.10) until it was astutely observed that the drawing was executed after the etching was in progress to help solve some of the problems that arose as the artist worked on his copperplate.[42] For example, in the unfinished etching it is evident that Rembrandt struggled with the length of the nude's legs and gave her two sets of feet and ankles, placing one set above the other. He also posed her upon a very tentative dais. These passages are resolved in the drawing. Equally important, the drawing is not indented for transfer to a plate.

The proportions of the nude's figure are similar to those used for the Getty's nude woman with a snake, datable about 1637, and Eve in the 1638 etching. There are also close similarities in style and technique with the artist's intermediate drawing for the composition of his portrait of *Maria Trip* of around 1639 (see fig. 3.20)—the gall-ink lines and washes have even eaten into the paper in the same manner. These factors point to a date in the late 1630s for both the British Museum drawing and the etching.

Rembrandt's original copperplate for the unfinished print, now in a private collection, shows that Rembrandt did not incorporate in his plate any of the corrections he made in his

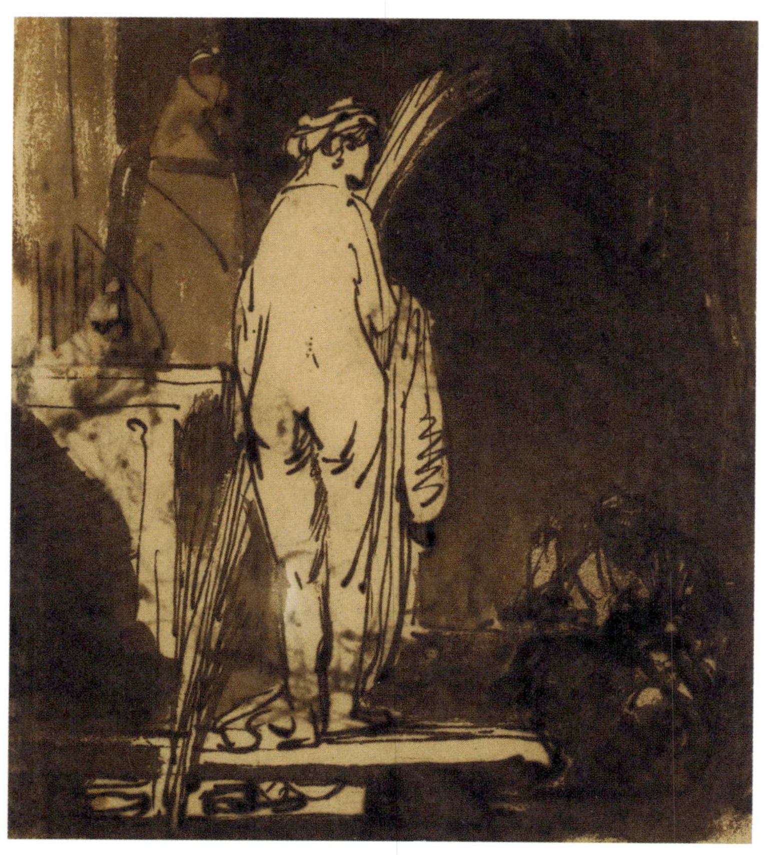

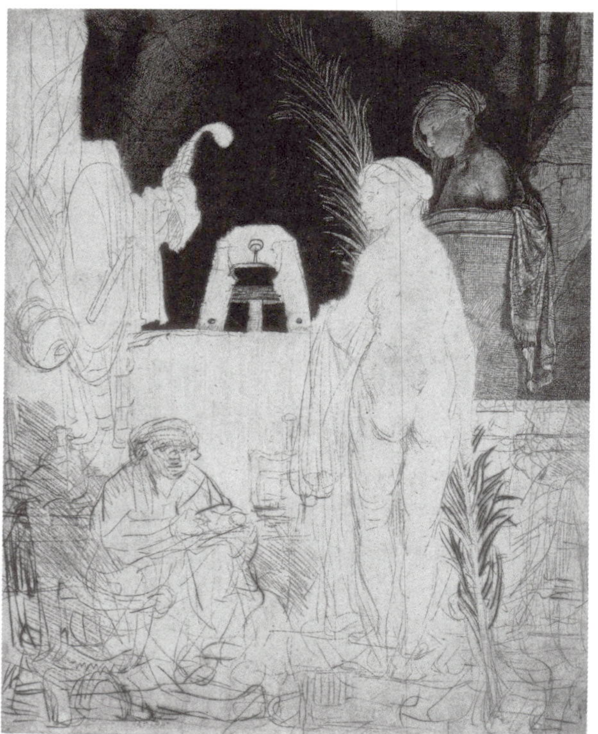

9.9 | *Artist Drawing from a Nude Model* (recto), ca. 1639. Pen and brown iron-gall ink, brown wash, on paper prepared with brown wash; 18.8 × 16.4 cm (7⅜ × 6½ in.). The British Museum, London, inv. Gg,2.248. Photo © The Trustees of The British Museum/Art Resource, N.Y.

9.10 | *Artist Drawing from a Nude Model*, ca. 1639. Unfinished etching with drypoint and burin; 23.2 × 18.4 cm (9⅛ × 7¼ in.). The British Museum, London, inv. 1895,1214.111. Photo © The Trustees of The British Museum/Art Resource, N.Y.

drawing. Why he didn't, and why he left his etching unfinished remain unanswered questions. The subject of the drawing and etching is not certain either. An eighteenth-century cataloguer of Rembrandt's prints wrote that in the Netherlands the etching was called "the statue of Pygmalion."[43] Additionally, it has been noted that the pose of Rembrandt's nude model seen from the rear closely resembles the pose given to the nude in an etching of Pygmalion made in 1615 by the painter, etcher, and poet Pieter Feddes van Harlingen.[44] By showing Pygmalion, a sculptor of ancient times, woefully contemplating the statue he created of a nude woman, Feddes van Harlingen follows the story as told by Ovid (43 B.C.–A.D. 17). After falling hopelessly in love with his statue, Pygmalion implored Venus to bring it to life. Venus granted his wish.

Ovid's story, of course, does not fit Rembrandt's drawing or print. They depict a draftsman hard at work in a painter's studio, not a lovelorn sculptor. The conspicuous long palm frond found in both the sketch and the print suggests that Rembrandt may have intended them to have an allegorical meaning, perhaps an allusion to the palm awarded to those who master the art of drawing.

A study that does not need an exegesis is Rembrandt's magnificent pen-and-wash drawing, now at Oxford, of a woman stripped to the waist seated in a lofty studio (fig. 9.11). The studio is generally accepted as a depiction of the one used by the artist for about two decades in his stately Jodenbreestraat house. The drawing helped serve as a model for the reconstructed studio in the house after it was purchased by the City of Amsterdam in 1908, and an effort was made to restore it to the state it was in when Rembrandt and his family occupied it. As mentioned earlier, the home is now the Museum het Rembrandthuis.

The half-nude woman is seated in glowing light. Thanks to the drawing we can see the source of the light and how Rembrandt managed to manipulate it on other occasions. Light streams into the studio through two high windows. A curtain attached to the ceiling is stretched above the windows; it serves as a reflector and most likely could easily be raised or lowered to control the amount of light admitted. The lower halves of the two windows are covered by shutters.

The drawing provides a good view also of the artist's high easel. On the table is a portable writing desk with a sloping top, which also could be used for drawing or working on etching plates. To the right of it is what has been recognized

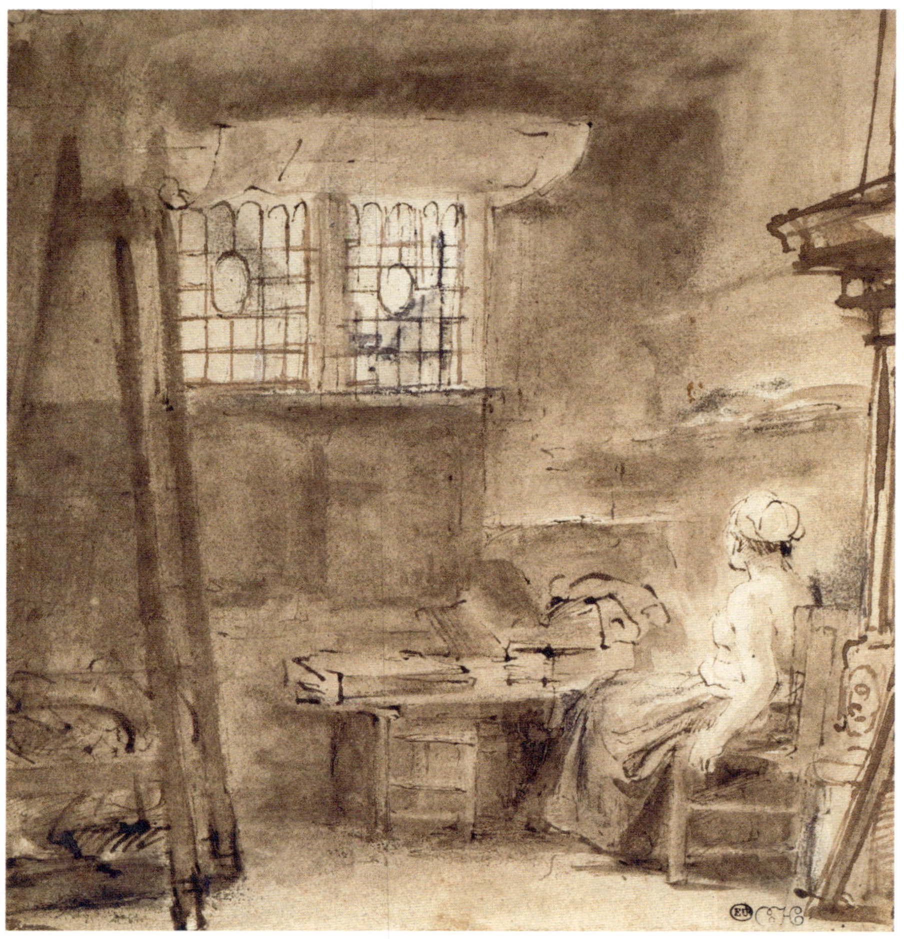

by some students as a cradle with a folded coverlet on its top. Since the drawing is datable to the mid-1650s, it has been suggested that the cradle is probably the one used by Cornelia, Rembrandt and Hendrickje's baby, born in 1654. If this is the case, the half-naked woman may be Hendrickje. Regrettably, Rembrandt offers only a lost-profile view of her head. Thus, it is impossible to check her features with her other putative portraits.

The artist's most touching drawings of female nudes are his late ones of humble models, at times depicted seated on simple studio stools (figs. 9.12, 9.13). They evoke a reponse to women devoid of all formal beauty that is seen again only in works by Courbet, Manet, and particularly Degas. The realism of his early nudes has not been abandoned, but in these superb works the mood has changed. It has become somber, and forms, shadows, and half-shadows have been stripped to essentials.

9.11 | *The Artist's Studio (with a Seated Woman Naked to the Waist)*, 1659. Pen and brown ink, brown and white wash; 20.5 × 18.9 cm (8 1/8 × 7 3/8 in.). Ashmolean Museum, University of Oxford, acc. no. WA1855.8, cat. no. PI 192. Photo © The Ashmolean Museum, University of Oxford.

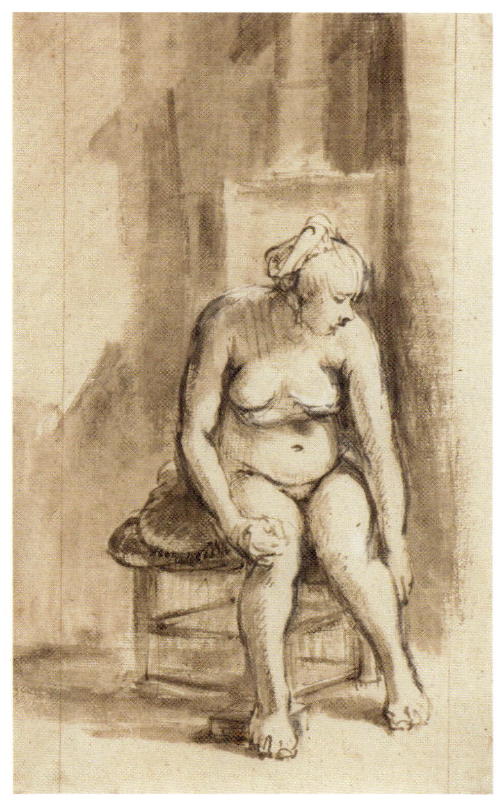

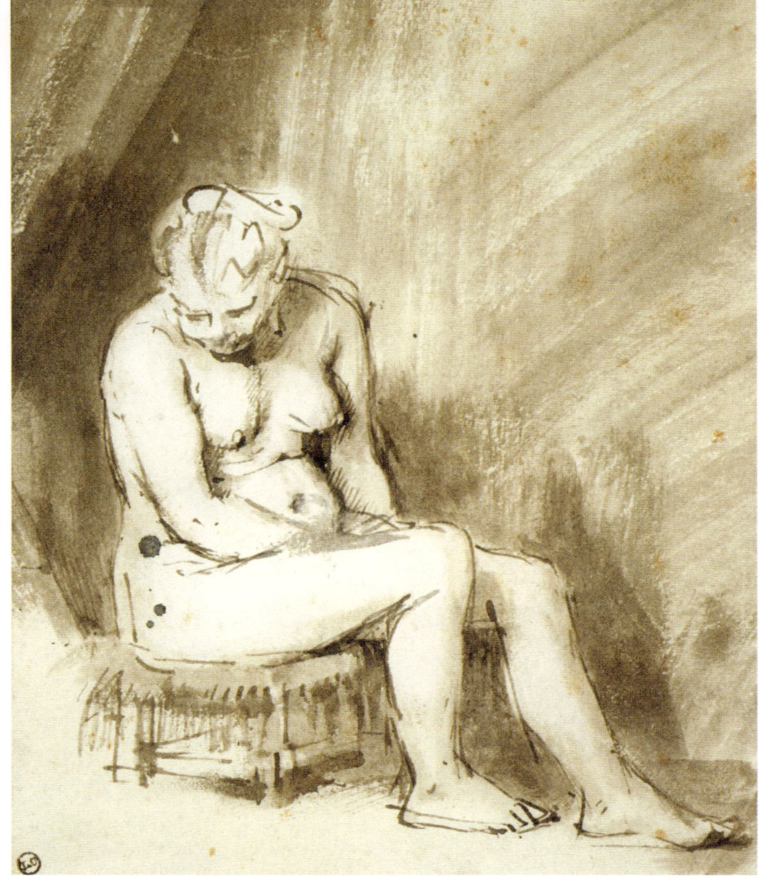

9.12 | *Nude Woman Seated in Front of a Stove*, 1661–62. Pen and brush and brown ink, black chalk, white gouache, on paper; 29.2 × 17.5 cm (11½ × 6⅞ in.). Rijksmuseum, Amsterdam, inv. RP-T-00-227.

9.13 | *Nude Seated Woman on a Stool*, 1654/56. Pen and brown ink, and brush and brown wash, on ivory laid paper laid down on cream laid card; 21.2 × 17.4 cm (8¼ × 6⅞ in.). The Art Institute of Chicago, Clarence Buckingham Collection, inv. 1953.38. Photo © The Art Institute of Chicago.

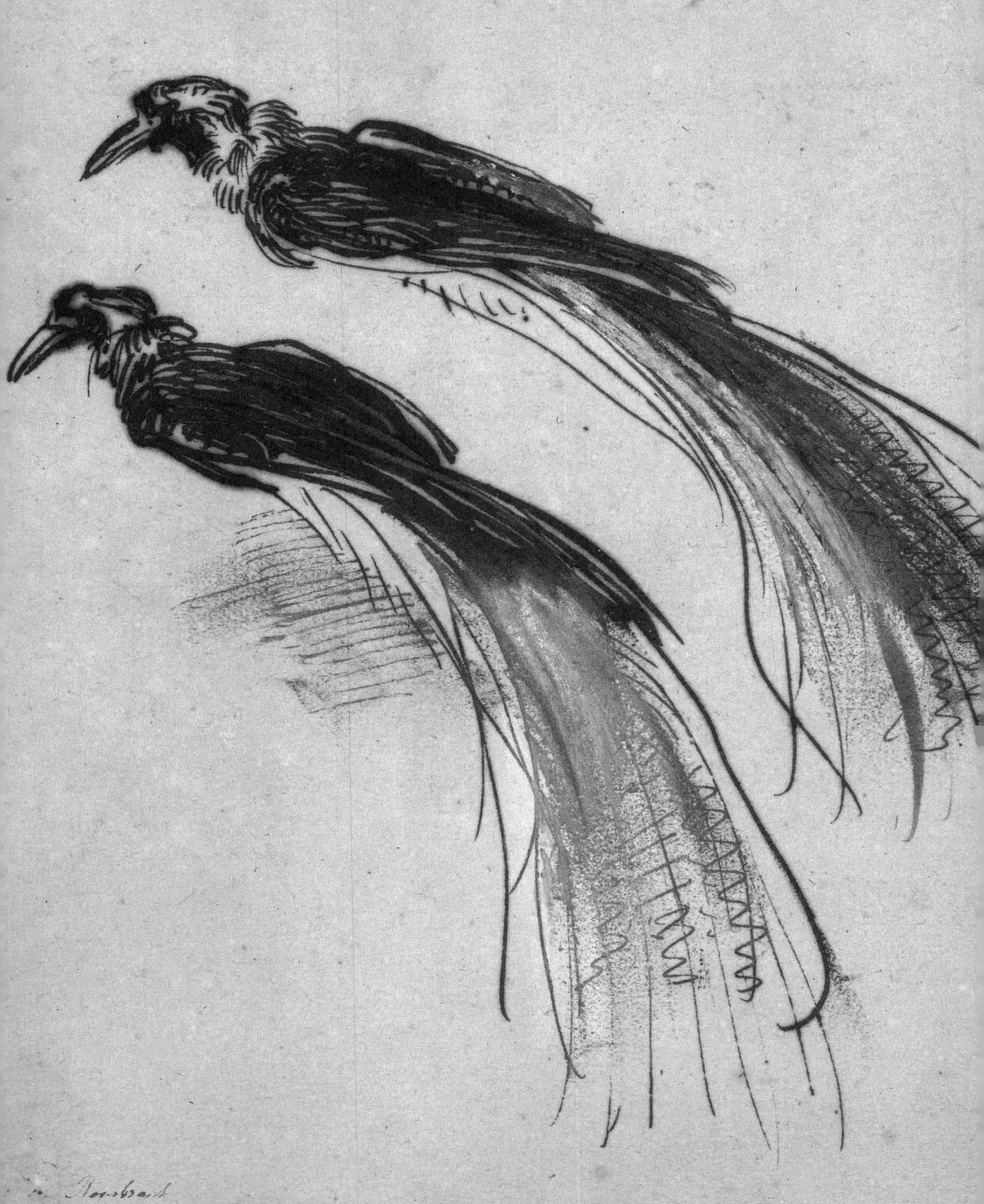

10 | Animals

THE ARTIST'S BLACK-CHALK DRAWING at the Albertina of an elephant (fig. 10.1) may have been in the book "filled with drawings by Rembrandt of animals done from life," which is listed in his 1656 inventory.[45] It also would have found a fitting place in the "book bound in black leather with the best sketches by Rembrandt" cited in the same inventory.[46] It is of unsurpassed quality. No drawing of an elephant does greater justice to the beast in a benign mood, content with its massive size and heavy, wrinkled skin.

The Albertina's drawing is proudly signed and dated 1637. About the same time Rembrandt made three other black-chalk sketches of this elephant. One, likewise at the

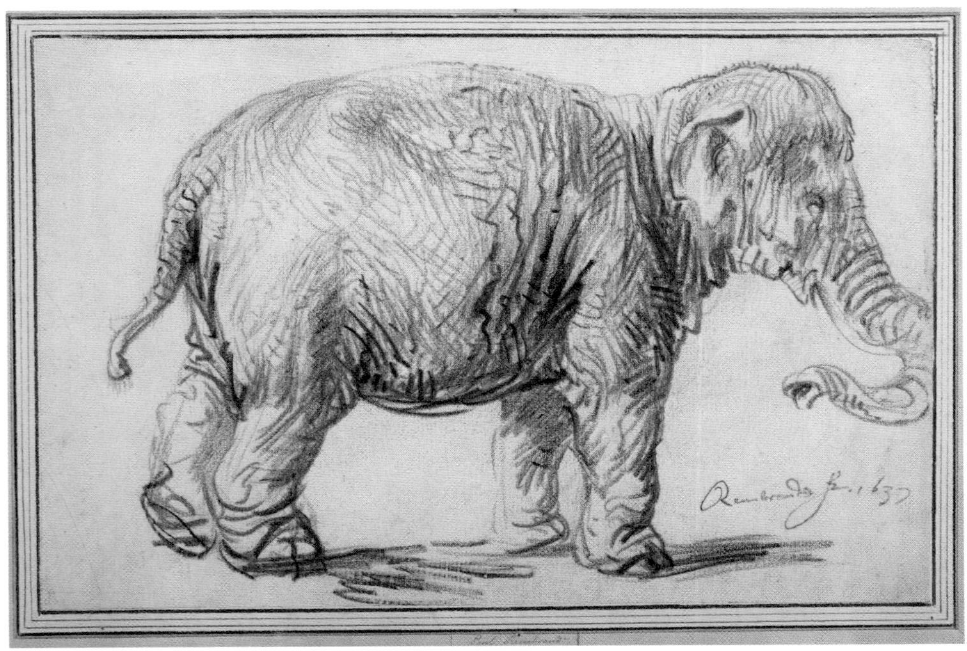

10.1 | *An Elephant*, signed and dated 1637. Black chalk; 23.5 × 35.4 cm (9¼ × 13⅞ in.). Graphische Sammlung Albertina, Vienna, inv. 8900. Photo: Erich Lessing/Art Resource, N.Y.

Albertina, depicts the beast in various poses; the second, at the British Museum, offers a profile view; the third, at The Pierpont Morgan Library, depicts its forequarters.[47] Rembrandt also included an elephant in the background of his 1638 etching of *The Fall of Man* (see fig. 15.8). According to an old tradition, its presence in the Garden of Eden is an allusion to virtue, in contrast to evil, represented by the serpent.

The elephant in the drawings is the female named Hansken, who toured Europe. She was born in Ceylon about 1630 and died in Florence in 1655. An example of the manner in which the beasts were exhibited at Dutch fairs, markets, and festivals is seen in a 1653 drawing at the Getty Museum by Jan van Goyen, *Village Festival*.[48]

Among the wild and exotic beasts exhibited in Europe during the artist's time were lions and lionesses. Since the stadholder Frederik Henry had a well-stocked zoo in a palace near The Hague, Rembrandt may have seen the majestic animals in it. In any event, it is evident that he seized opportunities to draw them. About a half-dozen of his studies of lions are known today. Exemplary of their superb quality are the charcoal[49]-and-gray-wash drawing at the British Museum of a rapacious lioness about to devour a bird held between her paws (fig. 10.2) and the Louvre's pen-and-wash drawing of an intensely alert recumbent lion (fig. 10.3). Rembrandt's close studies of the powerful beasts served him well in his depiction of a ferocious, double-chained lion in *The Concord of the State*—a complicated allegorical painting, now at Rotterdam, whose meaning is still debated—and in his drawing and etching of Saint Jerome's faithful lion (see figs. 15.5, 15.6).

Peter Schatborn has rightly observed that Rembrandt had a good instinct for choosing the best medium for drawing various animals.[50] Chalk was used for elephants; it is an exceptionally effective medium for rendering their rough, heavy skin. Lions, too, were done in chalk and in charcoal but more often in pen and wash—the latter used discriminately to distinguish between their heavy manes and supple skins. The Louvre's two studies of a bird of paradise on a single sheet are executed in a more elaborate technique (fig. 10.4). Their vulture-like heads and bodies were done with pen and iron-gall ink; in passages, the pen lines are so close they take on the quality of wash. The birds' display of feathers (not tails) are delineated with fine, sweeping long lines and even more delicate zigzag ones. White opaque watercolor has been added to give a suggestion of color and, here and there, to soften passages.

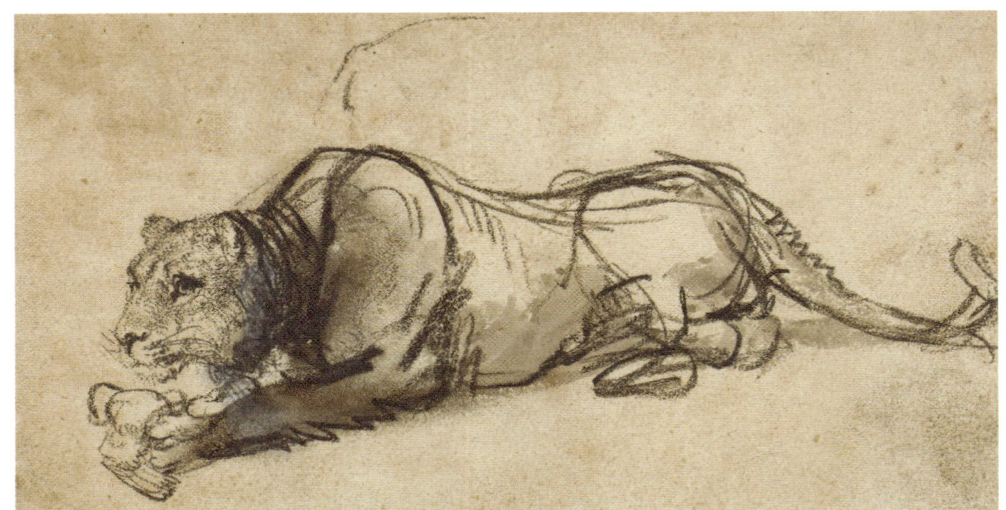

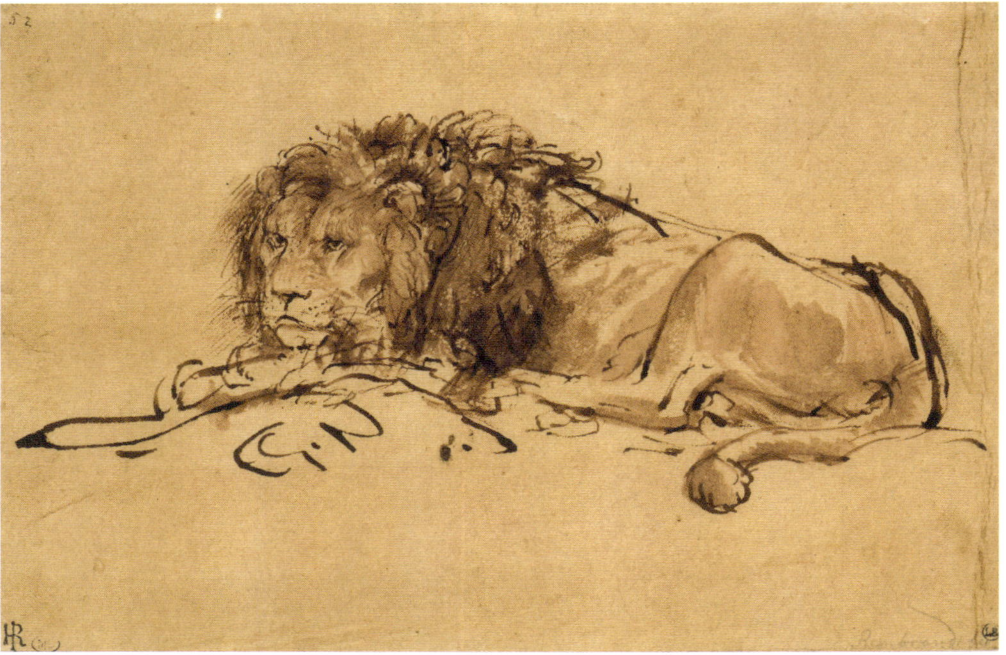

10.2 | *Lioness Devouring a Bird*, ca. 1638–42. Charcoal with gray wash, heightened with white, on paper prepared with brown wash; 12.6 × 23.9 cm (5 × 9⅜ in.). The British Museum, London, inv. Oo,9.71. Photo © The Trustees of The British Museum/Art Resource, N.Y.

10.3 | *Lion Resting*, ca. 1645–50. Pen and brown ink, brown wash; 13.8 × 20.7 cm (5⅜ × 8⅛ in.). Musée du Louvre, Paris, inv. RF4721. Photo © RMN—Grand Palais/Art Resource, N.Y. Photographer: J. G. Berizzi.

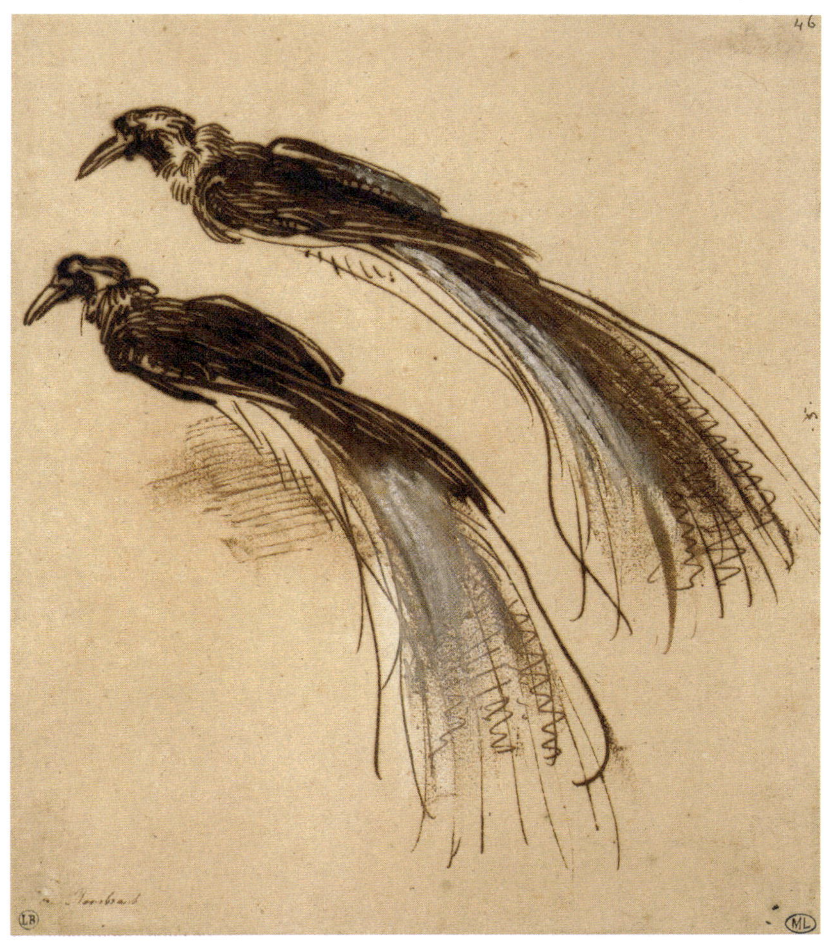

10.4 | *Two Studies of a Bird of Paradise*, ca. 1639. Pen and brown iron-gall ink, brown wash, heightened with white opaque watercolor; 18.1 × 15.4 cm (7⅛ × 6⅛ in.). Musée du Louvre, Paris, inv. RF4687. Photo © RMN—Grand Palais/ Art Resource, N.Y. Photographer: Jean-Gilles Berizzi.

Rembrandt's 1656 inventory lists "a bird of paradise and six fans in a drawer."[51] The bird was one of a number of natural objects in his encyclopedic collection (his *naturalia* also included skins of a lion and a lioness). Birds of paradise, native to New Guinea, were brought to the Netherlands on Dutch East India Company vessels. According to an apocryphal tale, the birds had no legs and had to spend their entire lives in flight. We know now that their legs were cut off and their innards removed when they were mounted in Asia. Rembrandt's drawing shows legless birds, indicating that the lifelike studies were done from a dead specimen treated by a taxidermist, not a live bird. Most likely the stuffed bird resting with six fans in Rembrandt's drawer in 1656 served as the model for both studies.

The total number of the artist's known drawings devoted to wild and exotic beasts is very small. If we include two not fully convincing sketches of camels, formerly at the

Kunsthalle, Bremen (presumably lost in World War II), merely fifteen have been identified.[52] The existing sketches of domestic animals are less than half that number: three of pigs and one each of a dog, a cow, and a study of two horses at a halt.[53] It is reasonable to assume that a considerable number have been lost; the 1656 inventory speaks of a book "filled with drawings by Rembrandt of animals done from life." Moreover, at least one of the existing drawings of lions is datable to about 1660 (Benesch no. 1216) and thus could not have been in the book cited in the inventory.

Before turning to two notable sketches of domestic animals, it is worth mentioning that Rembrandt broke with the long tradition—best represented by Albrecht Dürer, Joris Hoefnagel, and Jacques de Gheyn II—of making exquisitely precise depictions of insects, caterpillars, butterflies, snails, lizards, frogs, mice, and other small creatures. To judge from his existing drawings, Rembrandt had no interest whatsoever in depicting this aspect of the natural world.

Only Rembrandt's 1650 life-size etching of a single marble coned shell (*Conus marmoreus*; fig. 10.5) conjures up an image of him as artist-naturalist. The remarkable print stands alone in his oeuvre. However, the image cracks when we learn he made a significant error in his depiction of it. These

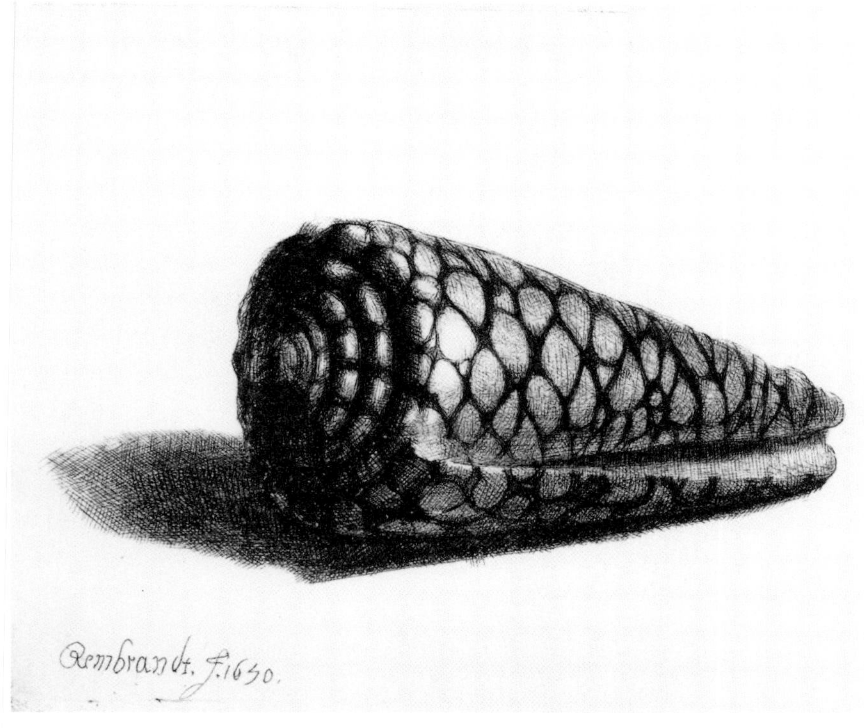

10.5 | *The Shell* (*Conus marmoreus*), signed and dated 1650. Etching, drypoint, and burin; 9.7 × 13.2 cm (3¾ × 5¼ in.). The Pierpont Morgan Library, New York, RvR 234. Photographer: David A. Loggie.

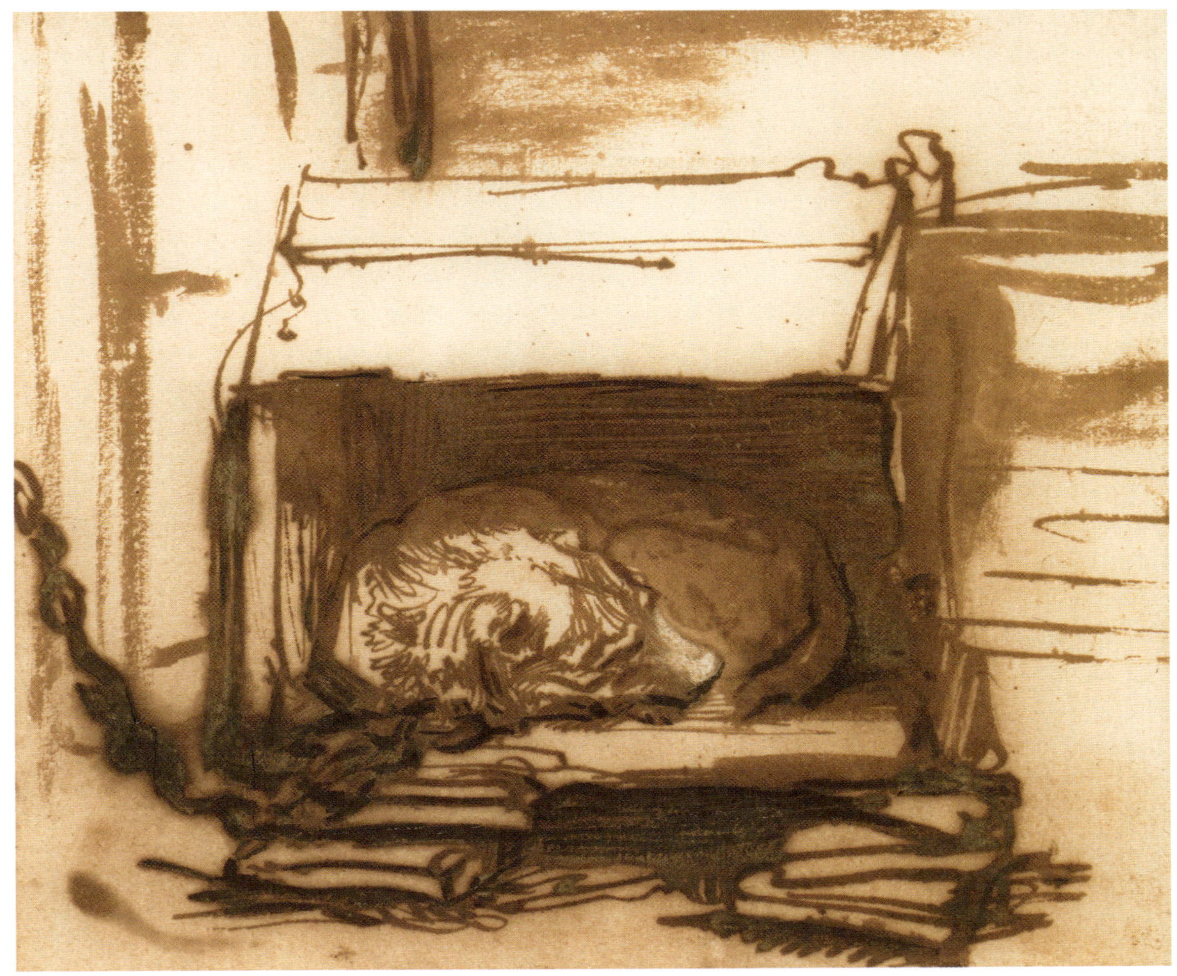

10.6 | *Sleeping Watchdog*, ca. 1637/40. Pen and brown ink with brush and brown wash, with touches of opaque white watercolor, on cream laid paper; 14.3 × 16.8 cm (5⅝ × 6⅝ in.). Museum of Fine Arts, Boston, John H. and Ernestine A. Payne Fund, inv. 56.519. Photo © 2009 Museum of Fine Arts, Boston.

shells, when seen from below, invariably coil clockwise. Rembrandt depicts his coiling in a counter-clockwise direction. Of course, he knew the etching of it that he made on his copperplate would be reversed when printed. He carefully inscribed his signature and date in reverse on his plate, so they appear the right way round, but not his depiction of the shell. The scientific accuracy as well as descriptive realism that conchologists demand did not interest him.

Boston's appealing iron-gall ink-and-wash drawing of a chained watchdog sleeping in its hutch set on wooden blocks (fig. 10.6) has the strong chiaroscuro effect the artist often favored during the first decades of his career. A similar sketch was probably used as a model for the sleeping dog in the shadows of the lower right foreground in the grisaille of *Joseph Telling His Dreams* of about 1633 at the Rijksmuseum (see fig. 5.6).

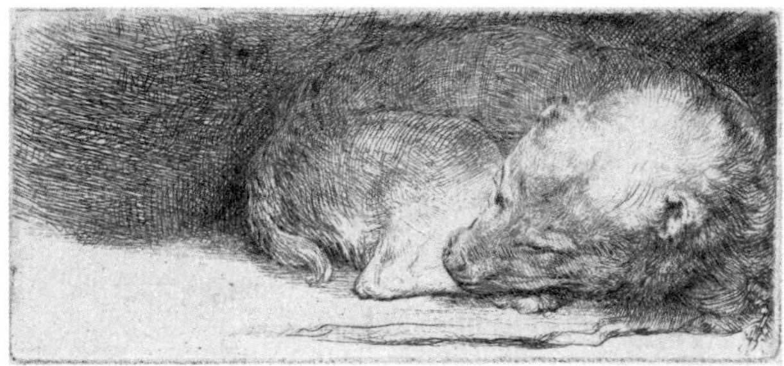

Rembrandt may have consulted the Boston drawing in the late 1630s for his etching of a curled-up sleeping puppy (fig. 10.7). In the little print the dramatic contrast between intense sunlight and deep shadows of the sketch remains pronounced.

As the sketch of two pigs at the Louvre shows (fig. 10.8), Rembrandt recognized that pen and ink are particularly suitable for portraying that animal's bristly hair coat. The sheet also includes a study of a pig's eye and ear. Datable to the late 1630s, the work was formerly related to the artist's 1643 etching of a huge sow ready for slaughter (fig. 10.9), but there is now consensus that they are based on independent studies from nature. Neither a preliminary nor a preparatory study is known for the etched sow, mercifully unaware of the pig butcher behind her preparing for his job.

10.7 | *Sleeping Puppy*, ca. 1639–40. Etching and drypoint, on paper, third state; 3.9 × 8.1 cm (1½ × 3⅛ in.). Rijksmuseum, Amsterdam, inv. RP-T-OB-240.

10.8 | *Studies of Pigs*, late 1630s. Pen and brown ink, corrected with white; 12.5 × 18.3 cm (4⅞ × 7¼ in.). Musée du Louvre, Paris, inv. RF4698. Photo © RMN—Grand Palais/Art Resource, N.Y. Photographer: Thierry Ollivier.

10.9 | *The Sow*, signed and dated 1643. Etching and drypoint; 14.5 × 18.8 cm (5¾ × 7⅜ in.). Harvard Art Museum, Fogg Art Museum, Cambridge, Massachusetts, Anonymous Fund for the Acquisition of Prints Older than 150 Years, inv. M23935. Photo © President and Fellows of Harvard College. Photographer: David Mathews.

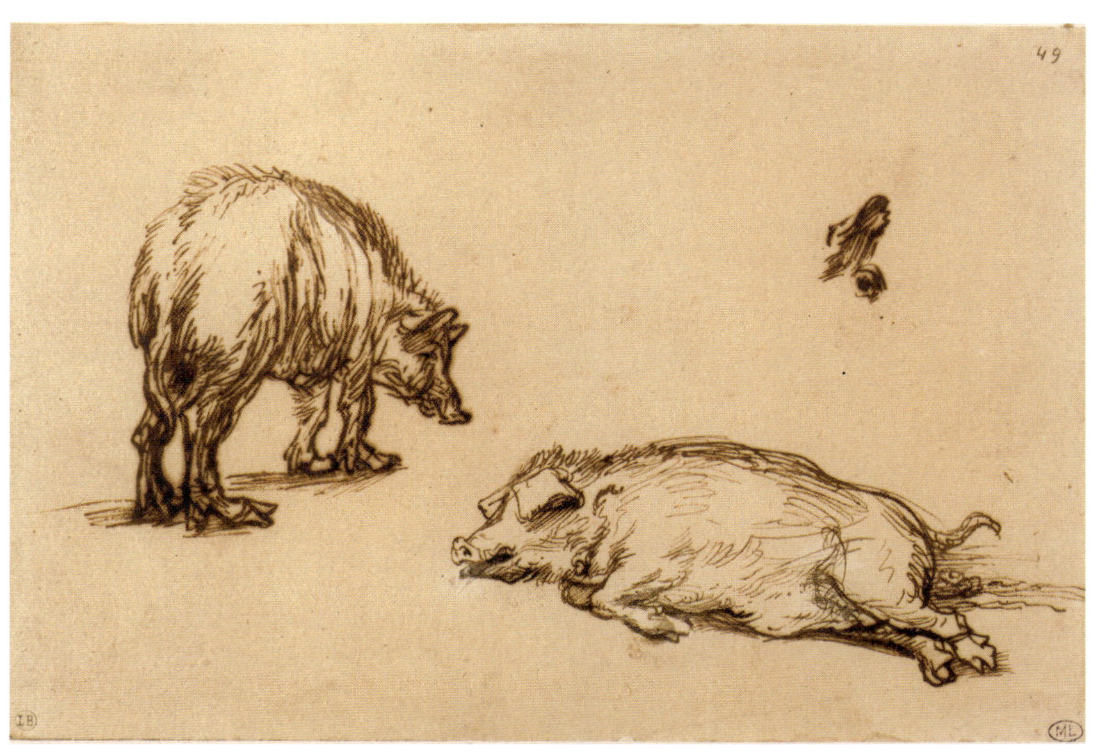

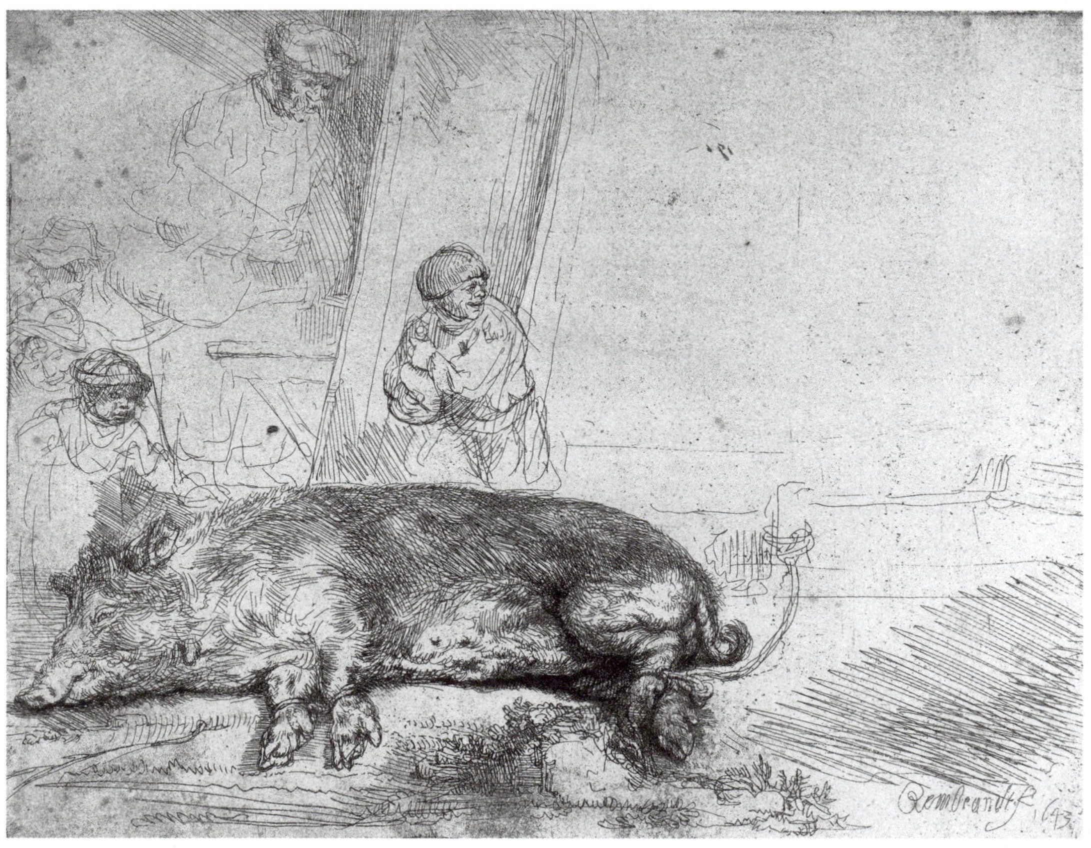

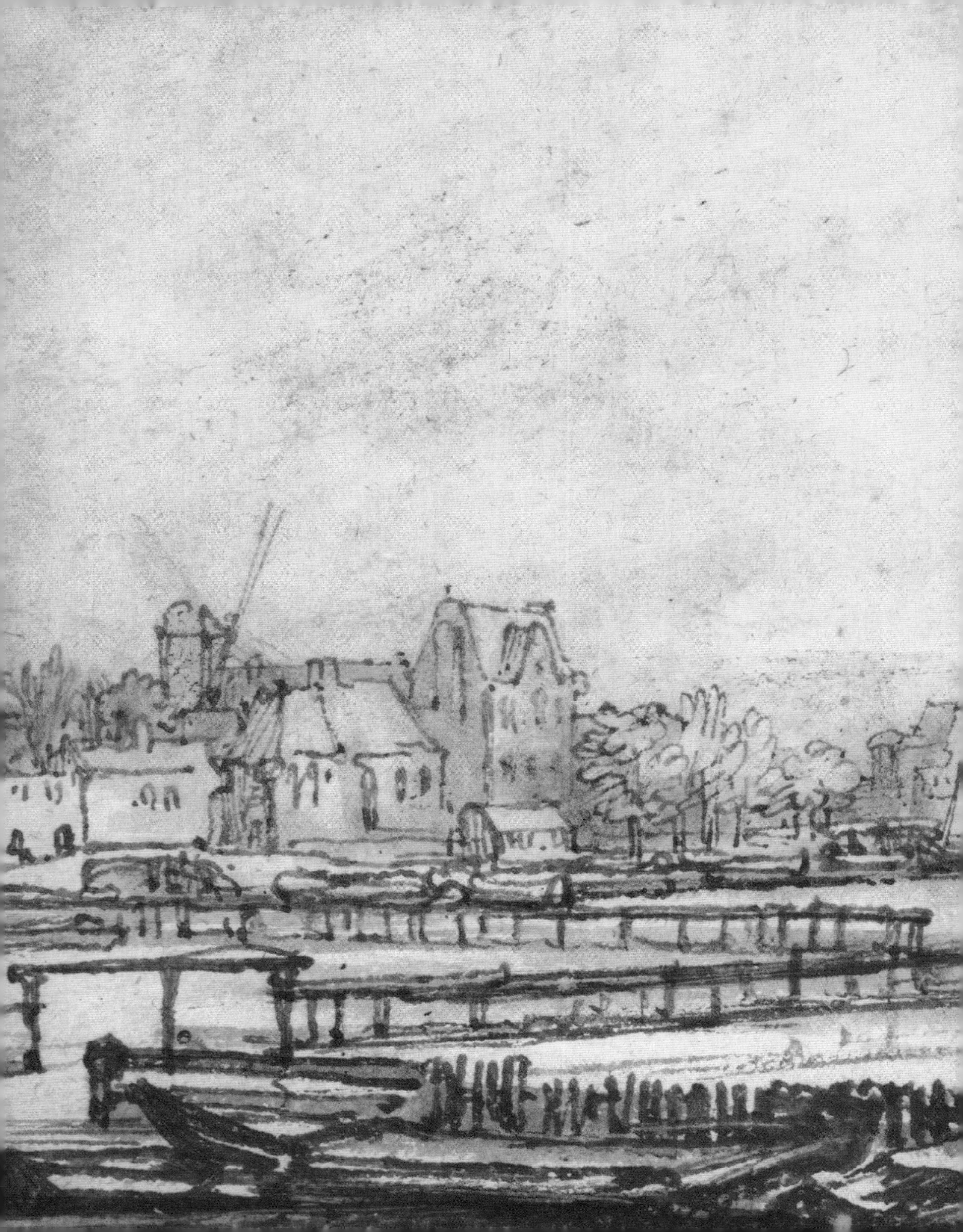

11 | Landscapes

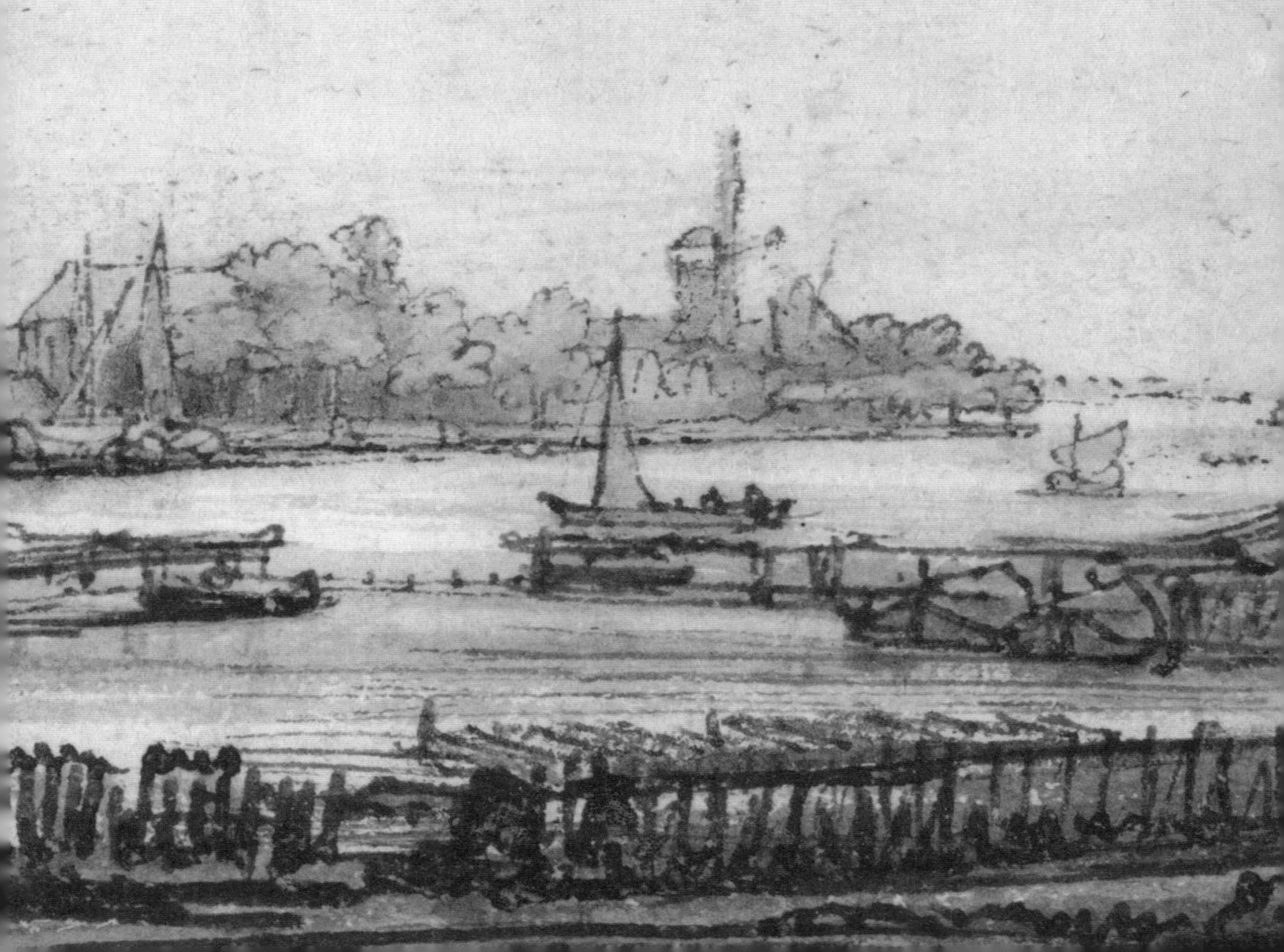

11 | LANDSCAPES

11.1 | *Cottage near the Entrance to a Wood*, signed and dated 1644. Pen and ink ranging from light to dark brown, brown wash, touches of red chalk, corrected with white; 29.9 × 45.5 cm (11¾ × 17⅞ in.). The Metropolitan Museum of Art, New York, The Robert Lehman Collection, inv. 1975.1.792. Photo copyright © The Metropolitan Museum of Art/Art Resource, N.Y.

11.2 | *Cottages under a Stormy Sky*, ca. 1635–40. Pen and brown ink, brown wash, white body color, on paper prepared with brown wash; 18.2 × 24.5 cm (7⅛ × 9⅝ in.). Graphische Sammlung Albertina, Vienna, inv. 8880. Photo: Erich Lessing/Art Resource, N.Y.

THE METROPOLITAN MUSEUM'S *Cottage near the Entrance to a Wood* (fig. 11.1) is Rembrandt's largest existing landscape drawing. The strict frontality of its composition and the extensive use of large areas of wash, some of it splashy, are exceptional. So are its autograph signature and the date of 1644 inscribed in the lower left (for an enlarged detail of the inscription, see fig. 16.3). It is the artist's only known landscape drawing that bears an authentic date.

Despite the paucity of dates on Rembrandt's almost two hundred drawings of nature, it is safe to say, on the basis of their style, that his passion for depicting landscapes began by the mid-1630s and cooled in the late 1650s. Those selected for this chapter show their extraordinary range.

A pinnacle of his early achievement in this category is the Albertina's dramatic view of cottages seen against a burst of sunlight dissipating a stormy sky (fig. 11.2). Sharp contrasts of bright light and deep shadow animate the composition and enhance its dynamic quality. Highly unusual are the ravening clouds. To be sure, dark clouds appear in every single one of the rare painted landscapes that can be attributed to Rembrandt (only seven or eight are generally accepted as authentic), but they hardly ever occur in his drawings. Although the sketch's composition was probably Rembrandt's invention, its cottages have been identified as an uncommon type found in an area near Amsterdam and in a few other parts of the Netherlands (see p. 146 and figs. 12.1, 12.2, 12.3).

In the early 1640s, soon after Rembrandt settled into his new house on Jodenbreestraat, he began to make drawings of Amsterdam's canals and streets as well as sights he saw in the environs of the metropolis.[54] Some are small black-chalk cityscapes done in the vicinity of his new home—black

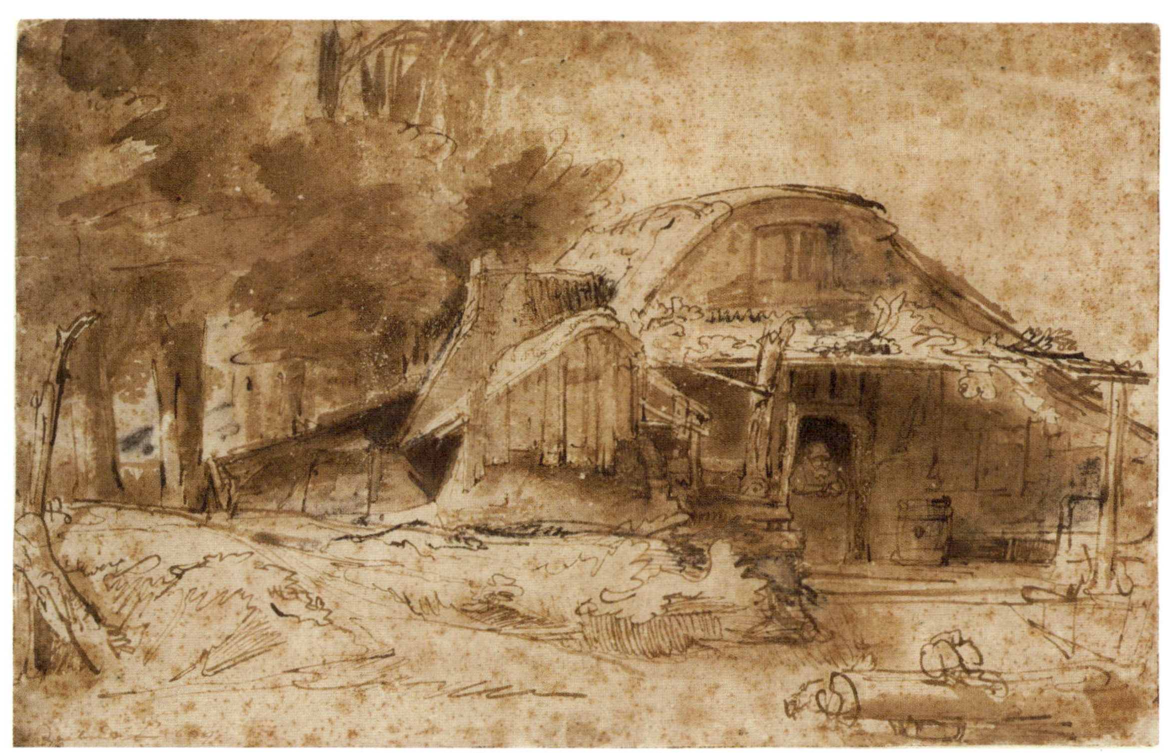

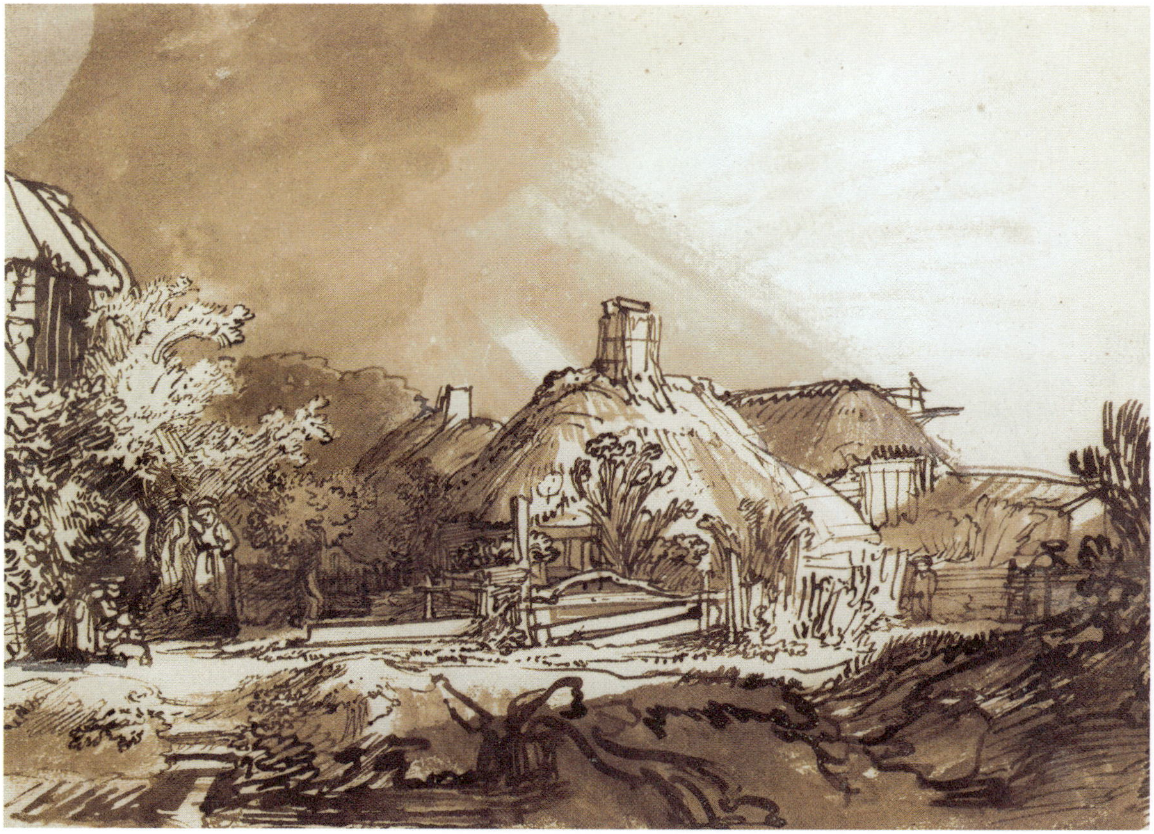

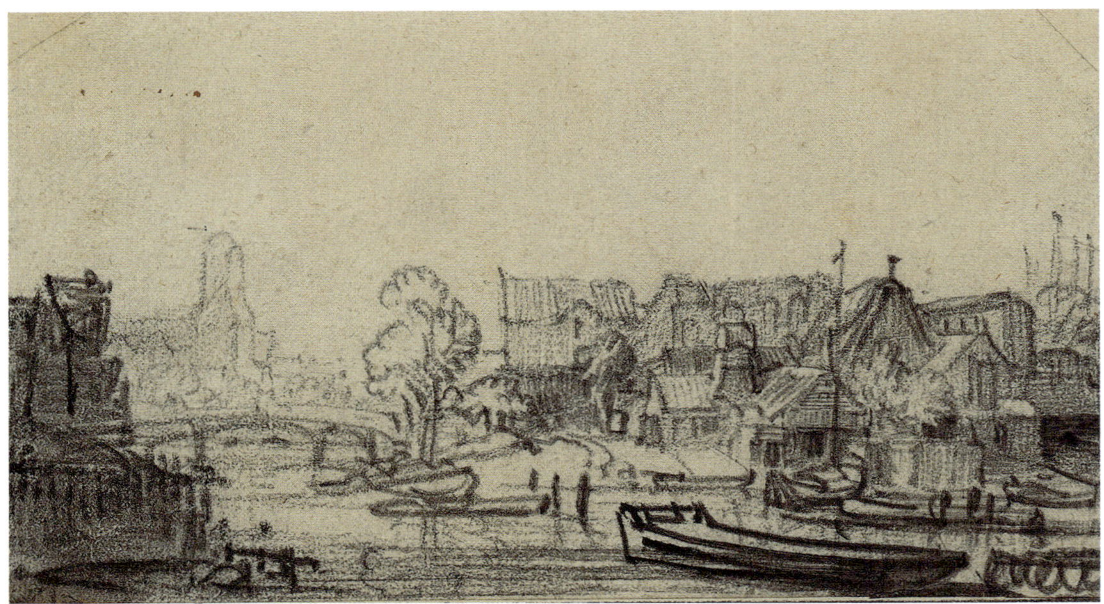

chalk was the medium he preferred when he worked outdoors from life. The black-chalk sketch illustrated here of a busy Amsterdam canal flanked by houses (fig. 11.3) is a sheet from a dismantled sketchbook.

Others, such as his black-chalk drawing of a ditch with overhanging bushes viewed from a modest wooden bridge visible at the bottom of the drawing (fig. 11.4), were probably done from nature during the course of an excursion into the countryside. When Rembrandt made his unusual 1645 etching *A Boathouse among Trees* (fig. 11.5), he may have had in mind the thick foliage of the above drawing's bushes and their reflection in the smooth, glistening water.

Consideration of Rembrandt's total production as an etcher establishes that he did not make many landscape prints. Fewer than thirty of his more than three hundred etchings belong to the category. Striking is the fact that Amsterdam's pen-and-wash *Cottage with a White Paling among Trees* (fig. 11.6) is one of the exceedingly rare drawings that qualifies as a preliminary study (in reverse) for one of them[55] (fig. 11.7). Rembrandt made significant changes when he worked his sketch into a print. He considerably reduced the size of the image, changed the shape of the trees, set the thatched-roof cottage back to the middle ground, devoted almost half of his composition to the sky, and added many little details—among them, a distant windmill, a tiny cow on the horizon, ducks in the pond, and a horse's skull in the right foreground.

11.3 | *View in Amsterdam of the "Houtkopersburgwal" on the Island of Uilenburg and the South Church*, ca. 1640–45. Black chalk; 9 × 16.2 cm (3½ × 6⅜ in.). Graphische Sammlung Albertina, Vienna, inv. 17572. Photo © The Albertina Museum, Vienna.

11.4 | *Canal Between Bushes*, ca. 1645. Black chalk on laid paper with a watermark; 15.5 × 11.7 cm (5⅛ × 4⅝ in.). Lubomirski Princes Museum at the Ossoliński National Institute, Wrocław, inv. I.r.o. 702 (D nr inw. 8782).

11.5 | *A Boathouse among Trees*, signed and dated 1645. Etching and drypoint; 12.7 × 13.4 cm (5 × 5¼ in.). The British Museum, London, inv. 1973.U.973. Photo © The Trustees of The British Museum. All rights reserved.

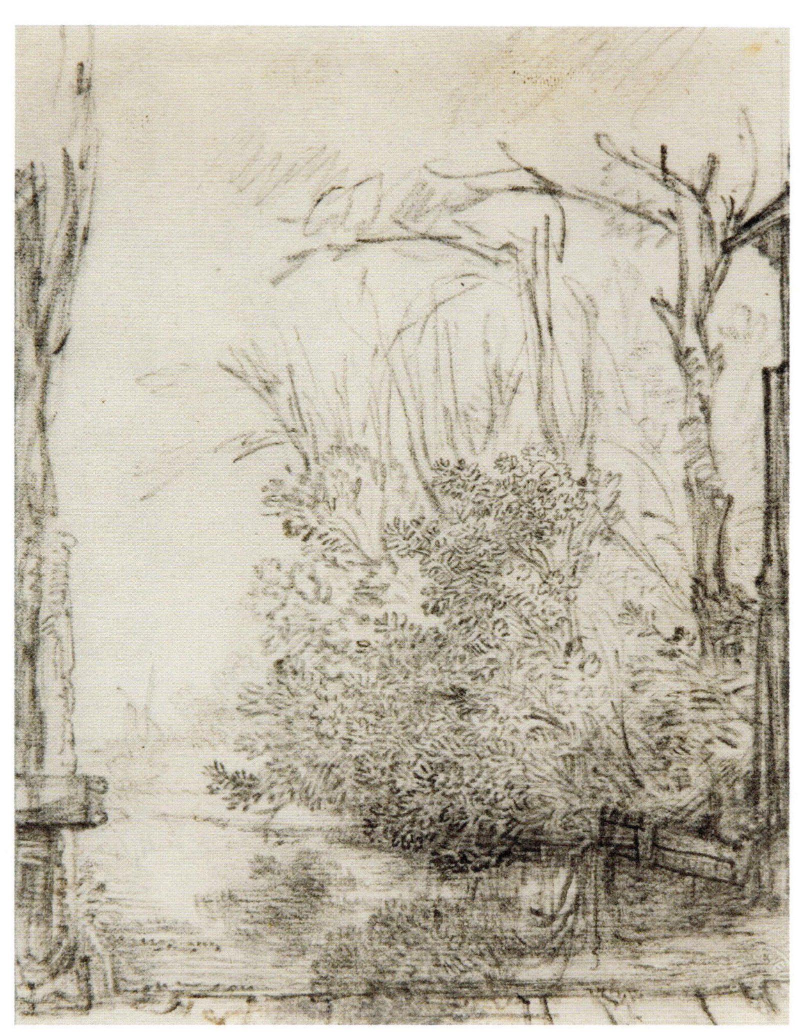

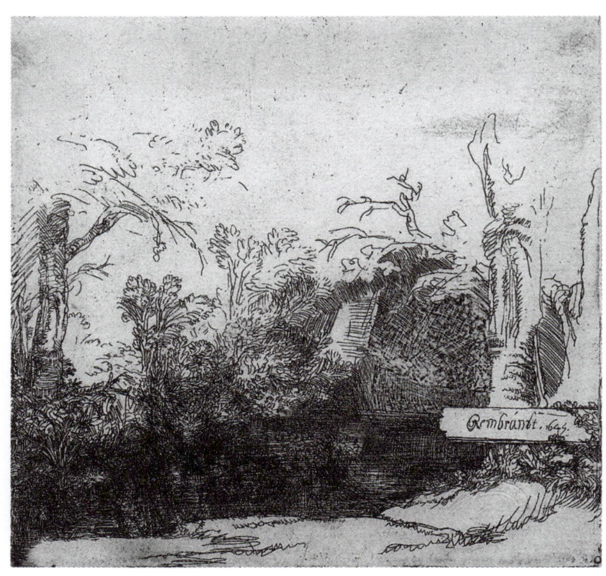
Rembrándt. 1645

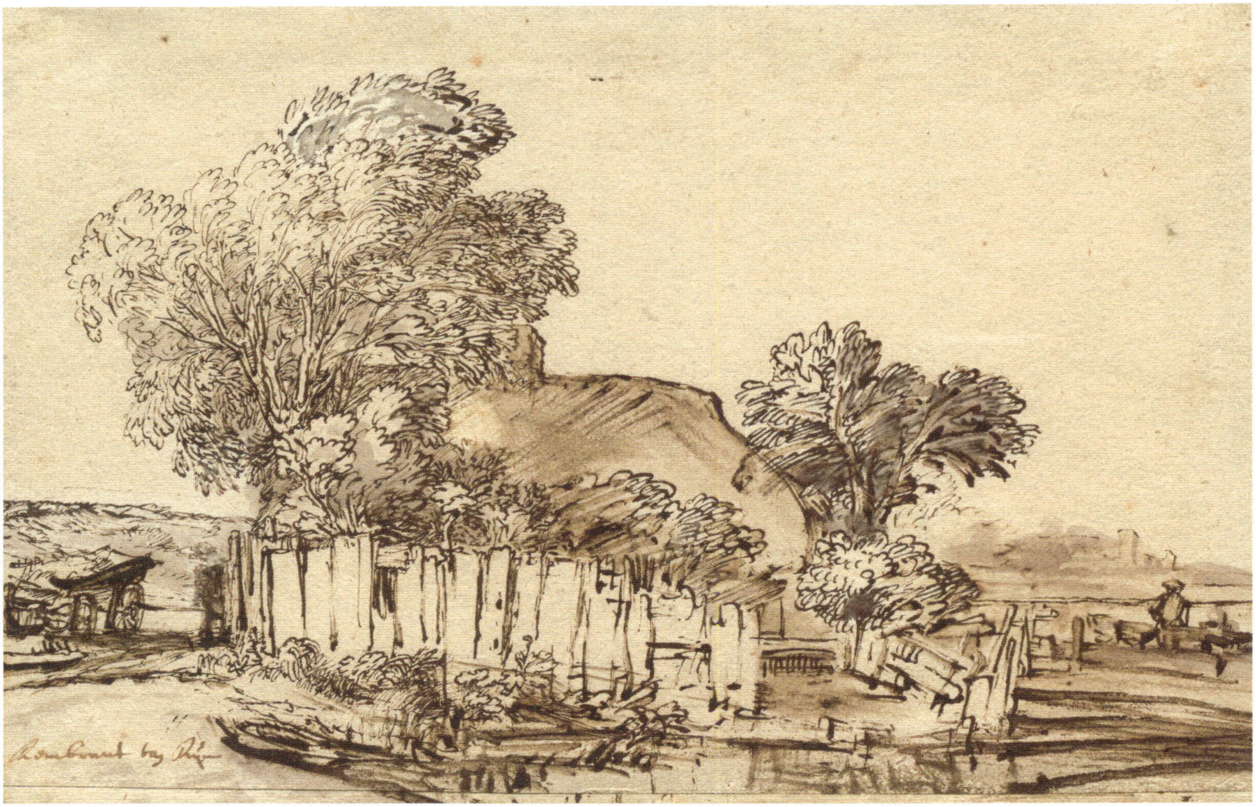

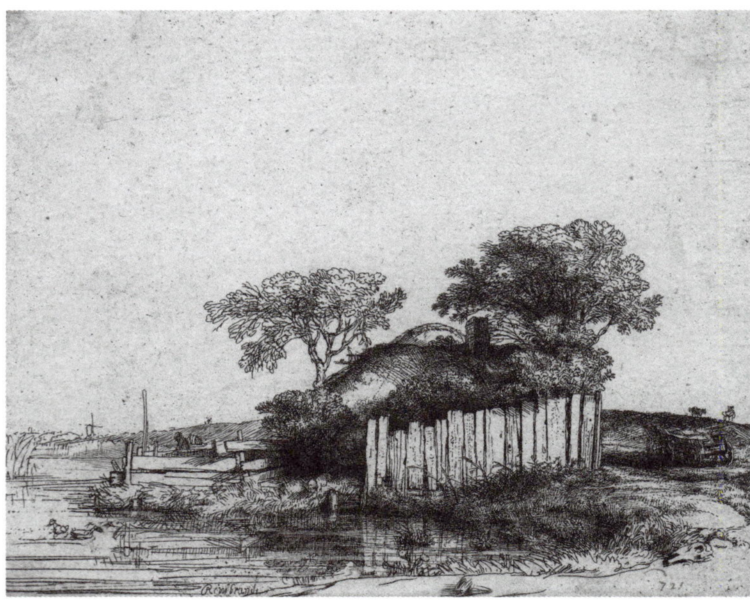

11.6 | *Cottage with a White Paling among Trees*, ca. 1648. Pen and brush and brown ink, brown and pale purple wash, white gouache, on paper; 17.1 × 25.5 cm (6¾ × 10 in.). Rijksmuseum, Amsterdam, inv. RP-T-1981-1.

11.7 | *Cottage with a White Paling among Trees*, signed and dated 1648. Etching and drypoint; 12.9 × 16 cm (5⅛ × 6¼ in.). The British Museum, London, inv. 1895,0915.430. Photo © The Trustees of The British Museum/Art Resource, N.Y.

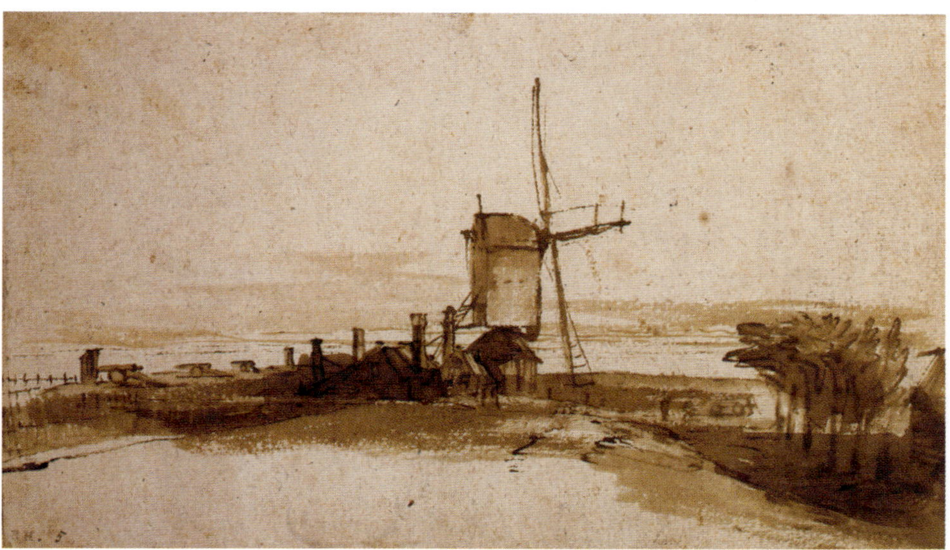

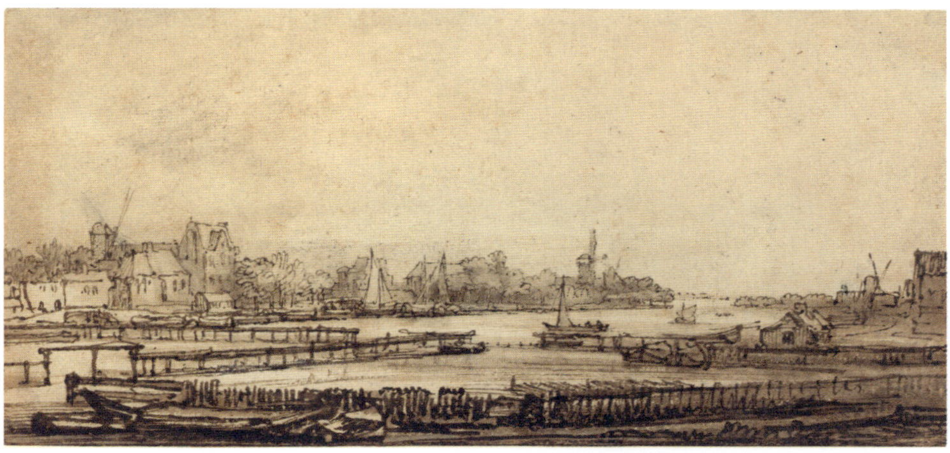

11.8 | *The Windmill on the Bastion "Het Blauwhoofd,"* ca. 1645. Pen and brown ink, brown and gray-brown wash; 11.6 × 19.8 cm (4 1/8 × 7 3/4 in.). Fondation Custodia, Collection Frits Lugt, Paris, inv. 5174.

11.9 | *The Amstel River Seen from the Bulwark beside the "Blauwbrug,"* ca. 1645–49. Pen and brown ink with brown wash; 8.9 × 18.5 cm (3 1/2 × 7 1/4 in.). National Gallery of Art, Rosenwald Collection, Washington, D.C., inv. 1954.12.114. Photo courtesy of the Board of Trustees, National Gallery of Art.

The artist made frequent trips along Amsterdam's city walls to sketch its bastions, which in many places were surmounted by windmills. Among the best results of this endeavor is his pen-and-wash drawing at the Fondation Custodia, Paris (fig. 11.8), of the bulwark popularly called *Het Blauwhoofd* (the Blue Headland), upon which were situated a few sentry boxes, cottages, and a post mill (a type whose entire body could be turned into the wind) affectionately named *De Bok* (the Billy Goat). The slender mill and its beautifully drawn vanes dominate the scene. Details of the landscape can be recounted: Cottages with tall chimneys are huddled to the left of the mill, and beyond them three cannons of the city's fortification. A clump of shadowed trees is seen at the bottom of an incline on the right. Extraordinary is the impression of vast space beyond the bulwark created by light washes.

The broad pen-and-wash drawing of the Amstel River sketched from a rampart near the Amsterdam bridge called the *Blauwbrug* (Blue Bridge), now in Washington, D.C., offers a faithful view of the southern gateway to the city (fig. 11.9). It can justly be called a rhapsody of palisades. With firm vertical and horizontal strokes of his pen and dark wash Rembrandt made a few rowboats and the extensive palisade in front of the rampart the strong foreground of his drawing. The palisades behind it on the left were situated in front of the *Blauwbrug*. To enter the city's canal system, vessels had to pass through their narrow openings. The one on the extreme left has been closed with a horizontal beam. Still open is the one in the outer palisade that stretches across the river. There, palisades as well as the shore on the right are done with lighter pen strokes and wash. The touch becomes even lighter as the river winds to the horizon. The sheet's high degree of finish suggests that it may have been made as an autonomous work intended for sale or as a gift.

Vastly more spacious and much more delicate than Washington's drawing of the Amstel is Rotterdam's bird's-eye *View of Haarlem with the Saxenburg Estate* (fig. 11.10). Its tremulous lines and light washes seem to have been blown gently upon the sheet rather than drawn. The view is seen from the high dunes at the village of Bloemendaal. On the distant horizon is the skyline of Haarlem, where it is possible to

11.10 | *View of Haarlem with the Saxenburg Estate in the Middle Ground*, ca. 1650–51. Pen and brown ink, brown wash, touches of white; 8.9 × 15.2 cm (3½ × 6 in.). Museum Boijmans Van Beuningen, Rotterdam, inv. 130 (Koenigs Collection).

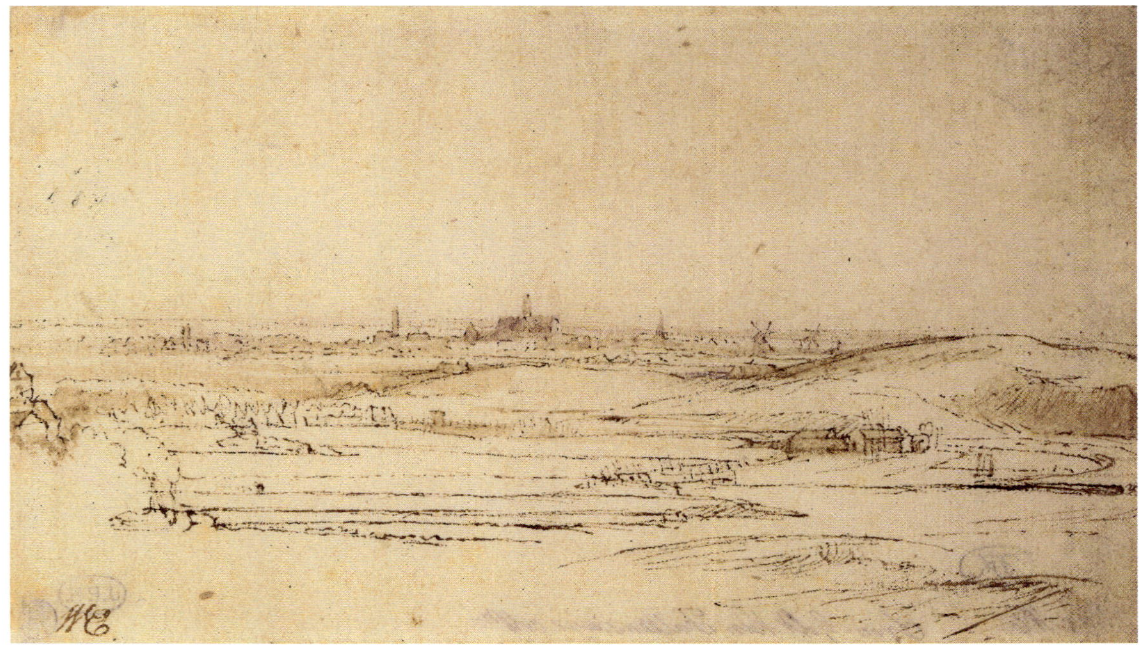

distinguish the nave and spire of Saint Bavo, the city's great church. Part of Bloemendaal's little church appears amid trees on the extreme left.

Saxenburg Estate was purchased in 1638 by the Amsterdam merchant Christoffel Thijsz, who was one of the owners of the house Rembrandt bought on Jodenbreestraat in 1639. He was still one of the artist's creditors in 1653. In 1651 Rembrandt made his unequaled panoramic etching of the same site (formerly wrongly entitled *The Goldweigher's Field*[56]). Rotterdam's drawing cannot justifiably be called a preliminary study for the print; however, it is certainly related to it and datable around the same time. Perhaps the artist made both during the course of visits to his creditor's estate. The trip of about twenty kilometers from Amsterdam to the estate would have been easy to make.

Among the walks Rembrandt favored was one that ran along the Diemerdijk east of Amsterdam toward the village of Diemen. At the end of the dike he reached the River IJ. A few taverns were situated in the bend of the dike. No one questions the thought that on occasion he probably stopped to refresh himself in one of them.

Certainty that he knew the area is provided by three drawings that have been identified as works made on the spot. Grandest is Chatsworth's pen-and-wash panoramic view of the bend (fig. 11.11). It captures the broad expanse of the river, which dwarfs the vessels ploughing it. On the far shore, from left to right, are Nieuwendam's church, the village of Schellingwoude, and Ransdorp's tower. Prominent in the right foreground is a wooden wall with thick wooden posts on it. The wooden wall and posts are more prominent in Rembrandt's other sketch of the view, now at Rotterdam (Benesch no. 1358); it is smaller and gives a more limited view

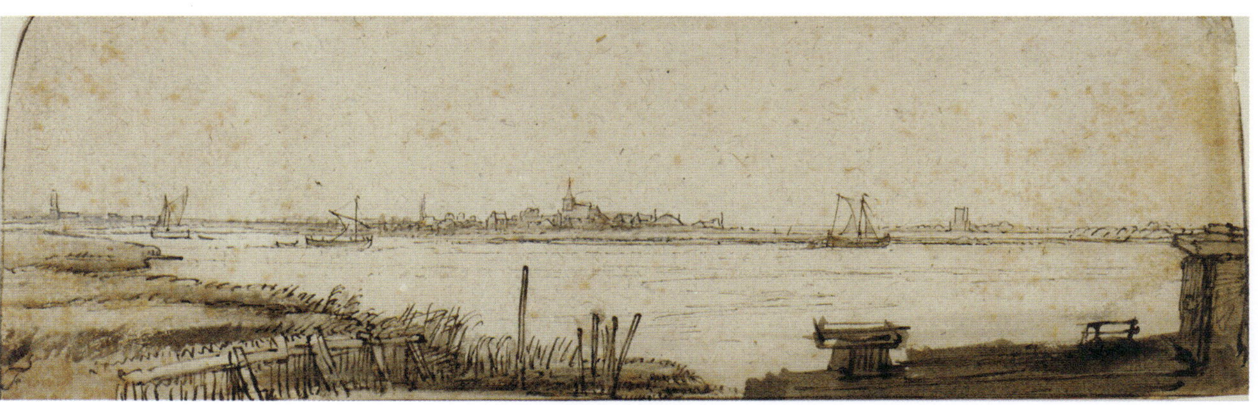

11.11 | *View over the River IJ from the Diemerdijk Looking toward Nieuwendam, Schellingwoude, and Ransdorp*, ca. 1650. Pen and brown ink, brown wash, touches of white, on grayish paper; 7.6 × 24.4 cm (3 × 9⅝ in.). Photo © The Devonshire Collection, Chatsworth, inv. 1030. Reproduced by permission of the Chatsworth Settlement Trustees.

of the distant shore than Chatsworth's drawing. The third sketch that belongs to the group is at the Louvre. It depicts a young artist drawing at a table in one of the vicinity's taverns (see fig. 8.12). Through the open window next to him one can make out a couple of the wooden posts, the IJ, and the village of Schellingwoude.

More frequent than his walks along the Diemerdijk were Rembrandt's excursions south of Amsterdam along the broad Amstel River, where he found landscape motifs for numerous drawings and a few prints. We have already seen a view of the noble waterway from a rampart near Amsterdam's *Blauwbrug* (see fig. 11.9). From that site the river wound its way southward for about eight kilometers to the little village of Ouderkerk on the Amstel, where it met a tributary that vessels could use for passage to Utrecht—or they could remain on the Amstel and make their way to Gouda.

Rembrandt was particularly attracted to an area in which there was a pronounced bend in the Amstel, about five kilometers south of Amsterdam. In addition to the four drawings of it illustrated here (figs. 11.12–15), he made a 1641 etching known as *Farmhouse with Hayrick* (Bartsch no. 225) that clearly shows (in reverse) the same curve in the river and much more of the manor virtually hidden by luxuriant, tall trees in most of the drawings.

The old manor often obscured by trees when seen from the Amstel or the road that flanked the river (in figs. 11.12, 11.13, 11.14 merely the top of its tower is visible adjacent to a tall pole) acquired the name Kostverloren as early as

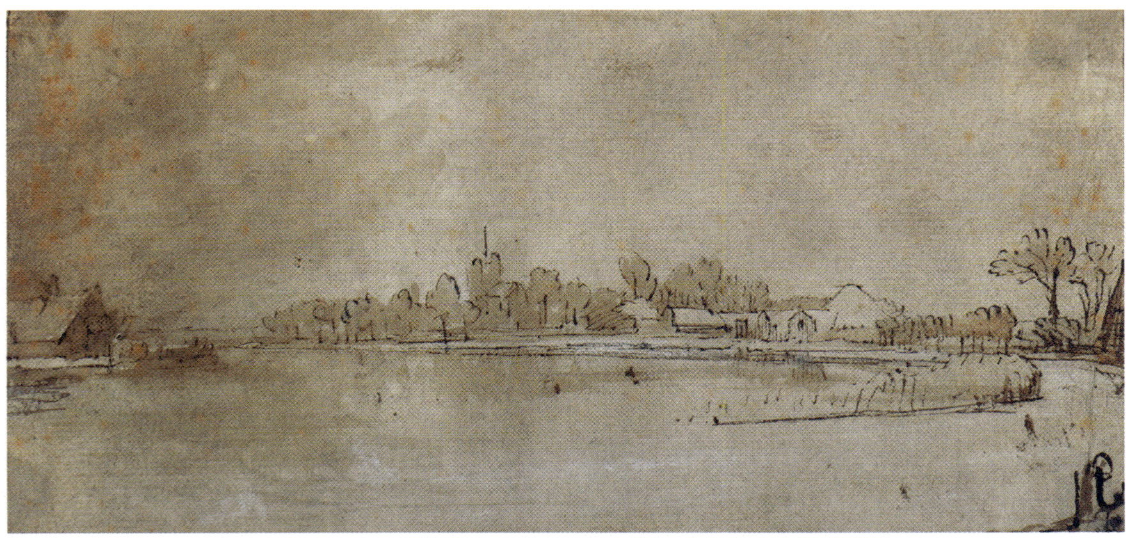

11.12 | *Panorama of the Bend in the Amstel River at Kostverloren*, ca. 1650. Pen and brown ink, brown wash, touches of white; 9.7 × 19.9 cm (3⅞ × 7⅞ in.). Photo © The Devonshire Collection, Chatsworth, inv. 1025. Reproduced by permission of the Chatsworth Settlement Trustees. Photographer: Ian Fraser-Martin.

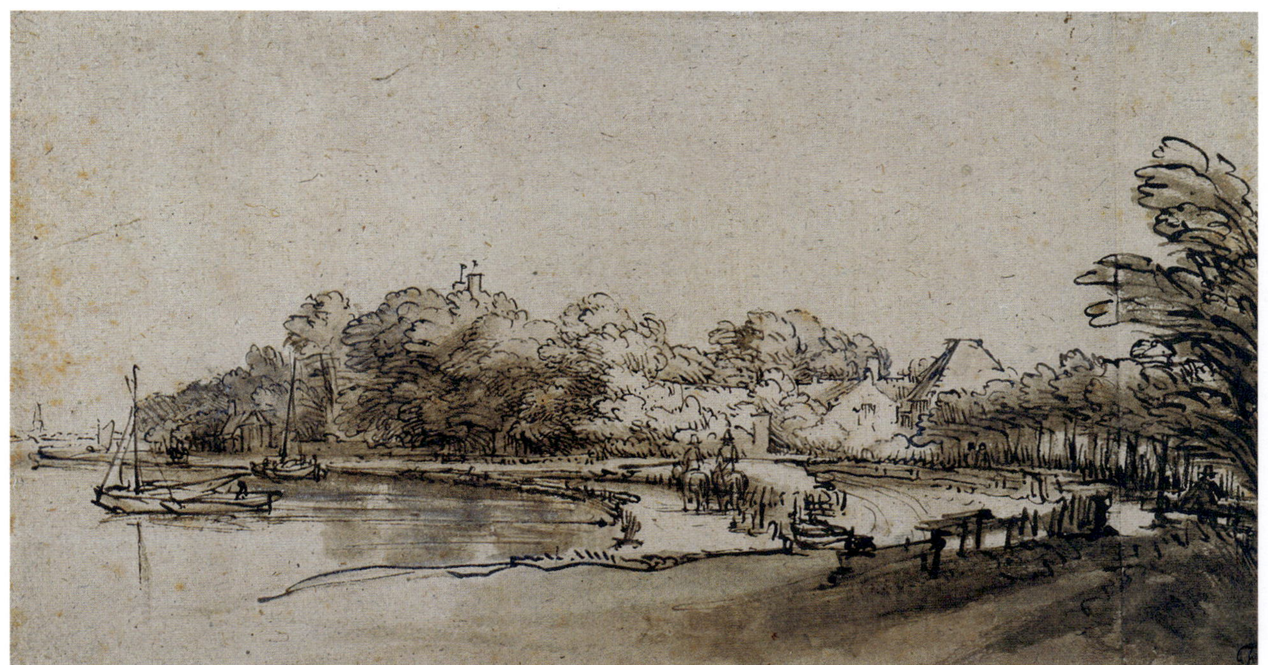

11.13 | *The Bend in the Amstel River at Kostverloren with Horsemen*, ca. 1650. Pen and brown ink, brown and gray washes, touches of white, on oatmeal paper; 13.6 × 24.6 cm (5⅜ × 9¾ in.). Photo © The Devonshire Collection, Chatsworth, inv. 1021. Reproduced by permission of the Chatsworth Settlement Trustees. Photographer: Ian Fraser-Martin.

about 1525. Kostverloren literally means "Lost Expenses"—the implication being "Money Down the Drain." According to tradition, the manor earned its nickname because of the seemingly endless cost of keeping the house's foundation intact in the marshy land on which it had been built.

Before the middle of the seventeenth century Kostverloren was the most conspicuous house in the vicinity. Its attractive location made it a notable landmark for people who viewed it from boats that plied the Amstel and for promenaders and travelers who used the river road. The manor's appeal was recorded by Dutch poets and artists. Among the latter, in addition to Rembrandt, were Jacob van Ruisdael, his pupil Meindert Hobbema, and his close follower Jan van Kessel.

In about 1650 Kostverloren was badly damaged by fire or by a natural disaster. However, its tower remained sound. For Rembrandt's haunting drawing of it in its ruined state, see fig. 12.8.

More than once did the artist make the short three-kilometer walk southward from Kostverloren along the road that follows the Amstel to the village of Ouderkerk. His familiar 1645 etching popularly but wrongly known as *Six's Bridge* depicts a view of the area;[57] the elegant spire of Saint Urban, Ouderkerk's village church, can be seen on its horizon. The church also appears in the distance of a pen-and-wash

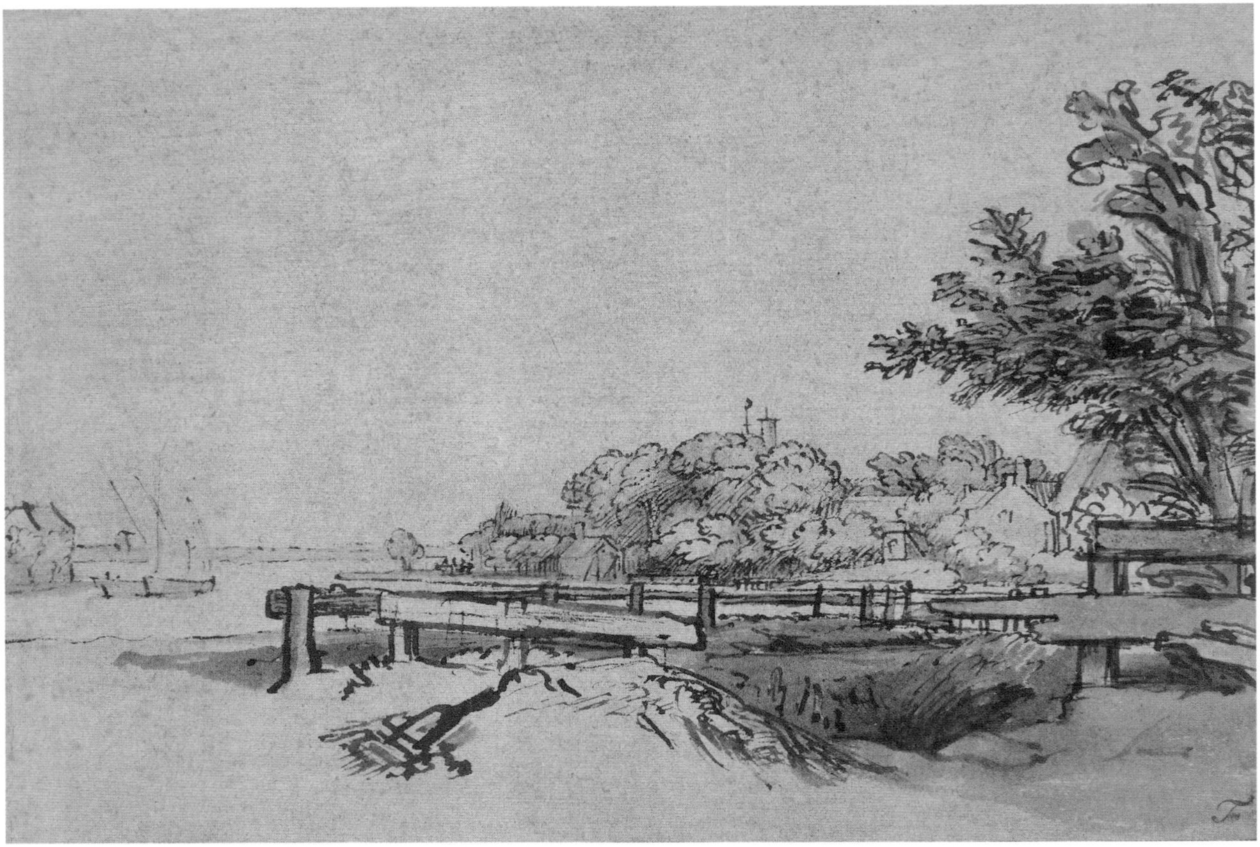

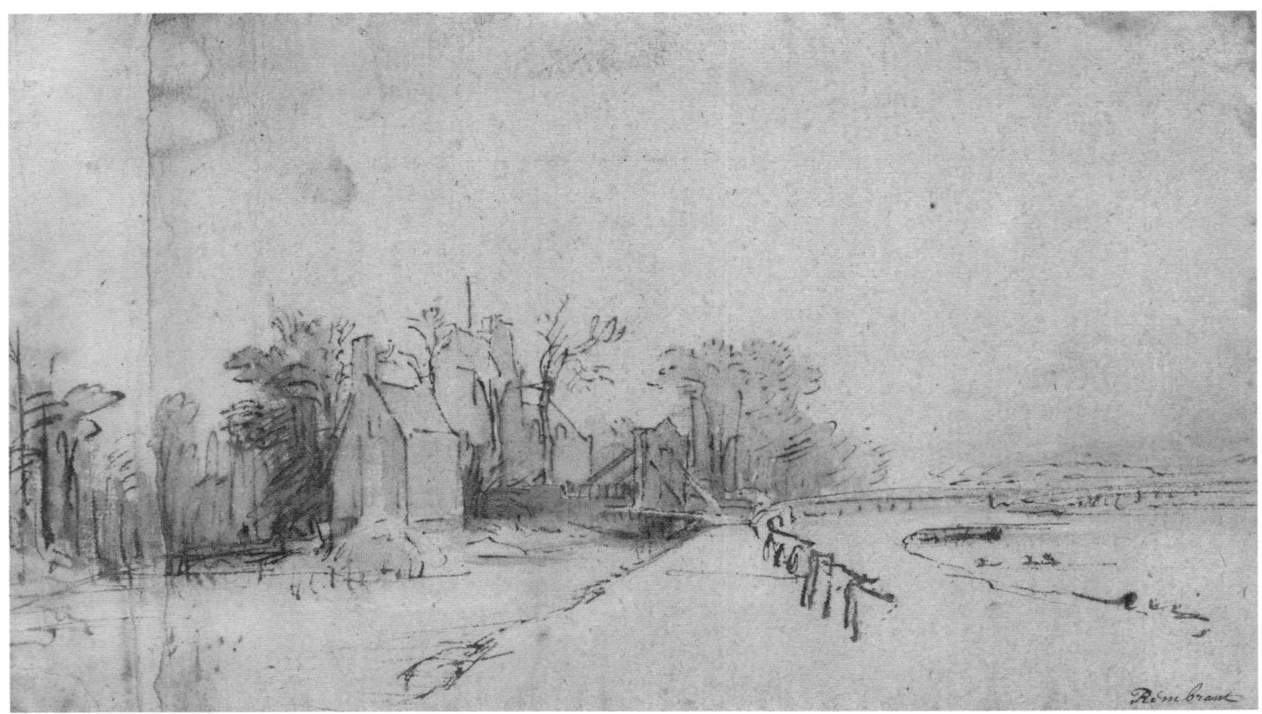

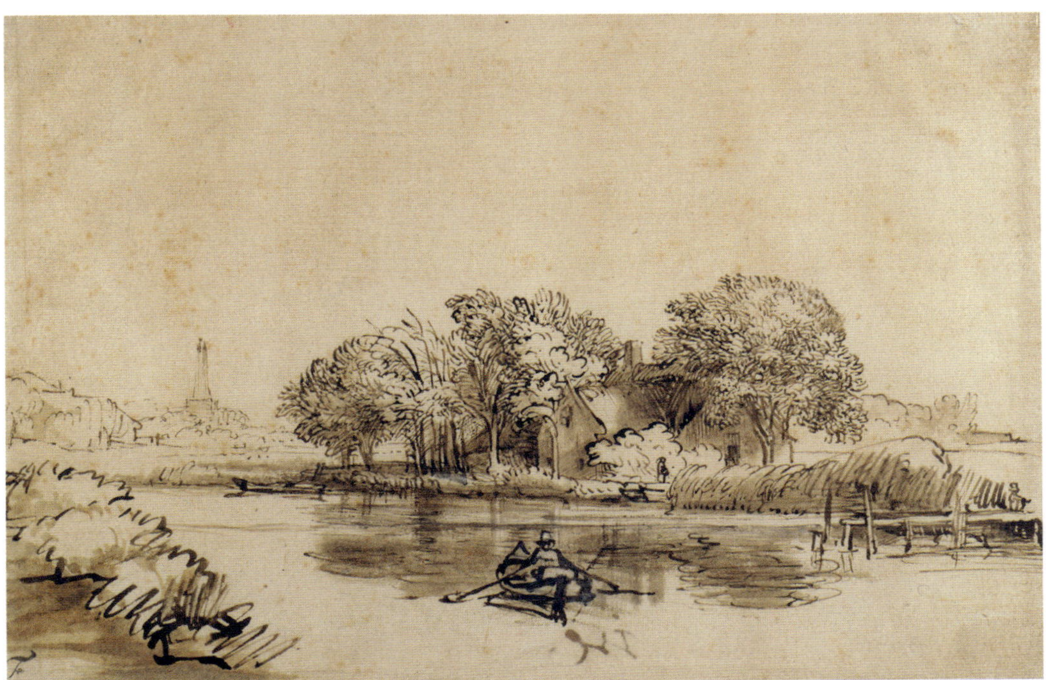

11.14 | *The Bend in the Amstel River at Kostverloren with Fences in the Foreground*, ca. 1650. Pen and brown ink, brown wash, touches of white, on paper prepared with brown wash; 14.1 × 21.3 cm (5½ × 8⅜ in.). The British Museum, London, inv. 19,841,110.90. Photo © The Trustees of The British Museum/Art Resource, N.Y.

11.15 | *View of Kostverloren*, ca. 1650. Pen and brown ink, pencil, brown wash on white paper; 13.1 × 22.8 cm (5⅛ × 9 in.). Kupferstich-Kabinett, Staatliche Kunstsammlungen Dresden, inv. C1910-52. Photo: Bildarchiv Preussischer Kulturbesitz/Art Resource, N.Y. Photographer: Herbert Boswank.

11.16 | *A Man Sculling a Boat on the Bullewijk, with a View toward Ouderkerk*, ca. 1648–50. Pen and brown ink, brown wash, touches of white; 13.3 × 20 cm (5¼ × 7⅞ in.). Photo © The Devonshire Collection, Chatsworth, inv. 1033. Reproduced by permission of the Chatsworth Settlement Trustees. Photographer: Ian Fraser-Martin.

drawing at Chatsworth (fig. 11.16) showing a man in a rowboat on a small tributary of the Amstel with a farmhouse amid trees on its bank. The reflections of the farmhouse and the trees in the calm river speak of a perfect summer's day.

Ouderkerk is the site of Beth Haim (Hebrew: House of Life), the cemetery of the Portuguese-Jewish congregation of Amsterdam, which was also a tourist site at least since 1641 when John Evelyn briefly visited the city and noted in his diary: "…I went to a place (without the Towne) called Over-kirk, where they [the Jews] had a spacious field assign'd them for their dead, which was full of Sepulchers, and Hebrew Inscriptions, some of them very stately, of cost."[58]

Jacob van Ruisdael, too, visited the cemetery in the mid-1650s. He made two highly finished drawings of some of its imposing tombs; his famous painting at Dresden of *The Jewish Cemetery* and another version of it at Detroit were inspired by the site. It seems that Rembrandt ignored the cemetery during his visits to Ouderkerk. Not a trace of it is found in any of his works.

Rembrandt's pen-and-wash drawing of a country view blanketed with snow is a treasure of the Harvard Art Museum (fig. 11.17). Few of the master's landscapes achieve its depth and atmospheric effect with more economy. Its farmstead and wide road were first sketched with a very fine pen and touches of

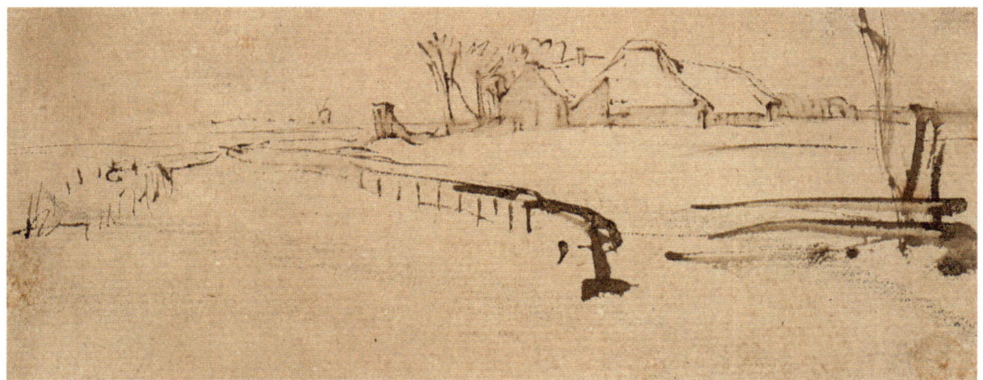

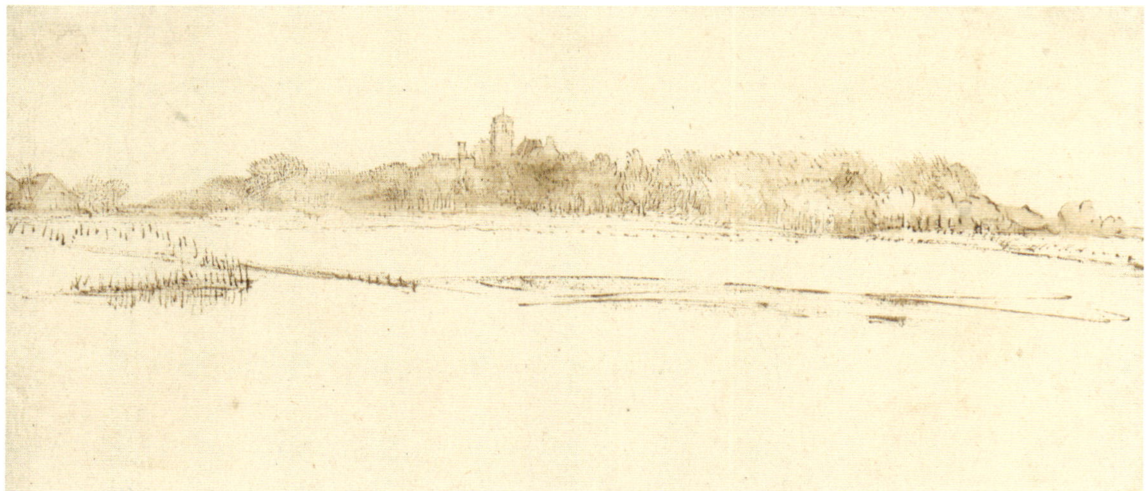

light wash. Then Rembrandt used an exceptionally broad-nibbed reed pen for the spectacularly bold foreground accents.

It has been suggested that Harvard's winterscape depicts a site along the Amstel River between Kostverloren and Ouderkerk. This may be the case. However, no topographical feature in the little drawing clinches the identification. Rembrandt's depictions of winter scenes are scarce. One of them, now at Dresden (see fig. 11.15), shows an unobstructed view of Kostverloren and the road that follows the bank of the Amstel on a dreary winter's day.

The wondrous economy that characterizes Harvard's winterscape is matched by the Getty Museum's incredibly subtle *Landscape with the House with the Little Tower* (fig. 11.18). The house with the little tower (*huis met het toorentje*) is seen in the far distance near the drawing's center. It belonged to Jan Uijtenbogaert, receiver-general of the United Provinces, who was portrayed by Rembrandt in an etching of 1639 (Bartsch no. 281). The drawing's site is on the River Shinkel

11.17 | *Winter Landscape*, ca. 1648–50. Pen and brown ink, pale brown wash, incidental marks in black chalk on cream antique laid paper, prepared with light rose-brown wash, mounted overall, framing line in brown ink; 6.7 × 16 cm (2⅝ × 6¼ in.). Harvard Art Museum/Fogg Museum, Cambridge, Massachusetts, Bequest of Charles A. Loeser, inv. 1932.368. Photo © President and Fellows of Harvard College. Photographer: Allan Macintyre.

11.18 | *Landscape with the House with the Little Tower*, ca. 1650. Pen and brown ink and brown wash; 9.7 × 21.5 cm (3⅞ × 8½ in.). J. Paul Getty Museum, Los Angeles, acc. no. 83.GA.363.

between Amsterdam and the nearby village of Amstelveen. Rembrandt's landscape etching (Bartsch no. 223) depicts the same site but from another view point. Both the etching and Getty's drawing are datable about 1650.

Almost the entire lower half of the drawing is absolutely untouched by pen or wash. At its middle merely two long horizontal virtually dry pen strokes indicate a low river bank, while delicate lines tell of a narrow canal joining the river. Stretching across the entire horizon is a miniature panoramic view of distant houses and heavily wooded areas, which seem to pulse with life thanks to the master's dissolution of some of their forms with light wash that contrasts with dark accents.

Rembrandt rarely made pure brush drawings, but when he did, he achieved phenomenal results. His surpassing *Young Woman Sleeping* at the British Museum (see fig. 6.10) is done solely with a brush. So is his sketch, now at the Louvre, of a river with trees on its banks at twilight (fig. 11.19). It is the artist's only known landscape drawing executed in this technique. The remarkable sheet brings to mind evanescent wash studies by Claude Lorrain or J.M.W. Turner rather than landscape drawings by our artist. Indeed, until it was discovered that on the verso of the Louvre's drawing is a partially legible inscription in Rembrandt's own hand (probably a recipe for stopping-out varnish for use in etching[59]), it is safe to say his name would not leap to mind when this extraordinary wash landscape is confronted.

11.19 | *River and Trees*, ca. 1655. Brush and brown wash; 13.6 × 18.6 cm (5⅜ × 7⅜ in.). Musée du Louvre, Paris, inv. RF4709recto. Photo © RMN—Grand Palais/Art Resource, N.Y. Photographer: Thierry Le Mage.

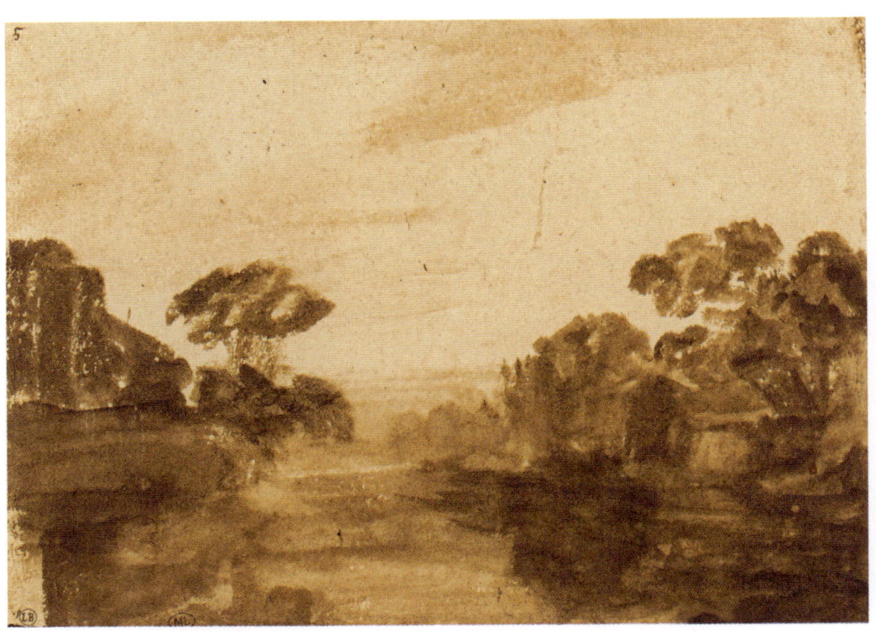

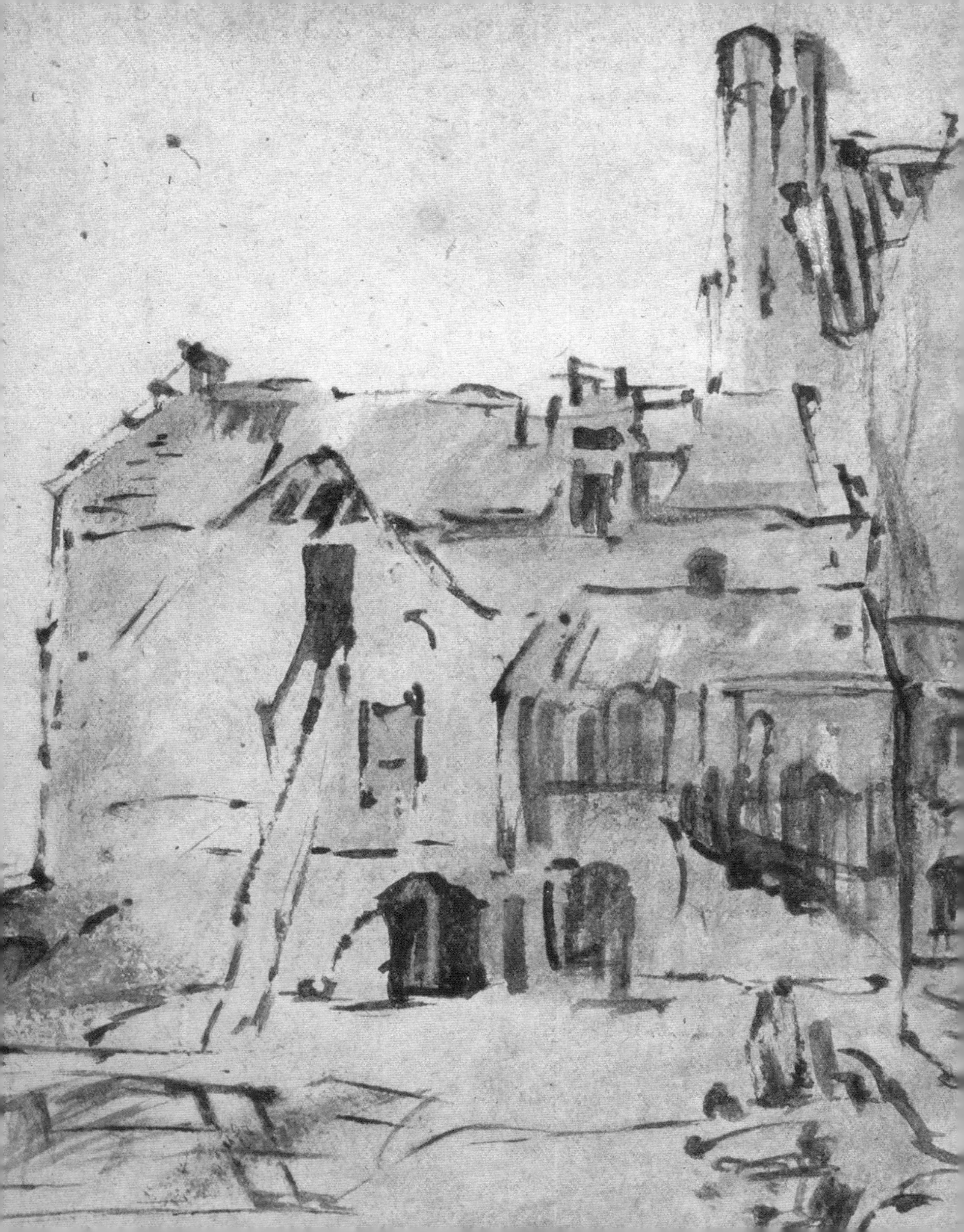

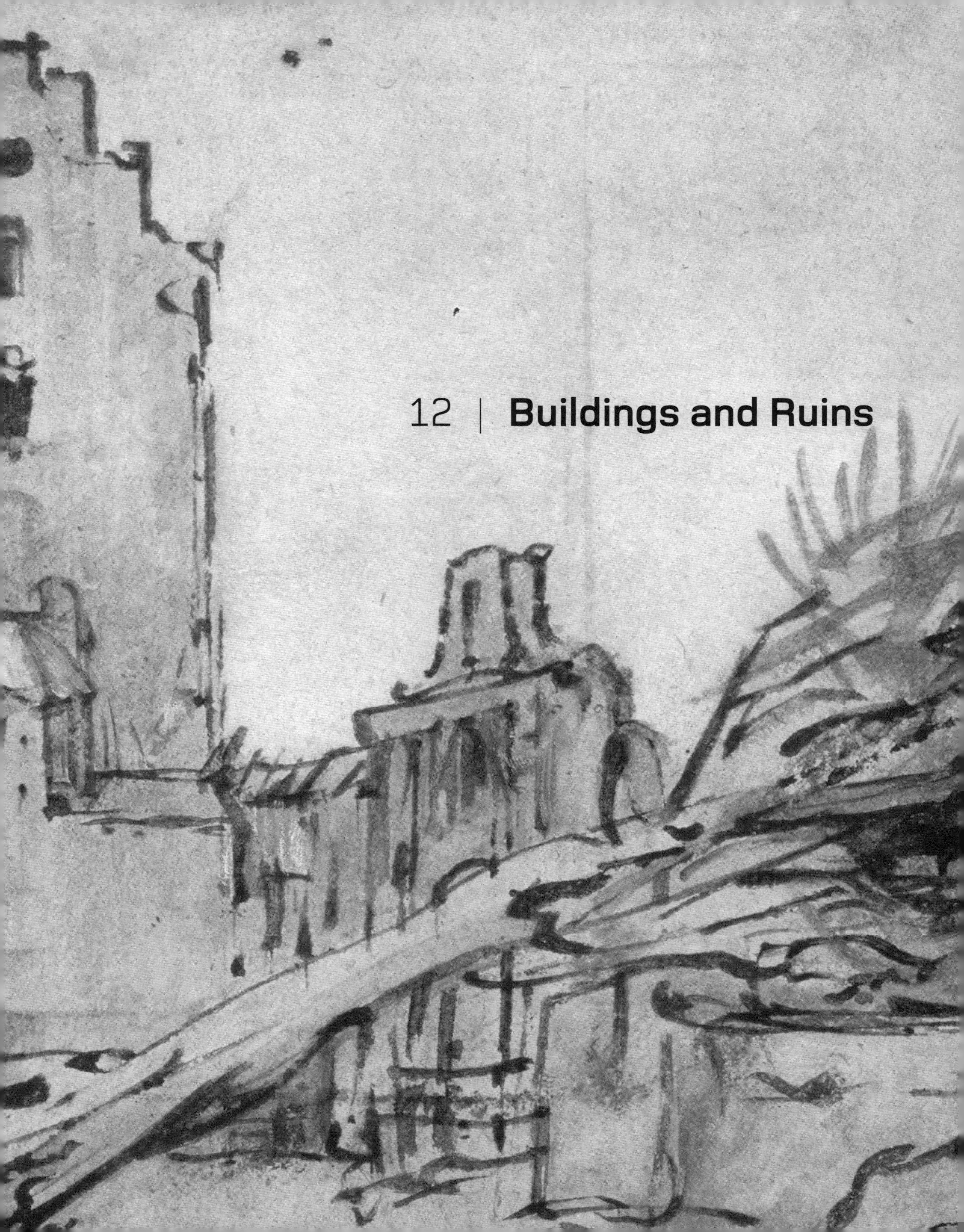

12 | Buildings and Ruins

12.1 | *Two Cottages with Thatched Roofs* (verso), ca. 1633. Silverpoint on vellum prepared with pale gray pigment; 8 × 13.4 cm (3 1/8 × 5 1/4 in.). Museum Boijmans Van Beuningen, Rotterdam, inv. R25 verso (Koenigs Collection).

12.2 | *Two Cottages with Thatched Roofs and Trees* (recto), ca. 1633. Silverpoint on vellum prepared with pale gray pigment; 10.9 × 19.2 cm (4 1/4 × 7 1/2 in.). Kupferstichkabinett, Staatliche Museen, Berlin, inv. KdZ 2317. Photo: Bildarchiv Preussischer Kulturbesitz/Art Resource, N.Y. Photographer: Jörg P. Anders.

REMBRANDT SHOWED AN INTEREST in an unusual type of cottage in his early drawings of buildings, which are datable to the 1630s. They are small, relatively short structures with hipped, thatched roofs, distinguished by chimneys in their front walls that extend through the ends of their roofs (see figs. 12.1, 12.2, 12.3; see also fig. 11.2). Cottages of this type were found in three parts of the Netherlands: in the Gooi, an area southeast of Amsterdam; in regions around Zwolle and Kampen in the eastern province of Overijssel; and in the northern province of Friesland.

After Rembrandt settled in Amsterdam around 1631 or 1632, the Gooi was easily accessible to him. There is no evidence that he ever traveled to the vicinity of Zwolle or Kampen. As for Friesland, in 1633 Rembrandt had a very special reason to make a journey to the province. He traveled there to seek permission to marry Saskia. At the time she was not residing in her native Leeuwarden, where her deceased father had been mayor, but with her guardian in the Frisian parish of Saint Anna, the main township of Het Bilt. The artist received the permission he sought.

We have seen that on 8 June 1633, three days after their betrothal, while Rembrandt was still in Friesland, he made his celebrated silverpoint drawing on prepared vellum of Saskia (see fig. 2.4). It has also been noted that silverpoint drawings on vellum are exceedingly rare in Rembrandt's oeuvre—indeed, they are unusual in seventeenth-century Dutch art.

Here the plot thickens a bit. The drawing of two cottages at Rotterdam is also in silverpoint on prepared vellum (fig. 12.1), and so is the one at Berlin of similar cottages, a few figures, and some scribbles that hint at the landscape setting (fig. 12.2). Additionally, both have silverpoint drawings on

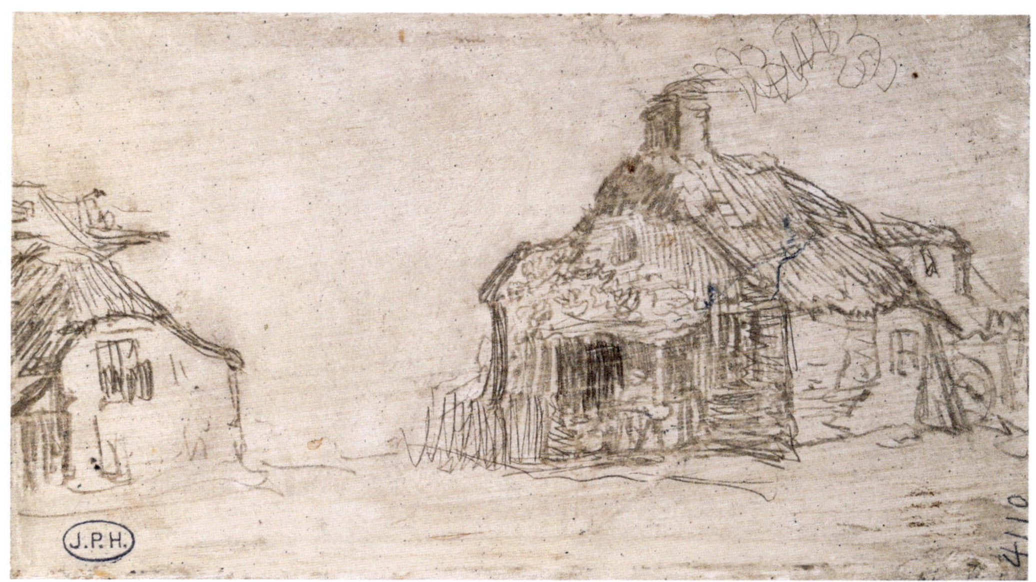
J.P.H.

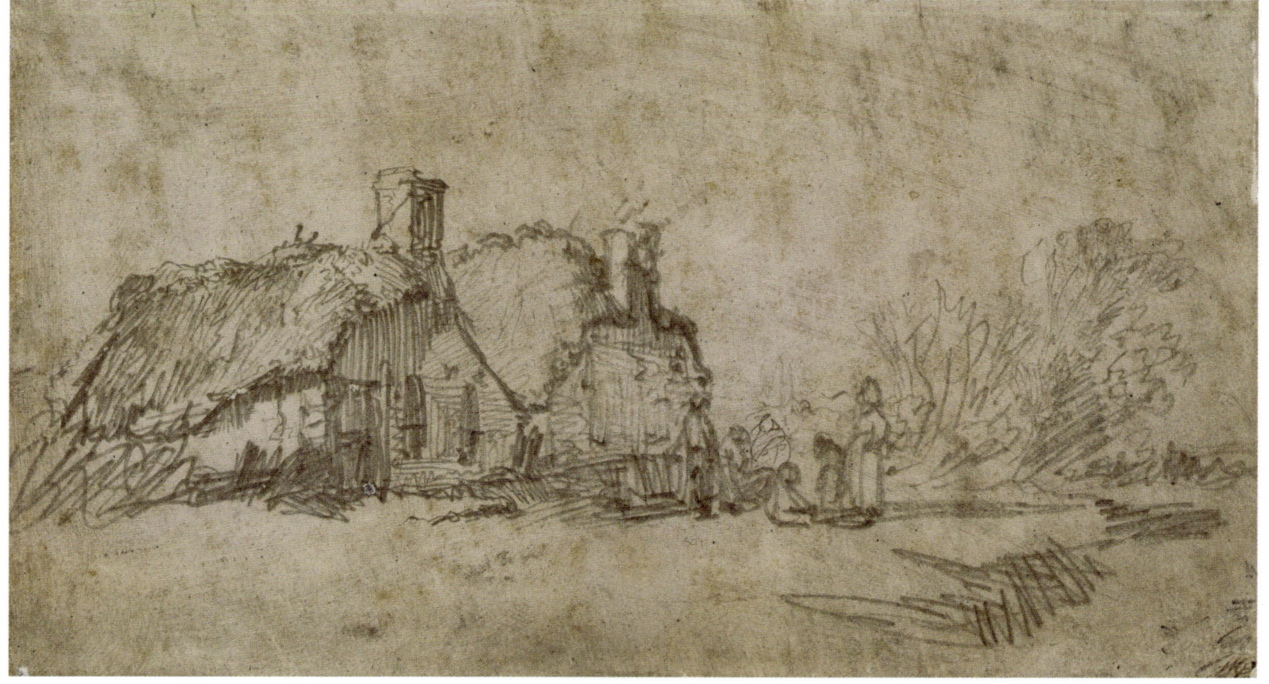

their reverse sides. The Rotterdam sheet has sketches of five heads (see fig. 4.4); its support most probably was cut considerably at a later date to balance the compositional arrangement of the heads. On the reverse of the Berlin sheet is a quick sketch of a panoramic landscape.

When we consider that Rembrandt's 1633 silverpoint drawing on prepared vellum of Saskia was made in the Frisian parish of Saint Anna, that his two silverpoint drawings on the same support of cottages of a type found in Friesland, and that it is arguable that originally all three vellum sheets had virtually the same dimensions, it is reasonable to hypothesize that the artist traveled to Friesland in 1633 with a sketchbook comprised of at least three pages of prepared vellum.[60] If the hypothesis is correct, the Rotterdam and Berlin sketches are among Rembrandt's earliest existing drawings of cottages and of cottages in a landscape.

An item listed in Rembrandt's 1656 insolvency inventory as "A vellum book full of landscapes done from life by Rembrandt" indicates that at that time the artist had some of his landscape drawings in a vellum sketchbook.[61] There is, however, no way of establishing whether the Rotterdam and Berlin sheets were in it.

The vigorous pen work of Getty's sketch of two cottages of a similar type, and just part of the thatched roof of a third (fig. 12.3), seems to anticipate Vincent van Gogh's

12.3 | *Old Houses with Thatched Roofs*, ca. 1640. Pen and brown ink, brush in white; 13.2 × 20.2 cm (4¼ × 8 in.). J. Paul Getty Museum, Los Angeles, acc. no. 85.GA.93.

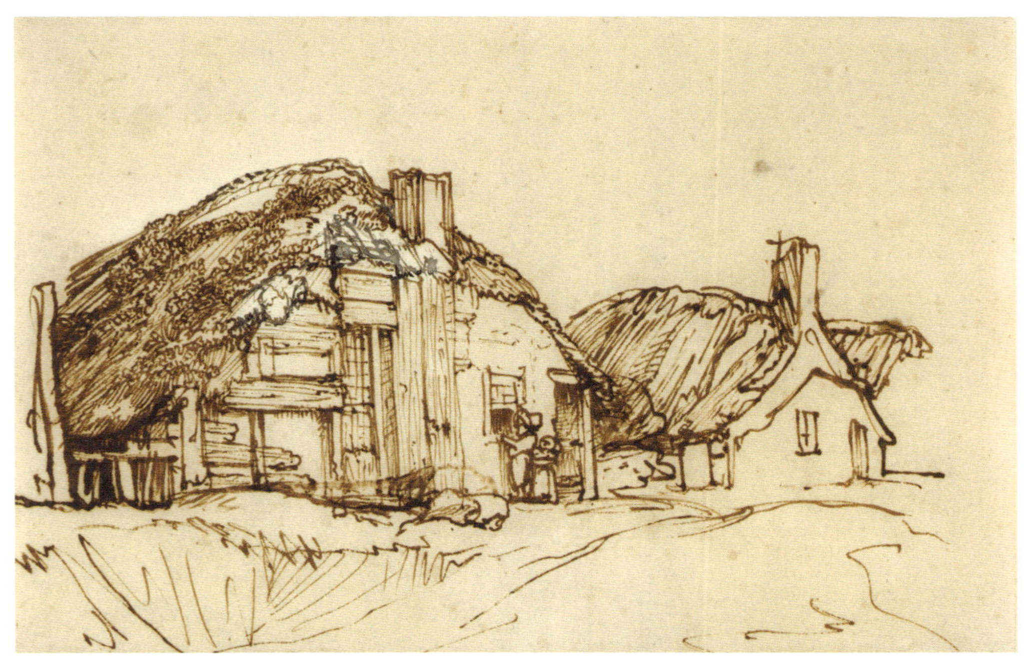

bold quill-and-reed-pen drawings, but there is no reason to believe Vincent ever caught a glimpse of it or comparable works by the master. Equally vigorous is Hamburg's pen drawing of a draw well beside a steep wooden staircase leading to the entrance of a farmhouse (fig. 12.4). In both drawings Rembrandt stresses the role wide, roughly sawn planks play in Dutch vernacular architecture. Identification of the Hamburg sheet as a study (in reverse) for the draw well and staircase leading to the inn in Rembrandt's large 1633 etching of *The Good Samaritan* is untenable.[62] Differences between pertinent elements in them are far greater than their similarities. Moreover, the Hamburg drawing most probably postdates the Good Samaritan etching by a few years.

The most majestic architectural drawing by the artist is Teyler Museum's pen-and-wash view of Rhenen's medieval *Westpoort* (West Gate; also known as the Utrecht Gate) as seen from within the town (fig. 12.5). The play of delicate and strong brown wash captures the character of the scene and gives a suggestion of the color and dull light on the building's fabric. Emphasis is upon the massive ancient gate viewed head on and extending to the very top of the sheet. Its cracks, crevices, and crumbling surface have not been ignored and neither have details of the flanking houses, but greater emphasis is given to the strong, blocky form of the tower, which dwarfs its cavelike portal. Beyond the portal are two barely distinct, minuscule figures—apart from them, not a soul is present.

Rembrandt made another drawing of Rhenen's West Gate seen from a different viewpoint and two expansive ones of its *Rijnpoort* (Rhine Gate), which has a turret and conical towers. The sights of the town situated on the Rhine about thirty-five kilometers southeast of Utrecht—particularly its beautiful late Gothic tower of Saint Cunera, which soars above the town's skyline and dominates the surrounding plain—attracted many Dutch artists. Among those who made Saint Cunera the focal point of panoramic landscapes are Hercules Segers, Jan van Goyen, Aelbert Cuyp, and Jacob van Ruisdael. Our artist does not belong to this group. He concentrated on views of two of the town's medieval gates.

Rembrandt's Rhenen drawings are datable around 1650. He made sketches also of other sites in towns and cities of the eastern provinces of the Netherlands (Arnhem, Amersfoort, Utrecht) that are datable to about the same time. Except for the drawings, there is no documentary evidence

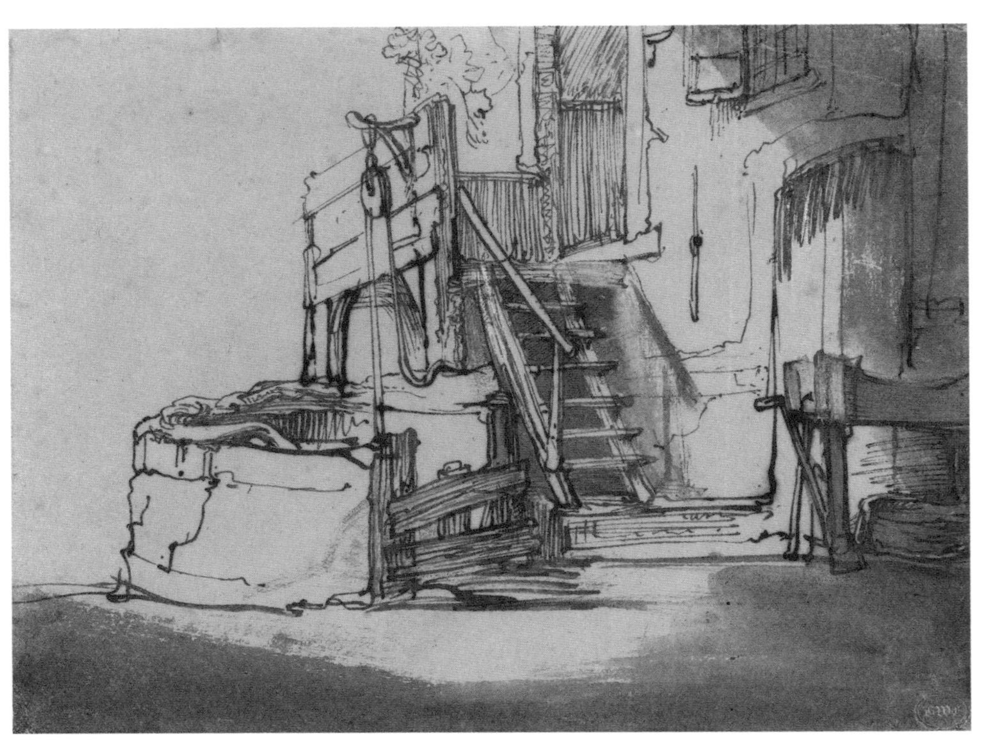

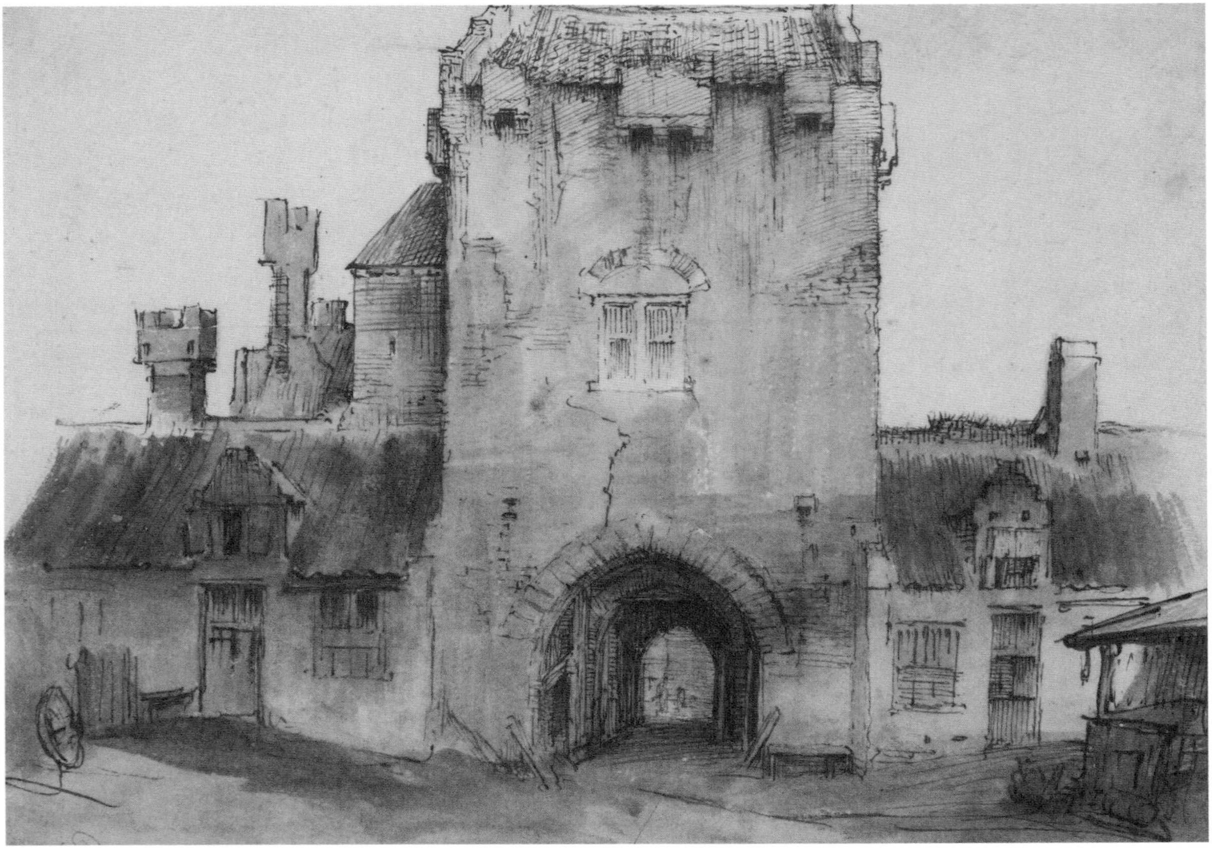

12.4 | *Entrance to a Farmhouse, with a Draw Well*, ca. 1635–38. Pen and brown gall-nut ink, heightened with white, outlined with black pen and with red in the upper left; 17.9 × 23.5 cm (7 × 9¼ in.). Hamburger Kunsthalle, inv. 22419. Photo: Bildarchiv Preussischer Kulturbesitz/Art Resource, N.Y. Photographer: Christoph Irrgang.

12.5 | *The Westpoort or Utrecht Gate at Rhenen*, ca. 1650. Pen and brown ink, brown wash, white heightening; 16.3 × 22.6 cm (6⅜ × 8⅞ in.). Teyler Museum, Haarlem, inv. O* 54.

to establish that he traveled to the eastern part of his country. However, he may have accompanied his close companion Hendrickje Stoffels when she went to her native town Bredevoort, near Arnhem, not far from the Netherlands' eastern border, to attend a baptism in July 1649.[63] Of course, if he did, his drawings, sketches, or *aides-mémoires* of sites in the area could have been made during the course of the trip. It has also been proposed that he made more than one journey to the eastern provinces either a few years before or after the middle of the century, and that some drawings of identifiable places there were made before or after about 1650. These trips remain as hypothetical as his journey to Arnhem with Hendrickje in 1649, but they are not implausible.

The artist's interest in old buildings was not a passing fancy. Proof of his predilection for depicting them instead of new ones is offered by his numerous sketches of Amsterdam views. Among them, not a single one includes a glimpse of the city's New Town Hall, now the royal palace, which still dominates the Dam, the metropolis's principal square. Begun in 1648, when the Eighty Years' War with the Spanish ended with formal *de jure* recognition of the independence of the republic, it was, in its monumental scale and wealth of decoration, the greatest European town hall up to that time. Contemporaries called it the Eighth Wonder of the World. Apparently Rembrandt was not impressed. The sad story of the part the mature artist played around 1660 in providing a colossal painting for the embellishment of the new building's great gallery is discussed in chapter 14 in the section devoted to the artist's drawings of historical subjects.

Even before 1648, when Jacob van Campen's design for the New Town Hall was accepted by Amsterdam's city council, a decision had been made to begin partial demolition of the Old Town Hall and some adjacent buildings. Rembrandt's quick chalk sketch at the Albertina shows the old structure partially demolished (fig. 12.6). The short bold strokes in the foreground depict the stumps of wooden piles used for support of buildings constructed on the city's watery soil. In the center, behind them, is the unmistakable tower of the Old Town Hall. On the right is part of the former Saint Elizabeth's Hospital and its steeple.

During the night between 6 and 7 July 1652, after construction on the New Town Hall had begun, a disastrous fire gutted what remained of the old municipal hall and adjacent, still-standing dilapidated structures. The pen-and-wash

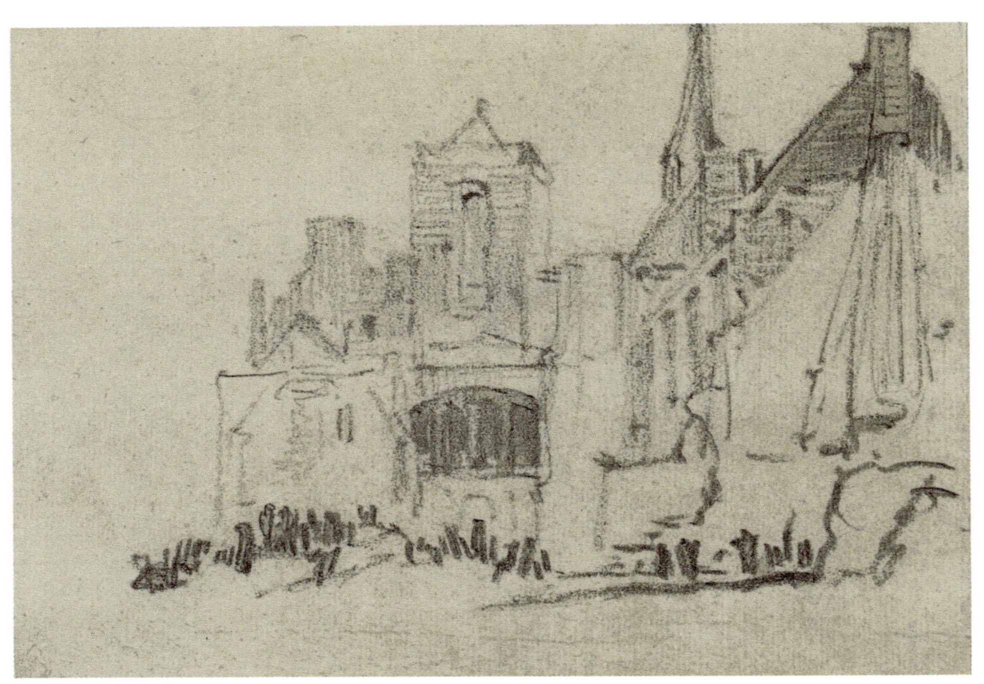

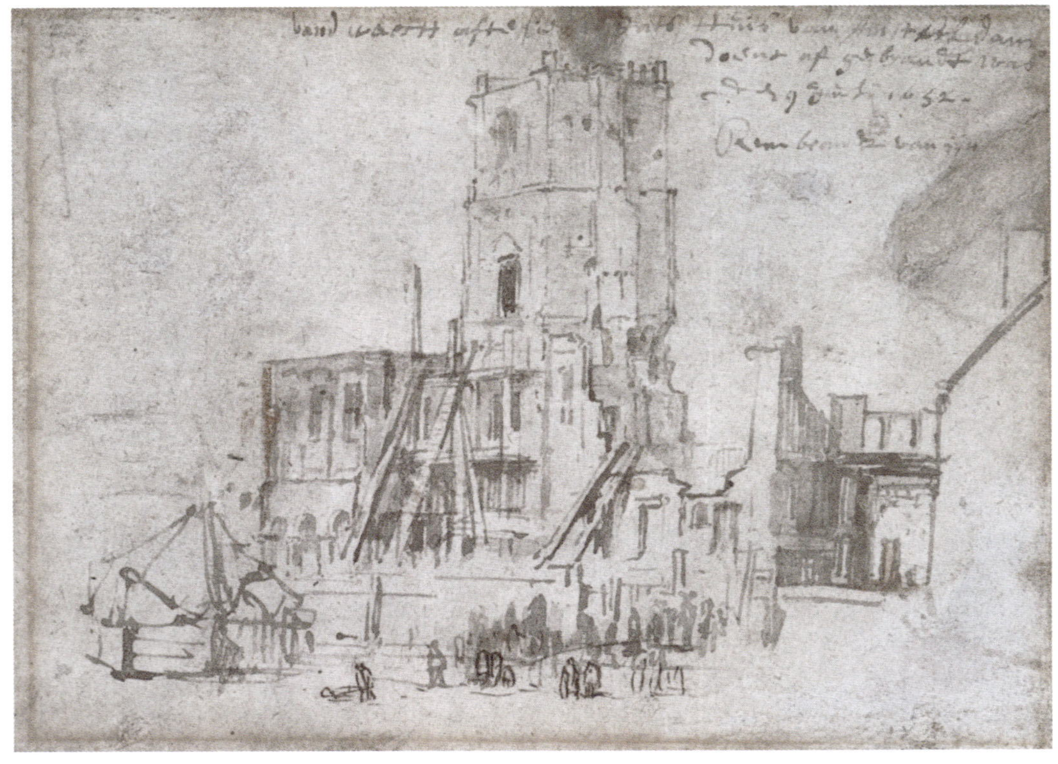

drawing Rembrandt made at the smoldering site two days after the fire is now at the Museum het Rembrandthuis (fig. 12.7). It is inscribed in Rembrandt's own hand: *"as seen from the Weigh-house the Town Hall of Amsterdam / when it burnt down / on 9 July 1652 / Rembrandt van rijn."*[64] The precious sheet is a rare production that does double duty as a written historical document and as a work of art.

In the center of the sketch is the ruined tower, and at the left is the roofless Court of Justice. Scaffolding has already been erected and ladders are in place to facilitate demolition of the ruin. The tentlike structure in the left foreground is the wood-and-canvas temporary quarters of the Exchange Bank, which was hastily built a day after the fire.[65] Even a devastating fire could not stop commercial activity at the Exchange Bank for more than a day in the city that at the time was northern Europe's financial center.

We have seen that Rembrandt made a group of landscape drawings at an attractive site along the Amstel where Kostverloren Manor was situated (see figs. 11.12–15). The manor was very badly damaged by a fire, flood, or storm around 1650; only its tower remained intact. In the late 1650s or early 1660s the ruined manor was acquired by new owners. Except for the tower, they razed it to the ground and rehabilitated the house, incorporating the old tower into the new structure.

Chicago now has Rembrandt's rough pen-and-wash sketch of Kostverloren when it was still in its ruinous state (fig. 12.8). Only a few touches of the pen outline its tower, the

12.6 | *Amsterdam's Old Town Hall Being Demolished*, ca. 1647. Black chalk; 11.3 × 16.1 cm (4½ × 6¼ in.). Graphische Sammlung Albertina, Vienna, inv. 8866. Photo © The Albertina Museum, Vienna.

12.7 | *Amsterdam's Old Town Hall after the Fire*, signed and dated 9 July 1652. Pen and brown ink, some red chalk; 15 × 20.1 cm (5⅞ × 7⅞ in.). Museum het Rembrandthuis, Amsterdam, inv. 245. Photo: The Rembrandt House Museum, Amsterdam.

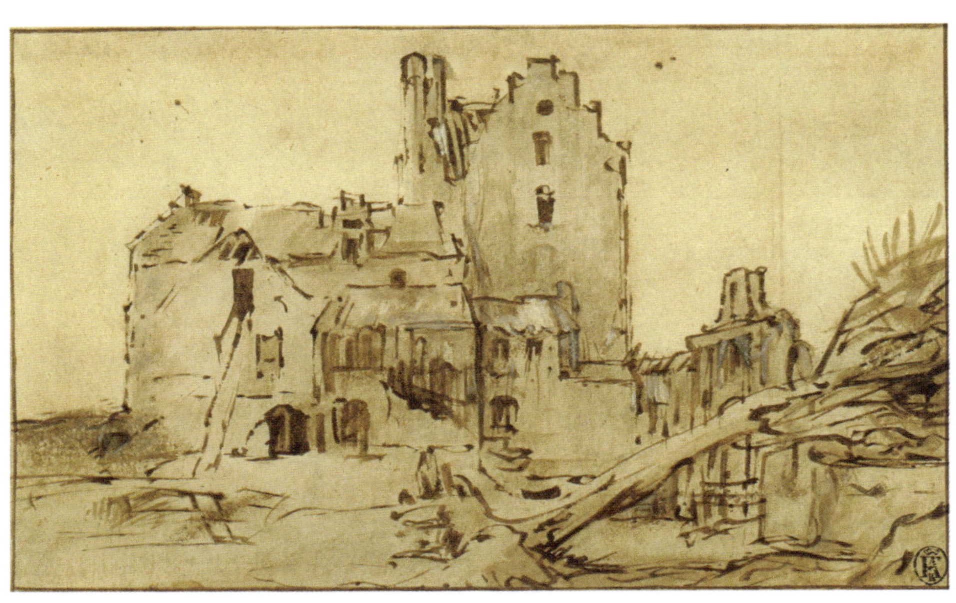

12.8 | *Kostverloren in a Ruinous State*, 1652/57. Pen and brown ink, with brush and brown wash, heightened with touches of white gouache, on cream laid paper; 10.9 × 17.5 cm (4¼ × 6⅞ in.). The Art Institute of Chicago, Clarence Buckingham Collection, inv. 1961.49. Photo © The Art Institute of Chicago.

house's wing, and the gaping holes in its devastated roof. A few more touches indicate rubble and the massive roots of a dead fallen tree in the foreground. Thin washes help define the ruins and its grounds. The tall trees with luxurious foliage that formerly surrounded the house have vanished. In its ruined state the deserted house looks ghostly. Though the connection is accidental, the broad-nibbed pen work of the sketch is found in another drawing by the master that can conjure up ghosts: *Skeleton Rider Mounted on the Skeleton of a Horse* (see fig. 16.8).

A building much closer to Rembrandt's Amsterdam house on Jodenbreestraat than Kostverloren was the Montelbaan Tower built on an embankment of the Oude Schans (Old Entrenchment). It was the most conspicuous monument in his neighborhood. The tower was constructed sometime after 1516 as part of the fortifications outside the walls of Amsterdam. After the city's expansion in 1591–93 brought the tower inside the walls, it lost its original function. In 1606 an octagonal brick structure and elegant, tall wooden spire were added to it. Installation of a prominent clock, vanes, and bells enhanced the addition. The way the tower and its

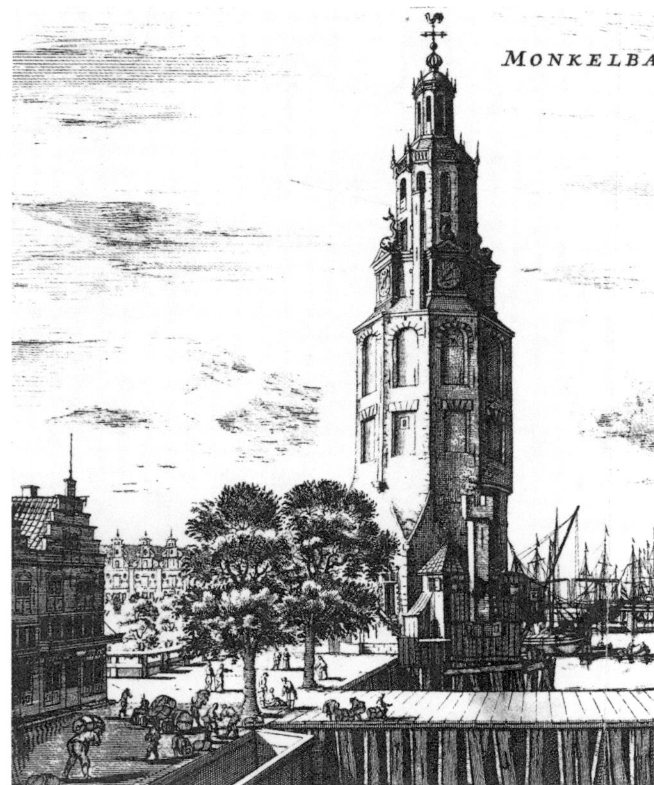

12.9 | Attributed to Jacob van Meurs (Dutch, ca. 1619–ca. 1680), *The Montelbaan Tower*, detail of an engraving in O[lfert]. D[apper]., *Historische beschrijving der Stadt Amsterdam*, Amsterdam, 1663.

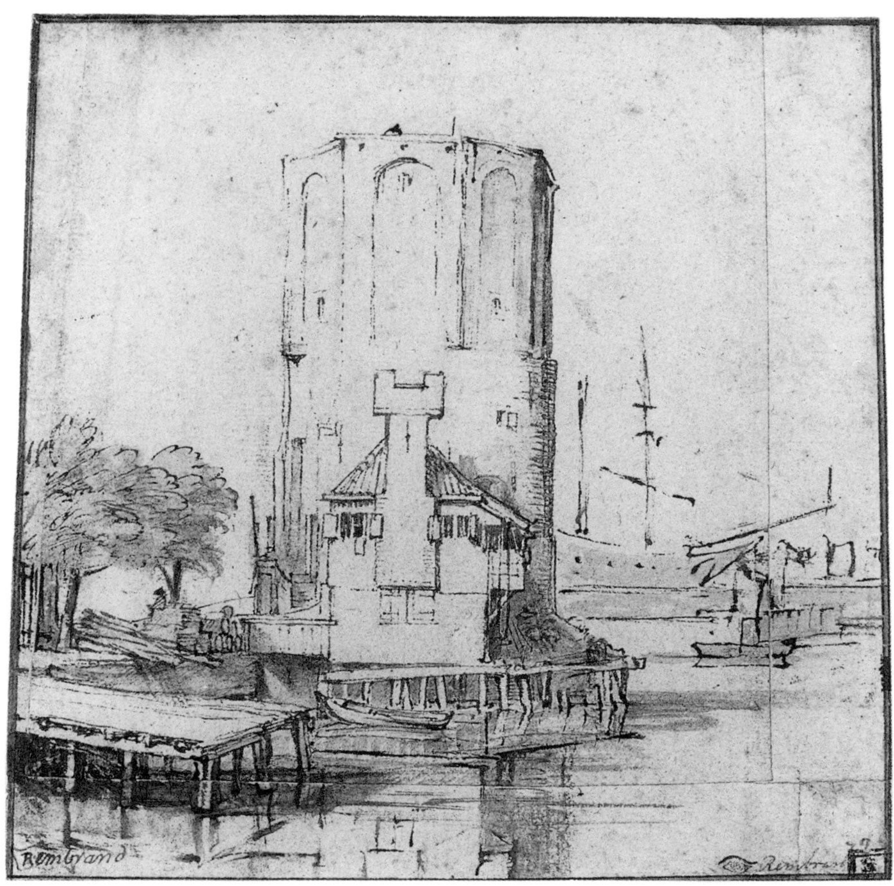

12.10 | *Montelbaan Tower at Amsterdam*, ca. 1644–45. Reed pen and brown ink, brown wash; 14.5 × 14.4 cm (5¾ × 5⅝ in.). Museum het Rembrandthuis, Amsterdam, inv. 244. Photo: The Rembrandt House Museum, Amsterdam.

addition looked in Rembrandt's time—and still does today—is seen in an engraving that appeared in a lavishly illustrated description of Amsterdam published in 1663 (fig. 12.9). But in Rembrandt's reed pen-and-wash drawing of the tower, now at the Museum het Rembrandthuis (fig. 12.10), the grand spire is omitted. He completely ignores it. So does Jacob van Ruisdael in his black chalk-and-wash sketch of the Montelbaan Tower at the Louvre (fig. 12.11).

Rembrandt's drawing of the spireless Montelbaan Tower is datable around 1645. Ruisdael's sketch of it was made about a decade or so later. Was Ruisdael inspired to make the radical change in Amsterdam's well-known landmark by having had a glimpse of Rembrandt's drawing? Although the answer to the question must be speculative, I lean toward a negative response to the query. "Influence" is not the only explanation for similar pictorial decisions.

Yet another question should be posed. Why did both artists omit the spire? There is no cut-and-dried answer to

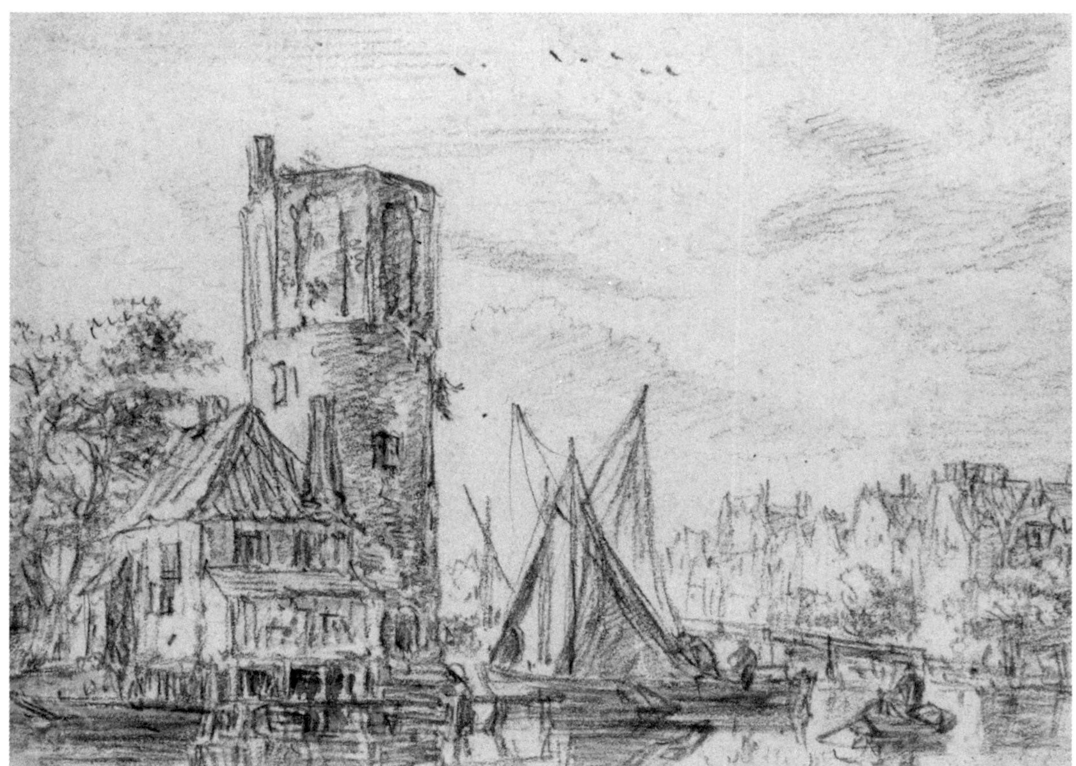

this query either. But it is not news that, like many of their contemporaries, neither artist had an unalterable commitment to making exact transcriptions of existing architectural monuments.

Rembrandt once again showed his preference for depicting ancient buildings without their later additions in his pen drawing, regrettably in less-than-fair condition, of *The "Swigh Utrecht" Tower at Amsterdam*, now at the Rijksmuseum (fig. 12.12; its name means "Utrecht be silent"). The fifteenth-century round castellated tower was originally part of the city's fortified wall. Later a prominent pointed roof was added to the squat tower; Rembrandt omitted the roof in his drawing.

To the left of the tower are a side wall and the chimney of the newly constructed wing of the Kloveniersdolen, the meeting place of Amsterdam's six militia companies. Construction of it was completed in 1636, and in 1642 *The Night Watch* was mounted in its assembly hall. Rembrandt showed little interest in the brand-new building where what was to become his most famous painting hung. He concentrated on the medieval "Swigh Utrecht" Tower stripped of its later addition.

12.11 | Jacob van Ruisdael (Dutch, 1628/29–1682), *Montelbaan Tower at Amsterdam*, ca. 1655–58. Black chalk, gray wash; 14.5 × 19.5 cm (5¾ × 7⅝ in.). Musée du Louvre, Collection Edmond de Rothschild, Paris, inv. 3532DR. Photo © RMN—Grand Palais/ Art Resource, N.Y. Photographer: Madeleine Coursaget.

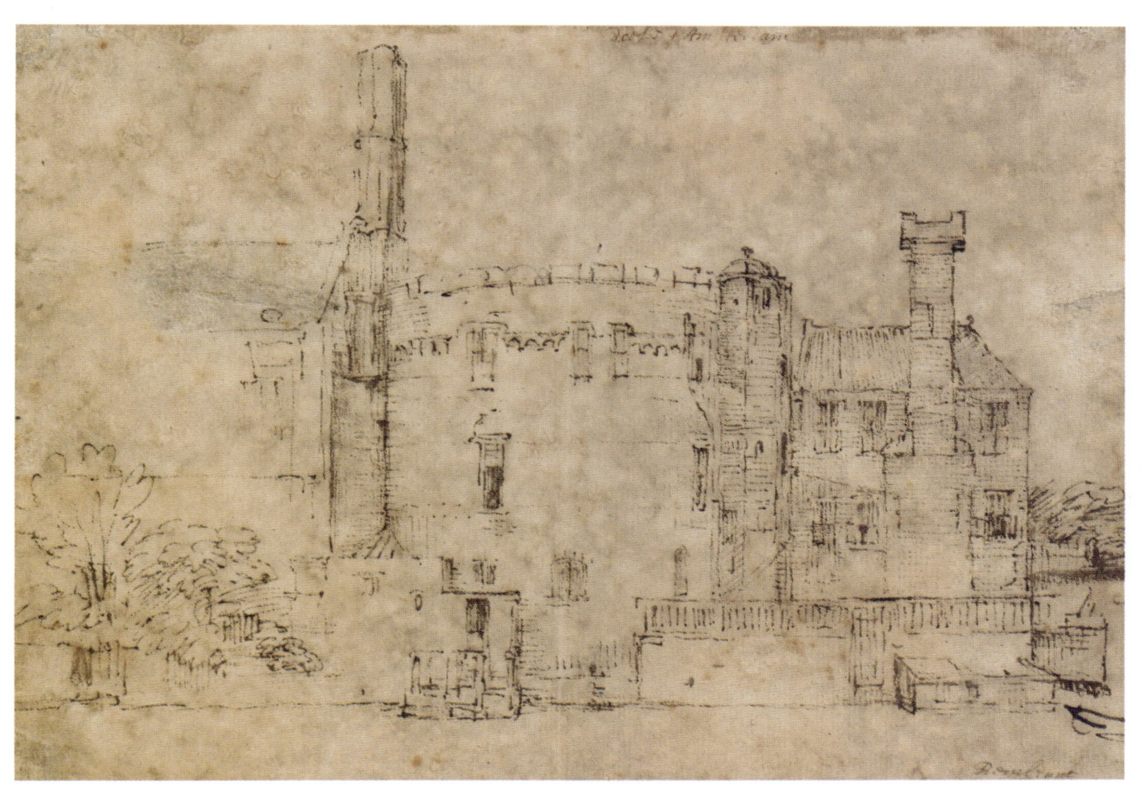

12.12 | *The "Swigh Utrecht" Tower in Amsterdam*, 1650–55. Pen and brown ink, on faded paper; 16.6 × 23.5 cm (6½ × 8⅞ in.). Rijksmuseum, Amsterdam, inv. RP-T-1969-222.

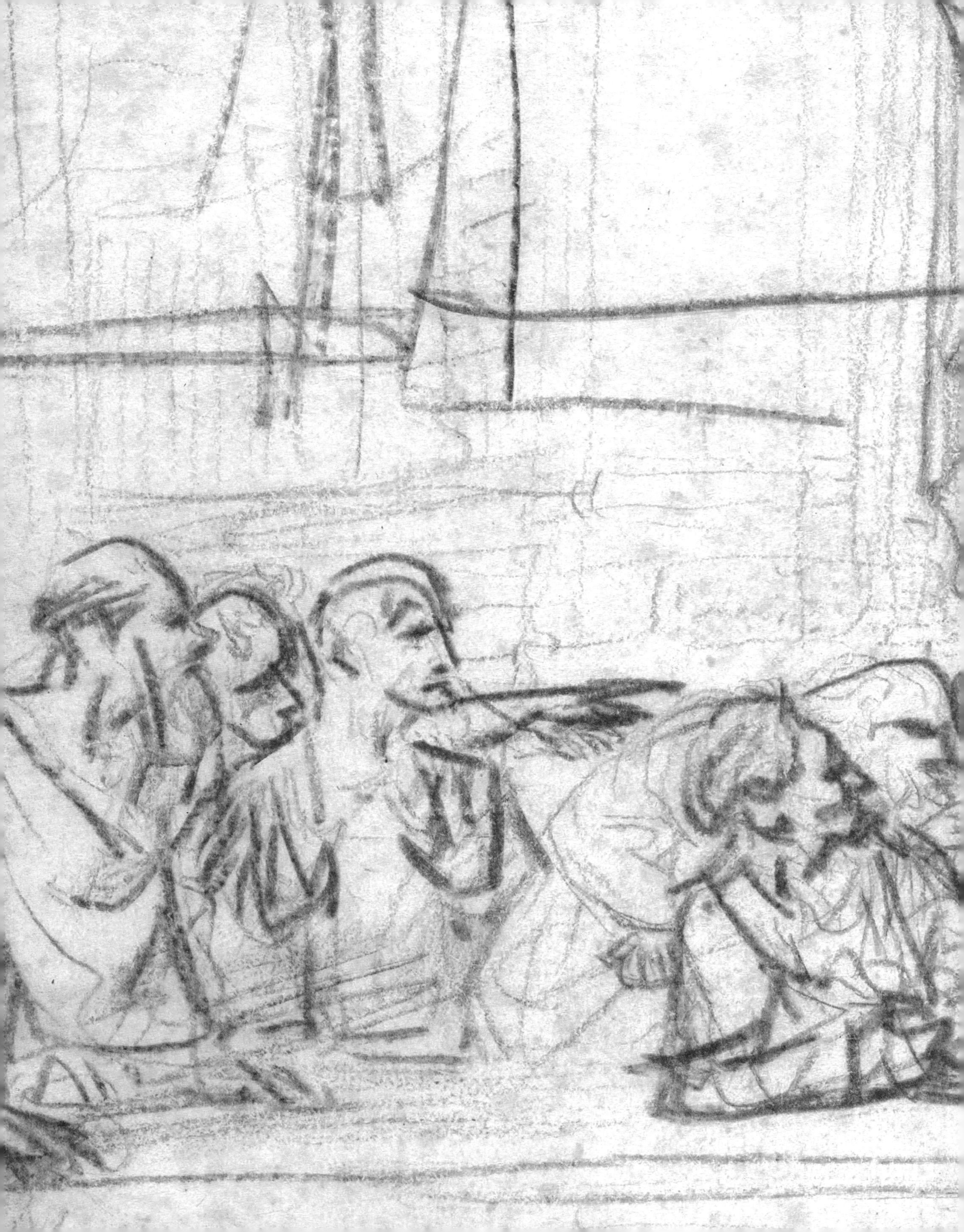

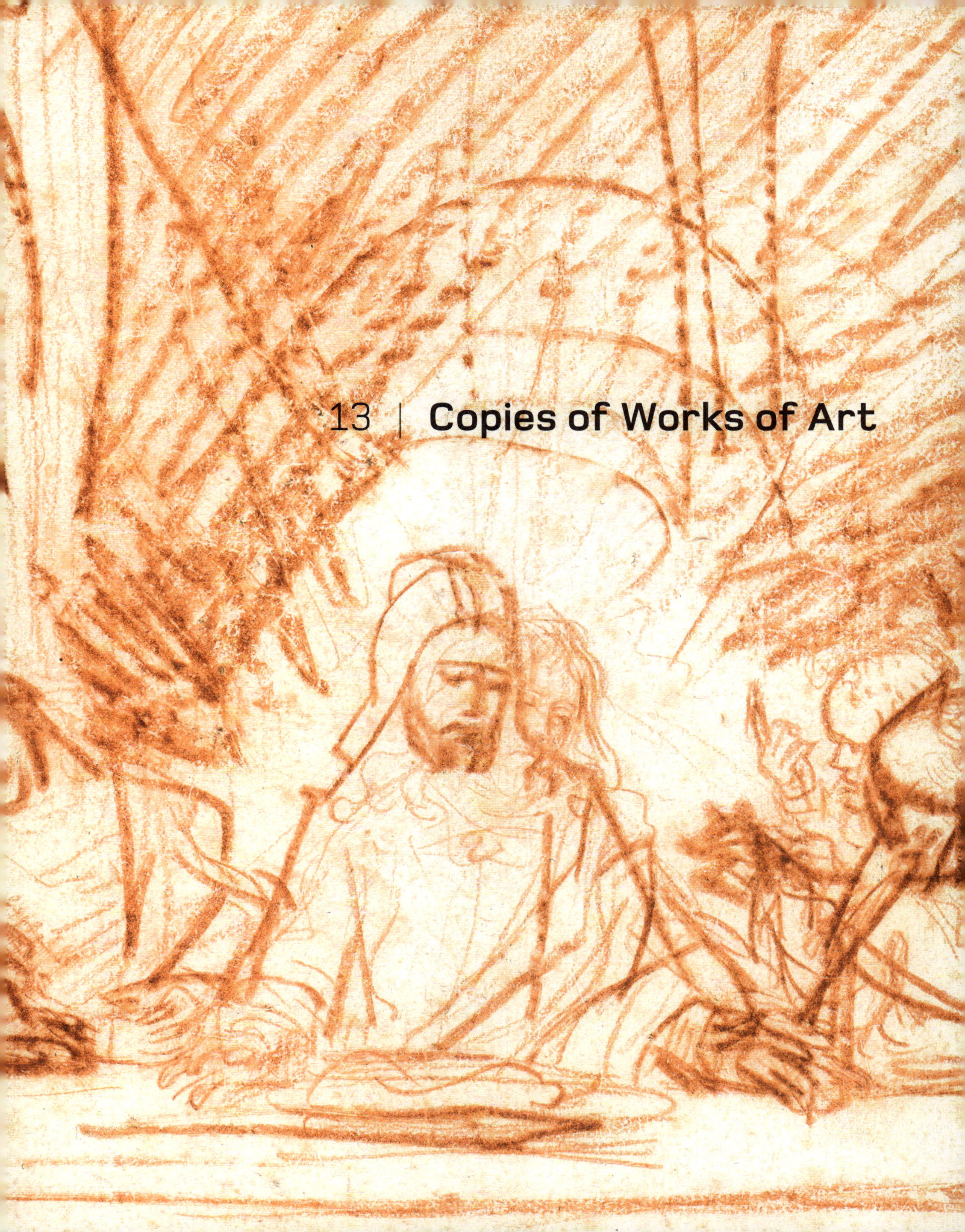

13 | Copies of Works of Art

"IF YOU TELL ME THE NAME of the artist you adore, I will tell you who you are," claimed Max J. Friedländer, the foremost twentieth-century connoisseur of early Netherlandish painting. Even a cursory examination of the works of art in Rembrandt's collection as described in his 1656 inventory indicates that the artist would have had great difficulty giving Friedländer an unqualified answer. His enthusiasm for art created by others was uncommonly diverse.

Sculpture was not wanting in his collection. More than sixty pieces of sculpture are listed, including twelve busts of Roman emperors (not the only evidence that he had more than a passing interest in ancient history). "A child by Michaelangelo" is also cited; it was most probably a partial cast or copy of Michelangelo's group of the Madonna and Child at the Church of Notre Dame in Bruges.

As for paintings and works on paper, apart from the large number that represented various categories of his own work, the range was wide. Among more than 130 paintings were works attributed to masters of the Italian Renaissance and the early Netherlandish school as well as contemporary Dutch artists. The names of Raphael, Jacopo Bassano, Van Eyck (the inventory does not state whether the reference is to Jan or to his brother Hubert), and Lucas van Leyden are listed—we can only guess if some of these attributions were overly optimistic.

Among more recent artists Hercules Segers was particularly well represented by eight paintings (Segers's etching plate of *Tobias and the Angel*, which Rembrandt partially scraped down and transformed into *The Flight into Egypt* not long before the inventory was compiled, is not mentioned). By Adriaen Brouwer there were seven works and a sketchbook. Paintings by Dirck Hals, Jan Lievens, Jan Porcellis, and Simon de Vlieger, among others, are mentioned. Additionally, the inventory offers two items that indicate Rembrandt dabbled in the art market. They state that the Amsterdam dealer Pieter de la Tombe owned a fifty-percent interest in paintings by Giorgione and Palma Vecchio; when the paintings were sold, half the proceeds were due to him.

The graphic section contained prints by Andrea Mantegna and Lucas van Leyden, by Martin Schongauer, Lucas Cranach, and Hans Holbein (although Rembrandt's modest book collection included Dürer's volume on proportions, curiously, any impressions of the preeminent German master's prints are missing). There were engravings after Raphael, Michelangelo, and Titian. The Bolognese school was well represented by Ludovico, Agostino, and Annibale Carracci and by Guido Reni. Netherlanders ranged from Maerten van Heemskerk, Frans Floris, and Pieter Bruegel to Peter Paul Rubens, Anthony Van Dyck, and Jacob Jordaens. Dutch mannerists included Hendrik Goltzius and Abraham Bloemaert.

Rembrandt also had works by his second and by far most influential teacher, Pieter Lastman. He owned two of Lastman's paintings, a book of his pen drawings, and another book that contained red-chalk drawings. Apparently he cherished his holding of works by the artist who played a seminal role in his early decision to become a history painter and from whom he continued to find inspiration in the following decades.

Today we know four of Rembrandt's red-chalk drawings that are copies of Lastman's history paintings. All are datable to around 1635, about a decade after Rembrandt left his teacher's studio. His copy of Lastman's *Susanna Surprised by the Elders*, and the original from which he worked, are illustrated here (figs. 13.1, 13.2). Rembrandt's variations on his study of Lastman's *Susanna* are found in his own *Susanna Bathing*, 1636, at The Hague, and again, more than a decade later, in *Susanna and the Elders*, 1647, now in Berlin.

Rembrandt made quick sketches as well as careful drawings after works in his collection. An example of the former is his pen sketch, now at Berlin (fig. 13.3), of a classical bust he owned, identified in his inventory as "an emperor Galba" (*Een keijser Galba*), that is inscribed [. .]LBA at its base. A version of the bust, traditionally called a portrait of the Roman emperor Servius Sulpicius Galba (3 B.C.–A.D. 69), in Stockholm, shows the same aquiline nose, sunken cheeks, high cheekbones, and bald head (fig. 13.4). The Stockholm bust

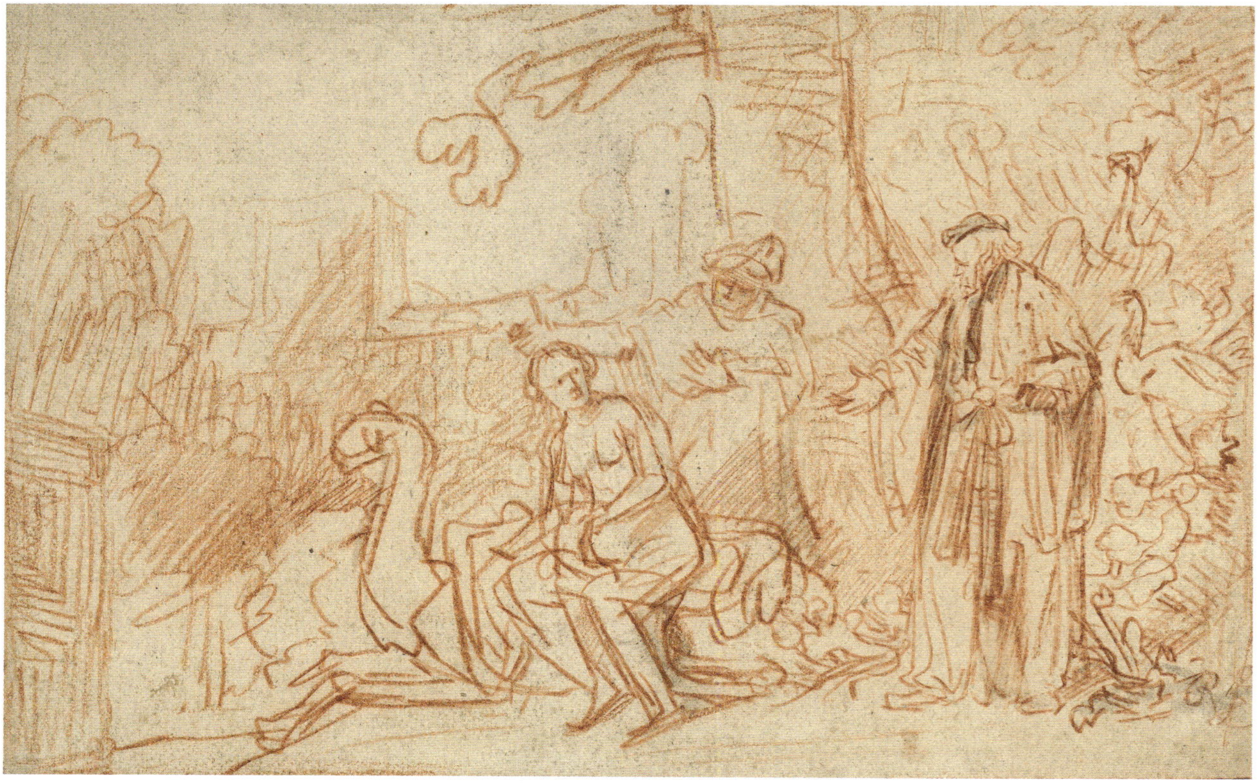

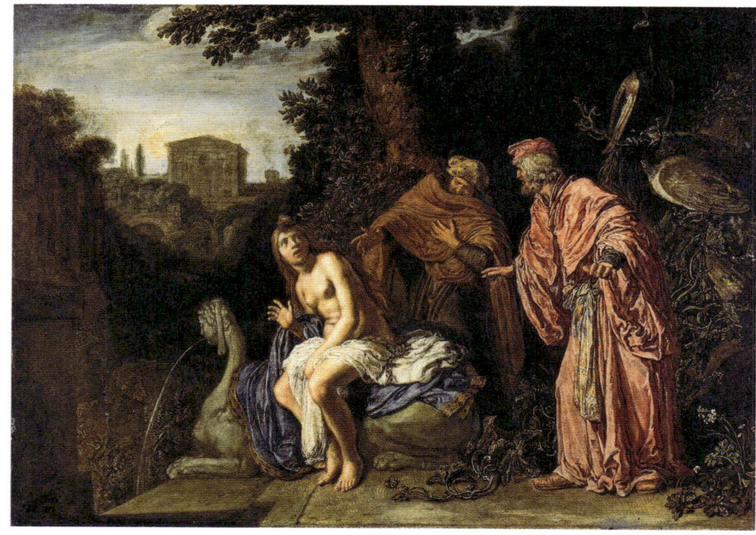

13.1 | *Susanna Surprised by the Elders*, after Pieter Lastman (Dutch, 1583–1633), ca. 1636. Red chalk; 23.5 × 36.4 cm (9¼ × 14⅜ in.). Kupferstich-kabinett, Staatliche Museen, Berlin, inv. KdZ 5296. Photo: Bildarchiv Preussischer Kulturbesitz/Art Resource, N.Y. Photographer: Jörg P. Anders.

13.2 | Pieter Lastman (Dutch, 1583–1633), *Susanna Surprised by the Elders*, signed and dated 1614. Oil on panel; 41 × 58 cm (16⅛ × 22⅞ in.). Gemäldegalerie, Staatliche Museen, Berlin, inv. 1719. Photo: Bildarchiv Preussischer Kulturbesitz/Art Resource, N.Y. Photographer: Jörg P. Anders.

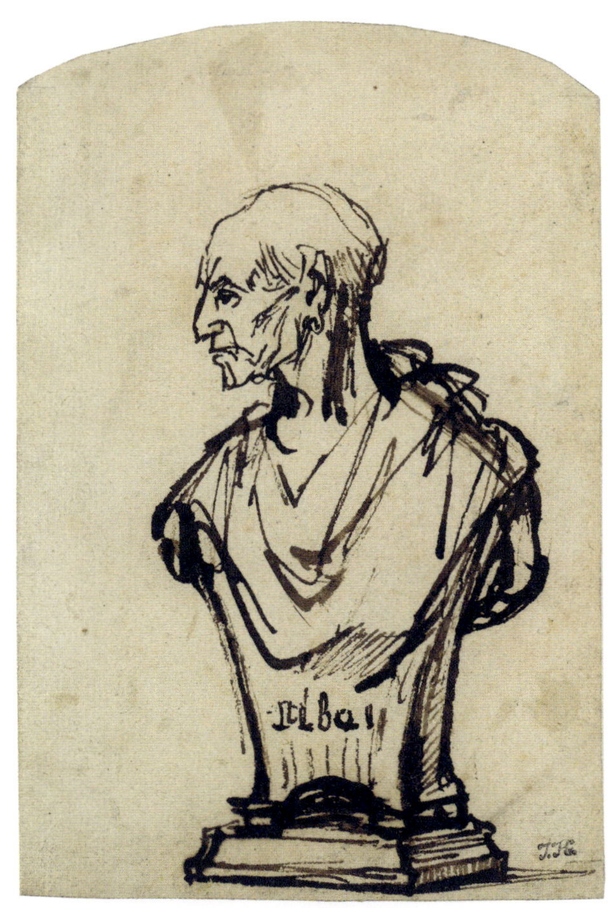

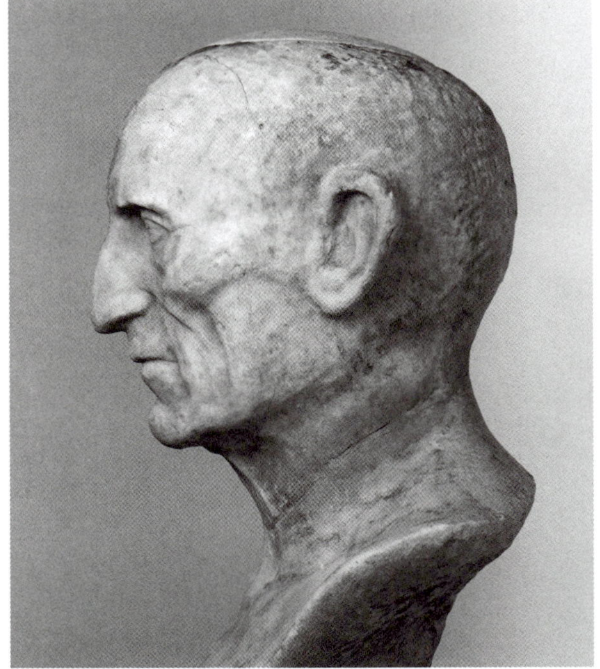

13.3 | *Bust of the Roman Emperor Galba*, ca. 1646–48, after a Roman bust. Pen and brown ink; 14.2 × 9 cm (5⅝ × 3½ in.). Kupferstichkabinett, Staatliche Museen, Berlin, inv. KdZ 15179. Photo: Bildarchiv Preussischer Kulturbesitz/Art Resource, N.Y. Photographer: Jörg P. Anders.

13.4 | Unknown artist, *Bust Presumed to Depict the Roman Emperor Galba*, first century A.D. Marble. Nationalmuseum, Stockholm, inv. SK87. Photo © The National Museum of Fine Arts.

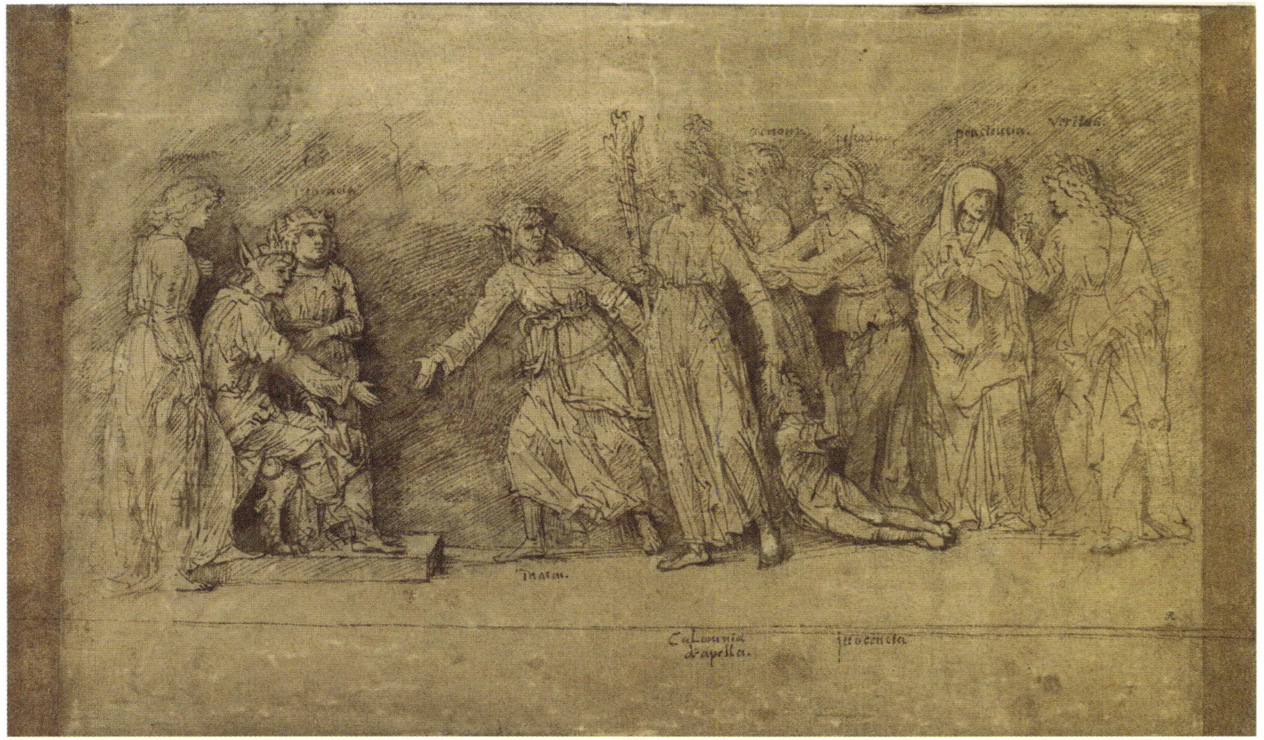

may well be the one Rembrandt owned, but it is an unlikely story that impulsive Queen Christina of Sweden arranged to purchase it at a sale of Rembrandt's effects and had it transported to Stockholm. Christina abdicated the Swedish throne in 1654 and made her first trip to Rome the following year. Both events occurred before the artist's inventory was compiled. By the time it was made and sales were arranged, Christina had abandoned her notion of making Stockholm the "Athens of the North" by importing culture.

A claim has been made that the Stockholm bust does not portray Emperor Galba but is a portrait of a private citizen executed by a sculptor active earlier, during the time of Rome's Republic. Rembrandt's inscription, however, indicates he thought the bust portrayed Galba, and so did later specialists until the identification was challenged in 1962.[66]

Rembrandt's copy of Mantegna's *Calumny of Apelles* in a pen-and-wash drawing on paper, which was prepared with brown wash and extended on each side by a couple of centimeters with different paper and different brown wash, is the artist's most meticulous and elaborate copy (fig. 13.5). The copy and Mantegna's original (fig. 13.6) are both in the collection of the British Museum. Perhaps the original was in

13.5 | *Calumny of Apelles*, after Andrea Mantegna (Italian, ca. 1431–1506), ca. 1652–54. Pen and brown ink, brown wash, on gray-brown paper prepared with wash; 26.3 × 43.2 cm (10 3/8 × 17 in.). The British Museum, London, inv. 1860,0616.86. Photo © The Trustees of The British Museum/Art Resource, N.Y.

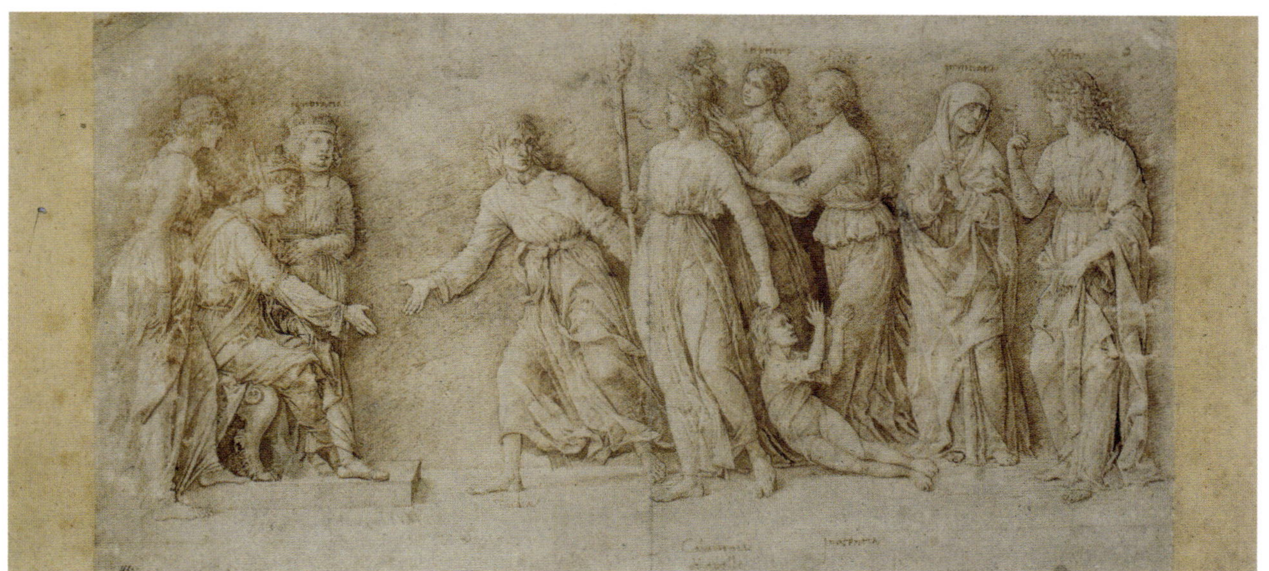

13.6 | Andrea Mantegna (Italian, ca. 1431–1506), *Calumny of Apelles*, ca. 1504–06. Pen and brown ink, heightened with white; 20.6 × 37.9 cm (8⅛ × 14⅞ in.). The British Museum, London, inv. 18,600,616.85. Photo © The Trustees of The British Museum/Art Resource, N.Y.

the book singularly described as "precious," which contained works by Mantegna, that is listed in the 1656 inventory (*'t kostelijcke boeck van Andre de Mantaingie*).[67]

Rembrandt must have had the original before his eyes as he made his close copy of the attitudes, drapery, gestures, and facial expressions of Mantegna's figures. He even imitated Mantegna's Latin inscriptions (although he made a few spelling errors and changes in his transcriptions). He also emulated the quattrocento master's fine pen lines and hatching, but Rembrandt's penmanship is more summary, and the suggestion of light that filters through Mantegna's relief-like composition is surprisingly not found in the copy that can be read as the mature Rembrandt's deeply respectful homage to the older master.

On the reverse side of the copy are various later inscriptions, including a lengthy one by the elder Jonathan Richardson (1667–1745), which relates the story of the calumny of Apelles as told by Lucian.[68] Richardson helpfully identifies the figures in the drawing. King Ptolemy, who stupidly believed the unjustified accusations against Apelles, is shown seated; he has been given ass's ears. Mistrust and Ignorance accompany him. Envy is conducting Calumny, who carries a burning torch and drags the accused Innocence by the hair. The figures exhorting her are Treachery and Deceit. Lastly come Truth and Repentance.

Richardson was a portraitist but is better known as an original art theorist and notable collector of drawings. The

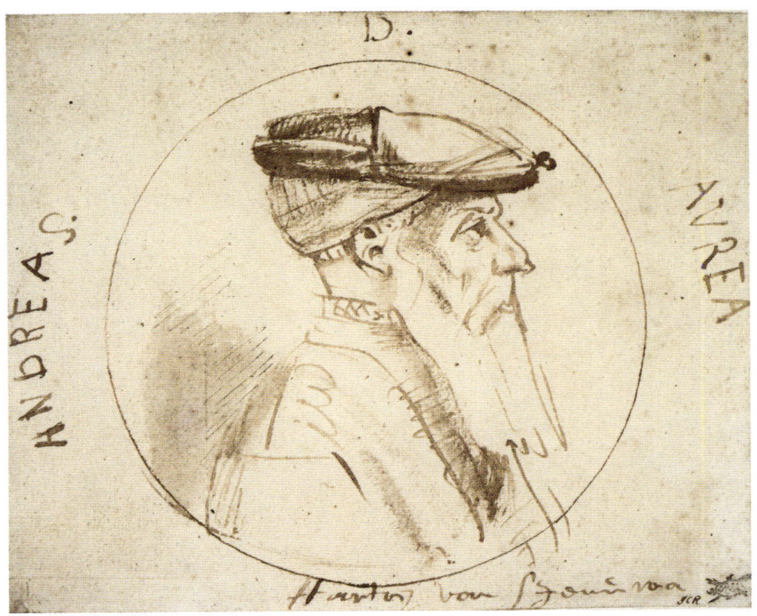

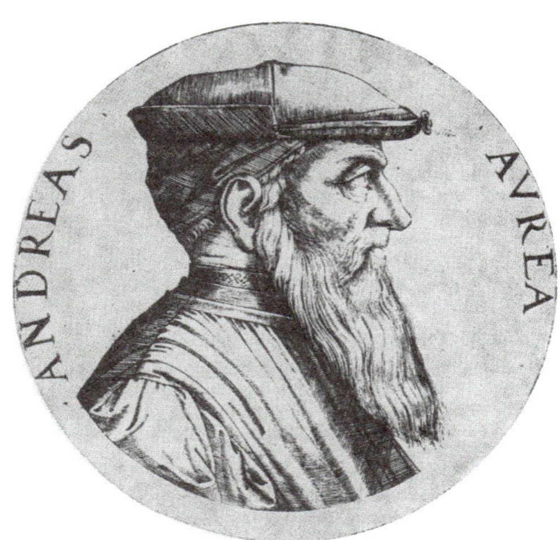

1747 posthumous sale of his drawings lists the staggering number of 120 drawings attributed to Rembrandt, including the artist's copy of Mantegna and a book that contained no less than twenty-five of the artist's copies of Mughal miniatures (for illustrations of two, see figs. 13.17, 13.18).

The pen-and-light-wash profile portrait of Andrea Doria (1466–1560), now in Berlin, is another Rembrandt copy of a Renaissance work, which was in Jonathan Richardson's collection (fig. 13.7). It is inscribed in the artist's hand: "ANDREAS. D. AVREA / *Herzog van S[tad] genuwa*." The source of Rembrandt's copy of a portrayal of the famous Genovese soldier of fortune and admiral is still an open question. Some historians say it is a copy of an unidentified medal or coin, which may have been part of the item listed in the artist's inventory as "A cabinet with medals."[69] It has also been suggested that it may be a copy of an unidentified bas-relief. A third proposal offers an engraved profile portrait of Doria in a tondo of the mid-sixteenth century as its source (fig. 13.8).[70] To be sure, there are congruencies between the two works, particularly in the caps. However, other engraved profile portraits of Doria wearing a similar cap are known,[71] and differences in physiognomy, and in the drawing of the ear, shoulders, and garments, raise some doubts regarding the cited engraving's status as Rembrandt's model.

There is no question whatsoever about the source of Rembrandt's signed red-chalk drawing after Leonardo's

13.7 | *Profile Portrait of Andrea Doria*, ca. 1655–58. Pen and brown ink, brown wash, the circle shaded with red chalk; 16.8 × 20.2 cm (6⅝ × 8 in.). Kupferstichkabinett, Staatliche Museen, Berlin, inv. KdZ 1557. Photo: Bildarchiv Preussischer Kulturbesitz/Art Resource, N.Y. Photographer: Jörg P. Anders.

13.8 | Unknown artist, *Profile Portrait of Andrea Doria*, ca. 1550–1600. Engraving. Biblioteca Marucelliana, Florence. From Bevers 2006, 176.

13.9 | *The Last Supper*, after Leonardo da Vinci (Italian, 1452–1519), ca. 1634. Red chalk, 36.2 × 47.5 cm (14¼ × 18⅝ in.). The Metropolitan Museum of Art, The Robert Lehman Collection, New York, inv. 1975.1.794. Photo copyright © The Metropolitan Museum of Art/Art Resource, N.Y.

13.10 | Giovanni Pietro da Birago (Italian, active 1470–1513), after Leonardo da Vinci (Italian, 1452–1519), *The Last Supper, with a Spaniel*, ca. 1500. Engraving. Kupferstichkabinett, Staatliche Museen, Berlin, inv. 83-24. Photo: Bildarchiv Preussischer Kulturbesitz/Art Resource, N.Y. Photographer: Jörg P. Anders.

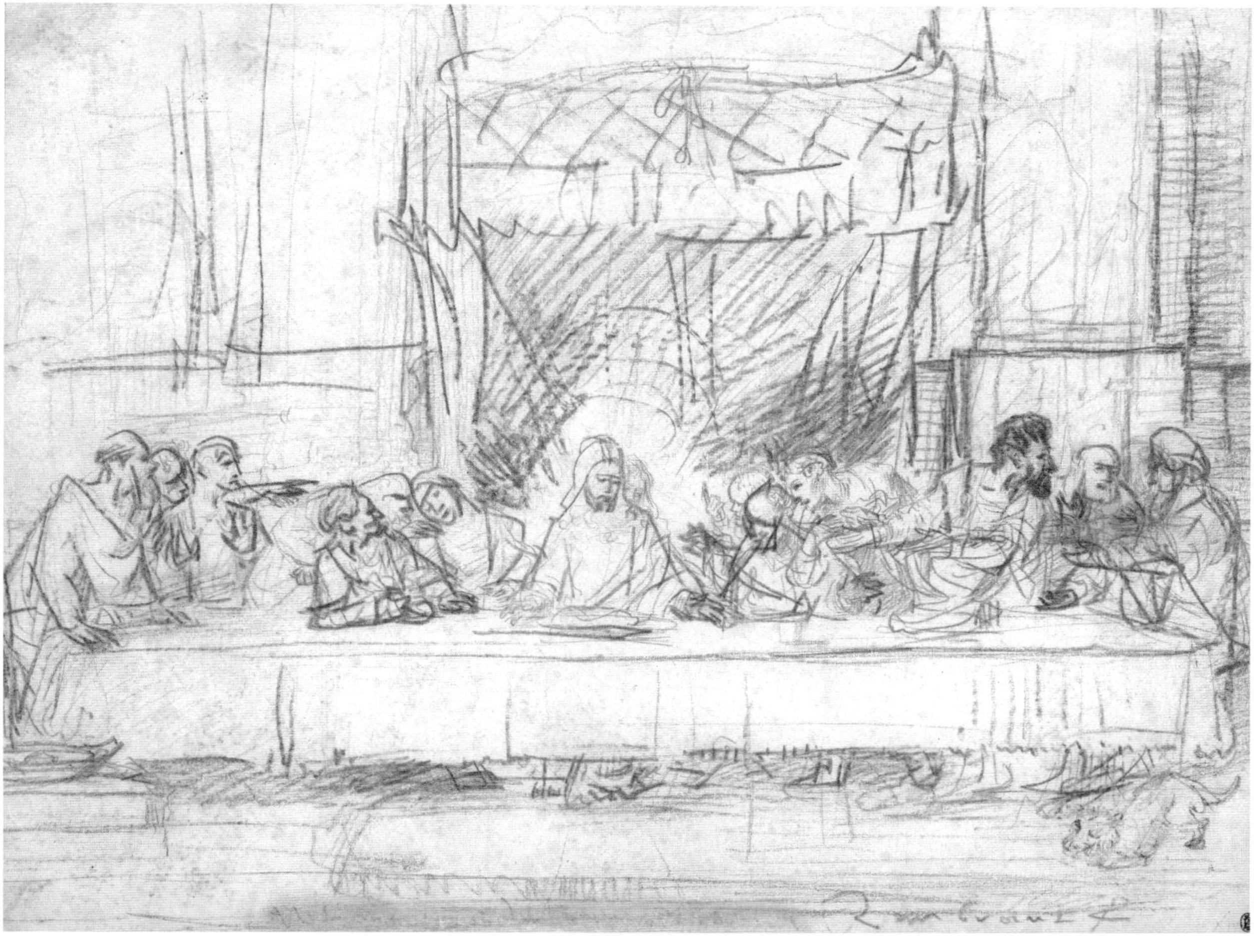

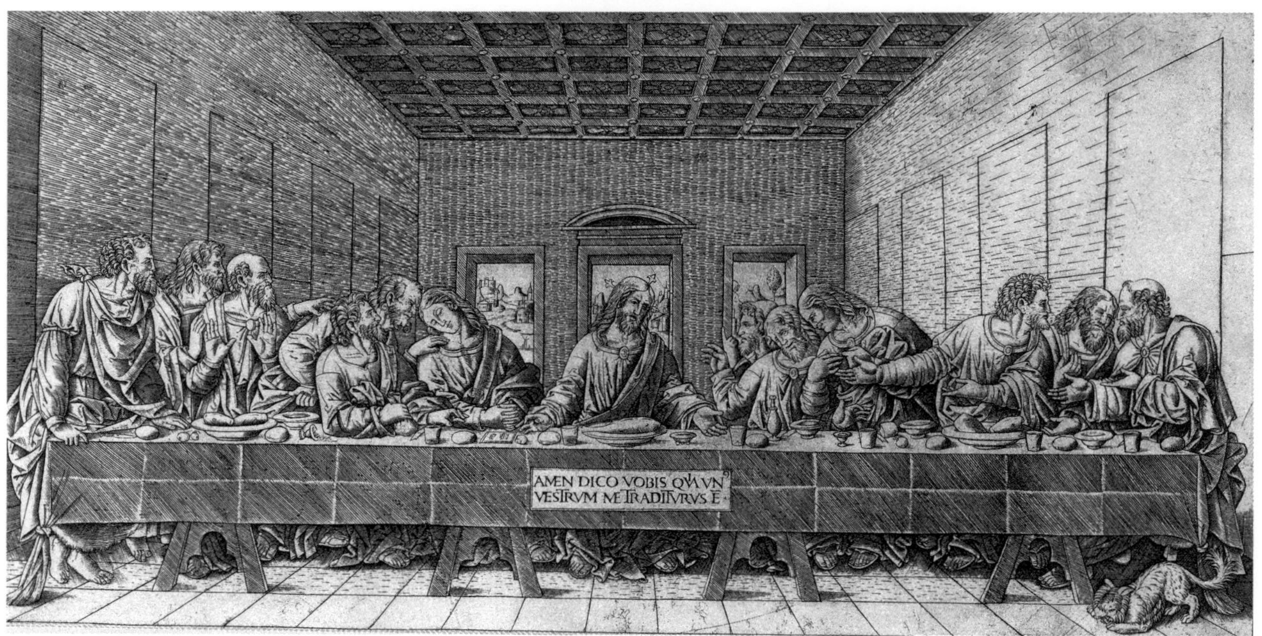
AMEN DICO VOBIS QVA VN
VESTRVM ME TRADITVRVS E

Last Supper, now at the Metropolitan Museum (fig. 13.9). The sheet, which is the artist's largest surviving drawing, is based on Giovanni Pietro da Birago's engraving of Leonardo's fresco in Milan (fig. 13.10). Birago introduced a playful spaniel into the right foreground in his print of the well-known work. The dog likewise appears in Rembrandt's copy.

After making a light sketch in hard red chalk of all the figures at the table, Rembrandt reworked them with powerful strokes of softer red chalk to stress each disciple's response to Christ's word that one of them would betray him (John 13:23). In the drawing Leonardo's deep room is radically transformed into a shallow space with curtained walls and a huge off-center canopy behind Christ's radiant figure. Among later reminiscences in the artist's work of this great drawing, datable about 1635, the most pronounced echoes are found in his painting of *The Supper at Emmaus* of 1648 at the Louvre and his 1654 etching of the same subject.

Two other drawings by Rembrandt that are variations on Leonardo's composition have survived. One, in the British Museum, also in red chalk, makes changes in the details of the six figures to the left of Christ (fig. 13.11); the artist's cropped signature is seen, lower left. The figures have been rearranged into two groups of three. Rembrandt's starting point for the rearrangement was not Birago's engraving, but a drawing, now at Chatsworth (or a now-unknown version of it), by the Flemish artist Pieter Soutman, who used it for his engraving of Leonardo's *Last Supper* after a lost design by Rubens. Possibly Rembrandt owned Soutman's drawing or a version of it.

Rembrandt's other variation on Leonardo's masterpiece is Berlin's pen sketch of the total composition (fig. 13.12). Here he departs from Leonardo by radically breaking his rigid symmetry and greatly intensifying the movement of all of the disciples. Not only by signing the Berlin variation but also by dating it 1635 (the year of execution is not found on his other copies), perhaps he was announcing that it was his final statement on the subject. In any event, depiction of the Last Supper is not found again in his oeuvre in any medium.[72]

If Rembrandt wanted to absorb aspects of Leonardo's achievement, he had to employ reproductions of his works. He never made a first-hand examination of any of them, for he never traveled to Italy. In fact, apart from a supposed trip to England that has generated occasional fevers of speculation,[73] to our knowledge, during the course of his life, he never crossed the border of his small country.

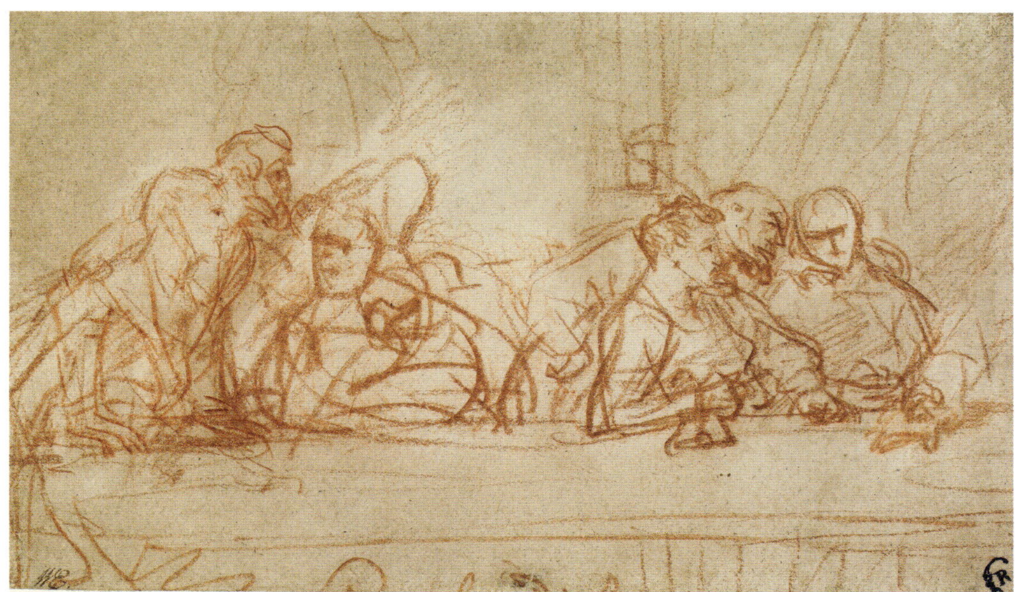

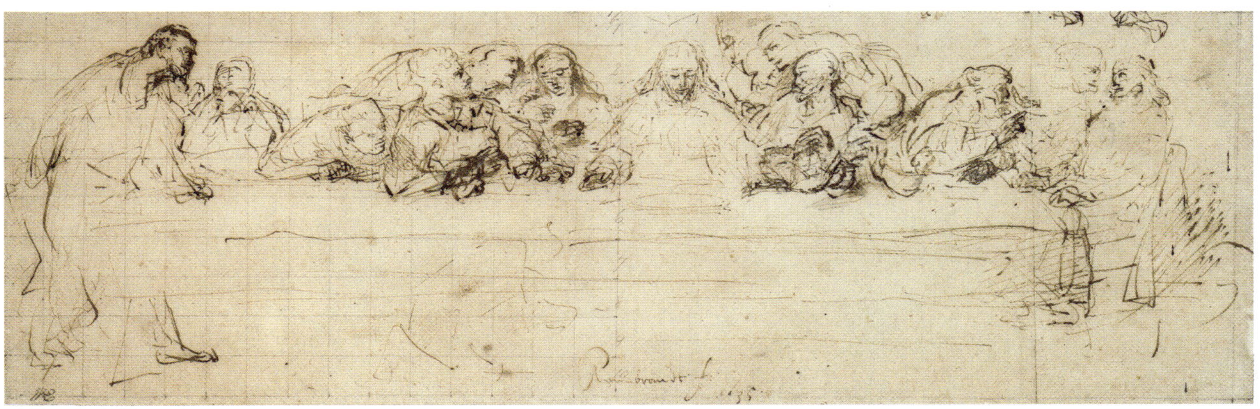

13.11 | *The Last Supper*, after Leonardo da Vinci (Italian, 1452–1519), signed with a signature that is cropped, ca. 1634. Red chalk, heightened with white, on paper probably washed with pale grayish brown; 12.5 × 21 cm (4⅞ × 8¼ in.). The British Museum, London, inv. 1900,0611.7. Photo © The Trustees of The British Museum/Art Resource, N.Y.

13.12 | *The Last Supper*, after Leonardo da Vinci (Italian, 1452–1519), signed and dated 1635. Pen and brown ink, brown wash, white, a few traces of red chalk; 12.5–12.9 × 38.5 cm (4⅞–5⅛ × 15⅛ in.). Kupferstichkabinett, Staatliche Museen, Berlin, inv. KdZ 3769. Photo: Bildarchiv Preussischer Kulturbesitz/Art Resource, N.Y. Photographer: Jörg P. Anders.

This was not the case for brilliant Constantijn Huygens, who knew Europe well. He spent more than half a century in the political service of the House of Orange. We have heard that, as Frederik Henry's secretary, he corresponded with Rembrandt about his commission to paint a series of five Passion pictures for the stadholder, and there is reason to believe Huygens procured the important job for him. In about 1630 Huygens began to write an autobiography, which, among other things, singles out Rembrandt and his friend Jan Lievens, who were not yet twenty-five years old, as artists who were on a par with the most famous painters. The autobiography also relates that Huygens suggested that they should go to Italy to study, for, if they became familiar with the works of Raphael and Michelangelo, they would reach the height of painting. They famously replied that now, in the flower of their

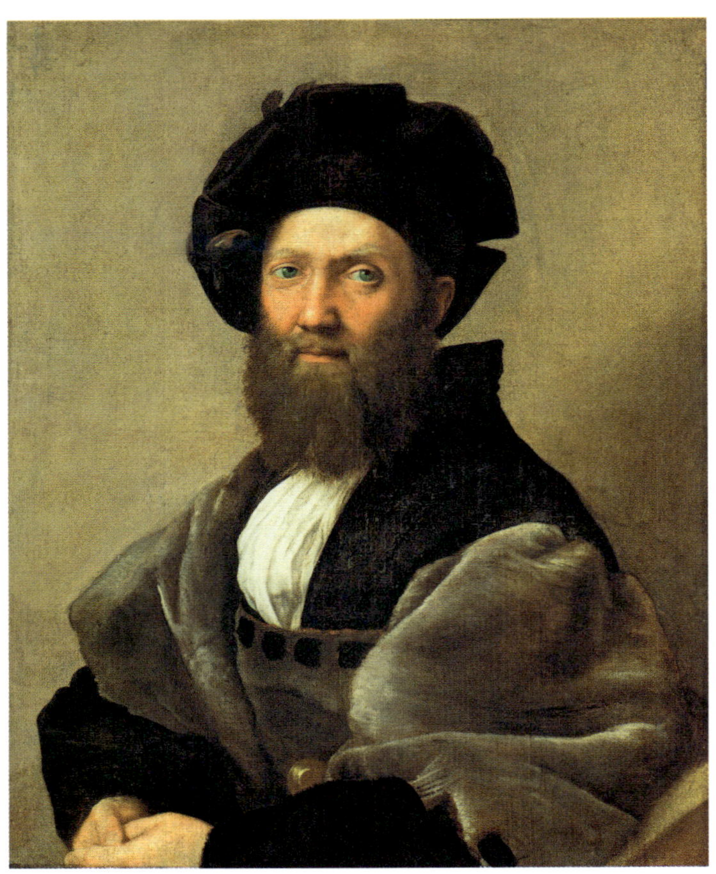

youth, they had no time for travel. Moreover, they added, the finest Italian works can be seen in Holland. Huygens, ever the diplomat, did not respond "nonsense," but the thought may have crossed his mind. He certainly knew that no contemporary Dutch collection could boast that it possessed Italian paintings that ranked with the finest.

To be sure, during Rembrandt's lifetime Amsterdam had a flourishing art market, and whenever superior paintings and works on paper appeared, they created a stir. Rembrandt was an active bidder at Amsterdam's auctions on more than one occasion. A minor sensation was created in the city when it was announced that the famous collection of Lucas van Uffelen, a merchant who had lived in Venice for many years, was scheduled for auction on 9 April 1639. The major accent in his sale was Raphael's *Portrait of Baldassare Castiglione*, now at the Louvre (fig. 13.13). It was purchased by Alfonso Lopez, a collector and agent of the French crown, who had a residence in the city at the time. Lopez already owned two masterworks by Titian: the so-called *Portrait of Ariosto* and *Flora* (the for-

13.13 | Raphael (Italian, 1483–1520), *Portrait of Baldassare Castiglione*, ca. 1514–15. Oil on canvas, 82 × 67 cm (32¼ × 26⅜ in.). Musée du Louvre, Paris, inv. 611. Photo: Erich Lessing/Art Resource, N.Y.

13.14 | *Portrait of Baldassare Castiglione*, after Raphael (Italian, 1483–1520), 1639. Pen and brown ink, white; 16.3 × 20.7 cm (6⅜ × 8⅛ in.). Graphische Sammlung Albertina, Vienna, inv. 8859. Photo: Erich Lessing/Art Resource, N.Y.

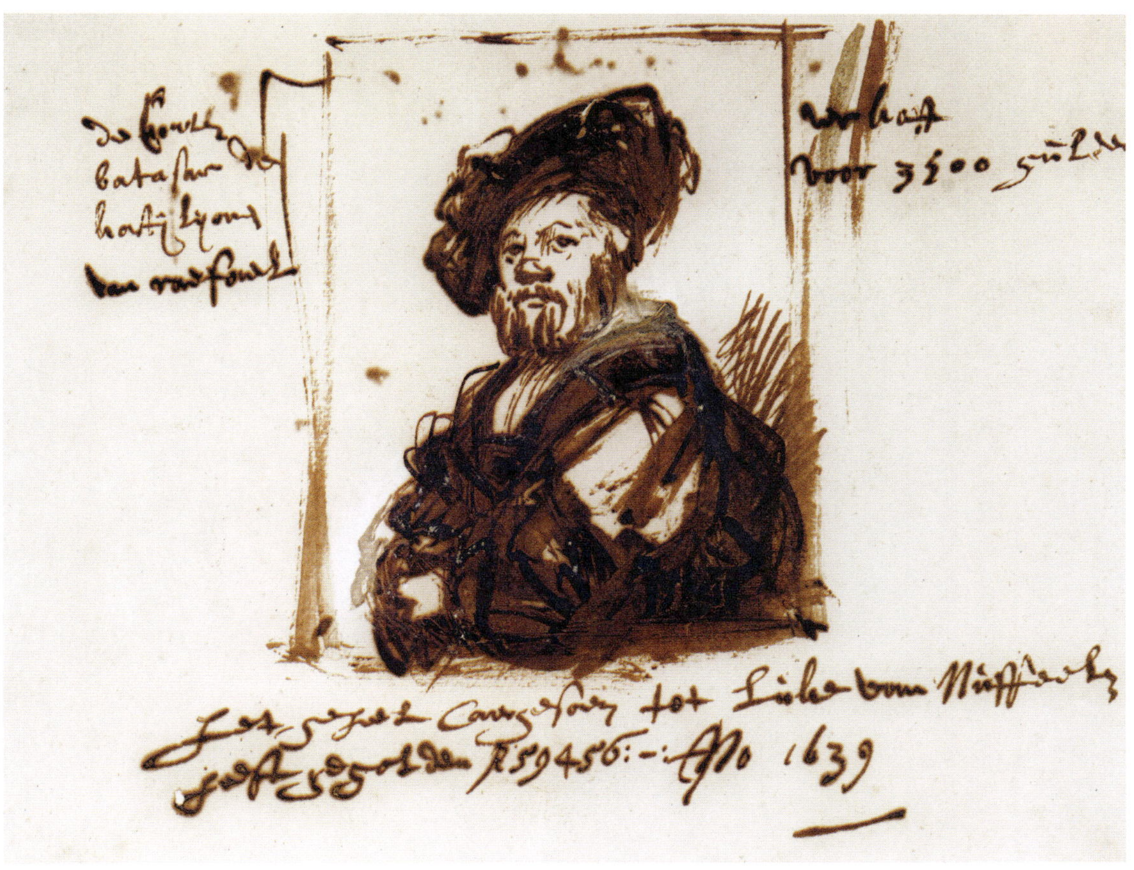

mer is now in the National Gallery, London, and the latter in the Uffizi).

The Albertina has a quick pen sketch Rembrandt made after Raphael's Castiglione, apparently at the sale. He made some changes in his copy (fig. 13.14), particularly in the angle of Castiglione's beret. The copy is inscribed in the artist's own hand. On the left he wrote: *"the Count Baldassare Castiglione by Raphael"*; on the right: *"sold for 3500 guilders"*; below: *"the whole cargo of Lucas van Nuffeelen* [sic] *fetched 59,456 guilders. Anno 1639."*[74] A measure of the value Amsterdam's art market placed on the Raphael in 1639 is obtained when we recall that three years later, when Rembrandt was at the height of his popularity as a face painter, he received about 1,600 guilders from sixteen civic guards as payment for their life-size portraits in *The Night Watch*.

It is well known that Rembrandt's copy of Castiglione had an impact on his celebrated 1639 etched *Self-portrait* (fig. 13.15). The influence of it, as well as of Titian's so-called *Portrait of Ariosto*, on the artist's 1640 painted *Self-portrait*

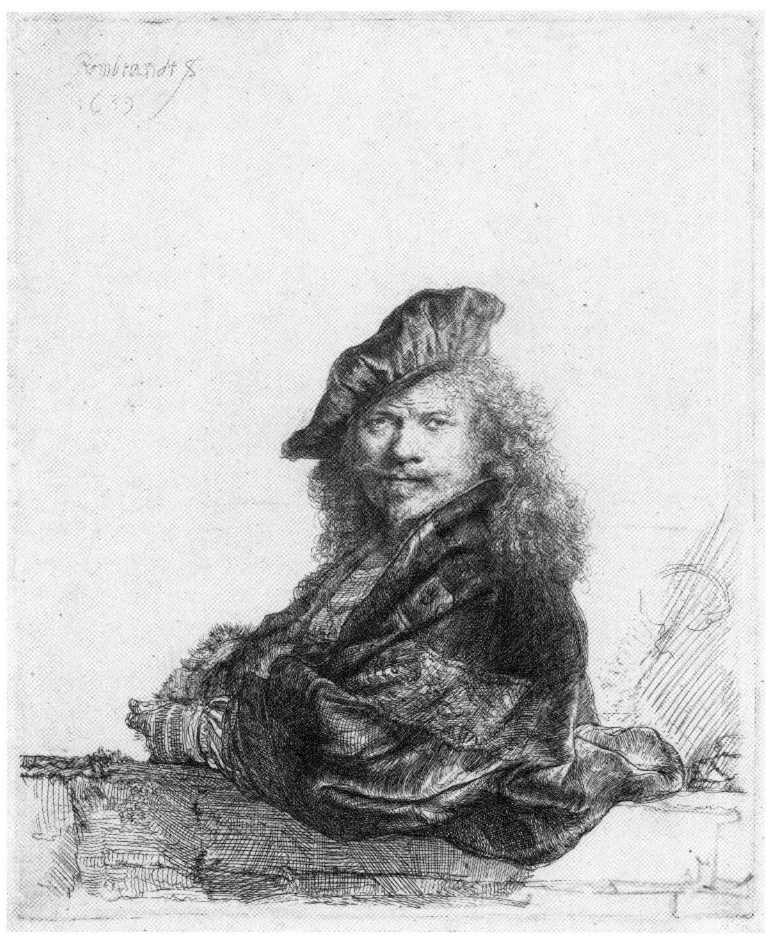

at the National Gallery, London, has also frequently been cited. Titian's so-called *Ariosto* was easily accessible to Rembrandt in Lopez's collection. The Venetian master's *Flora* was too. Proof that the Dutchman learned from it is offered by his 1641 painting of *Saskia as Flora*, at Dresden.

After the early 1640s Rembrandt's interest in Titian did not wane. On the contrary. In what I can only call an occult way, more than a few of his mature paintings reflect the Venetian master's mood, coloristic splendor, and technique. The resemblance between his mature drawn and etched landscapes and those by Titian is perhaps easier to explain by the reference in his inventory to "One ditto [book] very large, with almost all the works of Titian."[75] The book almost certainly was comprised of engravings as well as woodcut reproductions of his landscapes and other works.

13.15 | *Self-portrait Leaning on a Stone Sill*, signed and dated 1639. Etching; 20.6 × 16.4 cm (8⅛ × 6½ in.). Rijksmuseum, Amsterdam, inv. RP-P-OB-37.

Possibly the book also included Titian's original pen drawing depicting a characteristic Venetian Renaissance

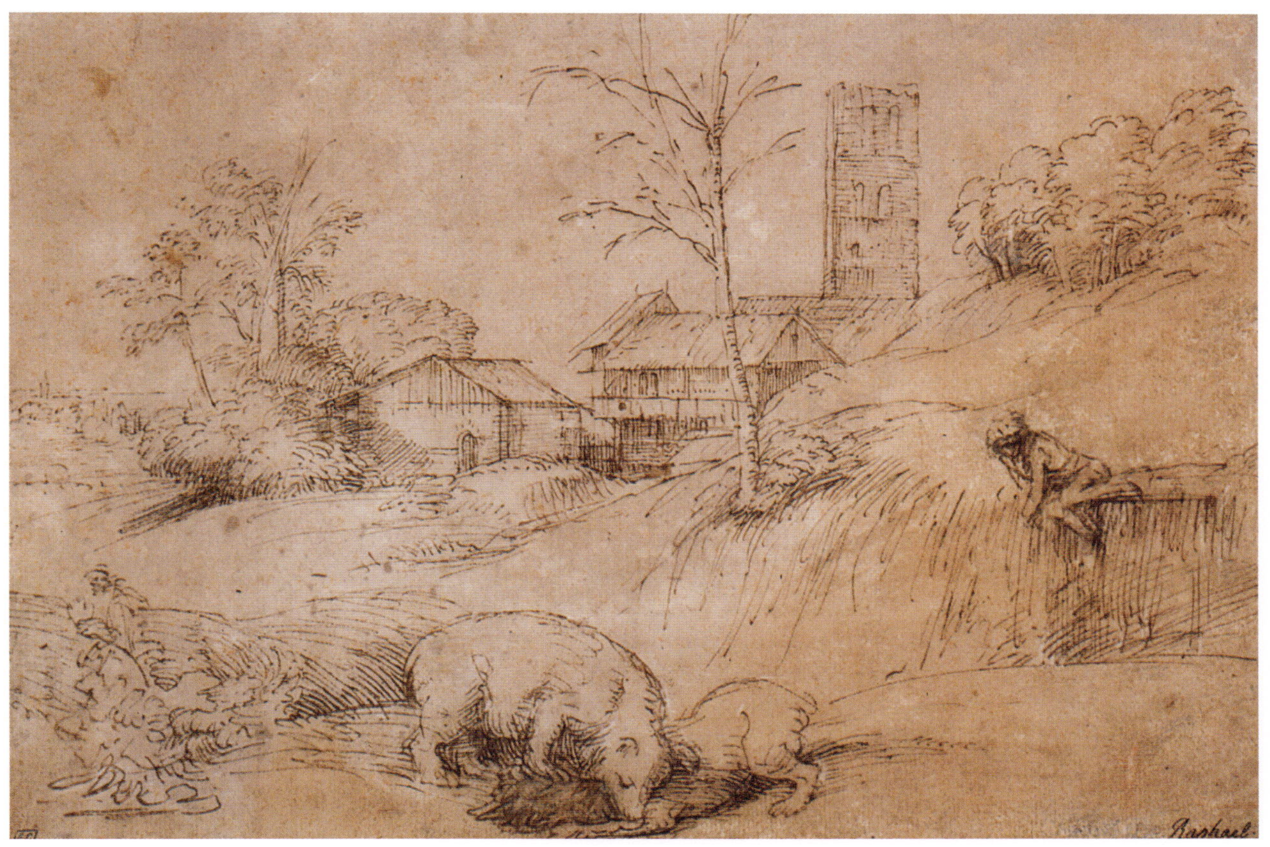

13.16 | *Landscape with a Bear*, after Titian (Italian, ca. 1488–1576), ca. 1650–53. Pen and brown ink, some corrections in white; 20.3 × 29.4 cm (8 × 11⅛ in.). Fondation Custodia, Collection Frits Lugt, Paris, inv. 6584.

landscape with a tower and farm building, before which a bear fights with a goat. Titian's original is now lost, but copies of it exist, including one by Rembrandt, now at Fondation Custodia (fig. 13.16). Before Christopher White published it as a drawing by our artist, it was attributed to Titian himself. White put what Rembrandt derived from his study of Titian's sketch in a nutshell: "[It] was not so much a way of drawing, as a type and mood of landscape which in his own works were no mere background but became an expression of the spirit of the subject he was illustrating."[76] A fine example of the landscape lesson he learned from Titian, or perhaps members of his circle, is seen in his etching of *Saint Jerome Reading in an Italian Landscape* (see fig. 15.6).

Rembrandt's most exotic copies are his late pen-and-wash drawings on Japanese paper,[77] sometimes lightly touched with colored chalk and watercolor, after seventeenth-century Mughal miniatures (figs. 13.17, 13.18). At least twenty-six of them are precious possessions of various collections today. Twenty-four can be identified as sheets that were, as we have heard, part of the book comprising twenty-five copies of the miniatures that appeared in Jonathan Richardson's 1747 posthumous sale. A few have earlier provenances.

The large group has often been identified as part of an item described in the 1656 inventory as a book "filled with curious drawings in miniature as well as woodcuts and engravings on copper of various costumes."[78] This identification is not certain, however. It has been noted that in Rembrandt's time works of the type he copied were usually specifically identified as "Mogolse," "Suratse," or "Oost-Idiaanse" miniatures.[79]

In the eighteenth century some of the miniatures Rembrandt studied were incorporated into the wall decoration of the "Millionenzimmer," a room in Schönbrunn Palace in Vienna. Comparison of the originals that can be identified as models indicate that Rembrandt's copies include radical alterations in perspective, background, color, and numerous details. His highly personal interpretations are freer and more sketchlike than his models. As usual, he worked directly. There is not a trace of underdrawing, fumbling, or groping. Few works among his copies of drawings match their surety and delicacy of line.

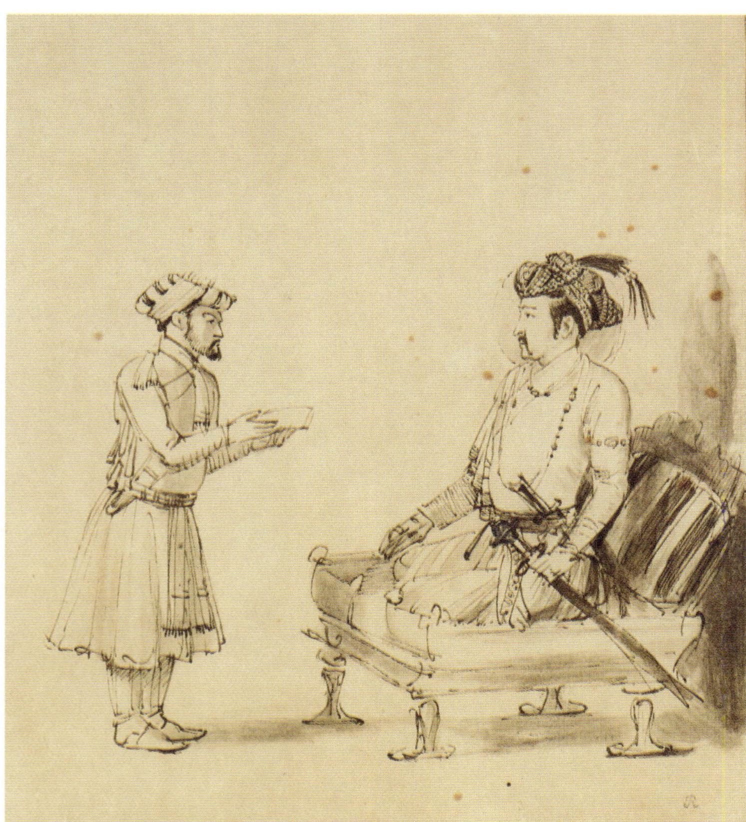

13.17 | *Emperor Jahangir* (ruled 1605–28) *Receiving an Officer*, after a Mughal miniature, ca. 1655–60. Pen and brown ink, brown and gray wash, touches of white, on Japanese paper; 21 × 18.4 cm (8¼ × 7¼ in.). The British Museum, London, inv. Gg,2.263. Photo © The Trustees of The British Museum/Art Resource, N.Y.

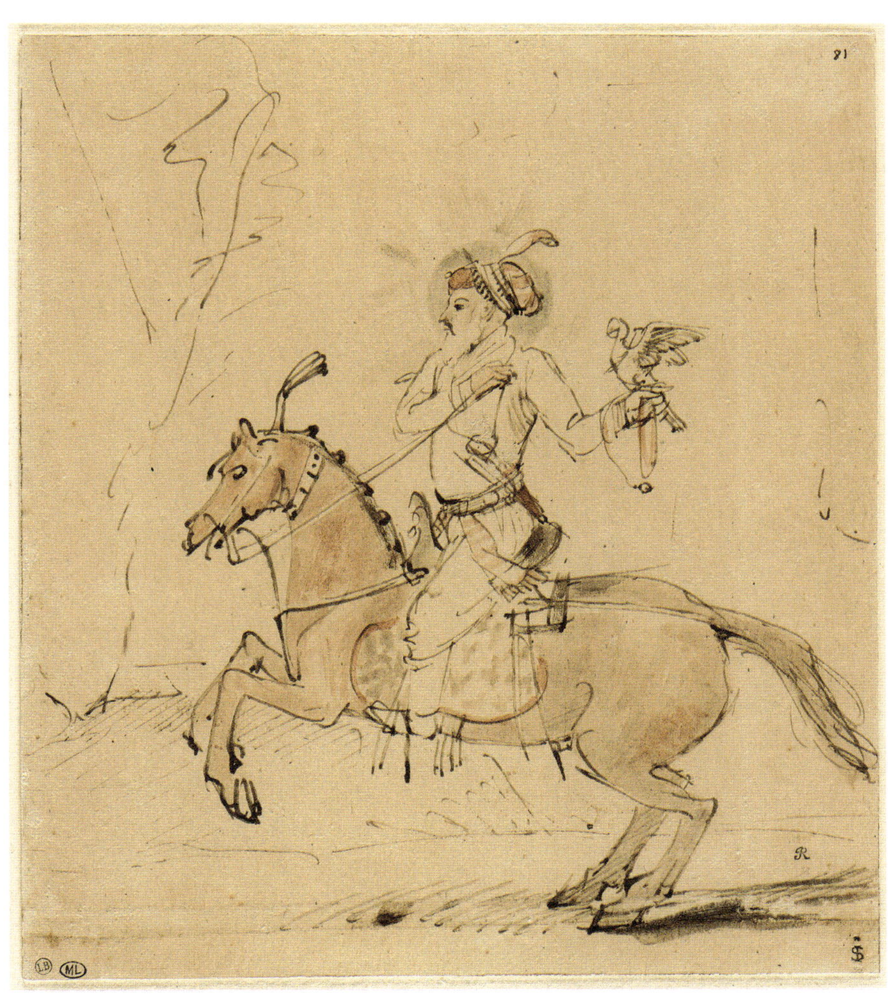

13.18 | *Shah Jahân on Horseback, Holding a Falcon on His Left Fist*, after a Mughal miniature, ca. 1655–60. Pen and brown ink, brown wash, watercolor, on Japanese paper; 21.9 × 19.2 cm (8⅝ × 7½ in.). Musée du Louvre, Paris, inv. RF4733. Photo © RMN—Grand Palais/Art Resource, N.Y. Photographer: Franck Raux.

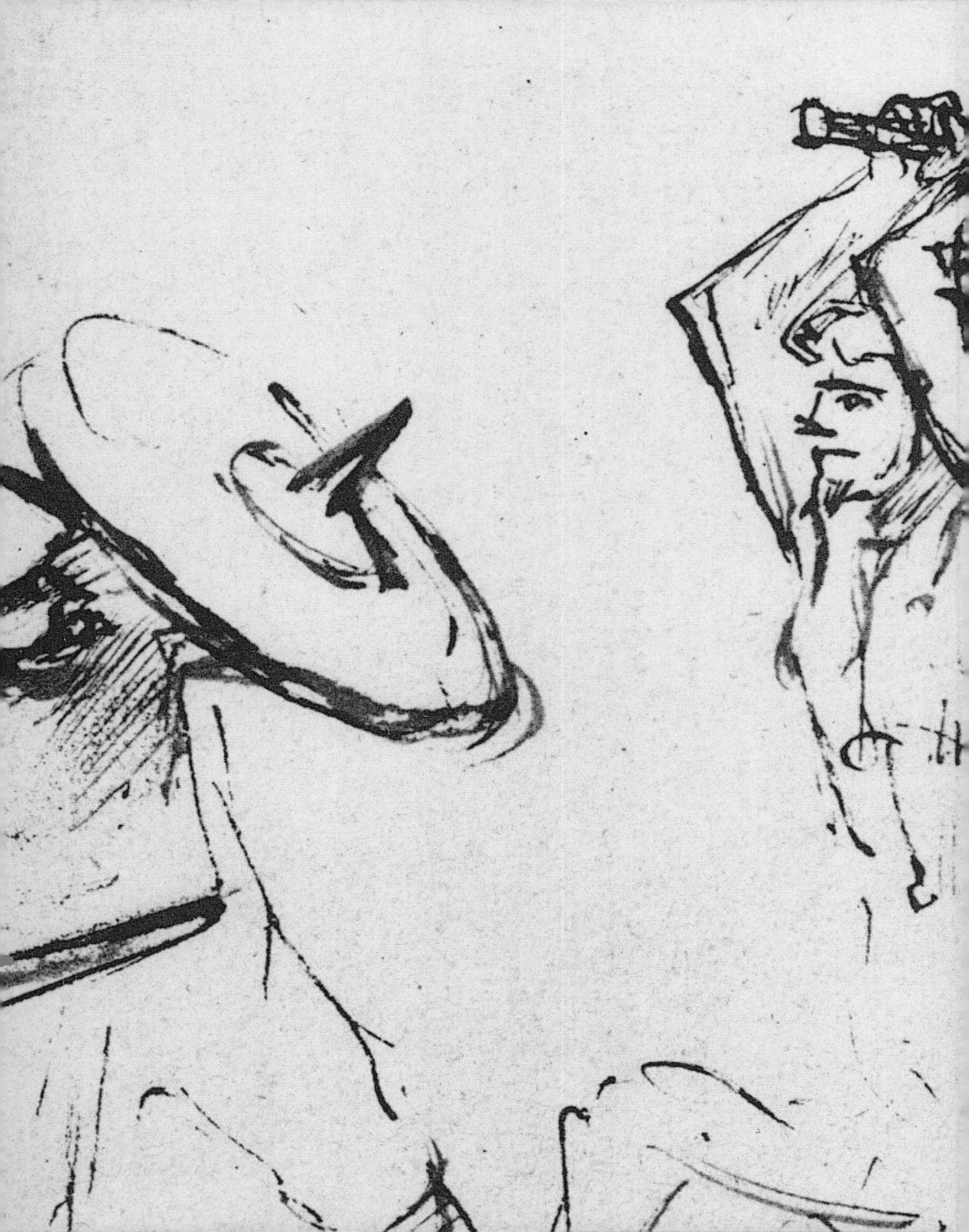

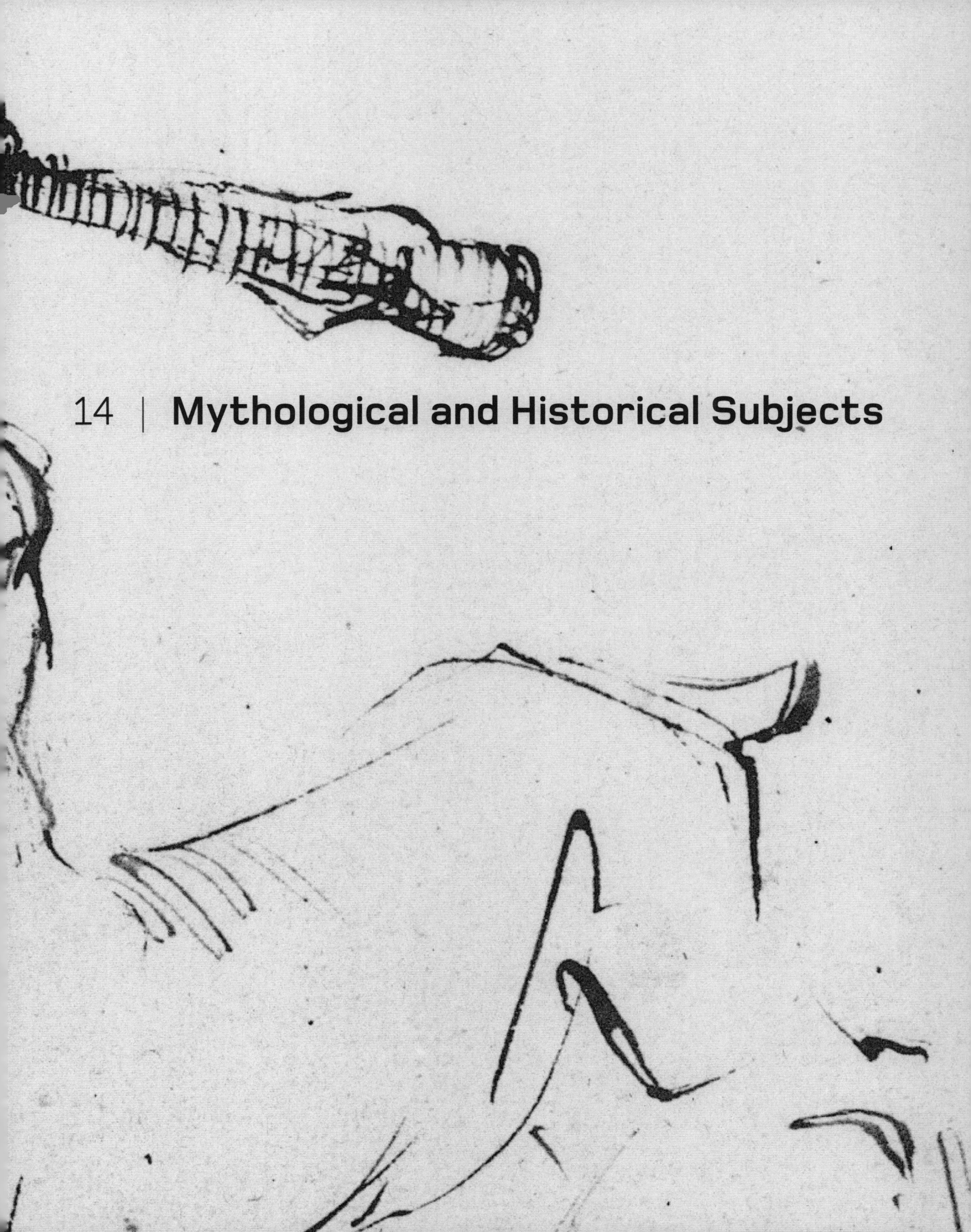

14 | Mythological and Historical Subjects

14 | MYTHOLOGICAL AND HISTORICAL SUBJECTS

DIANA, GODDESS OF HUNTING, wildlife, and maidens, was one of Rembrandt's favorite deities. We have heard that in the early 1630s he gave Diana's attributes—a quiver and a bow (but not her crescent-moon diadem)—to his earliest known drawing of a nude model, which served as a preparatory study for his etching of *Diana at the Bath* (see figs. 9.4, 9.5). Datable later in the decade is the pen-and-wash drawing of Diana accompanied by two greyhounds. She is seated with her feet firmly planted on the ground and her legs splayed with what a seventeenth-century stickler for decorum would call unladylike freedom (fig. 14.1). Here husky Diana (who bears a striking resemblance to Saskia) has completed her hunt. Holding her javelin, she rests. Her reclining hound pants; the other dog appears exhausted.[80]

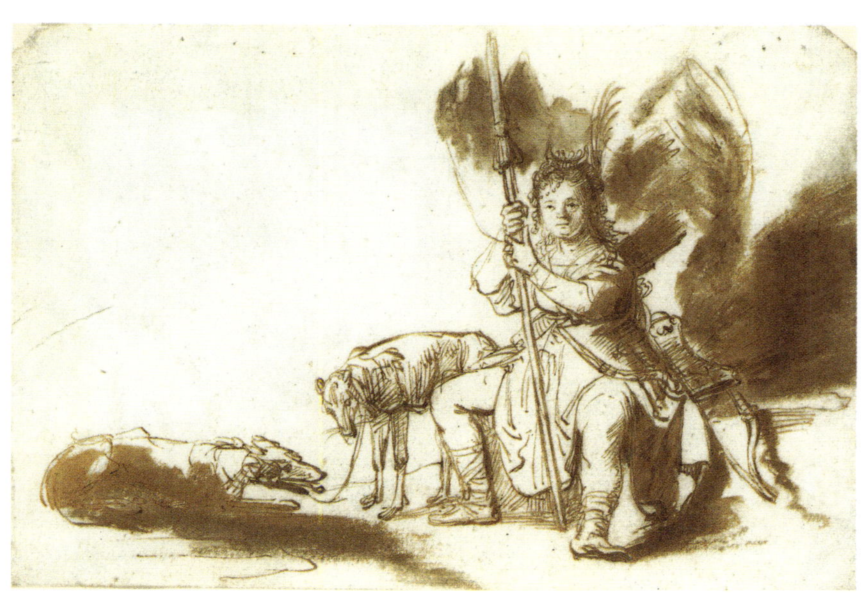

14.1 | *Diana with Two Dogs*, ca. 1638–40. Pen and brown ink, brown wash, over a preparatory drawing in black chalk on laid paper; 18.5 × 27.1 cm (7¼ × 10⅝ in.). Jan Krugier and Marie-Anne Krugier-Poniatowski collection, Geneva, inv. JK 3226.

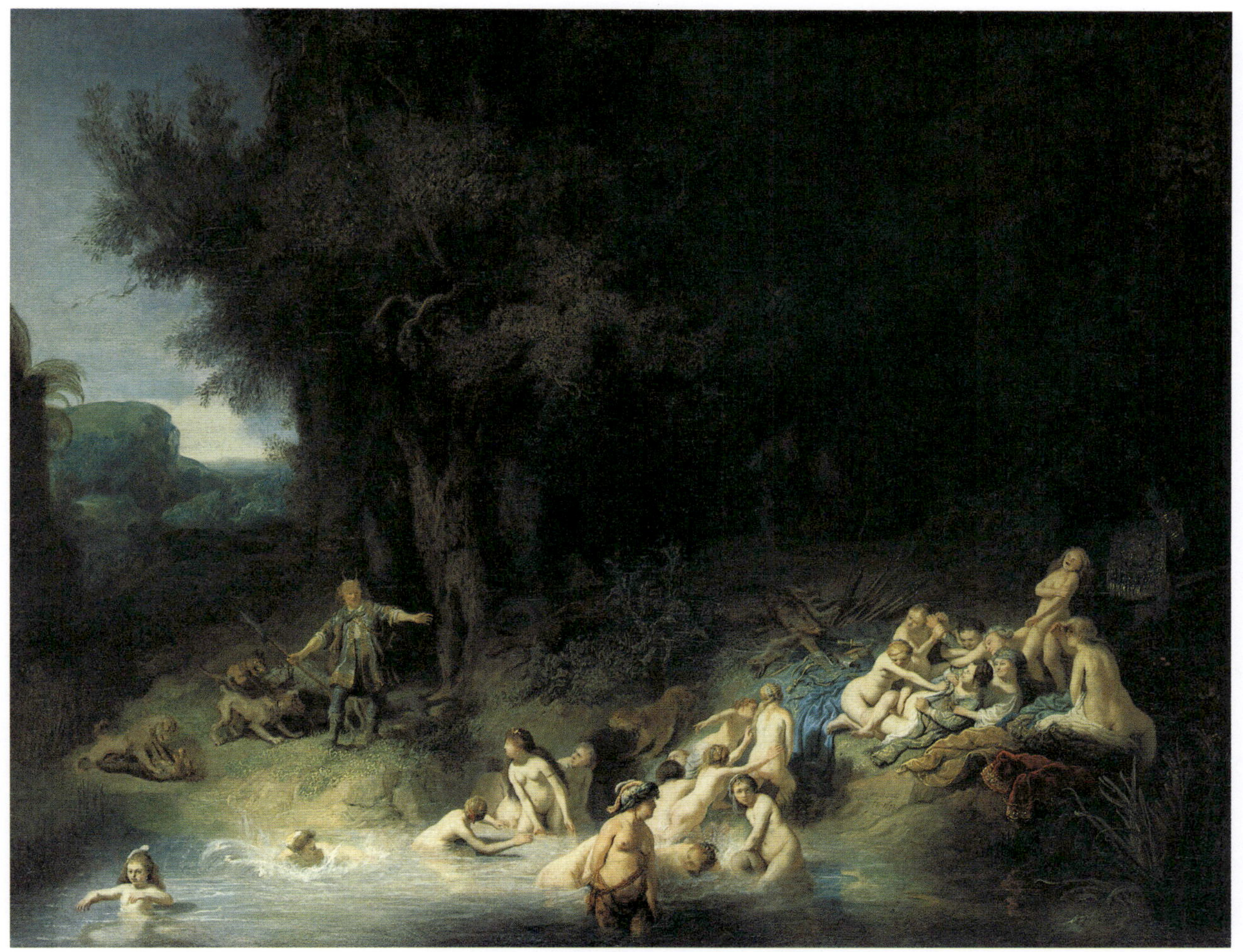

14.2 | *Diana Bathing with Her Nymphs, with the Stories of Actaeon and Callisto*, signed and dated 1634. Oil on canvas; 73.5 × 93.5 cm (28⅞ × 36¾ in.). Museum Wasserburg Anholt, Anholt, Collection Prince of Salm-Salm, inv. 391.

In contrast, Rembrandt's wooded landscape painting, datable about 1634, which includes a nude Diana bathing in a pool with a chain of more than a dozen naked, writhing nymphs, is full of action (fig. 14.2). The picture focuses on the climactic episodes of the stories of Actaeon and Callisto; combining both in one painting is unusual. Both stories are told by the Roman poet Ovid in his *Metamorphoses*, an epic narrative that, among other things, is a comprehensive source book for virtually all classical mythology.

Ovid relates (*Metamorphoses* 3.142f.) how unfortunate Actaeon, after a successful hunt with his companions, lost his way in a dark wood and came upon a pool where Diana, accompanied by her nymphs, was bathing to cool her naked beauty. When Diana saw him, she angrily scooped up a handful of water and dashed it into his eyes, shouting: "Now if you can, tell how you saw me naked." As she uttered her curse, a

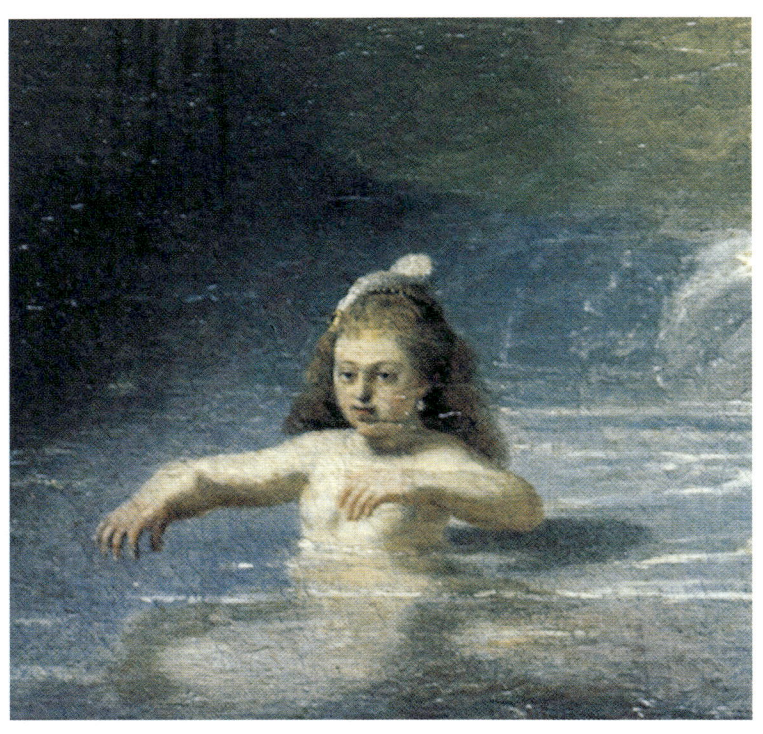

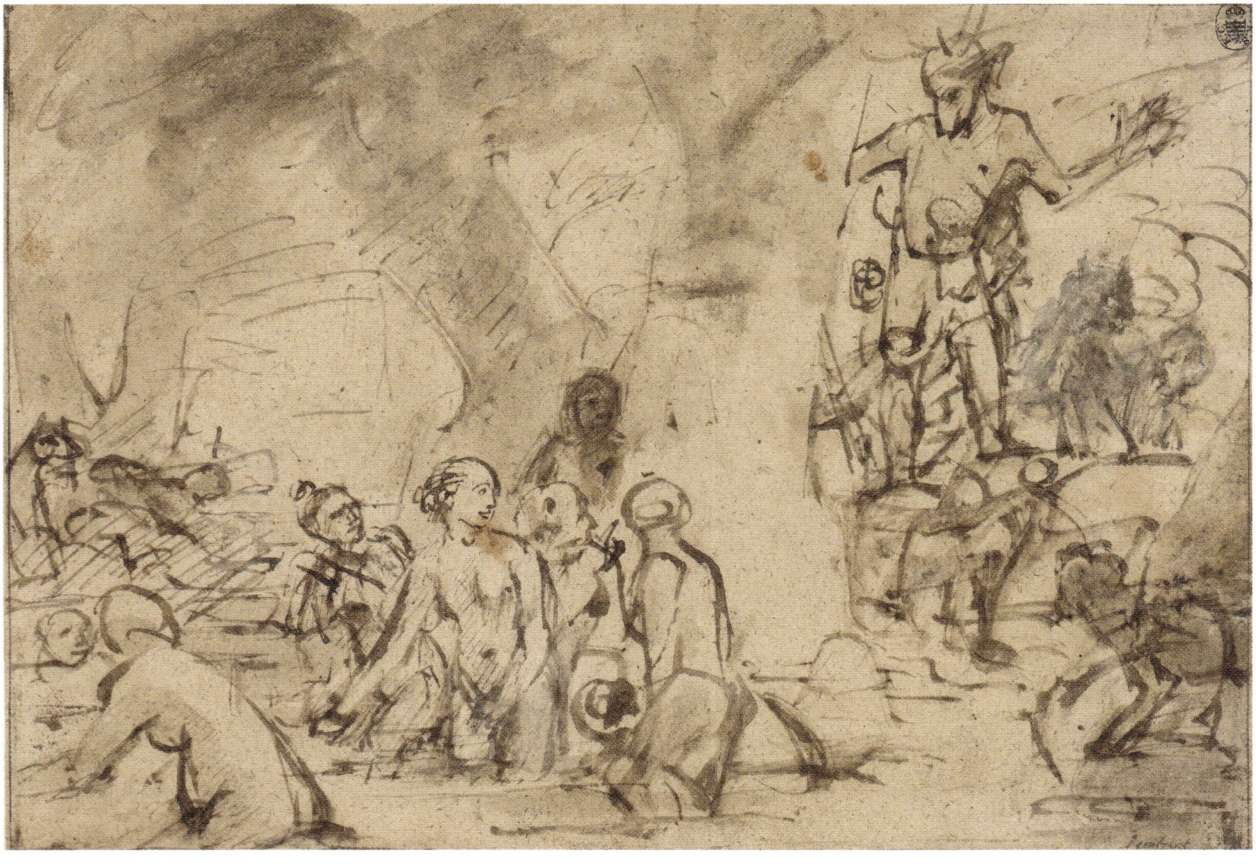

rack of deer's antlers sprang from Actaeon's forehead. This is the moment Rembrandt depicts on the left bank of the pool. Quick as a flash, Actaeon is metamorphosed into a deer, who is chased and finally devoured by his own pack of ferocious hunting dogs.

Notable is the lone smiling nymph wading in the water up to her bosom in the lower left foreground of the painting (fig. 14.3). The delight the pool gives her anticipates the pleasure Daumier's bathing ladies take in his lithographs of activities in nineteenth-century Parisian bathhouses. She also recalls the ploughman in Bruegel's well-known picture of the *Fall of Icarus*, the Flemish master's only mythological painting, which is likewise based on a story from Ovid's *Metamorphoses*. Like the ploughman, the wading nymph is completely oblivious to the tragedy taking place behind her.[81]

Aged Rembrandt returned to the subject of Diana and Actaeon in the 1660s in a powerful reed pen-and-wash drawing now at Dresden (fig. 14.4). There is only a suggestion of the dark forest. Emphasis is on the figures, particularly Diana, who has uttered her curse, and Actaeon, whose head and ear have already taken a deer's shape. His hand appears to become a hoof before our eyes. The suggestion that the mature Rembrandt found inspiration for his drawing in a print of the subject by Antonio Tempesta is not close to the mark. The Italian printmaker's anecdotal depiction of the episode takes place in an extensive fairyland forest. In the Dresden drawing Rembrandt concentrates, not on the woods, but on the dramatic action between the story's protagonists. The glances they exchange make us believe Ovid's claim that Diana not only metamorphosed Actaeon into a deer but also succeeded in planting fear within Actaeon's heart before uttering a word.

The right side of the artist's Diana painting depicts her nymphs' discovery of Callisto's pregnancy nine months after lusty Jupiter seduced her with his customary trickery. Her plight was revealed when Diana invited all of her companions to remove their clothing and bathe in a brook. All obeyed except Callisto, who only sought excuses for delay. "But her companions forced her to disrobe, and there her shame was openly confessed" (Ovid *Metamorphoses* 2.157f.). This brief passage is the basis for the nymphs' struggle with Callisto in Rembrandt's painting (fig. 14.5). Among them, one is behind her trying to pin her flat on her back; with a slight shift in her grip she would have the pregnant nymph in the hold wrestlers

14.3 | Wading nymph. Detail of figure 14.2.

14.4 | *Diana and Actaeon*, ca. 1662–65. Pen and brown ink, brown wash on coarse-grained Dutch paper; 24.6 × 34.7 cm (9⅝ × 13⅝ in.). Kupferstich-Kabinett, Staatliche Kunstsammlungen Dresden, inv. C1384. Photo: Bildarchiv Preussischer Kulturbesitz/Art Resource, N.Y. Photographer: Herbert Boswank.

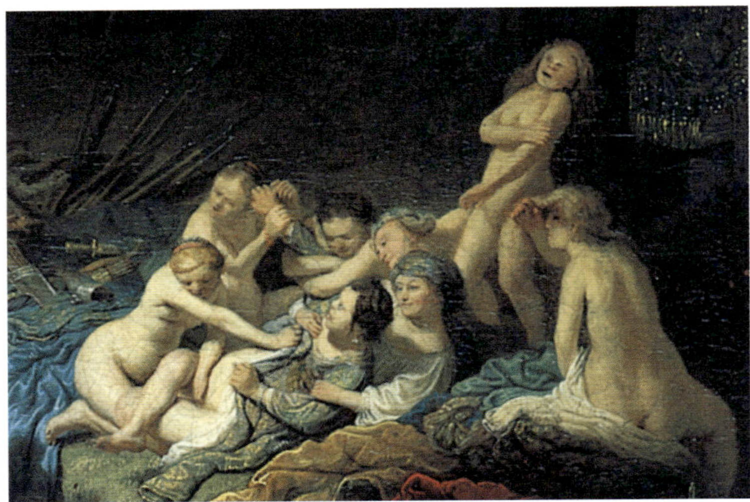

call a half nelson. Another nymph has raised Callisto's gown exposing her swollen belly. Yet another stands upright, laughing uproariously at the struggle.

Ovid tells that after the discovery of her condition Callisto stood terrorized, vainly trying to hide her state. Diana's judgment was harsh. She cried, "Begone! And pollute not our sacred pool," and so expelled her from her company. Rembrandt's pen-and-wash drawing of Callisto standing in shame before Diana (fig. 14.6) alters the mood of Ovid's account of the end of the affair. In the drawing nude Callisto appears with her head bowed and finds it impossible to conceal her pregnancy. But Rembrandt gives no indication that the seated goddess, who is having her hair dressed, is a hanging judge. Without prior knowledge of the sad end of this episode in the story of Callisto's life, it would not be astonishing to learn that Rembrandt's Diana did not righteously banish the seduced nymph, but mercifully forgave her.

The tale of Venus and Mars in Vulcan's net is found both in Homer's *Odyssey* (8.266–327) and in Ovid's *Metamorphoses* (4.168f.). Vulcan, god of fire and by trade a blacksmith, was the son of Jupiter and Juno. Though lame and ugly, thanks to his enormous wealth he managed to marry beautiful Venus, who proved an unfaithful wife. She repeatedly used their marriage bed to cuckold her husband with her lover Mars. When Vulcan learned of the scandalous affair, he got his revenge by forging a gossamer-fine bronze net, which even a god could not see. Then he cunningly draped the net from a beam in his bedroom and extended it over the bed. When bedded and stark-naked Venus and Mars were locked in embrace, Vulcan

14.5 | Callisto with nymphs. Detail of figure 14.2.

14.6 | *Diana and Callisto*, ca. 1640–45. Pen and brown ink, brown wash; 20.4 × 29.5 cm (8 × 11⅝ in.). Private collection.

14.7 | *Venus and Mars in Vulcan's Net*, ca. 1635. Pen and brown ink; 21.1 × 28.9 cm (8¼ × 11⅜ in.). Amsterdam Historisch Museum, inv. A10283.

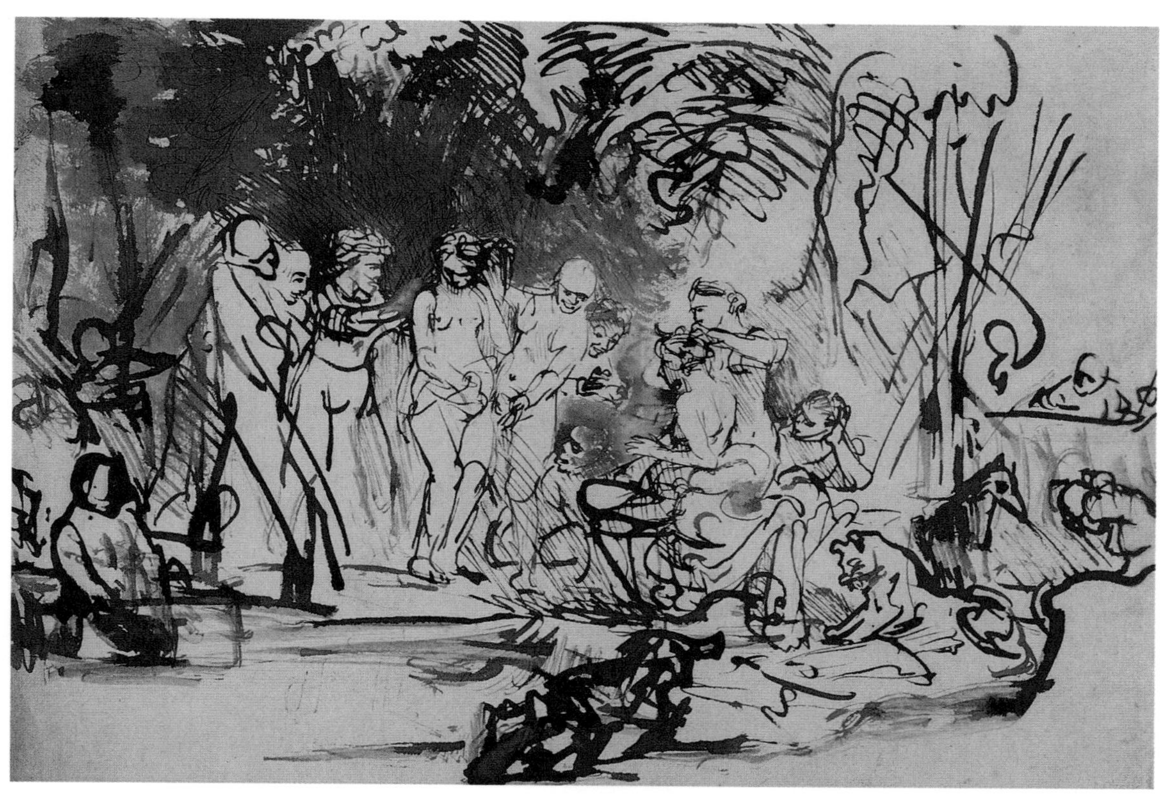

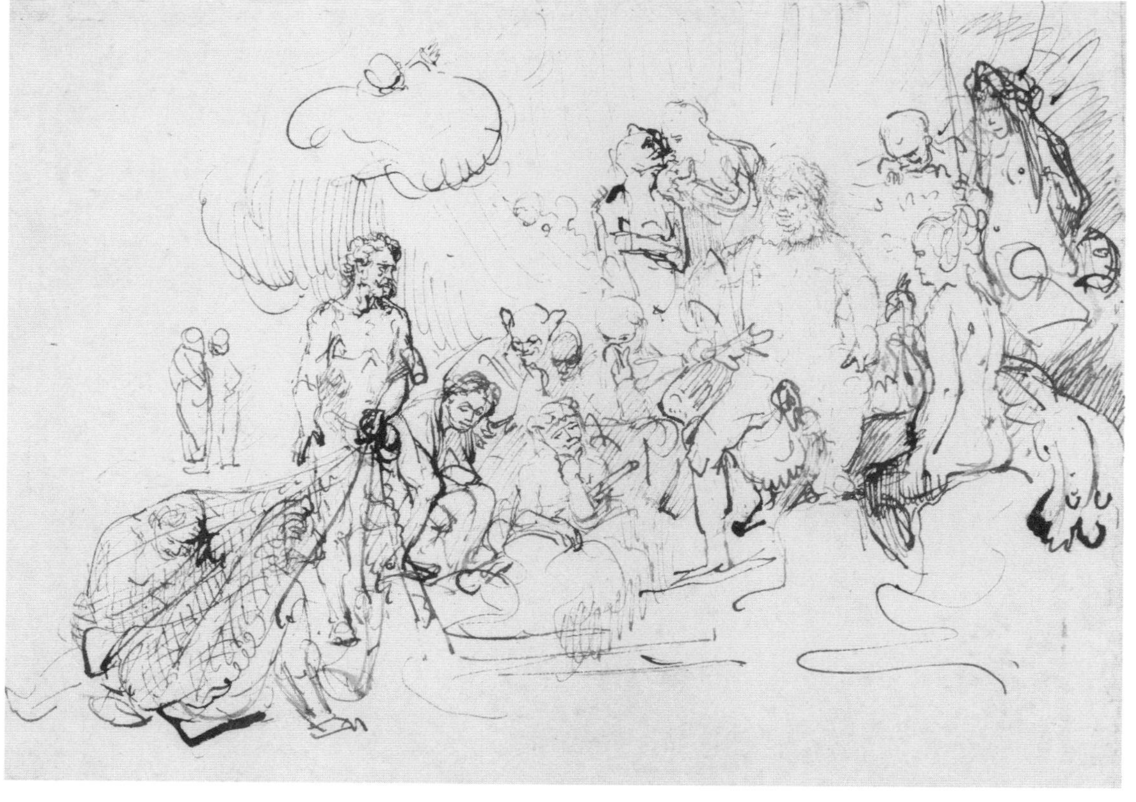

pinned them in his net. Straightaway, with a wail, he invited the other gods to see the netted cruel and comic couple.

The last part of the story is depicted in Rembrandt's pen drawing, now at the Amsterdam Historical Museum (fig. 14.7). Lame Vulcan, on the left, with his smith's hammer under his arm, presents the captured adulterers to seated Jupiter, with his symbolic eagle and bolts of lightning in his hand, and to seated Juno accompanied by a peacock, her attribute. The presence of nude Juno and the unidentifiable nude goddess behind her suggests that Rembrandt (or the person who advised him on the story's iconography) used Ovid's text, not Homer's version, as a source. Homer specifically states that Olympus's goddesses declined Vulcan's invitation to view naked Venus and Mars in his net. According to him, "Modesty kept each goddess to her mansion." Ovid omits this part of the story. However, both authors mention how some gods tittered when they saw the disgraced couple and prayed that they themselves be disgraced in the same manner. There can be little doubt that the smiles of a few of Rembrandt's gods were intended to express similar sentiments.

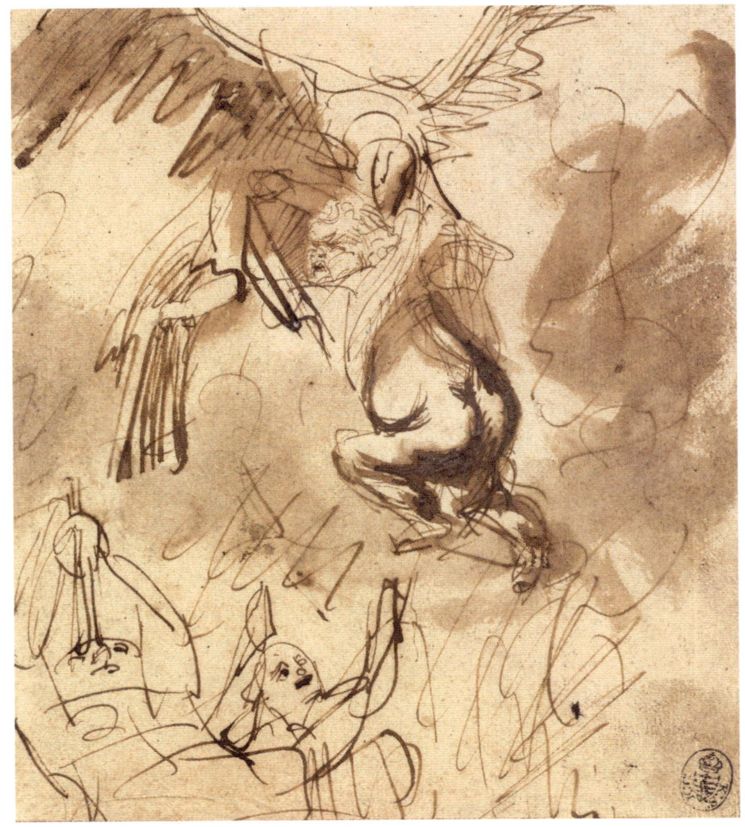

14.8 | *The Rape of Ganymede*, ca. 1635. Pen and brown ink, brown wash; 18.3 × 16 cm (7¼ × 6¼ in.). Kupferstich-Kabinett, Staatliche Kunstsammlungen Dresden, inv. C1357. Photo: Bildarchiv Preussischer Kulturbesitz/Art Resource, N.Y. Photographer: Herbert Boswank.

14.9 | *The Rape of Ganymede*, signed and dated 1635. Oil on canvas; 171 × 130 cm (67⅜ × 51⅛ in.). Gemäldegalerie Alte Meister, Staatliche Kunstsammlungen Dresden, cat. no. 1558. Photo: Erich Lessing/Art Resource, N.Y.

Dresden's rapid pen-and-wash sketch of the abduction of Ganymede by Jupiter in the guise of an eagle, bearing him to Olympus where he is destined to become cupbearer for the king of the gods, has a special status (fig. 14.8). It is a preliminary study for Rembrandt's life-size painting of the same subject, dated 1635, also at Dresden (fig. 14.9). No other preliminary or preparatory drawing for a mythological painting by the artist is known.

With good reason did Renaissance and Baroque artists traditionally represent Ganymede as an exceptionally handsome youth. After all, Homer describes him as the most beautiful of all mortal men (*Iliad* 20.232–34). Ovid puts it another way when

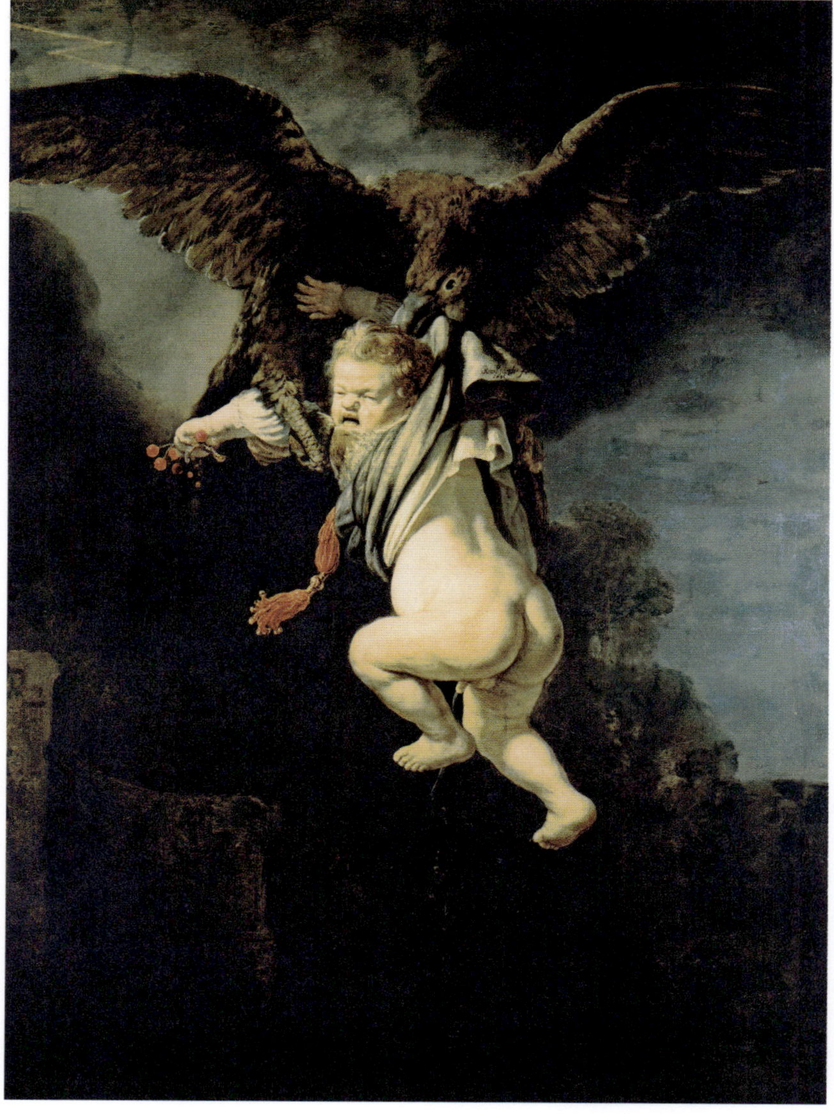

he sings that Ganymede was a boy for whom Jupiter so burned with love that he stole him as an eagle and flew him to Olympus, where he tends his cup (*Metamorphoses* 10.155f.).

By the time Rembrandt made his hasty sketch, he had already brought to the subject the uncompromising realism and originality characteristic of so many of his works of the 1630s. The most beautiful of all mortal men was not for him. He conceived of Ganymede as a toddler reacting as any toddler would if swept up by a tremendous eagle: He is crying with fright (similar wailing children are seen in other works by Rembrandt done about the same time; see pp. 87, 89 and figs. 4.7, 7.10). The eagle holds the little boy in a way that bares his fat bottom, potbelly, and back. These elements are unchanged in the completed painting. However, there Rembrandt adds an understandable physiological reaction Ganymede had to his abduction. As the little boy is raised sky-high, he is pissing (fig. 14.10).

The schematic, speedily sketched, gesticulating figures in the lower left foreground of the preliminary drawing are best interpreted as Ganymede's frantic parents reacting to the abduction of their young son. The figure plausibly identified as Ganymede's father holds a telescope through which he is looking. The parents and the telescope have, in turn, been connected with a passage in Karel van Mander's "Explanation of Ovid's *Metamorphoses*" in his *Schilder-boeck* published in 1604. Van Mander relates that the parents witnessed the disappearance of their young son, and he mentions that later Ganymede was transformed into the constellation Aquarius, which pours down water in sufficency.[82] The parents are not included in Rembrandt's painting—elimination of them was a good idea. As for the addition of Ganymede emptying his bladder in the finished picture, it has been proposed that the boy's action is a reference to his eventual transformation into the constellation Aquarius.[83] I am not wholly convinced by the astrological interpretation of this detail in the painting.

In a way, Rembrandt's mature reed-pen drawing of a swordsman with a shield battling a club-wielding Centaur (fig. 14.11) is as unusual as his sketch of Ganymede's abduction. To our knowledge, it is Rembrandt's only representation of the half-human, half-horse monster. The untraceable sketch, which I believe Picasso would have coveted, has reasonably been called a scene from the bloody battle that ensued after drunken, lustful Centaurs attempted to rape the Lapith bride of surpassing beauty and other women at a wedding to which

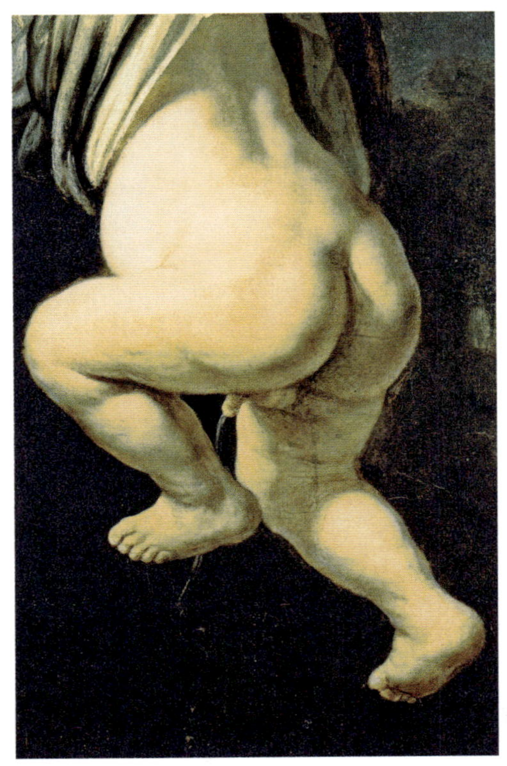

14.10 | Detail of figure 14.9.

14.11 | *Lapith Fighting a Centaur*, ca. 1655. Reed pen and brown ink; 14.5 × 19.3 cm (5 3/4 × 7 5/8 in.). Formerly H. Duval, Liège. Present whereabouts unknown.

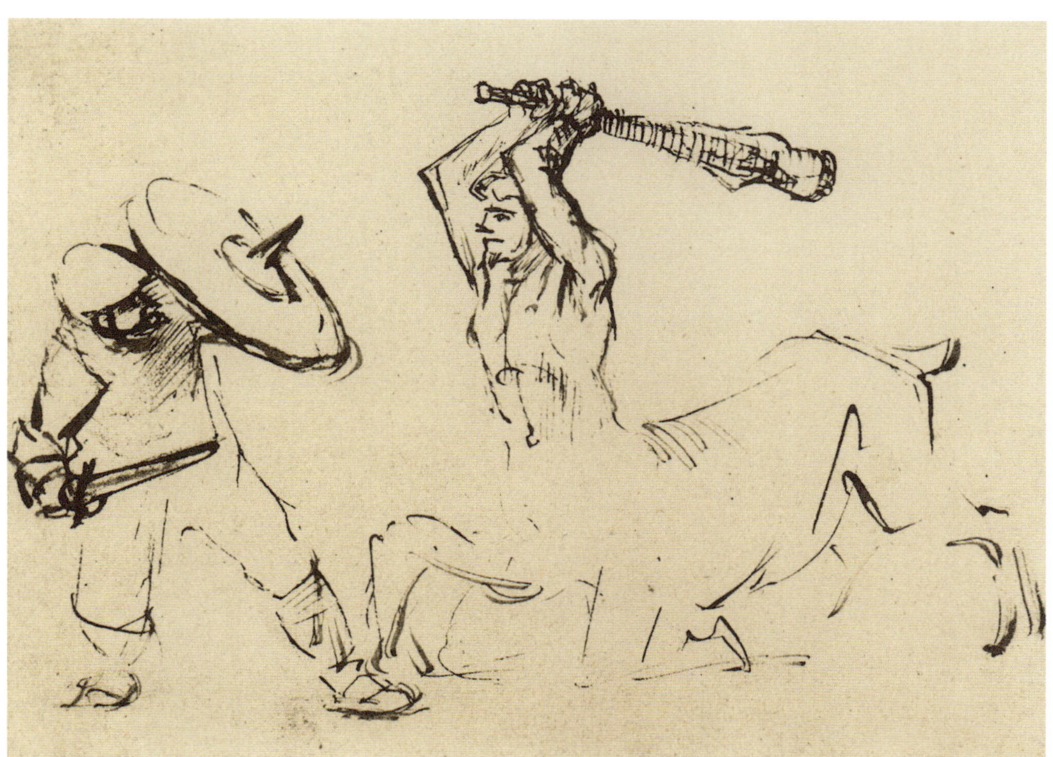

they had been invited. The famous story is told by Homer, Hesiod, and Ovid, among others.

Ovid's name appears frequently in discussions of Rembrandt's mythological drawings, and he is also the source for stories of some of the artist's best-known mythological paintings—for example, Getty's *Rape of Europa* or the Hermitage's *Danaë Visited by Jupiter as a Shower of Gold*. Rembrandt knew his Ovid. How he acquired his knowledge of him is less clear. Ovid's *Metamorphoses*, erotic poems, and other works were hardly reading given to boys enrolled in Leiden's Latin School, which young Rembrandt had attended.

It is appropriate to recall that no book by Ovid is cited in the 1656 inventory of the artist's effects. At the time his library was unimpressive; only twenty-four books are listed. Karel van Mander's *Schilder-boeck*, the hefty handbook for artists already mentioned, includes a lengthy exegesis in Dutch (more than two hundred pages) on Ovid's *Metamorphoses*, but it was not on Rembrandt's shelf either. Since the adventures of the ancient gods were a part of the stock-in-trade of a history painter, it is often assumed that Van Mander's commentary on the *Metamorphoses* received hard use in seventeenth-century Dutch studios. The assumption,

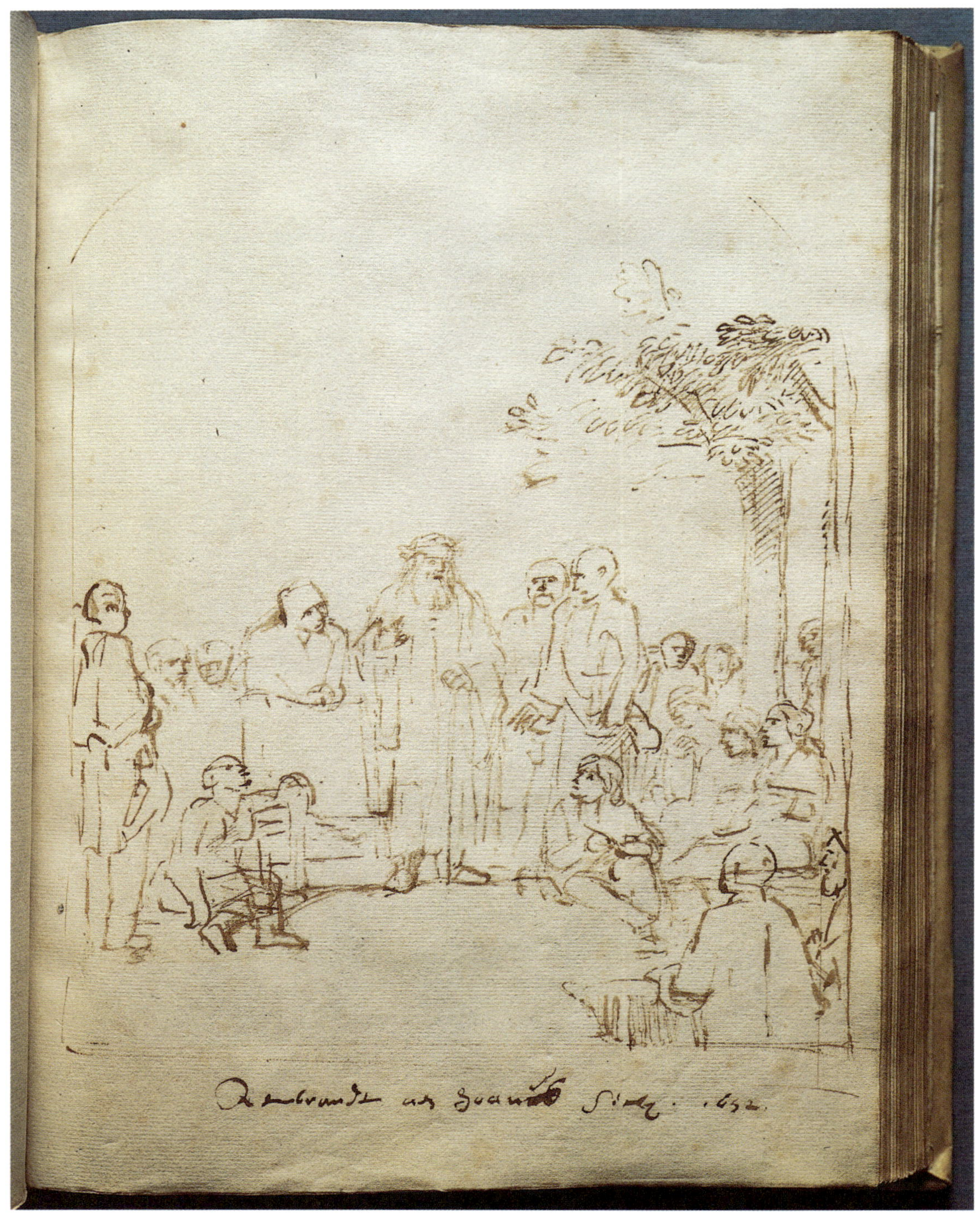

14.12 | *Homer Reciting Verses*, signed and dated 1652. Pen and brown ink; 26.5 × 19 cm ($10\frac{3}{8} \times 7\frac{1}{2}$ in.). Collectie Six, Amsterdam, collection no. 00208-77.

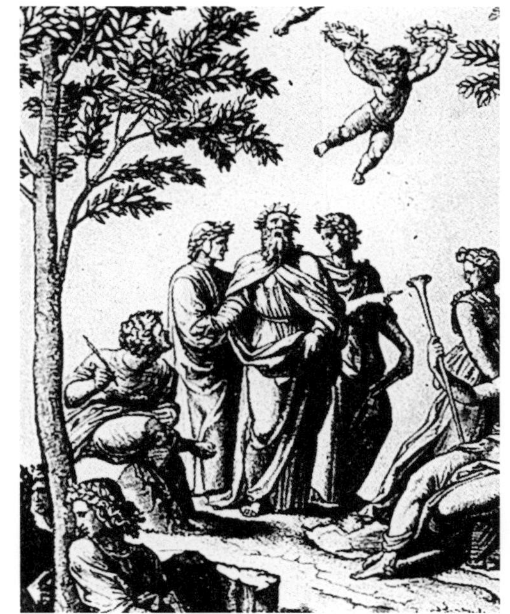

14.13 | Marcantonio Raimondi (Italian, ca. 1475/80–1527/34), after Raphael (Italian, 1483–1520), *The Assembly of the Gods on Mount Parnassus* (detail). Engraving. Harvard Art Museum, Fogg Art Museum, Cambridge, Massachusetts, Gift of Nelson Goodman, inv. M15695. Photo © President and Fellows of Harvard College. Photographer: Imaging Department.

however, is not supported by hard evidence. Rembrandt's inventory is not the only one that does not list *Het Schilderboeck*. A review of an eight-volume compilation of about 280 Dutch artists in inventories, almost all of which date from the seventeenth century, reveals that Van Mander's volume was hardly a best-seller. It is cited in only twelve inventories.[84] This fact suggests that in Dutch studios of the time there was more coaching by friends and patrons with knowledge of classical mythology—and, by extension, ancient history—than can be demonstrated.

With Rembrandt's beautiful pen drawing of *Homer Reciting Verses* (fig. 14.12) we turn to a historical subject. The drawing is on a sheet bound in an *album amicorum* owned by Rembrandt's friend and patron Jan Six; the album has remained in the collection of his heirs since it was compiled. At the bottom the artist signed and dated the drawings and dedicated it to Six: "*Rembrandt aen Joanus Six. 1652.*" It is his only drawing that bears a dedication.

An *album amicorum* is a friendship book in which drawings, poems, epigrams, epigraphs, emblems, autographs, and so forth, are collected. Rembrandt made a second drawing for Six's album, *Minerva in Her Study*, likewise signed and dated 1652 (Benesch no. 914). The state of preservation of both drawings is outstanding. For centuries both have been treasured in the same precious album and seldom exposed to light. For Rembrandt's equally well-preserved drawing of *The Presentation in the Temple* made about a decade later for another *album amicorum*, see figure 15.27.

The artist's choice of classical subjects for Six's album is understandable. Rembrandt responded to Six's distinct interest in classical antiquity. Not only does his *album amicorum* bear the name *Pandora* on its parchment cover, but Six also collected classical sculpture and in 1648 published his tragedy *Medea*, for which Rembrandt etched a frontispiece (it is one of the handful of books in the artist's small library that is listed by title in his 1656 inventory).

Rembrandt's *Homer Reciting Verses* shows his familiarity with Raphael's *Parnassus*, for it is clearly inspired by that painter's conspicuous depiction of the poet accompanied by listeners and an attentive scribe in his well-known fresco in the Vatican. Rembrandt almost certainly owned Marcantonio Raimondi's engraving after the fresco in one of the four albums of prints done after Raphael's works that are listed in his inventory. Figure 14.13 is a detail of the

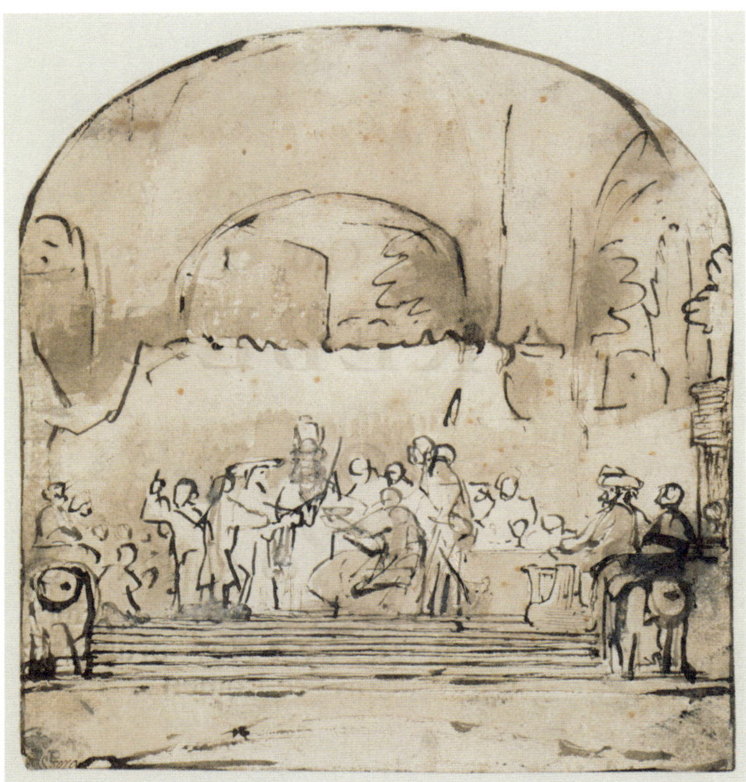

pertinent part of Raimondi's engraving. Six may have owned the print as well and possibly seized an opportunity to see the fresco in the flesh during the course of his tour of Italy in the early 1640s.

Homer Reciting Verses was the artist's private gift to Six, which the latter could share in his home with a few friends as they sat around a table leafing through his album. When Rembrandt made a pen-and-wash drawing, now in Munich, for his *Conspiracy of Claudius Civilis* (fig. 14.14), the greatest of all his works representing a scene from ancient history, he had quite another audience in mind. The finished painting—the largest he ever executed (larger than *The Night Watch*, it measured 5.5 meters in each dimension)—was intended for a lunette in the great corridor that surrounds the *Burgerzaal*, a vast public space in Amsterdam's glorious New Town Hall (fig. 14.15). The drawing's arched top takes into account the lunette for which the painting was designed.

Amsterdam's burgomasters determined the choice of subject when they agreed in the 1650s that all twelve lunettes should be decorated with episodes from the story of the revolt of Claudius Civilis (or, more correctly, Gaius

14.14 | *The Conspiracy of Claudius Civilis*, ca. 1661. Pen and brown ink, brown wash, white; 19.2 × 18.1 cm (7½ × 7⅛ in.). Staatliche Graphische Sammlung, Munich, inv. 1451 Z. Photo © Martina Bienenstein.

14.15 | Erik Kinell, Full-scale reconstruction of *The Conspiracy of Claudius Civilis* on the New Town Hall wall to which it belonged. Exhibited at the Nationalmuseum, Stockholm, 1956.

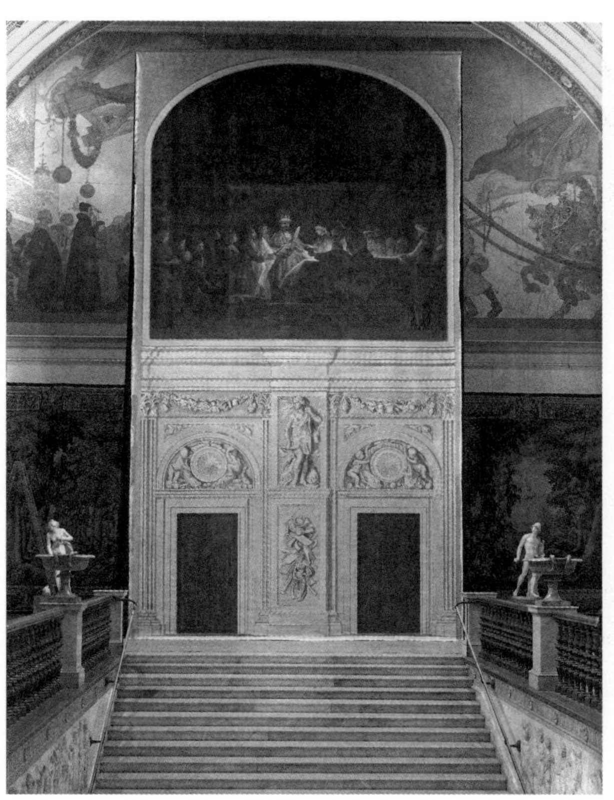

Julius Civilis), the Batavian who led an insurrection against the Romans in A.D. 69. The choice of subject was not unusual. During the seventeenth century parallels were frequently made between episodes of ancient history or the Bible and subsequent events of national history. For Dutchmen, their successful revolt against Spain, under the leadership of Willem the Silent, was prefigured by Claudius Civilis's rebellion. According to Rembrandt's contemporaries, Claudius was the prototype of Willem.

Rembrandt's pupil Govert Flinck, not the master himself, was originally asked to execute this vast project. It was the largest and most prestigious commission given to a seventeenth-century Dutch painter. Flinck prepared sketches for the paintings, and in November 1659 he was commissioned to execute twelve pictures for the New Town Hall's gallery. However, Flinck died in February 1660 before having made much progress on the scheme. The commission was then changed a bit and distributed among several artists. In January 1661 Jan Lievens and Jacob Jordaens were asked to paint scenes. In the same year Rembrandt probably received his order to paint the first episode of the story of the revolt.

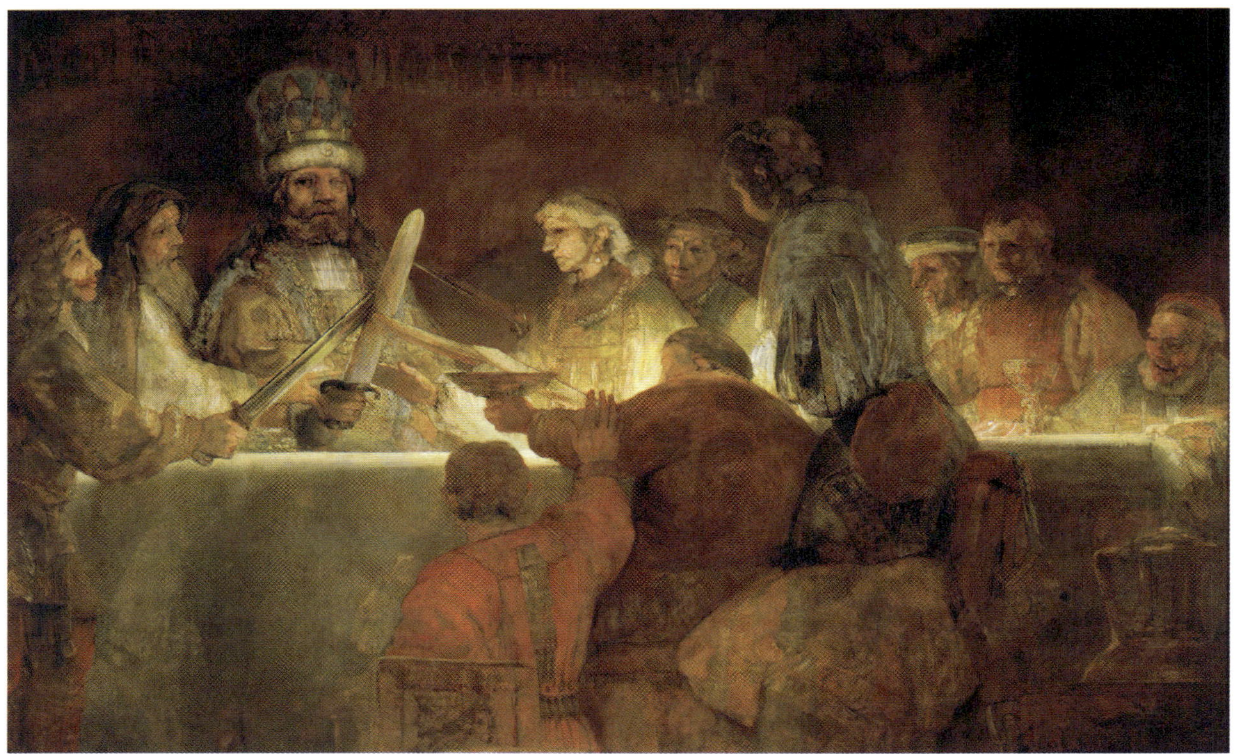

According to Tacitus (*Historiae* 4.13f.), the conspiracy began when Claudius Civilis, the mighty chieftain disfigured by the loss of one eye, summoned the chief Batavian nobles and tribesmen to a sacred grove. After they were excited by their revelry and the late hour of the night, he began to speak of the glorious past of the Batavians and the wrongs and enslavement they now suffered under the Romans. His impassioned speech inciting his countrymen to revolt "was received with great approval, and he at once bound them all to union, using the barbarous ceremonies and oaths of his country."

Rembrandt's night scene shows the Batavians taking their oath on Claudius Civilis's sword. The colossal painting was installed in the New Town Hall by 21 July 1662. Shortly after it was mounted, it was removed, and it was never again returned to the lunette for which it was designed. By 1663 its place had been taken by a painting by undistinguished Jürgen Ovens. His dull effort is still in situ.

Rembrandt's canvas was cut down, probably by the artist himself, to make it more saleable. He made some changes in the existing fragment, which preserves only the central group of the original huge picture, to make it a unified whole (fig. 14.16). The fragment is now on permanent loan at

14.16 | *The Conspiracy of Claudius Civilis*, 1662. Oil on canvas (fragment); 196 × 309 cm (77⅛ × 10 ft. 6⅝ in.) (originally 550 × 550 cm, or 18 ft. ¼ in. × 18 ft. ¼ in.). Nationalmuseum, Stockholm, inv. NM578 (on loan from Sweden's Royal Academy of Fine Arts). Photo: Erich Lessing/Art Resource, N.Y.

the Nationalmuseum, Stockholm, from Sweden's Royal Academy of Fine Arts. It and Munich's precious drawing give an idea of the artist's majestic conception for one of the most monumental history pictures ever painted.[85]

The artist's drawing is on the back of a fragment of a printed funeral ticket—there are other indications he was ready to draw on any piece of paper at hand (see p. 215 and figs. 15.24, 15.25). The missing part of the ticket bore the date 25 October 1661, which, of course, establishes that the sketch must have been made after the funeral ticket was printed. The drawing shows that the master of nocturnals set this night scene in a vast vaulted hall with open archways, not in the sacred grove Tacitus described. The change in setting was a significant one, enabling the artist to give his composition an architectonic grandeur and spaciousness that help emphasize the drama of the event. In the drawing the distribution of light and shade is of great importance for the total effect, and in the fragment of the painting, which has lost its architectural setting, the eerie light and iridescent grayish blues and pale yellows are even more important in bringing out the mysterious, barbaric character of the conspiracy.

A question remains: Why was the painting removed? Documentary evidence that would help answer the question is meagre and vague. Evidently his patrons wanted some changes, but we can only speculate what adjustments were requested. Perhaps the picture did not satisfy officials who endorsed classical ideals, which began to gain popularity in Holland after the middle of the century. Identification with early heroes was an acceptable idea, but possibly Rembrandt's conception of grizzly, one-eyed Claudius Civilis and his companions was too brutal for some of Amsterdam's powerful city fathers.

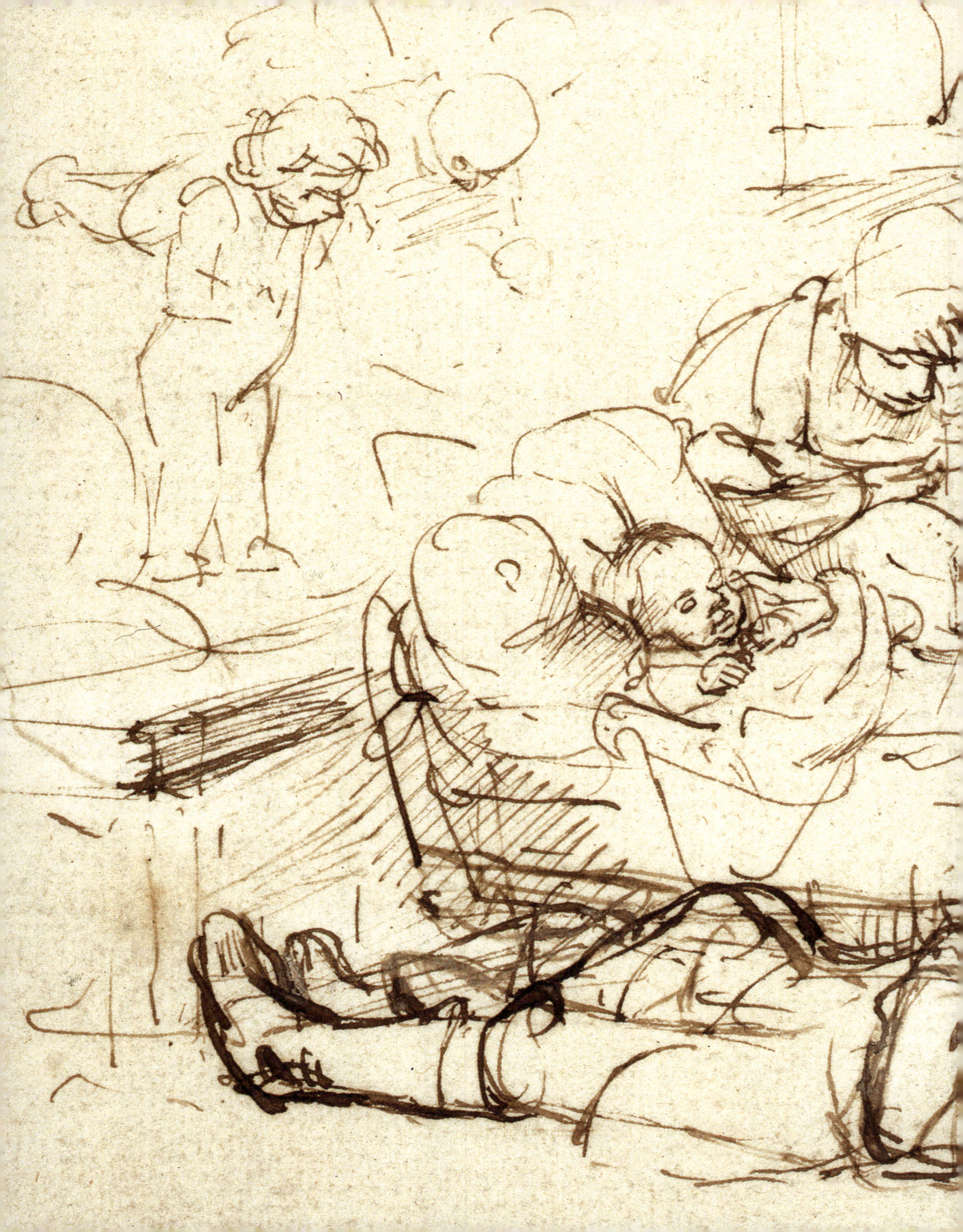

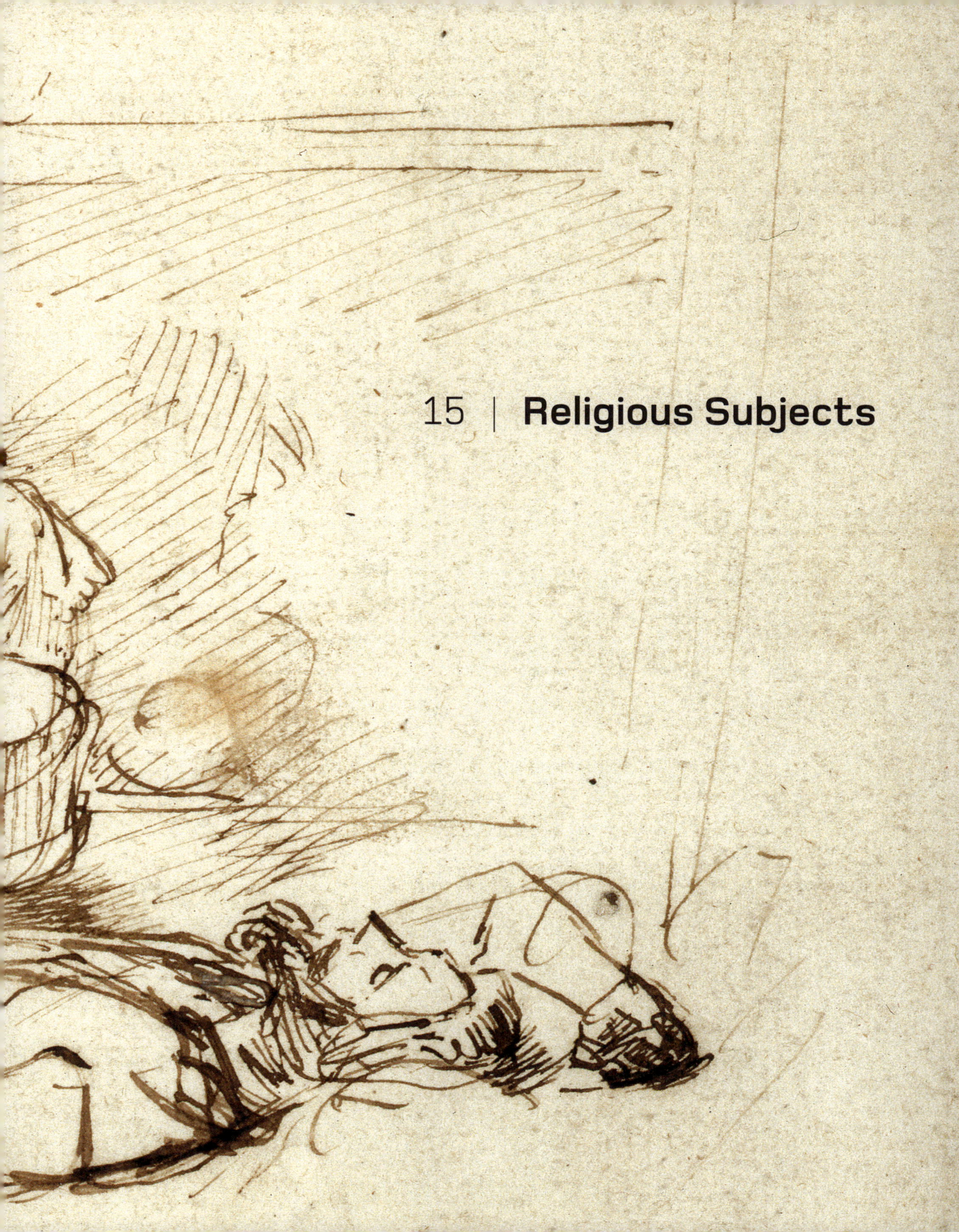

15 | Religious Subjects

15 | RELIGIOUS SUBJECTS

LITTLE IS KNOWN ABOUT REMBRANDT'S religious beliefs, but like other seventeenth-century Dutch protestants of every persuasion he must have found the Bible and episodes from the lives of saints a source of faith and edification. The Bible and stories of saints' lives were also the principal source, by far, for his activity as a draftsman. Many more of his drawings are devoted to these subjects than to the other categories discussed in the preceding chapters.

In view of their large number it may be astonishing to learn that not a single drawing can be connected to the vast majority of Rembrandt's best-known paintings of religious subjects. To name a few, no sketches can be related to Frankfurt's *Blinding of Samson*, Detroit's *Visitation of Mary and Elizabeth*, the Louvre's *Supper at Emmaus* or its *Bathsheba with David's Letter*, Kassel's *Jacob Blessing the Sons of Joseph*, Amsterdam's *Denial of Saint Peter*, or the Hermitage's *Prodigal Son*. And no drawing can be linked to any of the significantly different states of his monumental late etchings of *The Three Crosses* and *Christ Shown to the People*, prints that are universally acknowledged as two towering summits of his achievement as an etcher of biblical themes.

Happily there are a few notable exceptions—a good rule of thumb when assessing the character of Rembrandt's work is be mindful of exceptions. As we shall see, five drawings have been identified as studies for *The Hundred Guilder Print*, his most famous etching of a religious subject. Another is his preliminary compositional study at Bayonne (fig. 15.1) for his sympathetic painting of *The Holy Family with Angels*, dated 1645, at the Hermitage (fig. 15.2). With a few decisive scribbles the speedy pen sketch records what will become the picture's major elements: the seated Virgin peering into the cradle with an arm outstretched, Joseph as carpenter hacking with an axe at a yoke in progress, and an oversized angel descending into the interior. Finally, the composition is enclosed by a few hasty lines on the left and on the right; the latter will become part of a fireplace in the painting. Rembrandt made all sorts of additions to the finished work and had second thoughts about the single angel in the drawing. He replaced it with a half-dozen angels bathed in a burst of heavenly light. The most prominent angel, hovering above the Child's crib with outstretched arms, appears to have been painted from a suspended, manipulable wooden manikin of a child.[86]

Datable about the same time as the Bayonne sheet, but offering quite a different conception of the Holy Family with angels in an interior, is a brilliantly original pen sketch at the Fitzwilliam Museum (fig. 15.3). It belongs to the very large group of biblical drawings never used for a painting or etching. Here an exhausted Joseph is stretched out, flat on his back, dead to the world. Changes have been made to one of his legs and to the arm above his head to better express his deep sleep. Mary has fallen asleep next to baby Jesus sleeping in his cradle. Both mother and Child are done with lighter pen lines than Joseph. Two angels witnessing the silent scene are done with even finer lines. Perhaps Rembrandt intended to suggest they are making an appearance in the Holy Family's dreams. The sleeping infant in a cradle that is the subject of an untraceable small black-chalk drawing (fig. 15.4) is a mirror image of those seen in the works discussed above and may be related to them.

Hamburg's pen-and-wash drawing of *Saint Jerome Reading in a Landscape* (fig. 15.5) qualifies as another rare preliminary sketch for a religious work. It served as a study (in reverse) for the etching of *Saint Jerome Reading in an Italian Landscape* (fig. 15.6). The large drawing is virtually identical in size to the print; however, it was not indented for transfer to a copperplate. There are marked differences between the two works. In the etching Jerome and his lion are more prominent; the ancient giant tree's trunk and the shape of its foliage, hardly perceptible in the drawing, have been worked up; and buildings in the imaginary landscape in the distance show that the artist has absorbed what he learned from his study of prints he owned after works by Titian and possibly his followers.

There are also important differences in the treatment of light and shadow. Generous applications of wash are used in the drawing to place its large foreground rock,

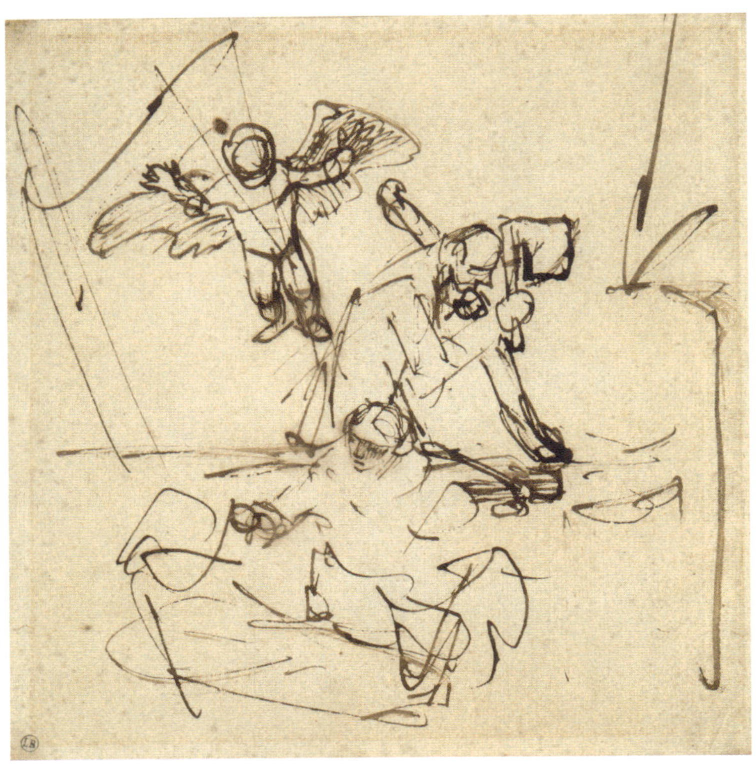

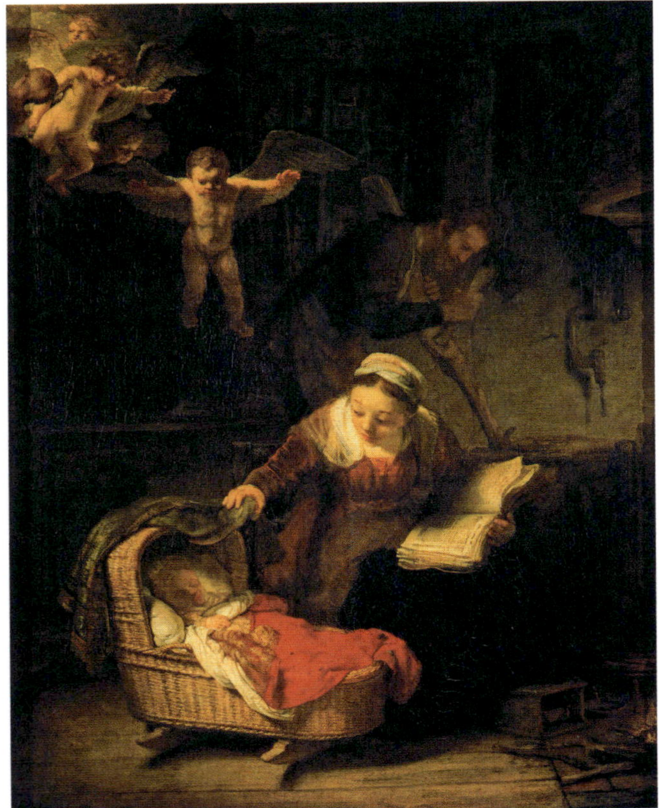

15.1 | *The Holy Family in the Carpenter's Shop*, ca. 1645. Pen and brown ink; 16 × 15.8 cm (6¼ × 6¼ in.). Musée Bonnat, Bayonne. Photo © RMN—Grand Palais/Art Resource, N.Y. Photographer: René-Gabriel Ojéda.

15.2 | *The Holy Family with Angels*, signed and dated 1645. Oil on canvas; 117 × 91 cm (46 × 35⅞ in.). Hermitage, Saint Petersburg, inv. 741. Photo: Scala/Art Resource, N.Y.

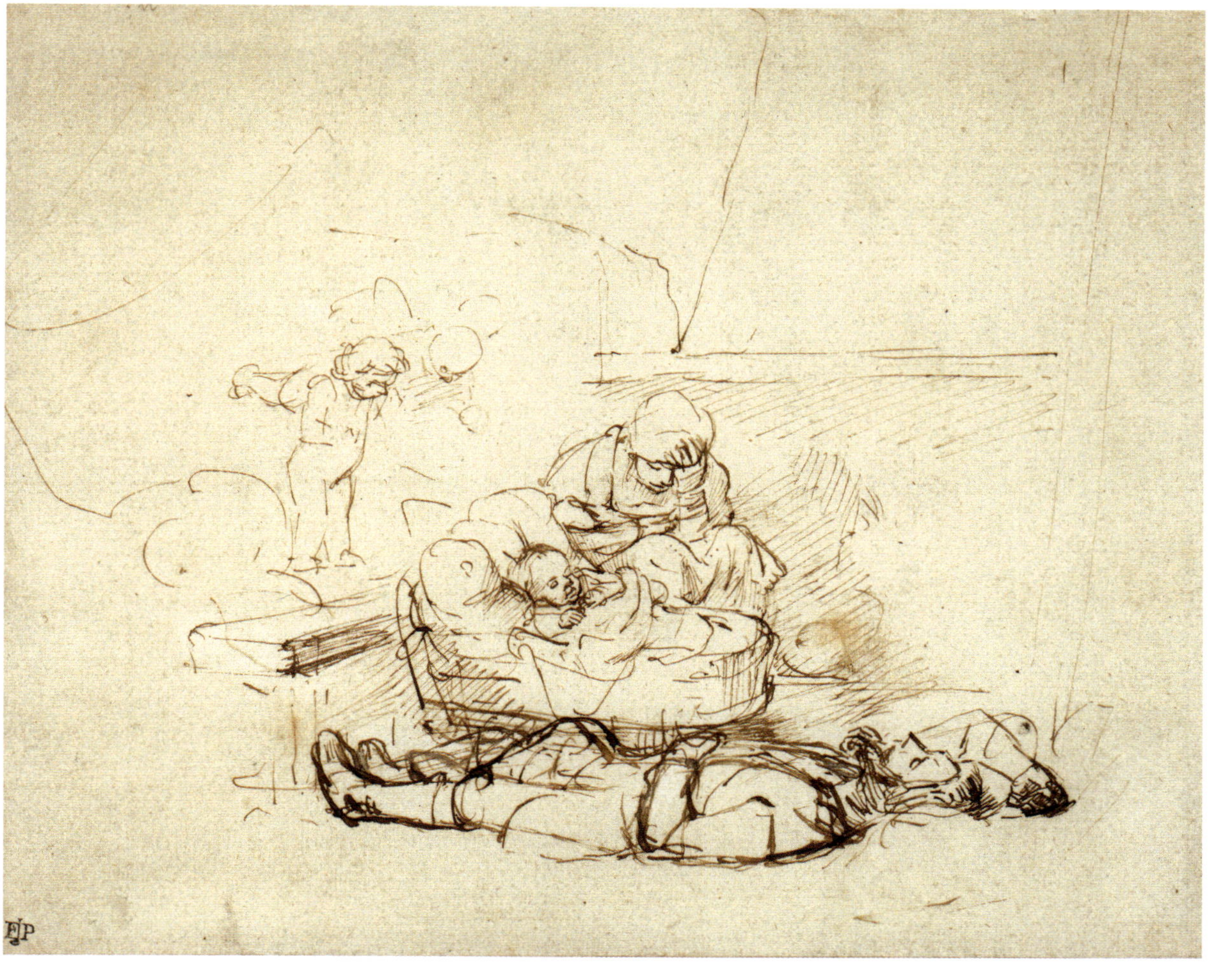

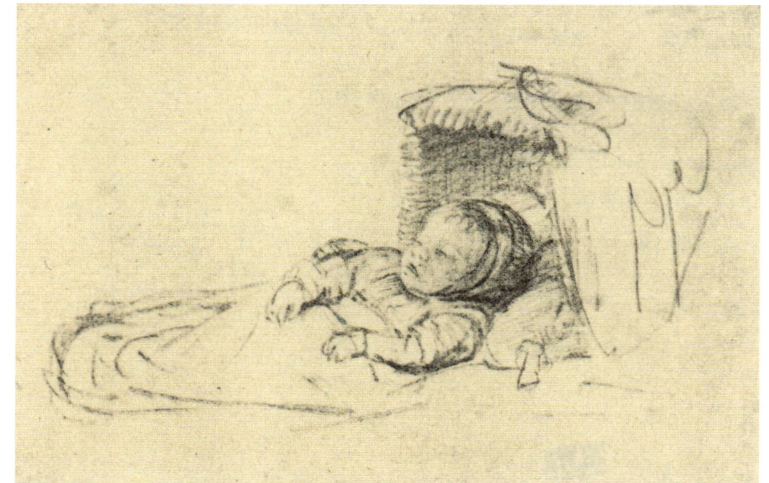

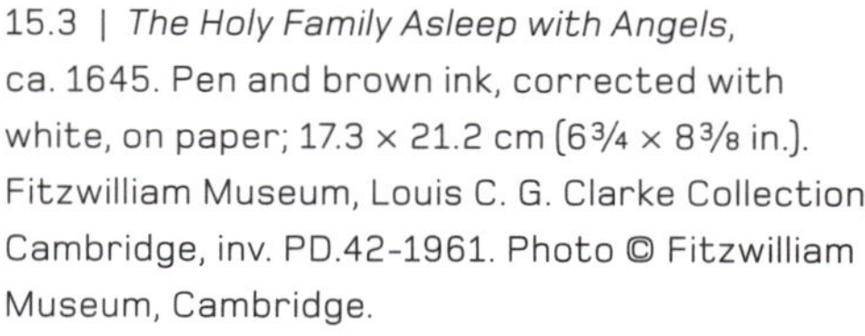

15.3 | *The Holy Family Asleep with Angels*, ca. 1645. Pen and brown ink, corrected with white, on paper; 17.3 × 21.2 cm (6¾ × 8⅜ in.). Fitzwilliam Museum, Louis C. G. Clarke Collection, Cambridge, inv. PD.42-1961. Photo © Fitzwilliam Museum, Cambridge.

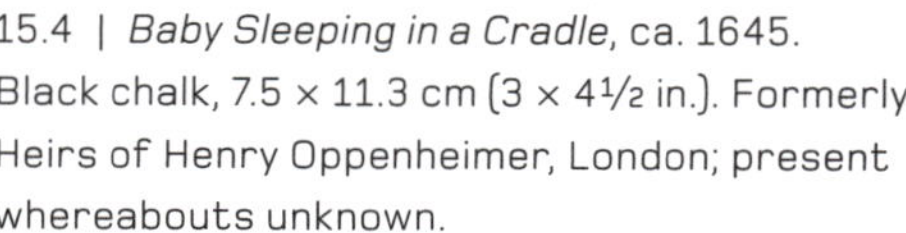

15.4 | *Baby Sleeping in a Cradle*, ca. 1645. Black chalk, 7.5 × 11.3 cm (3 × 4½ in.). Formerly Heirs of Henry Oppenheimer, London; present whereabouts unknown.

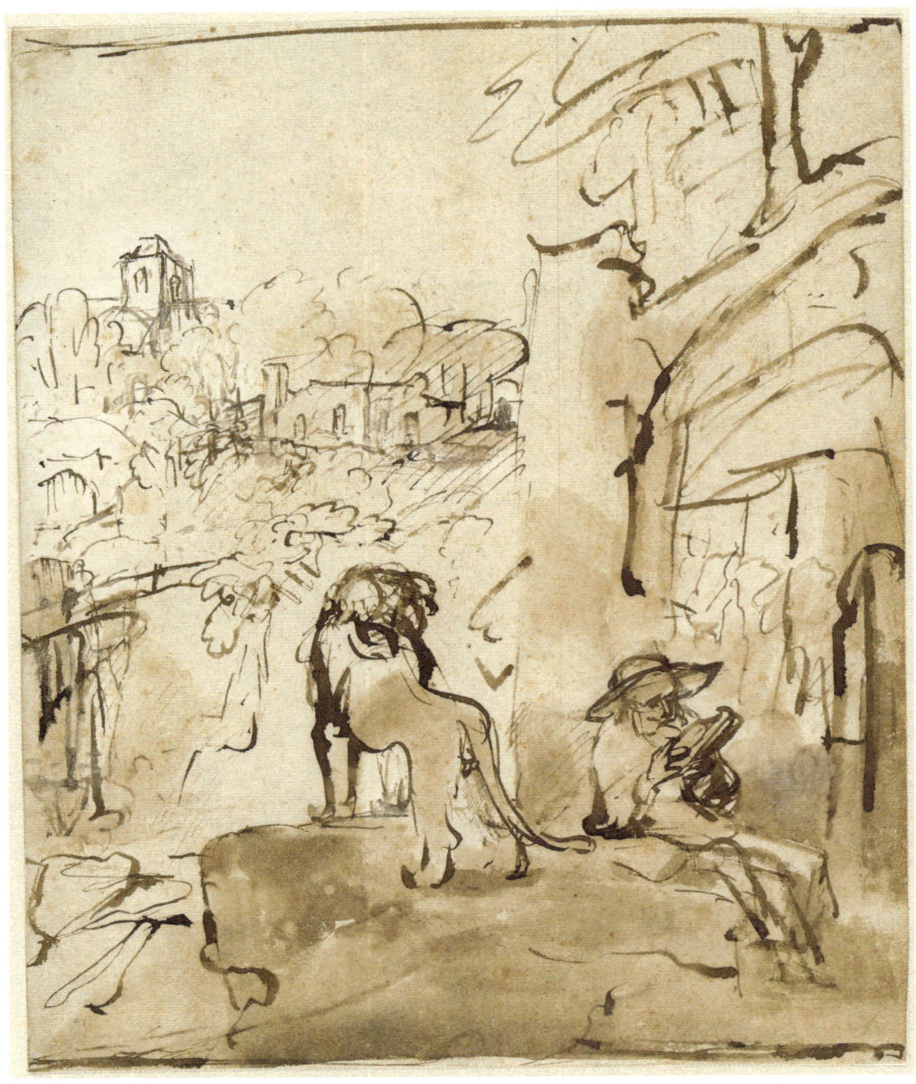

the lion's body and hindquarters, and the reading Jerome in shade. The etching reverses this effect and adds a light area in the middle ground. Dazzling light has been introduced into the print and, only after acquiring familiarity with excellent impressions of the etching with its many deep dark, velvety drypoint passages intact, is it possible to find a hint of the print's spectacular chiaroscuro effect in the drawing.

A few of Rembrandt's drawings show the genesis or struggle involved in developing an idea for a narrative based on a biblical passage. The summary pen sketch of a seated Eve offering Adam the fateful apple, which he either does not want to touch or is about to grab (fig. 15.7), can be read as an early idea for his extraordinary 1638 etching of the *Fall of*

15.5 | *Saint Jerome Reading in a Landscape*, ca. 1653. Pen and brown ink, brown wash, heightened with white, on white paper; 25.2 × 20.4 cm (9⅞ × 8 in.). Hamburger Kunsthalle, inv. 22414. Photo: Bildarchiv Preussischer Kulturbesitz/Art Resource, N.Y. Photographer: Christoph Irrgang.

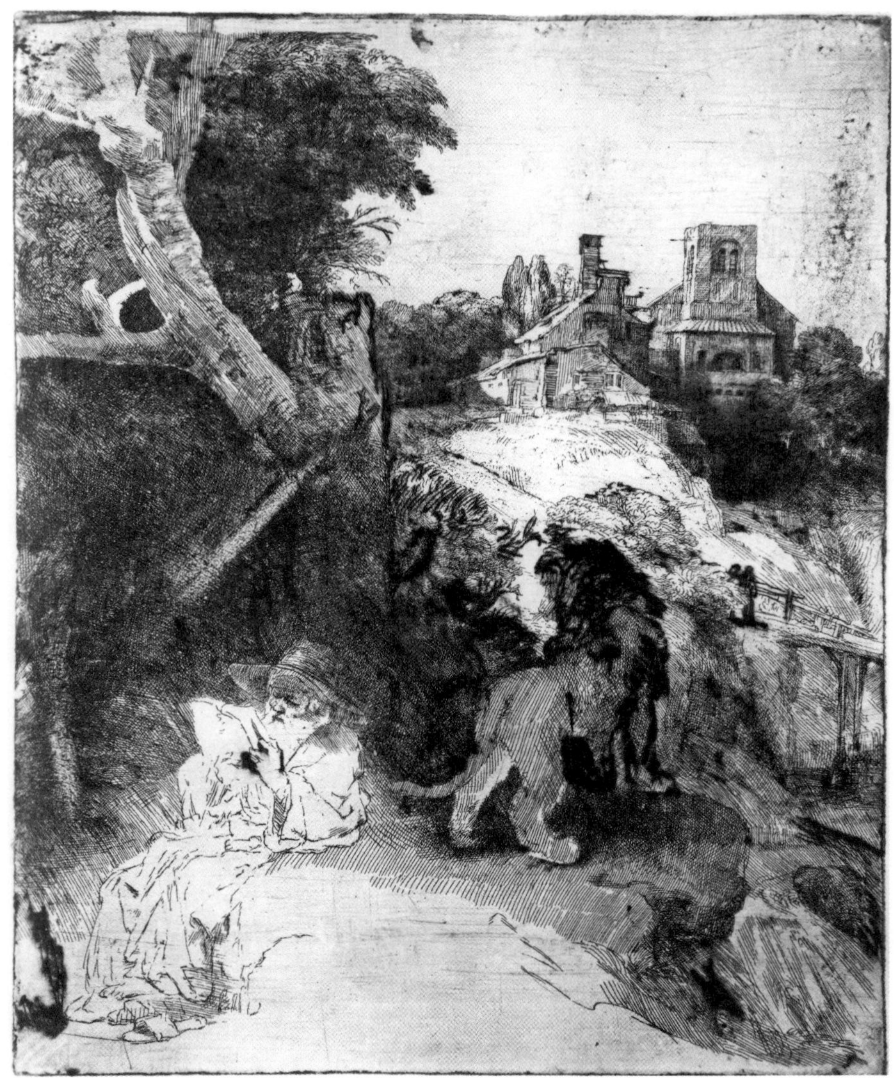

15.6 | *Saint Jerome Reading in an Italian Landscape*, ca. 1653. Etching, drypoint, and burin, on Japanese paper; 25.9 × 21 cm (10¼ × 8¼ in.). Graphische Sammlung Albertina, Vienna. Photo: Foto Marburg/Art Resource, N.Y.

Man (fig. 15.8). Though the sketch can be faulted for the poor drawing of Adam's outstretched leg, the convincing character of other passages permits acceptance of its traditional attribution to the artist.[87] Rembrandt, too, can nod.

On the other hand, there can be no doubt about the unmistakable connection between the etching and Leiden University's pen-and-wash sketch of two studies of Eve with the apple and Adam's reaction to her proposal that he take it (fig. 15.9). The arrangement of the couple in the Leiden study, with Eve on the left side and Adam on the right, is a mirror image of the way they appear in the etching. In the sketch the artist experiments with possible ways for Eve to hold the apple as well as positions for Adam's upraised hand. Neither

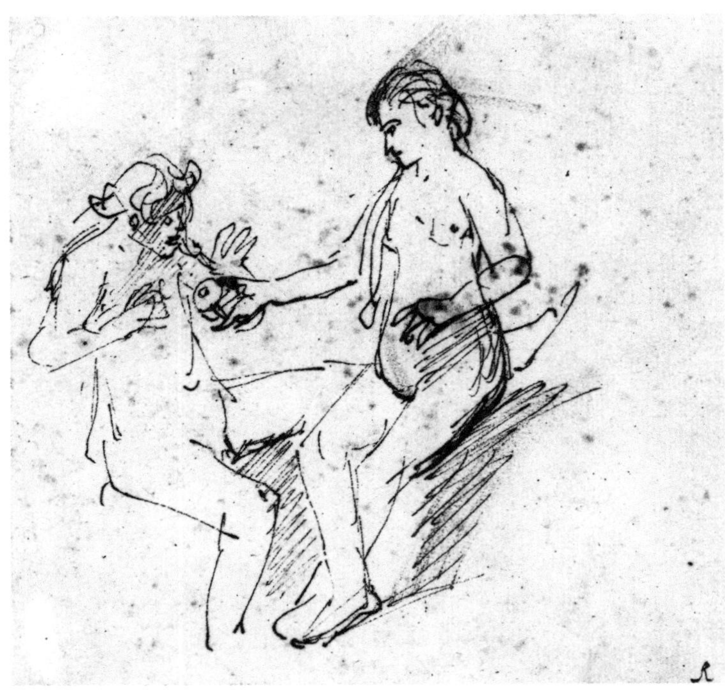

offers his last thoughts regarding the relationship of the pair. In the print they are of equal height, and their figures do not overlap. Eve's naked body, her apple, and one of Adam's hands have been positioned on the etching's central axis. Did Rembrandt make other sketches incorporating these changes, or did he make them directly on his copperplate?

Rembrandt's celebrated *Hundred Guilder Print* (fig. 15.10) is datable about 1648. It may have acquired its popular title soon after it appeared on Amsterdam's art market. In a letter written as early as 9 February 1654 by Jan Meyssens, an Antwerp print publisher and dealer, to Karel van den Bosch, Bishop of Bruges, he states: "Also here is the rarest [= finest] print published by Rembrandt, in which Christ is healing the sick, and I know that in Holland [it] has been sold various times for 100 guilders and more; and it is... very fine and lovely, but ought to cost 30 guilders. It is very beautiful and pure."[88]

The etching illustrates passages from chapter 19 of the Gospel of Matthew. Its text is treated with liberty. Successive events are merged into a simultaneous one, with Christ in the center preaching and performing his miracles. According to the text, Christ had come from Galilee, a large multitude following him, and he began to preach, healing the sick. Members of the crowd look to the Lord, waiting for their turn to be healed.

15.7 | *Eve Offering the Apple to Adam*, ca. 1635–38. Pen and brown ink; 11.9 × 11.4 cm (4¼ × 4 ½ in.). Formerly Mr. and Mrs. David Felix, Philadelphia, Pennsylvania; present whereabouts unknown.

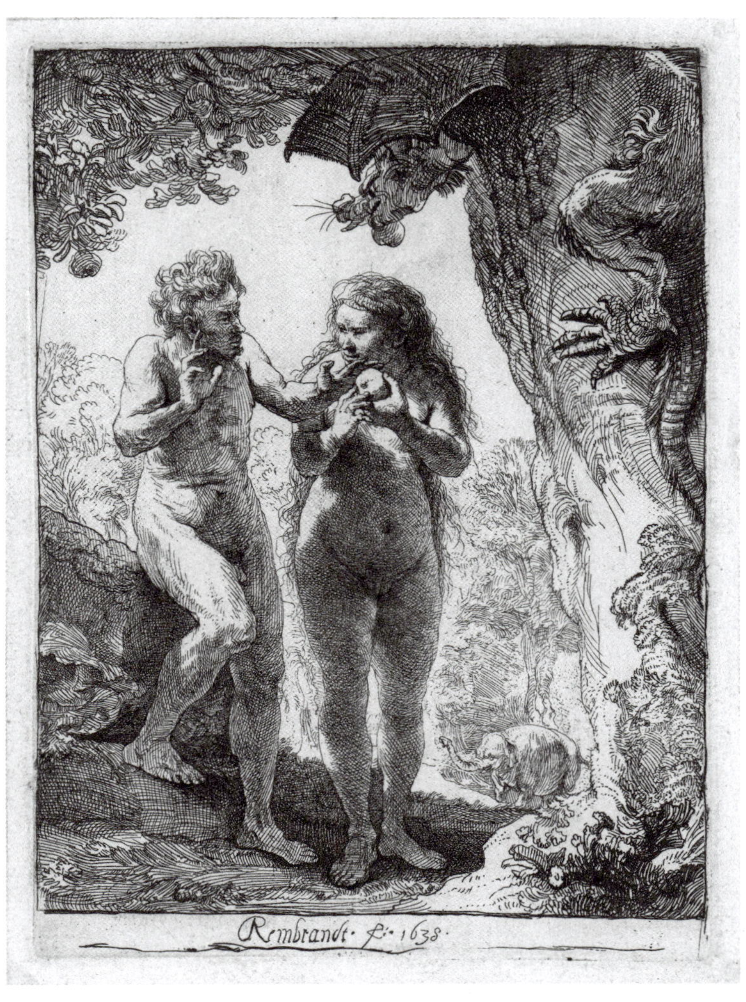

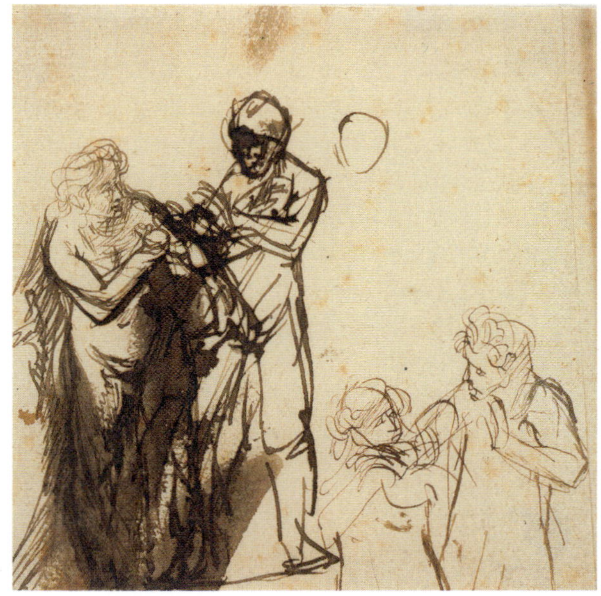

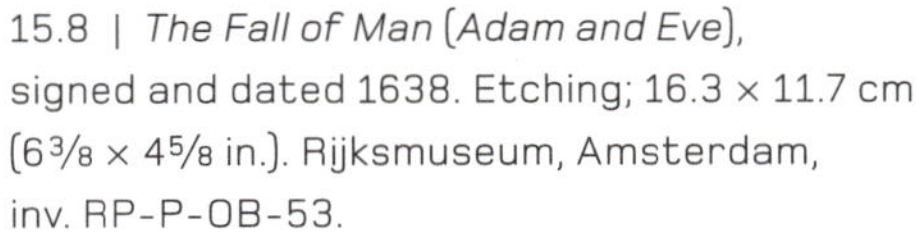

15.8 | *The Fall of Man (Adam and Eve)*, signed and dated 1638. Etching; 16.3 × 11.7 cm (6 3/8 × 4 5/8 in.). Rijksmuseum, Amsterdam, inv. RP-P-OB-53.

15.9 | *Studies for the Fall of Man*, ca. 1638. Pen and brown ink, brown wash; 11.5 × 11.5 cm (4 1/2 × 4 1/2 in.). Leiden University Library, shelfmark PK-T-AW-1097.

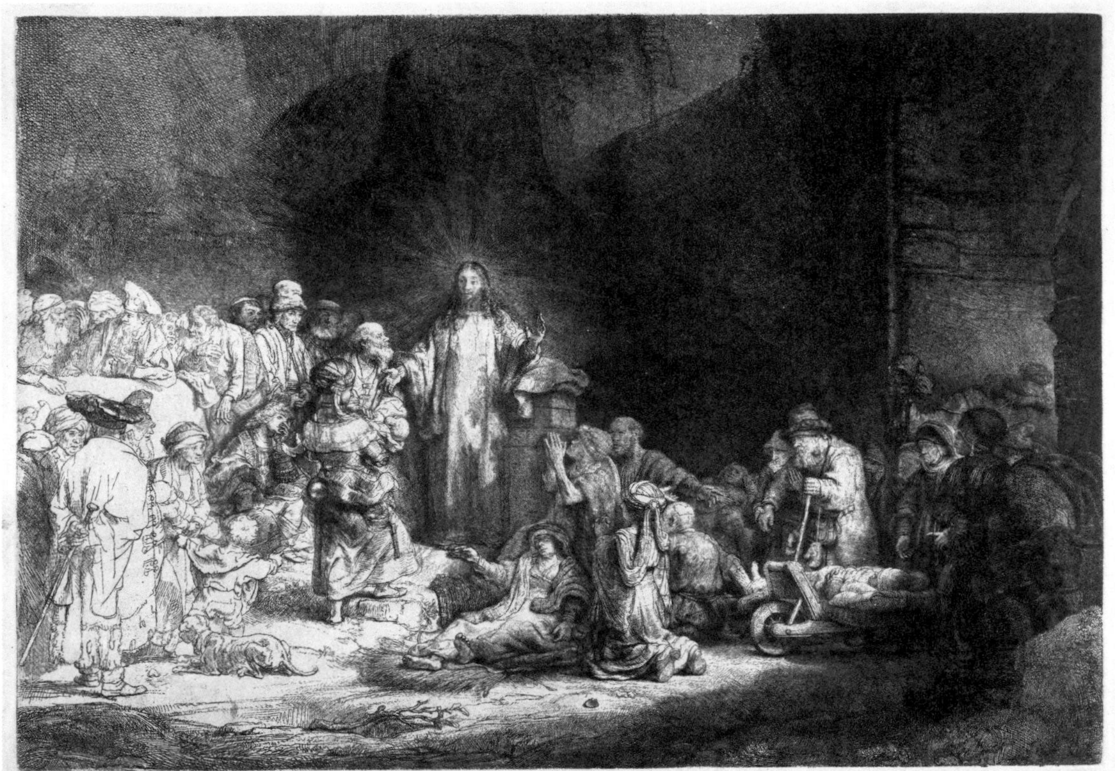

Near the center, a young mother with a child advances toward Jesus. Peter interferes, restraining her, but Christ makes a countermovement. It is the moment when he says the famous words: "Suffer the little children and forbid them not to come unto me, for such is the kingdom of heaven." The chapter also includes the story of the rich youth who could not decide whether to give his possessions to the poor and follow Christ's teachings. He is seen seated, in contemplation, to the left in rich attire. After his departure, Jesus says: "It is easier for a camel to go through the eye of a needle than for a rich man to enter into the kingdom of God." The camel passing through a gate on the right side of the etching may refer to this passage of the chapter. Pharisees are seen at the upper left. As in the text, they are arguing among themselves, not with Christ.

The print is one of many proofs that Rembrandt was an exceptionally attentive reader of Scripture. *Een oude bijbel* (an old Bible), one of the few books listed by title in the 1656 inventory, must have been the volume he opened most frequently.

Existing sketches for *The Hundred Guilder Print* unsurprisingly indicate that Rembrandt made many revisions to his

15.10 | *The Hundred Guilder Print* (*Christ Healing the Sick*), ca. 1648. Etching, drypoint, and burin, on Japanese paper; 27.8 × 38.8 cm (11 × 15¼ in.). The British Museum, London, inv. PD1973-U-1022. Photo © The Trustees of The British Museum/ Art Resource, N.Y.

initial idea for individual figures in the etching. Two pen sketches (both in reverse) are known for the woman with an outstretched arm lying at Christ's feet (fig. 15.11). In one of them she is sketched twice; on the left side she is looking up, on the right she has an arm raised (fig. 15.12). A separate sketch of her right hand and leg is in the lower left corner of the sheet. In the second sketch Rembrandt tried the idea of showing her praying (fig. 15.13), but in the end he discarded the thought. The same little sheet has another sketch of her head. A pen sketch (in reverse) of a standing man holding a cap (fig. 15.14) is a third study for the print. In the etching he appears without his cap standing next to the praying woman whose remarkable, prominent shadow falls upon Christ's garment. The cursory treatment of his legs in the sketch suggests that the artist knew they would be hidden in the completed etching.

A compositional study (again in reverse) that includes both the reclining woman and standing man as well as figures grouped around them (fig. 15.15) approximates Rembrandt's final solution for this area of the work. However, comparison of the drawing and print indicates that significant adjustments continued to be made.

Finally, there is a touching pen study (in reverse) for the feeble old blind man accompanied by an old woman (fig. 15.16). He has a conspicuous place on the right side of the print where he appears much weaker and more infirm than in the sketch (fig. 15.17). And who but Rembrandt would have thought of depicting the helpless old man with mittens dangling from a string secured to his waist? If one chooses, this tiny telling detail, usually associated with the care given to the apparel of little children, can be read as an emblem of the artist's signature. Rembrandt himself did not find it necessary to sign the famous etching.

Although surviving drawings for *The Hundred Guilder Print* give a hint of the imaginative power, intense concentration, and labor that went into its creation, they do not account for the etching's warmth of feeling that seems to emanate from Jesus, spreading balm on the suffering souls of the sick, the poor, and the humble, or the wondrous light that hovers and spreads over the deeply shadowed scene. These effects are mostly due to Rembrandt's incomparable control of his etcher's needle, his burin, and his use of drypoint burr.

Scores of the artist's drawings testify to his genius as a storyteller, but none more than his many sketches of biblical subjects. Among the most dramatic is Berlin's explosive

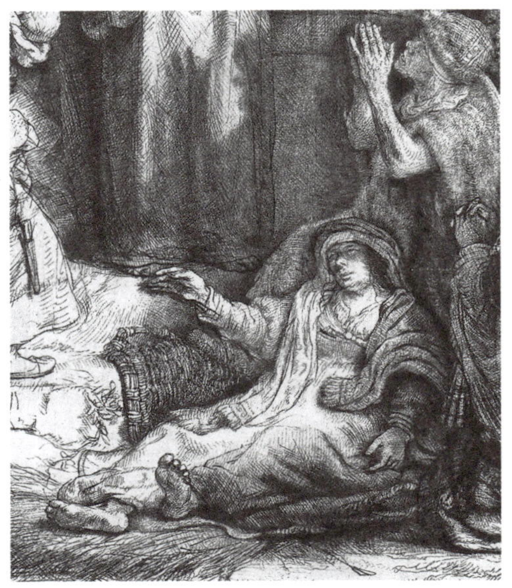

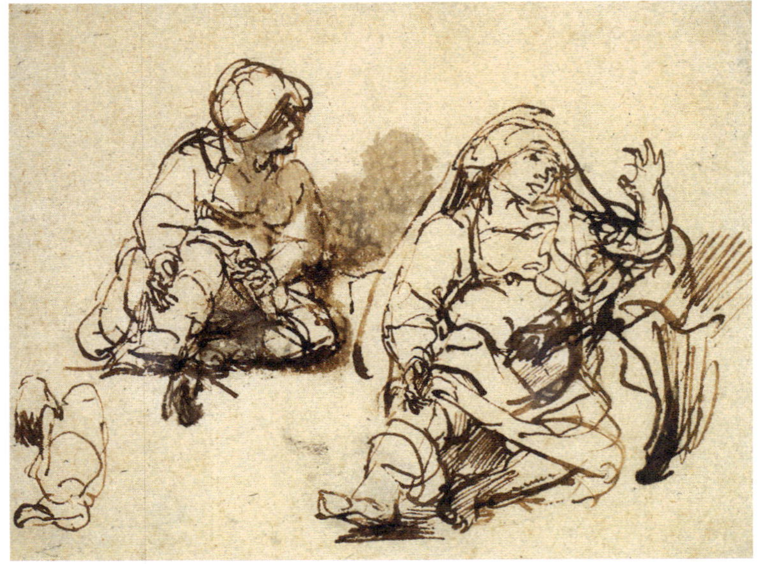

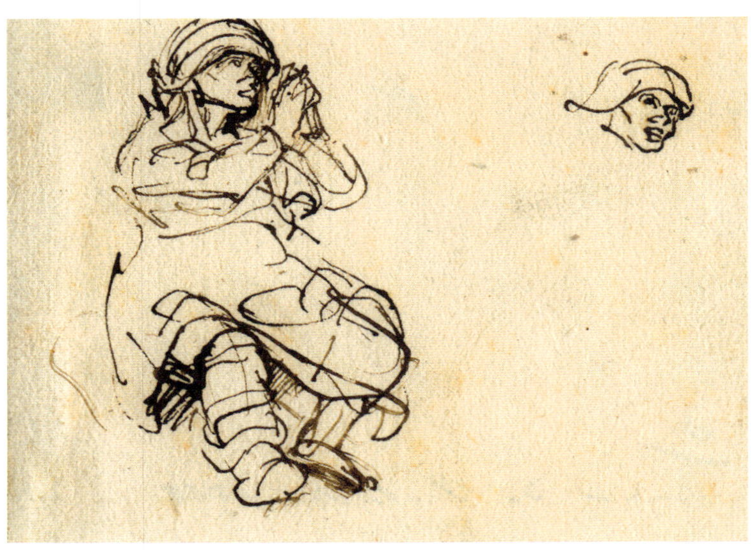

15.11 | Woman lying at Christ's feet. Detail of *"The Hundred Guilder Print,"* figure 15.10.

15.12 | *Studies for the Sick Woman in "The Hundred Guilder Print."* Pen and brush and brown ink, white gouache, on paper; 10.1 × 12.2 cm (3⅞ × 4¾ in.). Rijksmuseum, Amsterdam, inv. RP-T-1964-27(R).

15.13 | *Studies for the Sick Woman in "The Hundred Guilder Print."* Pen and brown ink; 8 × 10.9 cm (3⅛ × 4¼ in.). Collection of Clement C. Moore II. Photo courtesy of Clement C. Moore II.

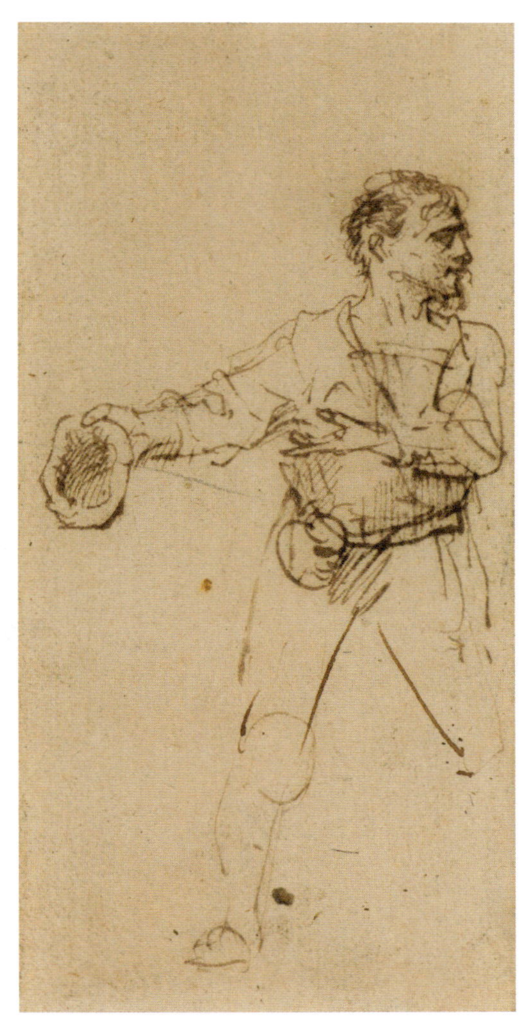

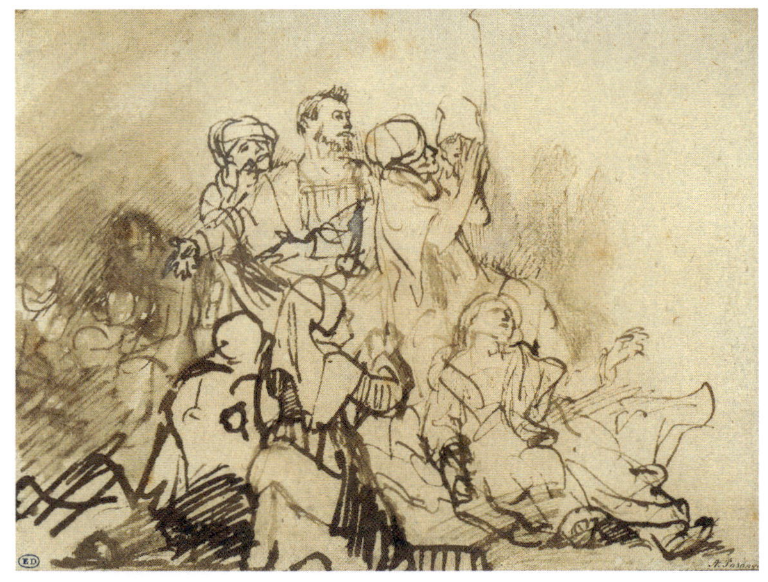

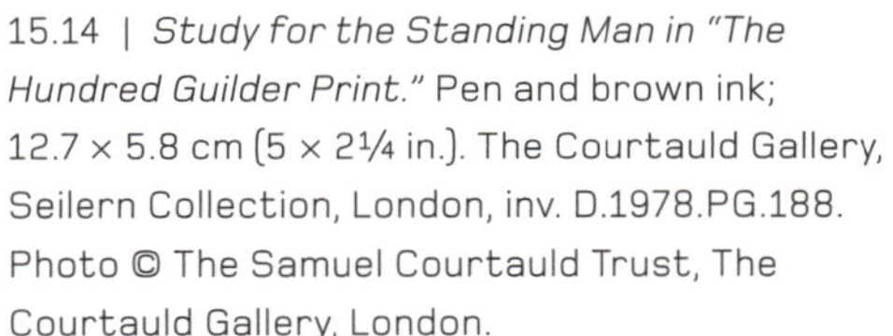

15.14 | *Study for the Standing Man in "The Hundred Guilder Print."* Pen and brown ink; 12.7 × 5.8 cm (5 × 2¼ in.). The Courtauld Gallery, Seilern Collection, London, inv. D.1978.PG.188. Photo © The Samuel Courtauld Trust, The Courtauld Gallery, London.

15.15 | *Compositional Study for "The Hundred Guilder Print."* Pen and brown ink, brown wash, heightened with white; 14.4 × 18.4 cm (5⅝ × 7¼ in.). Kupferstichkabinett, Staatliche Museen, Berlin, inv. KdZ2695. Photo: Bildarchiv Preussischer Kulturbesitz/Art Resource, N.Y. Photographer: Jörg P. Anders.

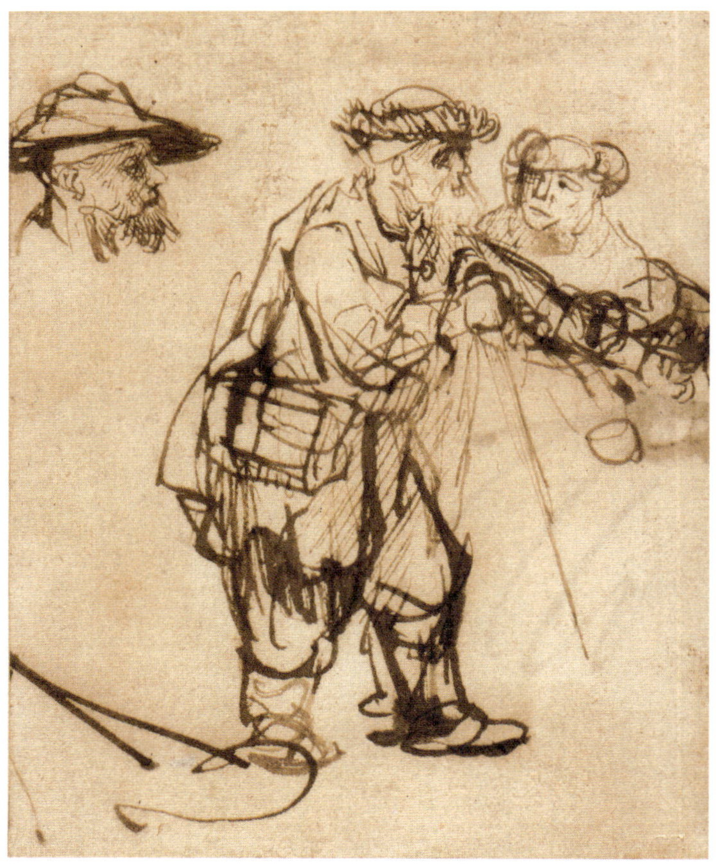

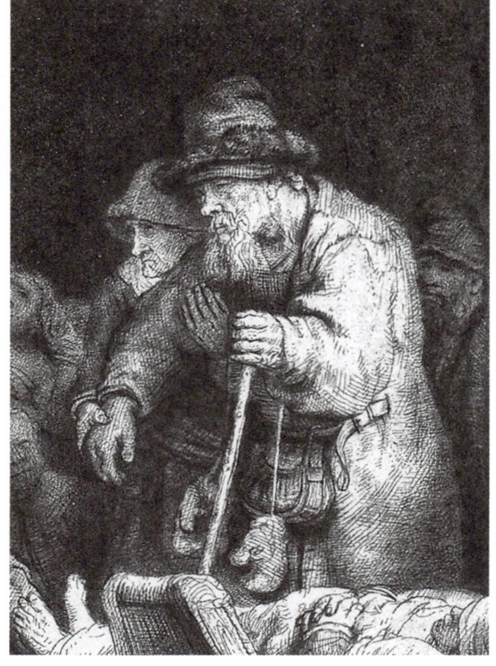

pen-and-wash drawing of Jacob lamenting at the sight of Joseph's bloodstained coat (fig. 15.18), the climax of a story told in Genesis (37:3–34). Jacob loved Joseph more than all his other children because Joseph was the "son of his old age." When Joseph's brothers realized this, they hated and envied him. Eventually they sold him to the Ishmeelites. To hide their wicked deed, they took Joseph's coat of many colors, which his father had made for him, and dipped it in the blood of a dead kid. Then they brought it to their father, exclaiming "This we have found; know now whether it be thy son's coat or no." And Jacob said: "It is my son's coat; an evil beast hath devoured him; Joseph is without doubt rent to pieces." And Jacob rent his clothes.

Rembrandt shows old Jacob with his hands clasped, his eyes rolling, his open mouth emitting what must be taken as a bloodcurdling cry at the very instant he recognizes his beloved son's bloodstained coat. The large splashes of wash on the left represent the son bearing the coat. He is more a fear-inspiring specter than a figure. Between them are two,

15.16 | *An Old Man Led by a Woman,* study for *"The Hundred Guilder Print."* Pen and brown ink; 12 × 9.8 cm (4¾ × 3⅞ in.). Musée du Louvre, Paris, inv. 22891. Photo © RMN—Grand Palais/ Art Resource, N.Y. Photographer: Thierry Ollivier.

15.17 | Old blind man. Detail of *"The Hundred Guilder Print,"* figure 15.10.

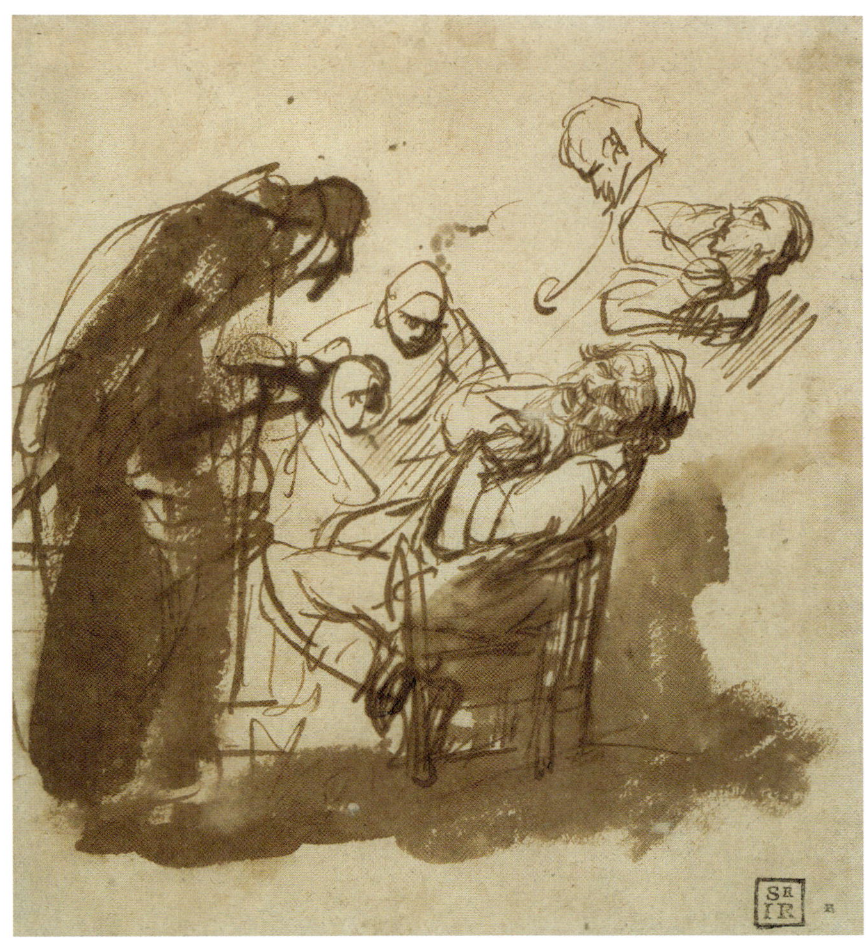

15.18 | *Jacob Lamenting at the Sight of Joseph's Bloody Coat*, ca. 1635–37. Pen and brown ink, brown wash, white; 17.2 × 15.5 cm (6¾ × 6⅛ in.). Kupferstichkabinett, Staatliche Museen, Berlin, inv. KdZ 52123. Photo: Bildarchiv Preussischer Kulturbesitz/Art Resource, N.Y. Photographer: Jörg P. Anders.

perhaps three, hastily sketched figures. Above, on the right, is a cursory variation of lamenting Jacob's head and arms. The adjacent head in profile may be a study for dejected Jacob mourning the loss of Joseph.

Not as dramatic, but equally affecting is the pen drawing at Besançon of the *Annunciation* (fig. 15.19). No other sketch of the subject by the artist is known, and he did not treat it in other media. The story has been depicted almost countless times by Western artists. Most popular is the moment the angel Gabriel came to the Virgin Mary and said: "Hail, thou art highly favored, the Lord is with thee, blessed art thou among women" (Luke 1:28).

Rembrandt decided to show what happened to Mary after the announcement. She is dazed and has collapsed. Incredibly fine lines delineate her tender expression. Solicitous Gabriel assists her. In Luke's account, she is troubled by the archangel's appearance and words. He comforts her and tells her she has found favor with the Lord (Luke 1:29–30). Word that she will conceive and bring forth a son, and call him Jesus, is given in the following verse.

Gabriel's magnificently drawn wings, which probably impress both ornithologists and aeronautical engineers, are the only element of the drawing that indicates that we are confronted by a scene from the Annunciation. All other traditional references to the subject have been eliminated: the Holy Spirit as a dove or rays of celestial light that signify the favor Mary has found with the Lord; lily branches, an allusion to Mary's virginity; a prayer book and a prie-dieu, indications of Mary's devoutness; and an ambassadorial staff in Gabriel's hand. The only props are a familiar armchair, a single slipper, and perhaps a hastily sketched kitten at the Virgin's feet. Elimination of all else focuses attention on Mary and Gabriel and their relationship.

Another drawing that depicts a crucial part of a story's climax is Cleveland's pen-and-wash sketch of the healing of blind Tobit (fig. 15.20), a story taken from one of the apocryphal books of the Old Testament. Pious Tobit, known for his acts of charity, became poor and blind in his old age. His son Tobias, with the indispensable help of the archangel Raphael (in Hebrew his name means God's help), heals Tobit's blindness.

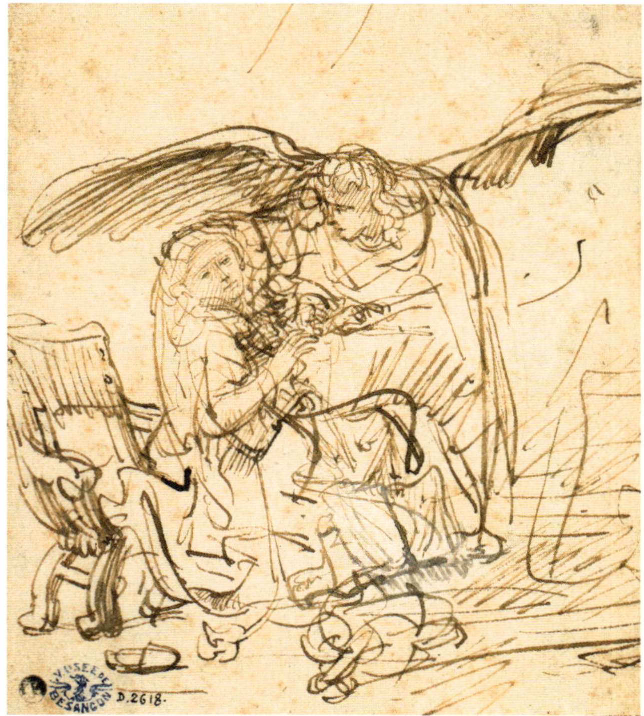

15.19 | *The Annunciation*, ca. 1635. Pen and brown ink, corrected with diluted gouache; 14.4 × 12.4 cm (5⅝ × 4⅞ in.). Musée des Beaux-Arts et d'Archéologie, Besançon (France), inv. D2618. Copyright Besançon, Musée des Beaux-Arts et d'Archéologie. Photographer: Pierre Guenat.

Cleveland's drawing shows Tobias performing a delicate surgical operation with a knife on one of his seated father's eyes—contrary to the text of the Book of Tobit, which states Tobias rubs the gall of a fish on his eyes, thereby peeling off the film that blinded him for eight years and making him see again. The archangel Raphael, more faintly drawn, closely watches the operation, while Tobias's aged mother, Anna, peers intently through her spectacles over her son's shoulder. She helpfully holds a cup. Sarah, Tobias's wife, stands at the side with hands clasped watching the procedure.

The Book of Tobit, like the other apocryphal books of the Old Testament, is not well known today, perhaps because it and the others are included in neither the King James nor the Douay versions of the Bible. But earlier ages were familiar with it, and it was a particular favorite of Rembrandt's. He illustrated aspects of it during every phase of his career in every medium he used. Members of his circle likewise show a predilection for the story.

It is hardly necessary to turn to the relevant passage in the Gospel of Saint John to discover the drama depicted in

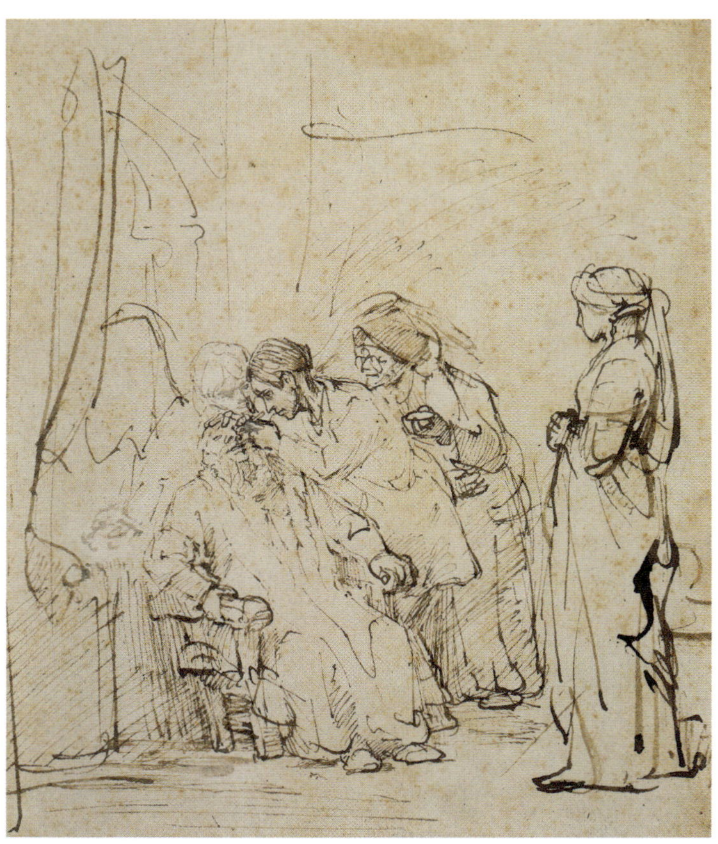

15.20 | *Tobias Healing His Father's Blindness*, ca. 1640–45. Pen and brown ink, touched with white gouache, framing lines in brown ink; 21.1 × 17.7 cm (8¼ × 7 in.). Photo © The Cleveland Museum of Art, Purchase from the J. H. Wade Fund, inv. 1969.69.

Amsterdam's fascinating drawing of squatting Jesus going about his business of washing Peter's feet. Peter, seated and leaning forward, grasps the arm of his chair, wondering why, in heaven's name, the Lord is doing such a thing (fig. 15.21). Before Peter sat in his armchair, he said to Christ: "Thou shalt never wash my feet." Jesus answered: "If I wash thee not, thou hast no part with me" (John 13:8). As depicted by Rembrandt, Peter's mien tells us he still lacks understanding of the Lord's humble humanity.

A love story in the Old Testament tells of Isaac and his wife Rebecca spied upon by Abimelech, King of the Philistines, as they enjoy their conjugal relationship (Genesis 26:6–9). It is the subject of a delicate pen drawing, now in the Werner H. Kramarsky collection (fig. 15.22). Isaac's wife Rebecca was a beauty. When the couple settled in Gerar, Isaac told the local men that Rebecca was his sister, not his wife, because he feared they would kill him for her. After the couple had been in Gerar for a long time, Abimelech "looked out at a window, and saw, and, behold, Isaac was sporting with Rebecca his wife" (Genesis 26:8). The king then called Isaac. After telling him what he saw, Abimelech remarked that Rebecca was surely his wife, not his sister. Isaac replied that was indeed the case and that he had lied because he feared to die for her. Subsequently, the sympathetic king offered the couple his protection.

In the upper right of the drawing the king is at the window; he is very difficult to spot in a reproduction, but be assured he is there. The loving couple is clearer. Isaac is seated on a balustrade. His wife is sitting on his lap. He is looking at her (his head has been drawn twice) and embraces her with one arm. His other hand touches Rebecca's breast and she, in turn, lays her hand upon his. This is precisely the position of two hands in Rembrandt's *The Jewish Bride* (fig. 15.23), arguably the second most famous hands in the history of Western painting. Top place in this category can be assigned safely to Michelangelo's hand of God about to give life to Adam by touching one of his fingers in the Italian master's fresco on the Sistine Chapel's ceiling.

The drawing of Isaac and Rebecca almost certainly served as inspiration for *The Jewish Bride*. Granted, the man's head in the painting is seen in three-quarters view, not in profile, but striking similarities remain. Hands are similarly positioned and so are the tender embraces. The plant on the right in the drawing also appears in the painting. And most important, X-radiographs of *The Jewish Bride* reveal that Rembrandt

15.21 | *Christ Washing the Disciples' Feet*, 1640–49. Pen and brown ink, on paper; 15.7 × 22.1 cm (6⅛ × 8¾ in.). Rijksmuseum, Amsterdam, inv. RP-T-1889-A-2049.

15.22 | *Isaac and Rebecca Spied upon by King Abimelech*, ca. 1655–60. Pen and brown ink, corrected with white, on paper; 14.4 × 18.3 cm (5⅝ × 7⅛ in.). Werner H. Kramarsky collection, New York, inv. 1582.

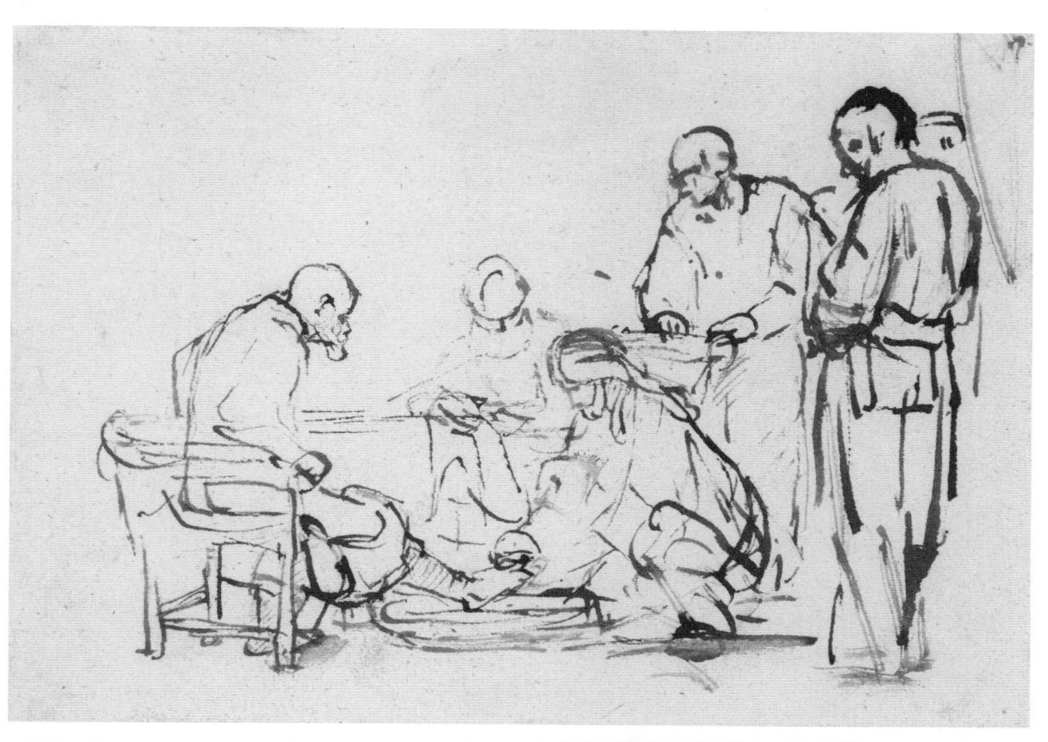

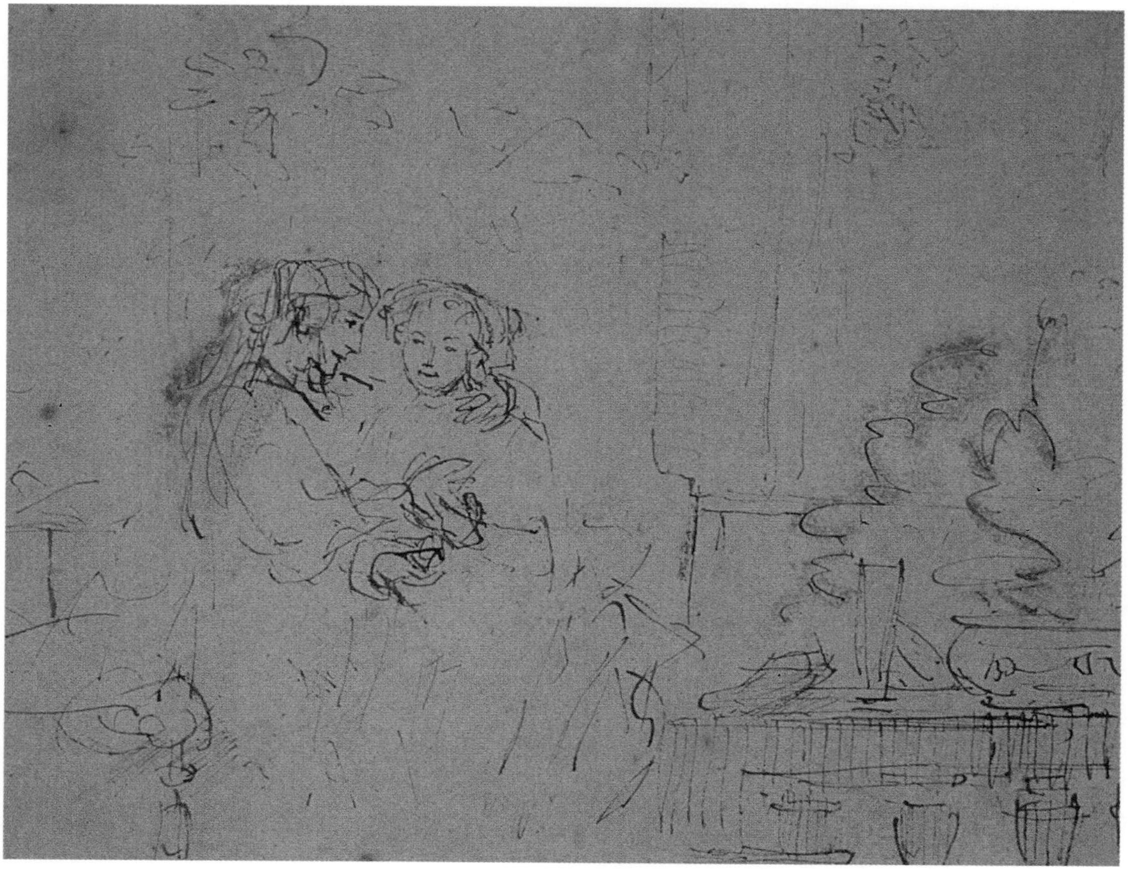

originally painted the figures closer to the way they are seen in the drawing, with the woman seated with her right leg over the man's left leg. Later Rembrandt changed his mind and made the revisions now seen in the masterwork.[89]

Identification of the sitters for *The Jewish Bride* has been much discussed (its popular title dates from the nineteenth century). It may be a commissioned portrait of a couple in the guise of a religious pair—historical portraits that showed sitters as biblical, mythological, or literary characters were *à la mode* in some circles in the Netherlands during the seventeenth century. In view of the double portrait's close connection with the drawing, perhaps a married couple had themselves depicted as Isaac and Rebecca. A precedent for this notion is offered by Rembrandt's pupil Ferdinand Bol's double portrait of an identifiable Dutch couple as Isaac and Rebecca that is datable not long after their marriage in 1645.[90]

Munich's late pen-and-wash drawing, with touches of gray and light red watercolor added by a later hand, of *Christ*

15.23 | *The Jewish Bride*, signed, ca. 1665–69. Oil on canvas; 121.5 × 166.5 cm (47⅞ × 65½ in.). Rijksmuseum, Amsterdam, inv. SK-C-216 (on loan from the City of Amsterdam).

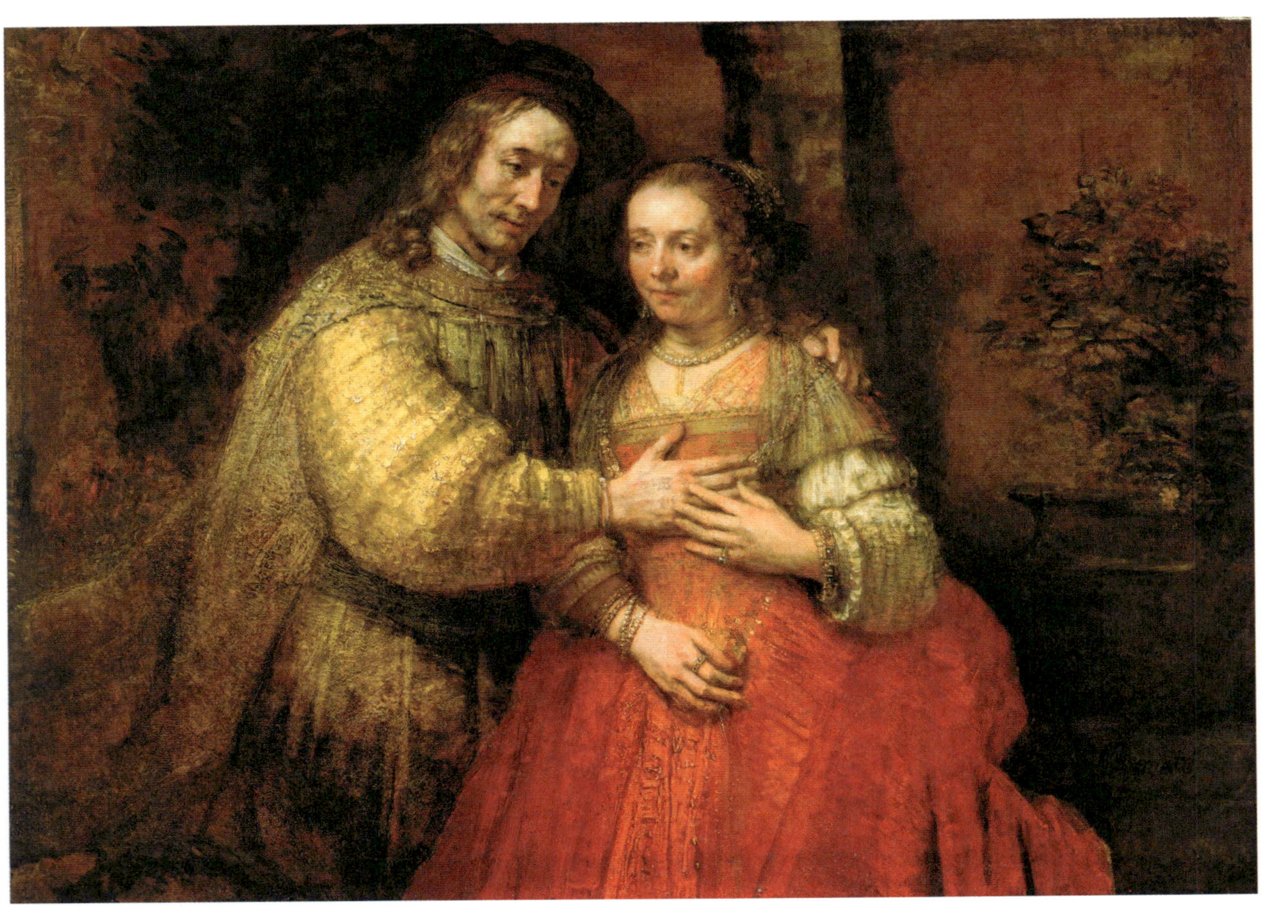

and the Woman Taken in Adultery (fig. 15.24) is drawn on the back of a fragment of a printed funeral ticket (fig. 15.25). It has been established that the funeral occurred on 14 May 1659; the drawing probably was executed soon afterward. We have already heard that the artist's compositional study for his colossal painting of *The Conspiracy of Claudius Civilis* is on the verso of part of another funeral ticket dated more than two years later (see p. 193 and fig. 14.14).

The Munich drawing depicts the opening of the story (John 8:2–6). While Christ was teaching in the temple, scribes and Pharisees brought him a woman taken in the very act of adultery. When she was set in their midst, they maintained that according to Mosaic law she must be stoned, "but what sayest thou?" they asked Jesus. They were trying to tempt him in order to discover whether the love he was preaching was above Mosaic law.

The Dutch inscription in Rembrandt's own hand, at the bottom of the drawing, summarizes the scene: *"So eager to ensnare Christ in his answer, they* [the scribes and Pharisees] *could not wait for a written answer."*[91] The inscription may have been written as an *aide-mémoire*, a note to a potential client considering commissioning a painting based on the drawing, or a note of instruction to his students. Such autograph inscriptions are rare in Rembrandt's production as a draftsman.[92]

The brief account (John 8:6–11) of what followed the episode depicted in the Munich drawing is worth telling. Christ did not respond to the question put to him by the scribes and Pharisees. Instead of answering, he ignored them and stooped down and began to write on the ground with his finger. When they continued asking, he stood up and said: "He that is without sin among you, let him cast first a stone at her." When they heard him, each convicted by his own conscience, they proceeded to leave one by one. When Jesus found himself alone with the adultress, he said: "Woman, where are those thine accusers? Hath no man condemned thee?" She replied: "No man, Lord." Then Jesus said: "Neither do I condemn thee. Go, and sin no more."

Rembrandt's painting, dated 1644, of the same subject is now in the National Gallery, London (fig. 15.26). Perhaps the Munich drawing, which has the character of a quick compositional sketch, was a study for a new painted or etched version of the story that was never executed. Comparison of the painting and the drawing is telling. The small figures of the main group of the painting gain distinction by the falling

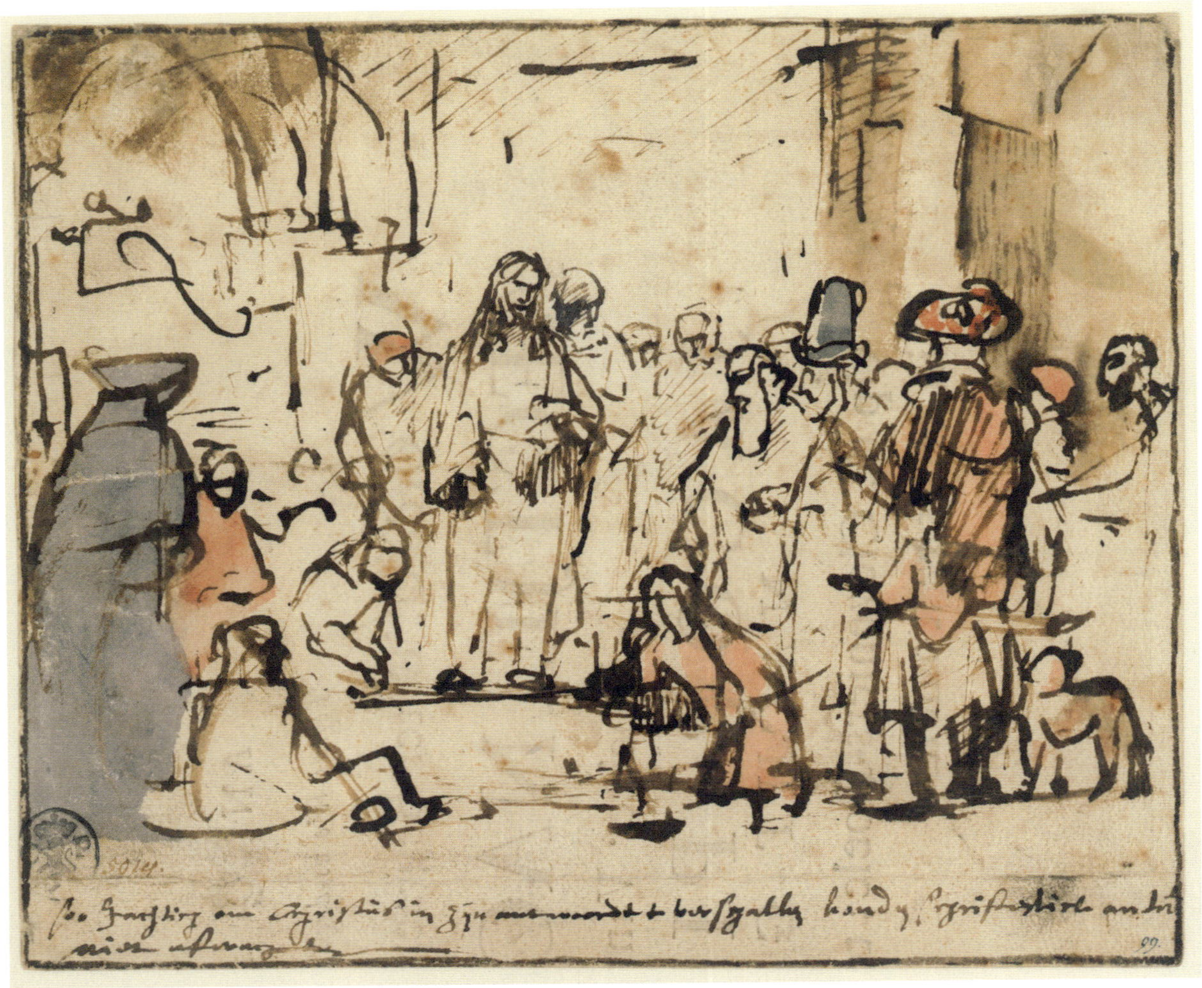

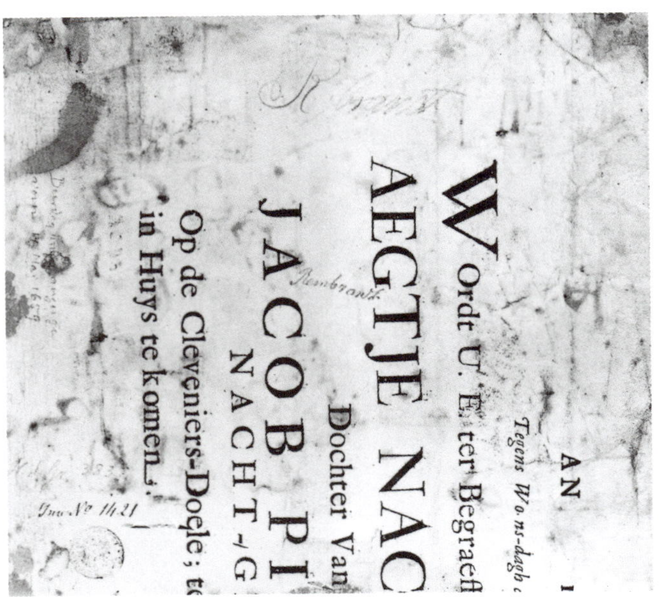

15.24 | *Christ and the Woman Taken in Adultery*, 1659. Pen and brown ink, brown wash, watercolor by a later hand; 17 × 20.2 cm (6¾ × 8 in.). Staatliche Graphische Sammlung, Munich, inv. 1421 Z.

15.25 | Verso of figure 15.24.

light that strikes them. Other figures in the dimly lit interior of colossal dimensions are difficult to distinguish. Fantastic columns, an ornate gilded altar, and deep shadows intensify the mysterious atmosphere. In the drawing there has been a profound change: Architecture is now clearly subordinate to the figures. Even though the drawing is schematic, it is evident Christ has gained in importance. The parapet upon which he stands is not obstructed by a figure. The composition recalls Rembrandt's well-known etching of about 1652 of *Christ Preaching* ("La Petite Tombe"). In it Jesus preaches frontally to a crowd standing on an unobstructed parapet, apart from a little child playing mindlessly in the dirt in front of it, and, as in the etching of Christ preaching, the figures in the drawing are on two levels.

Our discussion of the artist's biblical drawings closes with his signed and dated 1661 pen-and-wash drawing of *The Presentation in the Temple* (fig. 15.27) in the *album amicorum* that belonged to Jacob Heyblocq, an Amsterdammer who studied for the ministry but opted for a career as a master, then headmaster, of an Amsterdam grammar school. Contributions to his album, which consists of more than three hundred pages, were made from 1645 to 1678 and range from a few by Heyblocq's classmates at Leiden University to some by the most illustrious citizens of the new republic. In addition to Rembrandt's drawing there is a sketch by his successful pupil Govert Flinck, who has been mentioned as the artist who received the prize commission for paintings to decorate Amsterdam's New Town Hall. There are also drawings by other leading artists, among them Jan van de Cappelle, Gerbrandt van den Eeckhout, Aert van der Neer, and Jan de Bray, as well as some less-well-known artists and anonymous amateurs.[93]

Rembrandt's scene of *The Presentation in the Temple* is based on Luke 2:22–35. The same text inspired him to make a painting in about 1627/28, not long after he picked up his brushes as an independent artist in Leiden; to create another painting in about 1630; and to produce etchings in 1630, the late 1630s and again in the early 1650s. His very late representation of the subject is the poorly preserved unfinished painting of *Simeon in the Temple*, now in Stockholm, which, it has been suggested, was the one seen in his studio a few months before he died in 1669.[94]

According to Luke, it was revealed to Simeon that he would not die until he had seen Christ. In the drawing Simeon is viewed with the child Jesus in his arms, in the presence of

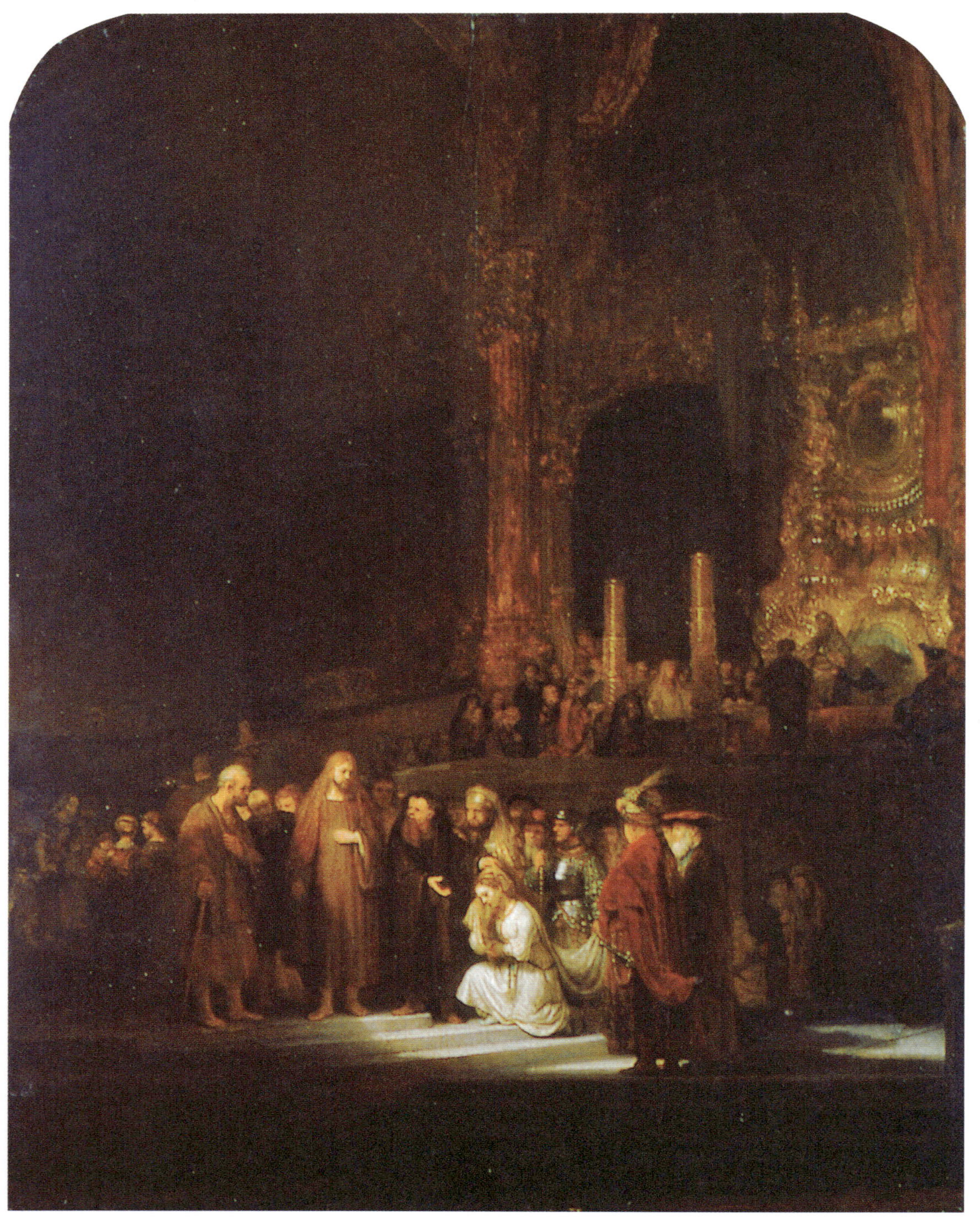

15.26 | *Christ and the Woman Taken in Adultery*, signed and dated 1644. Oil on panel; 83.8 × 65.4 cm (33 × 25¾ in.), upper corners rounded. National Gallery, London, inv. 47. Photo: Art Resource, N.Y.

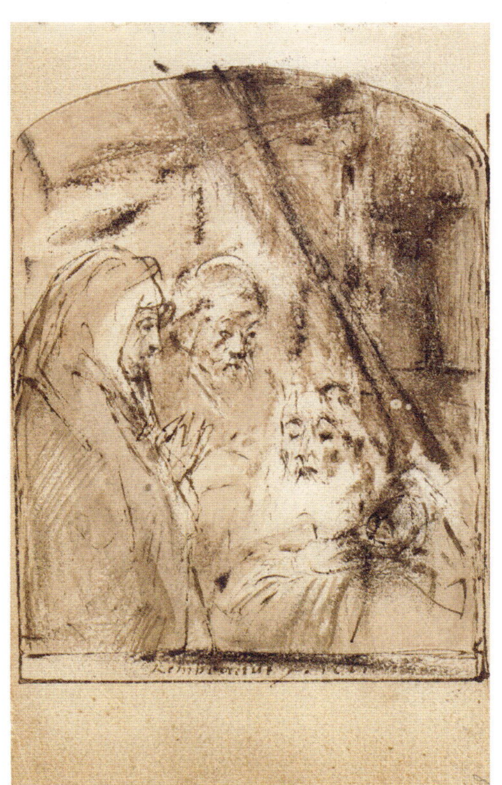

the devout Mary and Joseph, who had brought the Child to him in accord with Mosaic law. After blessing Jesus, Simeon said: "Lord, now lettest thou thy servant depart in peace... for mine eyes have seen thy salvation" (Luke 2:29–30).

The little drawing, with its rounded top, resembles a miniature devotional altarpiece. Generous use of different shades of brown wash define the four figures and engulf them in the temple's mysterious darkness. Only a few delicate touches of a fine pen define features. Light also plays a crucial role. In some passages a knife has been used to scrape away wash the artist wanted to lighten; and to suggest light, Rembrandt left some parts of the white paper untouched. He created Mary's halo and much of the heavenly light that descends upon Joseph and Simeon in a similar manner. We can only speculate if the drawing's celestial light should be taken as a reference to old Simeon's prophecy that Jesus should be "a light to lighten the Gentiles."

15.27 | *The Presentation in the Temple*, signed and dated 1661. Pen and brown ink, brown wash, white; 12 × 8.9 cm (4¾ × 3½ in.). Royal Library, The Hague.

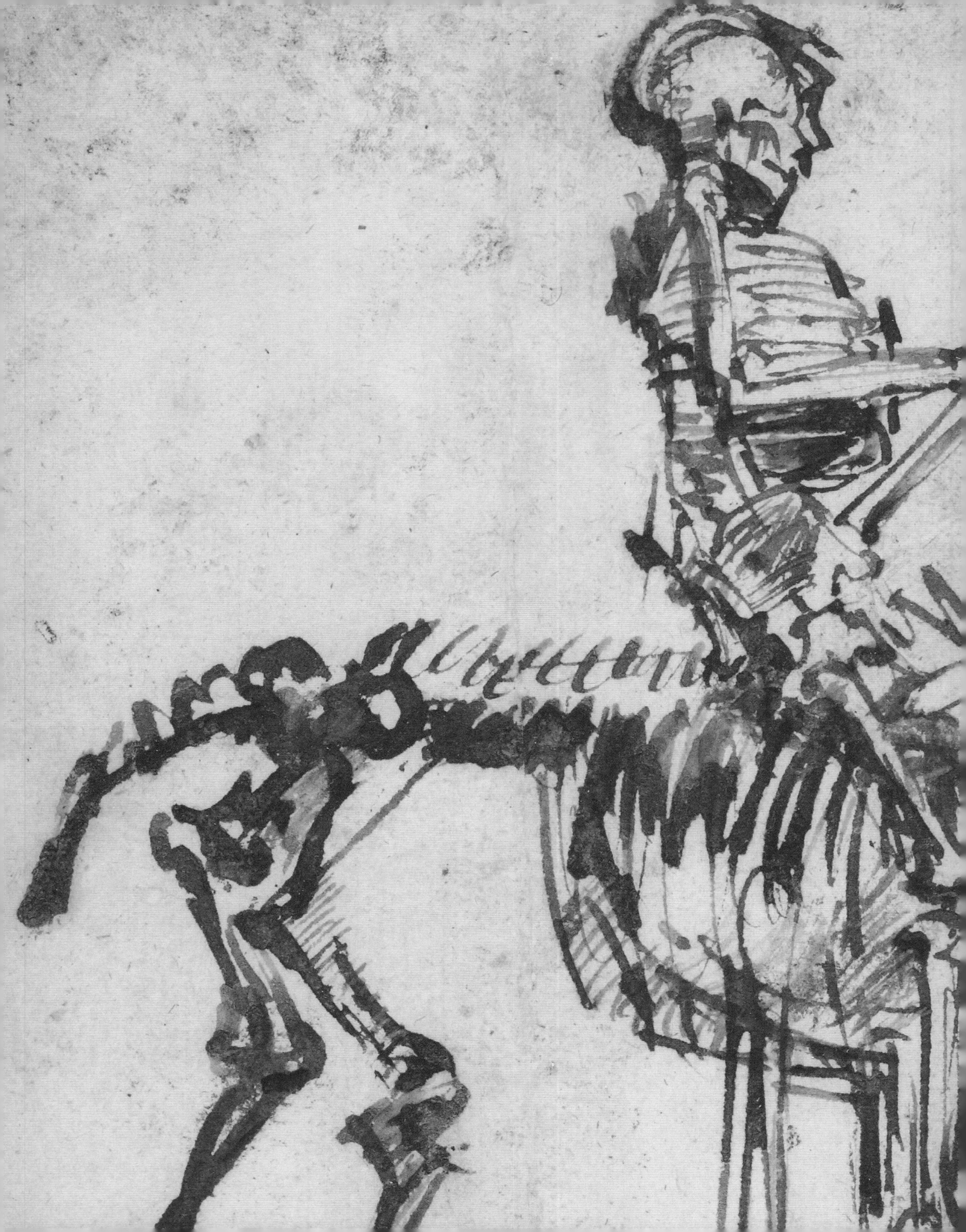

16 | Varia

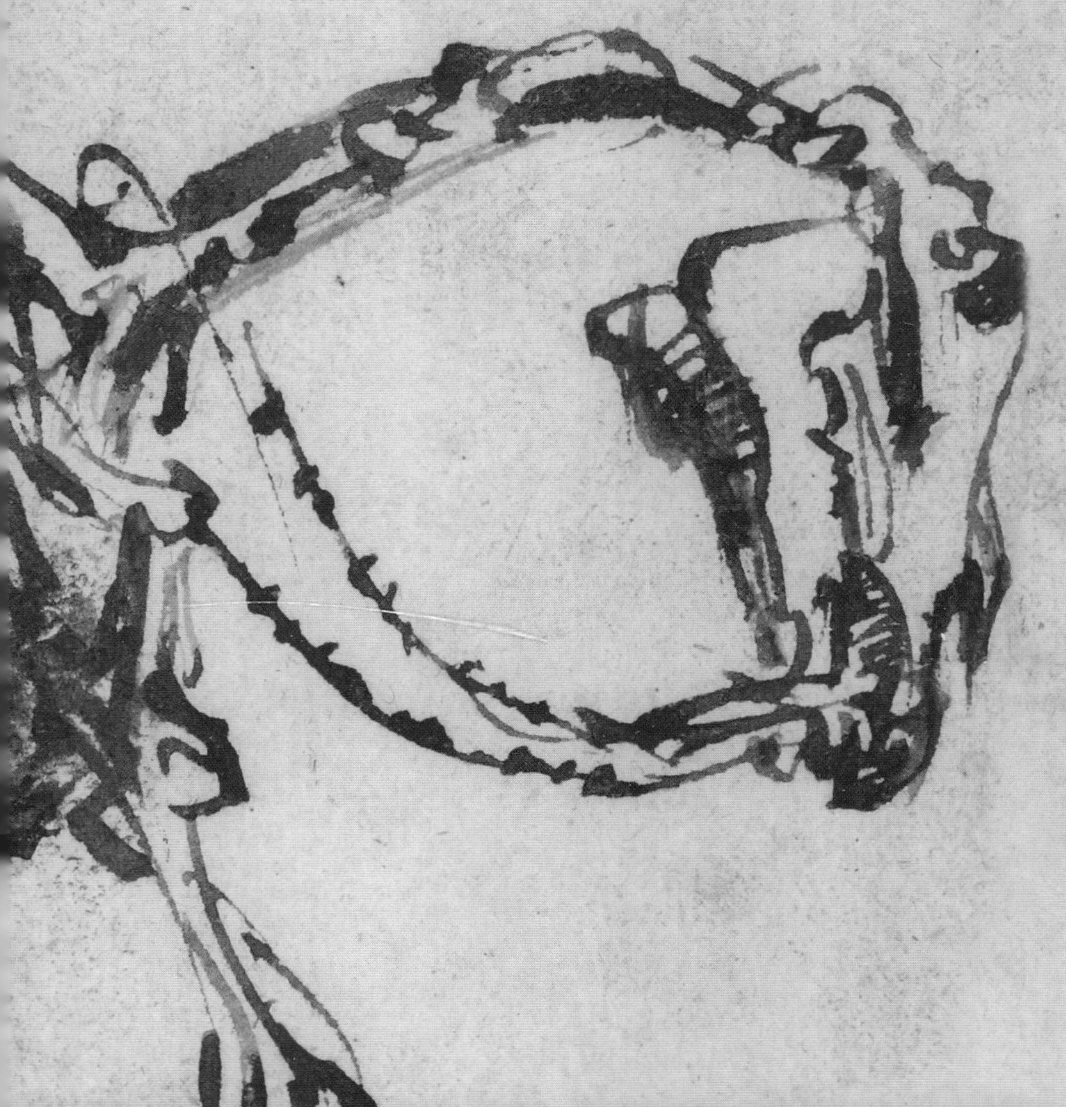

16 | VARIA

THE FIVE DRAWINGS discussed in this chapter are a mixed lot: a satire, a study of two Dutch working boats, a design for a picture frame, a sketch of a coach, and one of the skeleton of a rider seated upon the skeleton of a horse. Although none fits the thematic categories discussed earlier, they merit attention because of their revelation of additional aspects of the broad scope of Rembrandt's work, which continues to astonish.

For more than a century the pen drawing *Satire on Art Criticism*, now at the Metropolitan Museum in New York (fig. 16.1), has generated discussion and often disagreement.[95] Its attribution to Rembrandt has been challenged; the date written on its lower margin in Rembrandt's hand has been read in different ways; there is a consensus that the drawing's short inscriptions, which are not autograph, may be the key to the drawing's meaning; but there also is agreement that, except for a few words, they are indecipherable.

Figures in the drawing have been variously identified and assigned different interpretations, but there can be no question about the part played by the man with large ass's ears seated on a barrel pontificating about a framed painting that has been placed before him. As nearly everyone knows, since antiquity ass's ears have been used to signify stupidity. We have seen that the stupid, enthroned, crowned man has them in Mantegna's drawing of the *Calumny of Apelles*, which Rembrandt copied in the mid-1650s (see figs. 13.5, 13.6). However, there is no reason to conclude that Rembrandt was inspired by Mantegna to give ass's ears to the man. Moreover, it is unclear whether Rembrandt had encountered Mantegna's drawing by the time he made his satire. Put another way: Searching for the source of ass's ears worn by a character is asinine.[96]

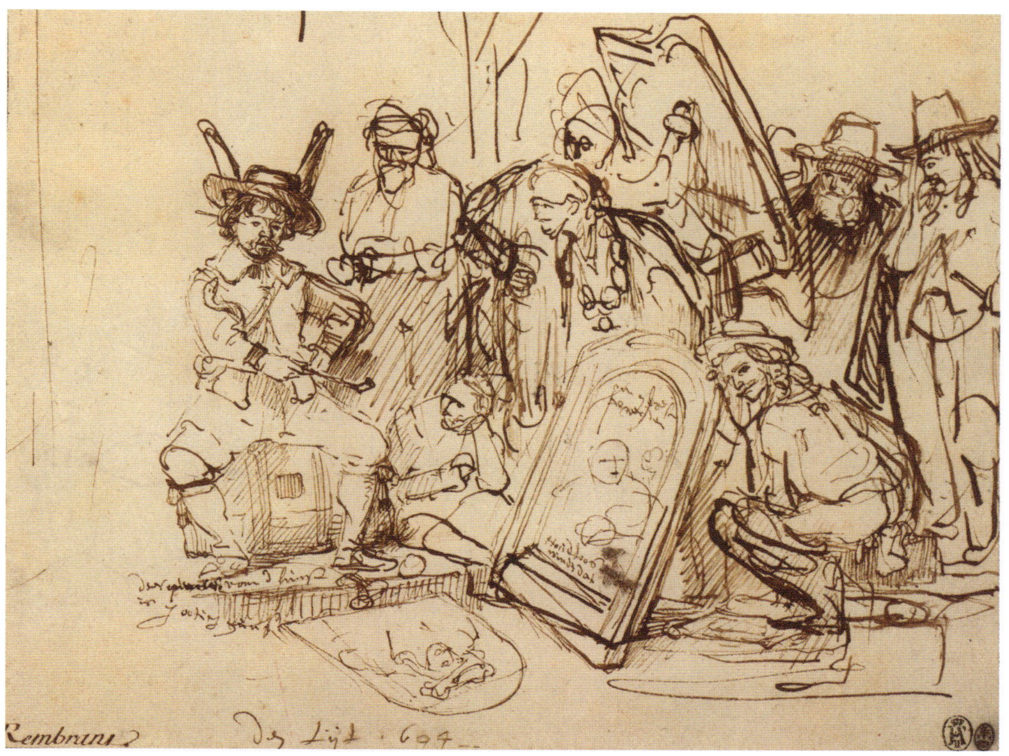

16.1 | *Satire on Art Criticism*, 1644. Pen and brown ink, corrected with white; 15.5 × 20.1 cm (6⅛ × 7⅞ in.). The Metropolitan Museum of Art, New York, The Robert Lehman Collection, inv. 1975.1.799. Photo copyright © The Metropolitan Museum of Art/Art Resource, N.Y.

Other things that accompany the seated man, who can safely be called a stupid critic, may very well signify his foolishness. The empty barrel upon which he is seated (its bunghole is open) may be a reference to his empty speech; his pipe used as a pointer may suggest his words are as ephemeral as the smoke a pipe emits; the pince-nez at his feet may be a play on the proverb: "If a man can't see, spectacles are worthless."

Certain (but not all) features of the depiction of the seated critic are weak, particularly his legs and feet, and the figure seated next to him is unusually awkward. The figures behind the man displaying the framed painting are difficult to read. Such passages probably explain why some connoisseurs have doubted the drawing's attribution. However, other parts of it, especially the critic's head and the two men on the right show a great similarity to those in *The Star of the Kings* (see fig. 8.11). They speak for the drawing's authenticity, a conclusion now generally endorsed. It is appropriate to add, however, that the signature "Rembrant" in the lower left corner is not in Rembrandt's hand.[97]

The conspicuous, defecating man in the right foreground, looking directly at the viewer and wiping his behind with a sheet of paper (from the book or pile of papers in front of him?), is showing his contempt for the proceedings. The bending man holding a framed picture has been identified as a factotum of an artist's guild because of the chain of metal discs he wears, or as an artist wearing a golden chain such as those worn by Titian, Rubens, and Van Dyck in their self-portraits. Behind him is a standing figure bearing aloft a large object at an angle. It has been proposed this figure is the helmeted goddess Minerva, holding a heart-shaped shield,[98] an identification difficult to follow. Whether the other figures have special meaning, as has been argued, or are merely extras remains an open question. The special significance—if it has one—of the half-length portrait painting with a rounded top at the stupid critic's feet has not been determined.

Finally, a word about the unusual inscription written by the artist at the bottom of the drawing; an enlargement of it is reproduced here (fig. 16.2). It has been variously read as *"den tijt·1604"* ("the time·1604") and *"den tijt·1644"* ("the time

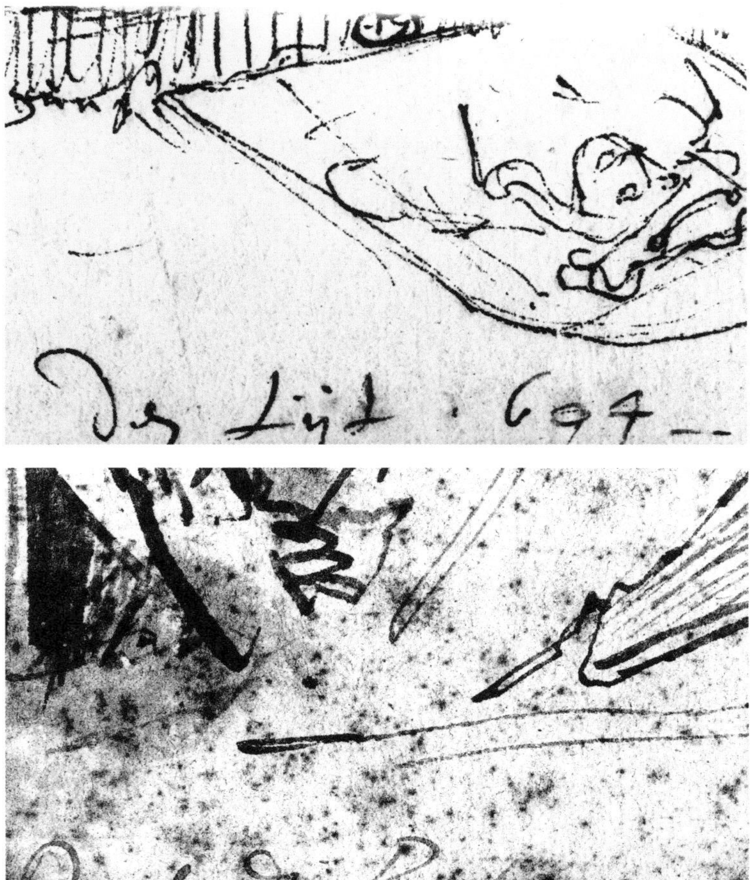

16.2 | Enlarged detail of inscription on figure 16.1.

16.3 | Enlarged detail of inscription on figure 11.1.

1644"). Now, if the 1604 reading is correct, at least part of the riddle that the sarcastic drawing poses is possibly solved. It may be a criticism of Karel van Mander's theoretical treatise for budding and established artists as well as amateurs: *Den grondt der edel vry schilder-const*, the first work in Dutch on the fundamentals of painting, which is a section of Van Mander's *Schilder-boeck* published in 1604.

The objections that this hypothesis explains neither why characters in the drawing wear costumes of the 1630s or 1640s nor why the critic's remarks directed at a portrait that seems to have been painted much later than 1604 are anachronistic. The type of historical accuracy called for by this criticism began to gain currency only in the nineteenth century.

More telling is the fact that Rembrandt wrote the third digit of the date in the same way (as a loop with a tail) on two other drawings he dated in the 1640s. One is the very large landscape also at the Metropolitan (see fig. 11.1); figure 16.3 shows an enlarged detail of its signature and its date of 1644. The other drawing, signed and very faintly dated 1641, of *Studies of Two Standing Men* (Benesch no. 500a), is at the Courtauld Gallery. This slim evidence for reading the date on the satire as 1644 is supported by the style of the sketch's penmanship.

Possibly a specific unpleasant personal incident impelled Rembrandt to make the sardonic drawing. Or possibly his loathing of the empty blathering of all windbags who assume they are qualified to make sound judgments about works of art found expression in the drawing. The two possibilities are not mutually exclusive.

More straightforward is the black-chalk drawing of two boats at anchor, now at the Albertina (fig. 16.4). It is datable to the early forties, when the artist made a number of black-chalk sketches of views of Amsterdam and its environs that were close to the spacious house he had purchased on Jodenbreestraat in 1639; one of them is illustrated in the chapter on landscape (see fig. 11.3).

The drawing of the boats was most probably done from life. Reflections of their bows in the flat, calm water and the bright light that dissolves some forms of their hulls indicate the day was sunny. The breeze was light; flags at the tops of the masts hardly flutter. The type of boat depicted is a boyer (*boeier*), a small open vessel with a standard gaff rig, normally used for coastal and inland trade. Midship on the hull of the near boat is a leeboard, used on either side of a vessel that sailed Dutch waters so shallow that the use of deep,

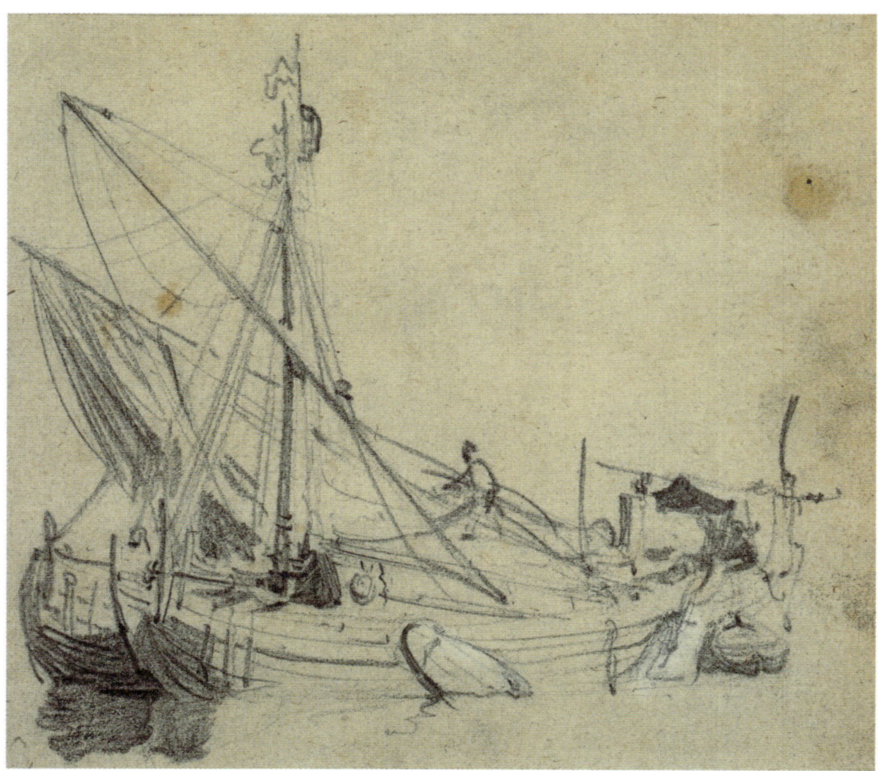

fixed keels was precluded. Leeboards prevent a vessel with a shallow draft from sliding leeway and enhance its ability to gain headway.

Without loss of its aesthetic appeal, Rembrandt's little sketch manages to incorporate an extraordinary number of other details of the two boats, which are tied together. The foremost one has a large anchor resting on its bow and below it three fenders on the hull. Aft is the boat's little dinghy. The long, bare yardarm indicates that the boat's sail has been stowed. In the boat tied to it a man is busy with a sail. The rigging of both boats is accurately and exquisitely drawn.

The artist could hardly avoid including boats in his sketches and etchings of the Dutch countryside in many places where water commands as large a part of the landscape as fields. However, the vessels that appear in his works of historical or religious subjects can be counted on the fingers of one hand.

16.4 | *Two Boats at Anchor*, ca. 1640–42. Black chalk, heightened with white; 14 × 15.8 cm (5½ × 6¼ in.). Graphische Sammlung Albertina, Vienna, inv. 17561. Photo © The Albertina Museum, Vienna.

Naturally, a boat has an important role in his 1633 historical etching of *The Ship of Fortune* that served as an illustration for a book by E. Herckmans, *Der Zee-Vaertlof* (In Praise of Seafaring, Amsterdam, 1634). It depicts the closing of the

Temple of Janus after Marc Anthony's defeat at Actium in 31 B.C. It is one of the artist's least successful prints.

The boats in his drawings of religious subjects are found in a sketch of *Christ in the Storm on the Sea of Galilee* (Dresden) and two of *Christ Walking on the Waves* (both at the British Museum[99]). The only painted example appears in his 1633 highly dramatic *Christ in the Storm on the Sea of Galilee* (stolen in 1990 from the Isabella Stewart Gardner Museum, Boston, along with Vermeer's *Concert* and other valuable works, and not yet recovered). It has been noted that in the Gardner painting Rembrandt took impossible liberties with the shape of the hull of the disciples' ship and with the size of its mast and its rigging.[100] Similar charges cannot be brought against his sketch made about a decade later of two working boats at anchor.

Early specialists thought the Louvre's pen-and-wash enframed drawing (fig. 16.5) of Rembrandt's grisaille painting of *Saint John the Baptist Preaching* of about 1635, now at Berlin, was a preliminary study for the picture. Later it was recognized

16.5 | *Design for a Frame for "Saint John the Baptist Preaching"* (recto), ca. 1655. Pen and brown ink, brown wash, corrected with white; 14.6 × 20.4 cm (5¾ × 8 in.). Musée du Louvre, Paris, inv. RF4667. Photo © RMN—Grand Palais/ Art Resource, N.Y. Photographer: Michele Bellot.

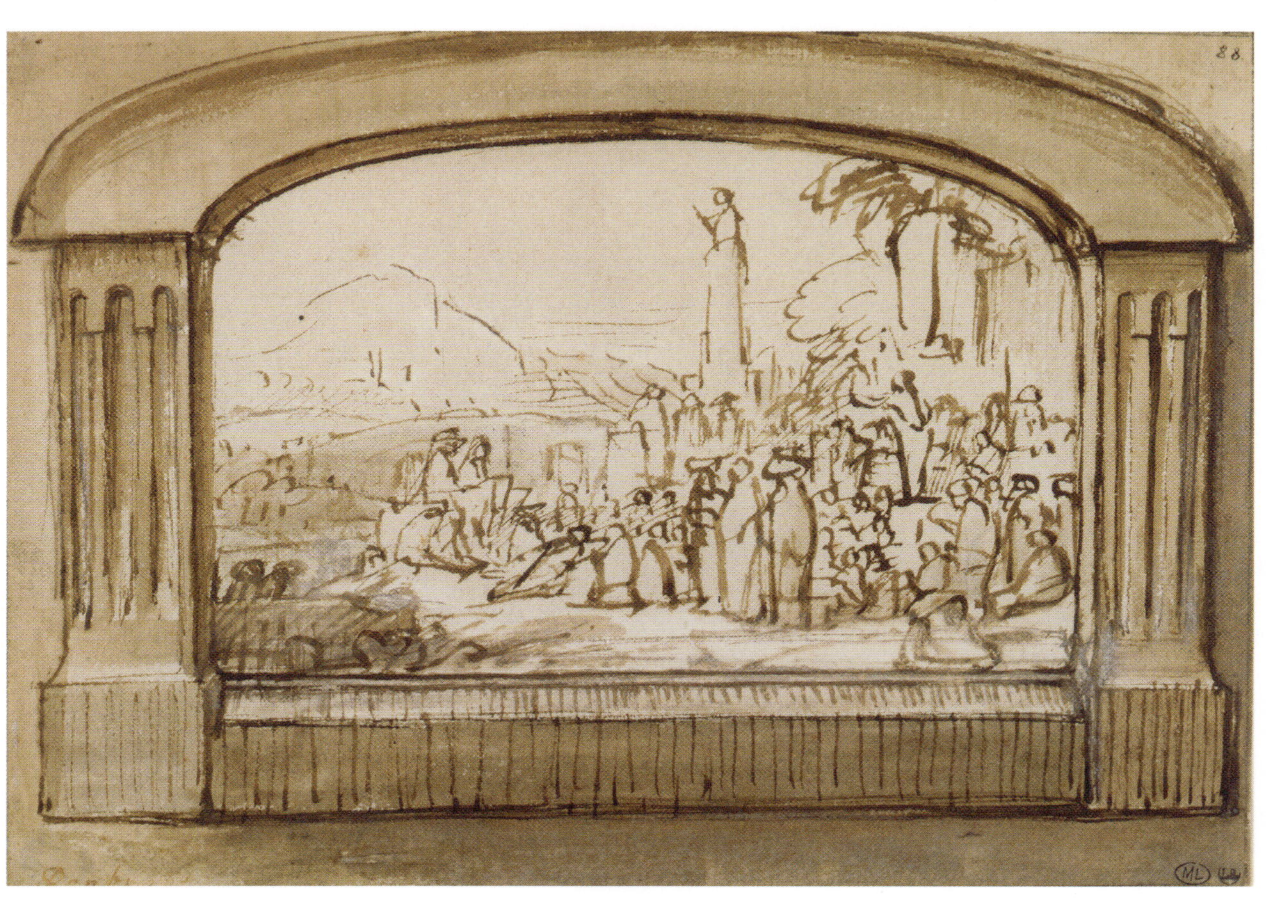

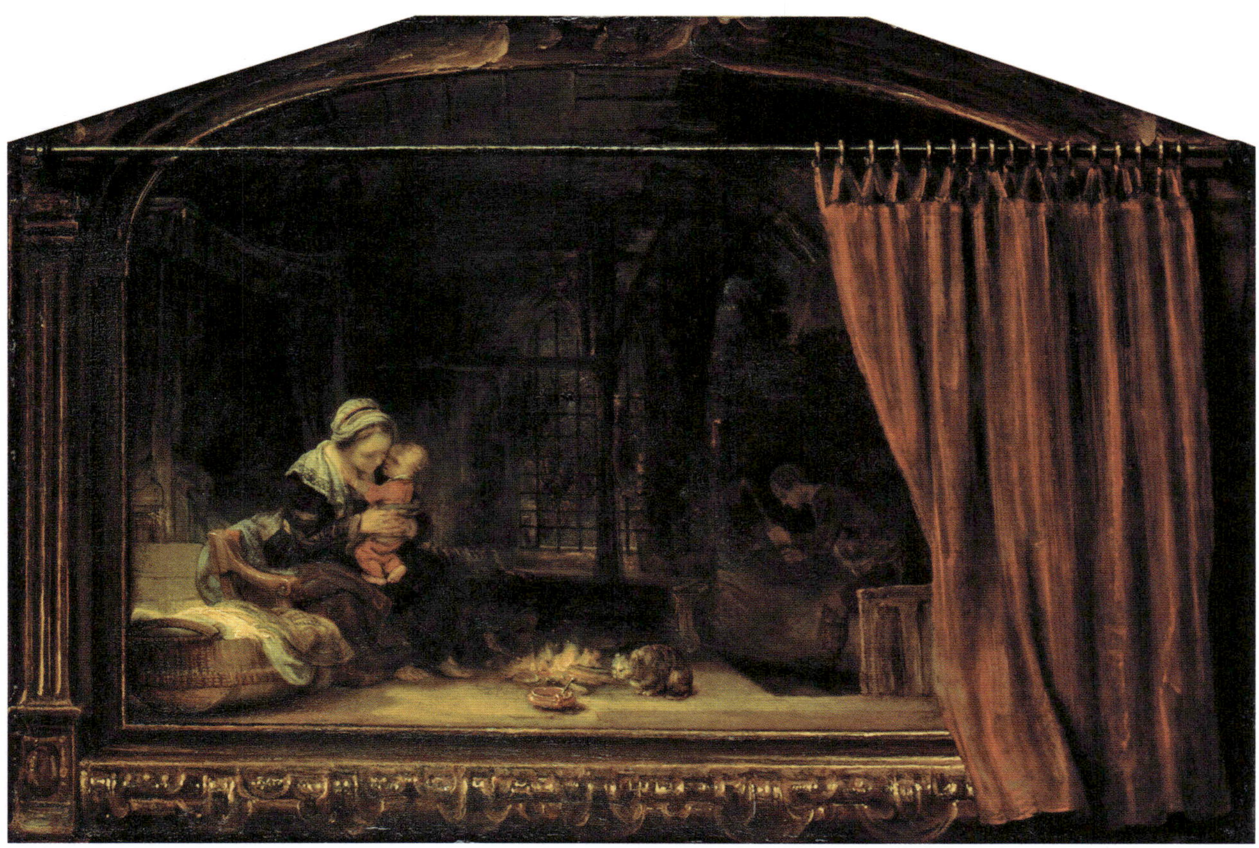

that this notion must be rejected, for the sketch within the frame is done in the abbreviated style the artist used around the mid-1650s; most probably it was done from memory, for there are significant compositional differences between it and the grisaille painted about two decades earlier.

There is now general acceptance of the ingenious hypothesis that the drawing is Rembrandt's design for a frame for the grisaille, which was ordered by his patron and friend Jan Six after he purchased the painting in the mid-fifties.[101] Knowledge that the grisaille was in Six's collection (it appears in the 1702 posthumous sale of his estate) bolsters the supposition. There is a simpler design for the same frame on the verso of the drawing. It probably precedes the one on the recto, which is illustrated here.

The deep frame, with its arched top, fluted pilasters on bases, and heavy bottom, seems to set a stage for the grisaille. A glimpse of the frame for Rembrandt's *Anatomy Lesson of Dr. Joan Deyman* from 1656, which can be seen in his sketch showing how it would look hanging near a window in

16.6 | *The Holy Family with Painted Frame and Curtain*, signed and dated 1646. Oil on panel; 46.5 × 68.8 cm (18¼ × 27⅛ in.). Gemäldegalerie, Museumslandschaft Hessen Kassel, Kassel, inv. GK240. Photographer: Ute Brunzel.

16.7 | *A Coach*, ca. 1660–63. Pen and brown ink with brown wash; 19.4 × 25.4 cm (7⅝ × 10 in.), upper corners rounded. The British Museum, London, inv. Oo,9.112. Photo © The Trustees of The British Museum/Art Resource, N.Y.

the surgeons' guildhall (see fig. 3.7), likewise has fluted pilasters and broad bases; however, its top is pedimented. Who designed the Deyman frame is not known.

In contrast, it is certain that Rembrandt painted the elaborate trompe-l'oeil frame around his heartwarming painting of *The Holy Family* of 1646 in Kassel (fig. 16.6). Its painted frame, which has an arched top and fluted pilasters, is partially covered by an unforgettable, red trompe-l'oeil curtain on a rod that stretches across part of the painting as well. The very top of the painted frame is no longer visible; it was badly damaged by fire. A copy of the painting, ascribed to Rembrandt's pupil Nicolaes Maes[102] and made before it was damaged, shows that the top of the painted frame was arched with an opening in the middle.

Rembrandt made a few drawings that include wagons and carts, but the British Museum's pen-and-wash drawing of a top-of-the-line coach is unique in his existing production as a draftsman (fig. 16.7). Strong sunlight falling upon

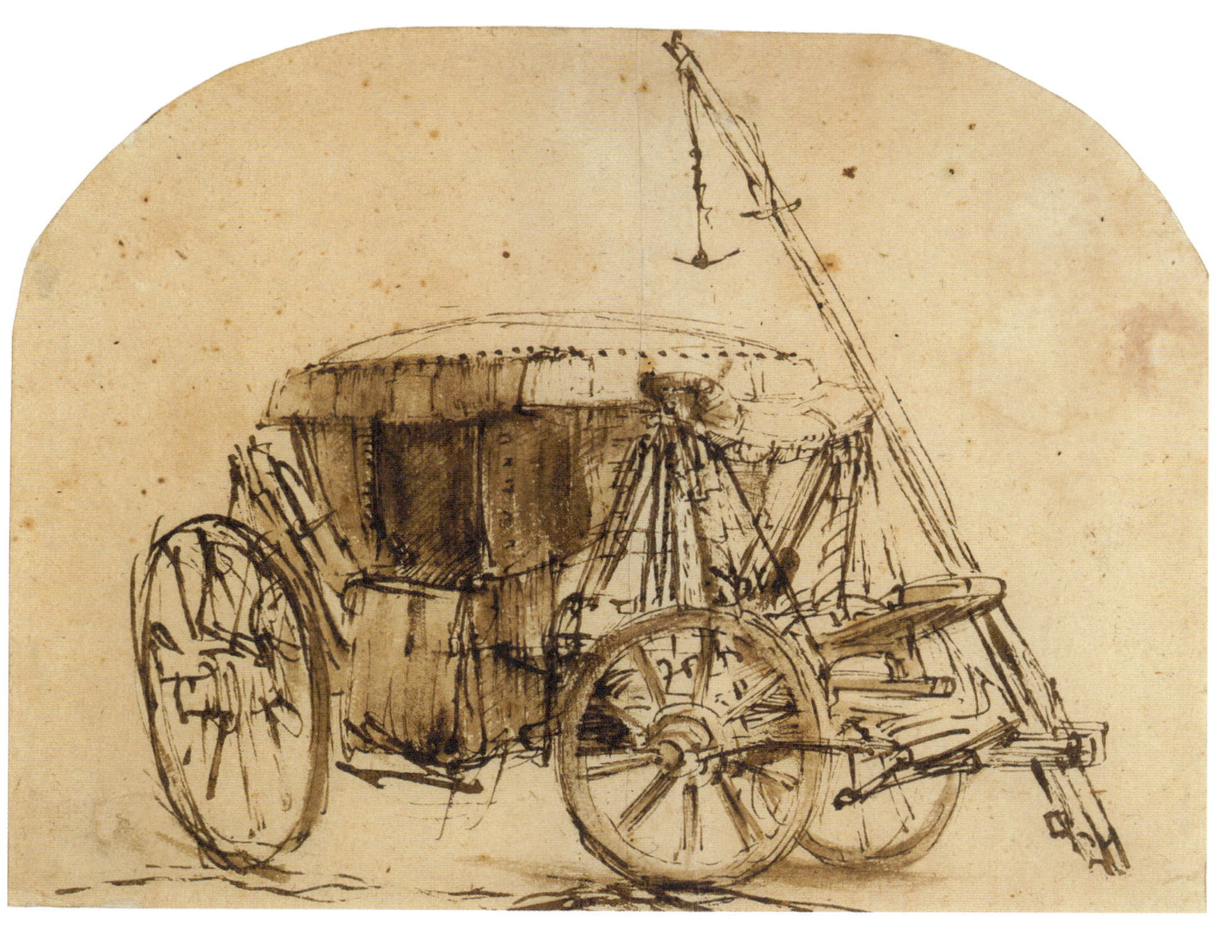

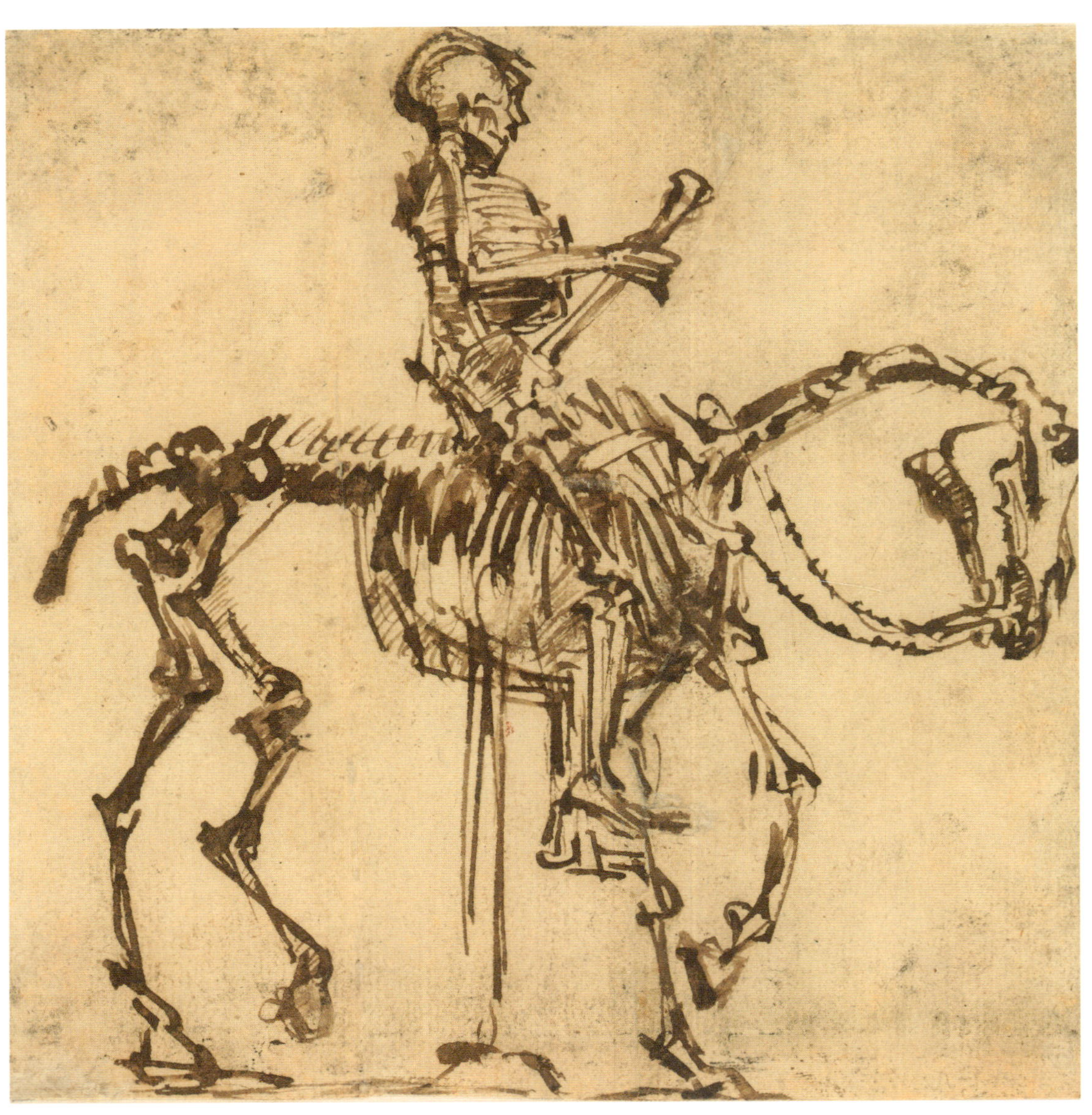

16.8 | *Skeleton Rider Mounted on the Skeleton of a Horse*, ca. 1655. Pen and brown ink; 15.7 × 15.4 cm (6⅛ × 6 in.). Hessisches Landesmuseum Darmstadt, inv. AE-670. Photographer: Wolfgang Fuhrmannek.

16.9 | Willem van Swanenburgh (Dutch, 1581–1612), after Jan Cornelisz Woudanus (ca. 1570–1615), *The Anatomy Theater, Leiden, in 1610*. Engraving. Academisch Historisch Museum, Leiden.

the vehicle throws its side in shadow not devoid of reflected light. The sketch's nervous pen strokes could hardly be more suggestive, and touches of wash are beautifully integrated with its fine and bold pen lines. The artist's matchless touch with both pen and brush is seen in the way the coach's slightly askew front wheels are rendered. Though the coach is perfectly static, if Umberto Boccioni had been given a chance to see the drawing of the coach's rear wheel, he would have applauded the artist as a forerunner of the futurists who claimed that light as well as motion destroys the substance of objects. It is noteworthy that Rembrandt found no need to indicate the coach's fourth wheel. Neither do I.

The drawing has been connected to Rembrandt's imposing life-size *Portrait of Frederik Rihel on Horseback*, presumably dated 1663, at the National Gallery, London—a painting that is also unique: It is the artist's only commissioned

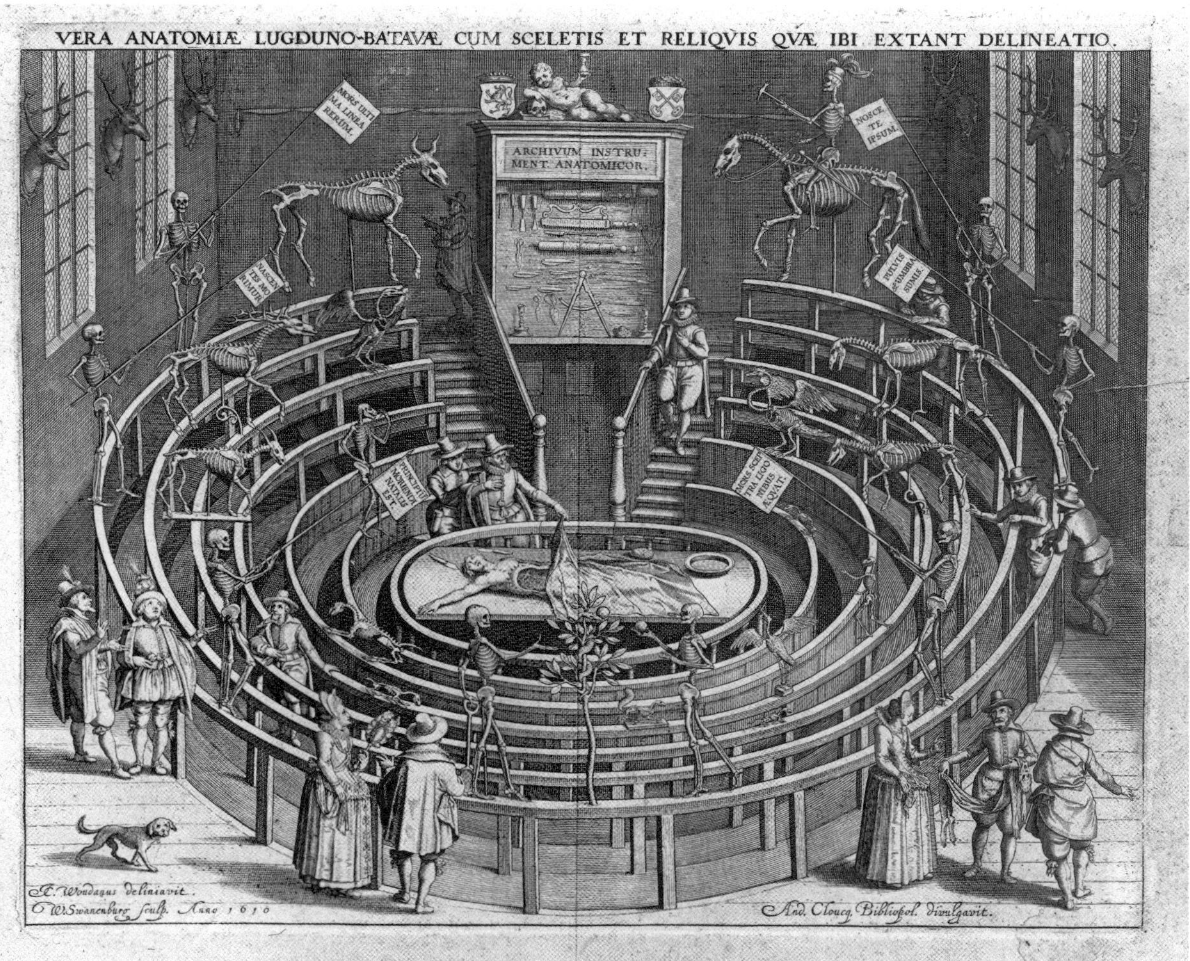

equestrian portrait. A vaguely similar coach, with passengers and a coachman, is in the painting that shows Rihel taking part in a procession, probably the one that honored Willem III's entry into Amsterdam in 1660. An inscription, not in the artist's hand, on the verso of the drawing reads: *"De Ryskaets v. Rembrandt"* (The State Coach by Rembrandt). Martin Royalton-Kisch writes that the identification may be accurate: "Rembrandt could have been asked by the sitter to include it in the painting, hence the artist's need to make the drawing in preparation for the detail."[103]

Darmstadt's vigorous pen drawing of a skeleton of a horse mounted by a skeleton rider (fig. 16.8) was probably made from a specimen of the pair mounted in Amsterdam's anatomical theater, where dissections were demonstrated. In 1663 a German tourist, while thoroughly doing the city's sights, recorded that among the things he saw in the theater was a man's skeleton on a skeletal horse.[104]

Leiden also had a specimen of the macabre pair in its world-famous anatomical theater. An idea of its appearance is given by a 1610 engraving of the theater's interior by Willem van Swanenburgh (fig. 16.9), younger brother of Jacob van

16.10 | *The Polish Rider*, ca. 1655. Oil on canvas; 116.8 × 134.9 cm (46 × 53⅛ in.). The Frick Collection, New York, inv. 10.1.98. Copyright The Frick Collection, New York.

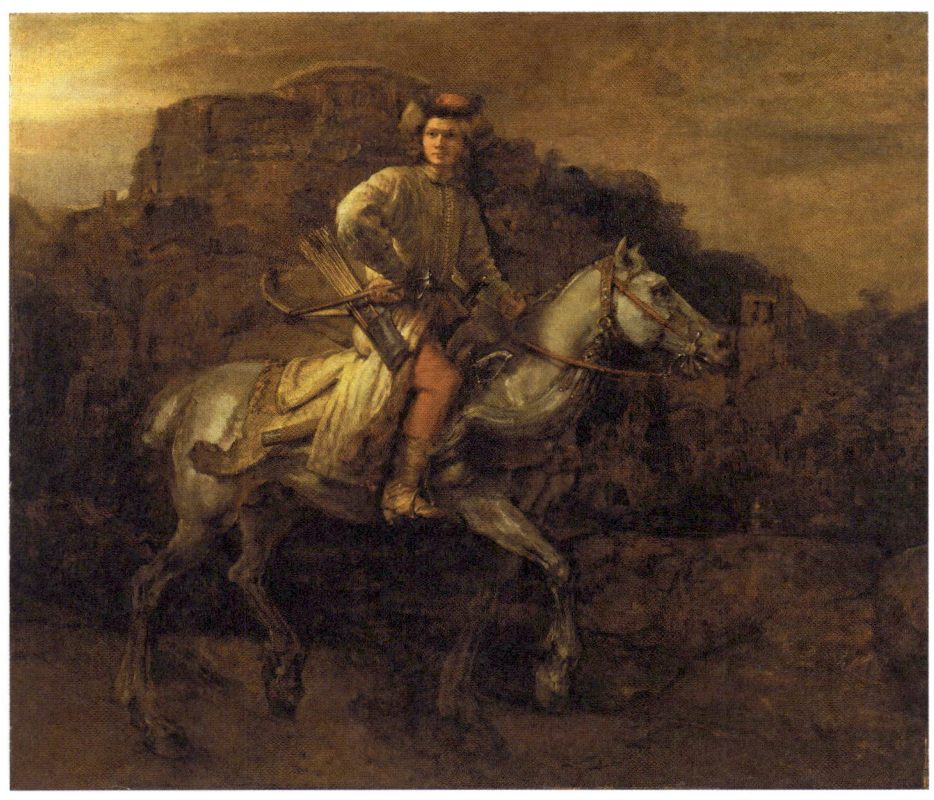

Swanenburgh, Rembrandt's first art teacher. A conspicuous skeleton rider on a skeleton horse is found in the upper right corner of his print. Like the horse and rider in Rembrandt's drawing, they are supported by a stand.

Of course, we cannot exclude the possibility that the skeletons were still on display in Leiden in the 1650s, when the Darmstadt sketch can be dated, and that Rembrandt executed it during the course of an unrecorded trip to his native town. But it is more likely that the pair in Amsterdam was his model. He was no stranger to various sites used as anatomical theaters in the great metropolis. He had an opportunity to gain familiarity with one while working on his *Anatomy Lesson of Dr. Tulp* in 1632 and with another in 1656 while painting the *Anatomy Lesson of Dr. Joan Deyman*.

Like many of the mature ones, Darmstadt's singular sketch was done with a broad-nibbed reed pen mostly loaded with ink. To make its fine lines here and there, Rembrandt held his reed pen at an angle. The more the drawing's details are studied (such as the horse's gait), the more tantalizing is the suggestion that Rembrandt had the drawing in mind when he painted the Frick's *Polish Rider* (fig. 16.10). News that in the Frick painting the horse's two hooves touching the ground are twentieth-century reconstructions on an added piece of canvas[105] does not dispel the intriguing relationship.

Consideration of the distinctive character of the five Rembrandt sketches discussed in this chapter extends our estimate of the artist's extraordinary range as a draftsman, and when we recall the great host of other subjects he depicted in remarkable drawings done during every phase of his career that are discussed in earlier chapters, it is perhaps not an exaggeration to claim that Rembrandt's range is matchless.

NOTES

1 Hinterding 2006, vol. 1, 74–77.

2 See note 3 below.

3 Van de Wetering et al. 2005, 101–8, 373–74, no. IV 10, 429–39, argues persuasively that Gole's mezzotint gives a more reliable image of the lost original than six known painted versions of it. In ibid., which is an exhaustive catalogue of Rembrandt's painted self-portraits, Van de Wetering also discusses the artist's drawn self-portraits. He finds reason to doubt the authenticity of the Berlin *Self-portrait* (see fig. 1.7): ibid., 155–56. He also suggests that the full-length *Self-portrait* at the Museum het Rembrandthuis (see fig. 1.11) may be by Rembrandt's pupil Willem Drost, who may have created it by combining the body of the Vienna *Self-portrait* (see fig. 1.12) with the head and shoulders of Rembrandt's etched *Self-portrait Drawing at a Window*, 1648 (Bartsch no. 22): ibid., 151–52. I do not share his doubts regarding the authenticity of these two drawings.

4 See note 3 above.

5 *"getekend door Rembrandt van Rhijn naar sijn selves / sooals hij in sijn schilderkamer gekleet was."* Pasted below the Dutch inscription on a separate piece of paper is a French translation of it written by the powerful French collector Pierre-Jean Mariette (1694–1774).

6 An X-radiograph montage of the Louvre painting shows that Rembrandt initially portrayed himself wearing a huge beret. Then he changed his headgear by giving himself the white cap now seen in the self-portrait. Illustrations of the X-radiograph montage are in Van de Wetering et al. 2005, 509, fig. 2; and Ducos and Mottin 2008, 85, fig. 53.

7 Valentiner 1905, 29–31.

8 Van Eeghen 1956.

9 *"dit is naer mijn huijsvrou geconterfeijt / do sij 21 jaer oud was den derden / dach als wij getroudt waren / den 8 Junijus / 1633."*

10 Schatborn et al. 2006a, 176, no. 64 (entry by C. van Tuyll van Serooskerken).

11 Van Eeghen 1977 first published the document. She sensibly insists it does not provide conclusive evidence for identification of the sitter. The document's pertinent passage reads: *"tekening van sijn persoon gedaen door Rembrandt van Rijn hangende in sijn testateurs voorhuys."*

12 Van Schendel 1956.

13 Before Van Regteren Altena 1950 published his findings on the drawing's intent, it was erroneously accepted as a preliminary study for the group portrait.

14 There is no consensus regarding the authenticity of the Louvre's drawing. It is accepted by Benesch (no. 661); Haverkamp-Begemann (1982, 15–16); and *Corpus* (vol. 3, 470). It is rejected by Lugt (1933, 61, no. 1317), by Schatborn (1985a, 210, under no. 103), and by Starcky (1988a, 199–200, no. 285). Starcky (ibid., 200) records that C. Hofstede de Groot and W. Sumowski also doubt the drawing's attribution to the master in hitherto unpublished statements. I align with the critics who question its ascription to Rembrandt.

15 Data given here on the relation of the drawing of Maria Trip to the painted version of the portrait is based on the discussion in Royalton-Kisch 1992, 78–79, no. 26.

16 Ruyter's portrait, unknown to Benesch, was introduced to the literature by Schatborn and de Winkel 1996.

17 Du Mortier 1989, 56.

18 Van de Wetering has doubts, which I do not share, that the head is a self-portrait. He finds it "difficult to accept that this figure with its wrinkled face and sagging skin could represent Rembrandt. Moreover, the figure is not 'looking in the mirror'" (Van de Wetering et al. 2005, 145, note 125).

19 Strauss and Van der Meulen 1979, 161, no. 1639/2: "*...want deesen twe sijnt daer die meeste / ende die naetuereelste beweechgelickheijt in / geopserveert is dat oock de grooste oorsaeck is dat / die selvijge soo lang onder handen sij geweest.*" Also see Gerson 1961, 34. Gerson's monograph includes facsimiles, transcriptions, and English translations of Rembrandt's seven letters to Huygens, his only existing correspondence. A facsimile and transcription of a forged Rembrandt letter dated 12 February 1662 is included in Visser [= W. Martin] 1906, 12–14. M. C. Visser was the pseudonym of W. Martin. For more on the false and genuine documents he published as a supplement to Hofstede de Groot 1906a, see Slive 1953, 45, note 1.

20 Schatborn 1985a, 18–19, no. 7: *"een dijvoot thr[?]eesoor dat in een fijn harte bewaert wert tot troost harer beleevende siel."*

21 Rembrandt's earliest biography was published in Jan Jansz Orlers, *Beschrijvinge der Stadt Leyden*, 2nd edn. (Leiden, 1641), 375. For a reprint and English translation, see Strauss and Van der Meulen 1979, 216–17, no. 1641/8.

22 Schatborn 1989, 118–19.

23 Van Berge-Gerbaud 1997, 2–4, no. 1.

24 Lieure 1924, no. 288.

25 Klessmann 1973, fig. 15.

26 The accessories are identified by De Winkel (2001, 56).

27 The suggestion was made by J. H. van Borssum Buisman, cited in Plomp 1997, 301, no. 327.

28 Ibid., 300: *"de minnemoer / van Titus soon / van Rembrant."*

29 Strauss and Van der Meulen 1979, 270, no. 1649/6: "*...zij t soontge van den voorn: Rembrant genaemt van Rhijn jonger sijnde hadde droogh gemint.*"

30 Van Eeghen 1969a.

31 In my view unconvincing doubts are expressed about the authenticity of the drawing in Vignau-Wilberg 2001, 146–47, sub no. 35.

32 Bredius 1892, 37, no. 6: *"Een dito [portfolio] daerin 56 tekening van Rembrandt historyen"*; and no. 17: *"Een dito [portfolio] daerin sijn 135 tekeningen sijnde het vrowenleven met kinderen van Rembrandt."*

33 Schatborn (1985a, 26–27, sub no. 11) gives compelling reasons for the identification.

34 According to Schatborn (1978, 134), another hand added some touches to the lower sketch. The hasty study, perhaps part of a larger sheet, may have looked unfinished to a later artist who did what he could to complete it.

The practice is not unusual. The suspicion that Ambroise Vollard, the first dealer to represent Cézanne, did the same to some of the French master's hardly touched watercolors is occasionally heard, but I have never seen proof that substantiates the allegation.

35 The helpful link between the drawing and the emblem in Cats's volume, along with a suggestion that the sketch may have been a sheet in an *album amicorum*, were first noted by Vignau-Wilberg (2001, 122–24, no. 26).

36 Bergström 1966.

37 Mayer-Meintschel 1970–71.

38 Strauss and Van der Meulen 1979, 612, no. 17: "*'t vel dar aen ende voorte de rest bysleepende.*"

39 Ibid., 373, no. 1656/12, no. 239: "*Een boeck, vol teeckeninge van Rembrant gedaen, bestaende in mans en vrouwe; neackt sijnde.*"

40 Municipal Archives, Amsterdam, notarial archive, J. Hellerus, fol. 555 (film 2579); A. Bredius, "Het geboortejaar van Jacob van Ruisdael," *OH* 8 (1888): 21–22.

41 Pels 1681, 35–36; for a Dutch transcription of pertinent lines of the poem, see Slive 1953, 210.

42 Royalton-Kisch 1992, 79–83, no. 27. The verso has an autograph drawing of *Joseph Interpreting the Dreams of the Butler and the Baker* (Genesis 11:1–20); it is reproduced and discussed in ibid., 82.

43 Pierre Yver, in his *Supplément au Catalogue Raisonné de MM. Gersaint, Helle et Glomy* (Amsterdam, 1756), no. 184, writes that the print is known in Holland as *het beeldt van Pigmalion*.

44 Saxl 1910, 42–43.

45 Strauss and Van der Meulen 1979, 375, no. 1656/12, no. 249: "*Een dito [boeck], vol teeckeningen van Rembrant, bestaende in beesten nae 't leven.*"

46 See introduction, p. viii, note 1.

47 Benesch nos. 458, 459, 460, respectively. Benesch and others have incorrectly listed the Morgan Library drawing as a counterproof. A technical examination of it made in 2003 established that it is, in fact, an abraded original; see Turner and Stampfle 2006, vol. 1, 141–42, no. 213. Abbing and Tuynman 2006 is a rewarding study of Hansken's life and Rembrandt's drawings of her (although the authors still classify the Morgan drawing as a counterproof). They discuss other seventeenth-century images of elephants as well.

48 Goldner 1988, 244–45, no. 108.

49 The suggestion that the drawing is probably done with a greasy crayon is wrong. Royalton-Kisch (1992, 93–94, no. 33) rightly notes that the drawing and another sketch of a lioness at the British Museum (Benesch no. 774) are in charcoal, an unusual medium for the artist.

50 Bevers et al. 1991, 67, no. 15 (entry by P. Schatborn).

51 Strauss and Van der Meulen 1979, 379, no. 1656/12, no. 280: "*Een laede, daer in een paradijs vogel en ses waijers.*"

52 Reference to the fifteen identifiable drawings includes a splendid unpublished sketch of a recumbent lioness, now in a New York private collection, which is similar in style and medium to the two drawings of the beast now in the British Museum (Benesch no. 775, here fig. 10.2; Benesch no. 774); William W. Robinson kindly informed me of its existence. Rembrandt's other drawings of lions are Benesch nos. 1211; 1214, here fig. 10.3; 1215; and 1216). The artist's four drawings of elephants are cited on pp. 120–21 and in note 47 above. In addition to the Louvre's sketch of birds of paradise (Benesch no. 456, here fig. 10.4) there is a study sheet that includes a dead bird of paradise, which is also at the Louvre (Benesch no. 158). Understandable doubts have been expressed about the attribution to Rembrandt of Bremen's untraceable drawings of camels (Benesch nos. 453, 454).

53 One of the sketches of pigs is at the Louvre (Benesch no. 777, here fig. 10.8) and two are at the British Museum (Benesch nos. 778, 779). The drawing of a dog is at Boston (Benesch 455, here fig. 10.6). The Rijksmuseum possesses the sketch of a cow and the sheet depicting two horses at a halt (Benesch nos. 393, 461).

54 All students of the artist's works on paper are indebted to Lugt 1915 (see Lugt 1920 for a German trans.), the first comprehensive study to identify numerous sites in and near the city that the artist depicted in drawings and prints. Bakker et al. 1998 provide extensive valuable material that supplements Lugt's findings.

55 Benesch (vol. 4, 222, no. C41) published it as a copy; White (1968) recognized it as an original.

56 Bartsch no. 234. The site was correctly identified by Van Regteren Altena 1954.

57 As early as 1751 Edmé-François Gersaint (162–64, no. 200) gave currency, in his posthumously published catalogue of Rembrandt's etchings, to the erroneous tradition that the print was made in the neighborhood of Six's country house as a result of a wager that the artist would be able to finish it during the time it took a servant to fetch mustard from a village for a meal the friends were sharing. Evidence has never been found proving that Six owned property in the vicinity of Ouderkerk.

58 *The Diary of John Evelyn*, ed. E. S. de Beer, vol. 2, *Kalendarium, 1620–1649* (Oxford, 1955), 43.

59 See White 1999, 262, note 15, for a discussion of the cryptic inscription.

60 See Van de Wetering 1997, 47–48, 69–74; and Broos 2005.

61 Strauss and Van der Meulen 1979, 375, no. 1656/12, no. 256: "*Een parckement boeck vol lantschappen nae 't leven, van Rembrant.*" Hinterding (2006, vol. 1, 179, note 299) first noted, with good reason, that this item is best translated as cited in the text, not as a book "bound in vellum" as proposed by Hofstede de Groot (1906a, 203) and Strauss and Van der Meulen (1979).

62 Bartsch no. 90. The link was wrongly made by Benesch (no. 462). He also erroneously related the drawing to the painting of the same subject in the Wallace Collection, which was formerly given to Rembrandt but is now ascribed to Govert Flinck (see Bredius, no. 545; and *Corpus*, vol. 2, 607–16, no. C48).

63 Abbing 2006a, 40, no. NRD 25 [RD 1649/2A].

64 Strauss and Van der Meulen 1979, 286, no. 1652/2: "*vand waech afte sien / stats Huis van Amsteldam / doent af gebrandt was / den 9 Julij 1652 / Rembrandt van rijn.*"

65 Cited in Bakker et al. 1998, 163.

66 See Bevers 2006, 115, note 4, for references in Berlin's curatorial files that maintain that the traditional identification as Galba is wrong.

67 Strauss and Van der Meulen 1979, 369, no. 1656/12, no. 200.

68 For a full transcription of Richardson's inscription, see Royalton–Kisch 1992, 123.

69 Strauss and Van der Meulen 1979, 367, no. 1656/12, no. 185: *"Een kassie met medalien."*

70 Broos 1972, 83–84.

71 See Benesch no. 1186.

72 Haverkamp-Begemann's entry on the New York drawing (Haverkamp-Begemann et al. 1999, 204–11, no. 66), which includes a discussion of the London and Berlin copies, is the best source for additional material on the three drawings and their impact on Rembrandt's later work.

73 Speculation on Rembrandt's trip to England is based on four drawings of English views, none of which is topographically accurate: *Saint Alban's Cathedral* (signed and dated 1640; Teyler Museum; Benesch no. 785); *View of London with Old Saint Paul's* (Berlin; Benesch no. 788); *View of London with Old Saint Paul's* (Albertina; Benesch no. 787); and *Windsor Castle* (signed and dated 1640; Albertina; Benesch no. 786). For more than a century specialists have debated their authenticity, and, if they are authentic, whether they were done on the spot in England or are copies after prints of works by other artists. The authenticity of their signatures has also been disputed. Plomp (1997, 309–10, no. 333) offers a succinct account of opinions about the group. Additionally he notes that the Berlin drawing is the only one of the four that has been universally accepted. He also proposes that it is reasonable to maintain the attribution of the Teyler Museum's *Saint Alban's* drawing to Rembrandt. He adds that its signature looks authentic and its date of 1640 is in accord with the drawing's style. Royalton-Kisch (1998, 669, no. 333) disputes Plomp's conclusions. He maintains that all four English views are now rejected implicitly if not always explicitly, and that the signature on the Teyler drawing does not look authentic. Schatborn writes (Schatborn et al. 2006, 17) that *Saint Alban's* and *Windsor Castle*, probably done after models, remain controversial because comparable Rembrandt landscape drawings are unknown. In his opinion, their signatures and dates appear feeble. It seems safe to predict that the last word regarding the status of the four English views has not yet been uttered.

74 Strauss and Van der Meulen 1979, 177, no. 1639/8: *"de Conte / batasar de / kastijlyone / van raefel / verkoft / voor 3500 gulden / het geheel caergesoen tot Luke van Nuffeelen / heft gegolden f 59456-: Ano 1639."*

75 Ibid., 371, no. 1656/12, no. 216: *"Een dito [boeck] seer groot met meest alle de wercken van Titian."*

76 White 1975, 378.

77 Upon the occasions when Rembrandt uses oriental paper, he most frequently employs Japanese paper, which is normally made of the inner bark of mulberry, gampi, or mitsumata plants. (European paper at the time was usually made of cotton or linen rags.) Generally yellowish in color, Japanese paper ranges from very thin to sturdier sheets, has a remarkably smooth surface, and is less absorbent than European paper. In Rembrandt's time it was imported into the Netherlands by the Dutch East India Company. He began using it for works on paper after the mid-1640s.

78 Strauss and Van der Meulen 1979, 369, no. 1656/17, no. 203: *"Een dito [boeck] vol curieuse minijateur teeckeninge nevens verscheijde hout en kopere printen van alderhande dragt."*

79 Lunsingh-Scheurleer 1980, 15.

80 Martin Royalton-Kisch, author of the catalogue entry on the drawing in Lange and Diederen 2007 (112, no. 48), notes that its pen-and-wash are over traces of a preliminary black-chalk sketch, a highly unusual procedure for Rembrandt, who almost invariably sketched directly in ink without use of underdrawings. The exceptional technique raises the possibility that the drawing is an excellent copy after a lost original by a very gifted pupil. For the suggestion that the pupil may have been Govert Flinck, see ibid. I am indebted to both Gregory Rubenstein and William W. Robinson for signaling Royalton-Kisch's observations.

81 There are unresolved questions regarding the status of the celebrated but unevenly preserved *Fall of Icarus* ascribed to Pieter Bruegel at the Musées Royaux des Beaux-Arts, Brussels. Some specialists attribute it to Bruegel, others claim it is a copy by another artist, and there are those who argue that it is a mélange of Bruegelesque elements put together by an unknown hand. Students of Rembrandt's oeuvre obviously cannot claim to have a monopoly on vexing attribution problems.

82 Karel van Mander 1604, *Het Schilder-boeck, "Wtlegghingh op den Metamorphosis Pub. Ovidii Nasonis,"* 87, recto.

83 See *Corpus*, vol. 3, 166, no. A113. Relevance of a neoplatonic interpretation of Ganymede's abduction as the blameless soul taken by God for Himself to Rembrandt's painting is likewise moot (see ibid.; and Russell 1977).

84 Brenninkmeyer-de Rooij 1984, 63. Her study is based on her trawl through artists' inventories in A. Bredius, *Künstler-Inventare*, 8 vols. (The Hague, 1915–20).

85 E. Haverkamp-Begemann (1973, fig. 6) proposes that a quick pen sketch at the National Gallery of Scotland, Edinburgh, is a preliminary study for the painting, and that it precedes the Munich drawing. Its composition differs significantly in more than one respect from the one finally used. The sketch's authenticity is exceedingly difficult to judge because it is a "deplorable wreck" (Andrews 1985, vol. 1, 85–86, no. D2862; vol. 2, 109, fig. 441). Some specialists, including Benesch (vol. 5, 2nd edn., 1973, under no. 1061, reproduced p. 291), call it a copy by a pupil; others see traces of Rembrandt's hand in the badly battered work. I would like to postpone judgment until I have had an opportunity to make a fresh, firsthand examination of it.

86 Perhaps the *houtkintgen* (wooden child) Rembrandt purchased at an Amsterdam auction on 22 February 1635 served as the model; see Strauss and Van der Meulen 1979, 116, no. 1635/1.

87 A fuzzy reproduction of the untraceable drawing, or a close copy of it, is illustrated in Rotermund 1963 (26, fig. 2; also see ibid., 311, no. 2). Its dimensions (12.5 × 12.5 cm; 4⅞ × 4⅞ in.) are very close to those of the ex-Felix drawing. Rotermund states that the sheet was

formerly in the Hermitage, Leningrad. Thus, the ex-Felix drawing may have had a stay in Russia. However, Benesch (no. 163) does not cite the Hermitage as part of its provenance, and Hofstede de Groot does not include it in his catalogue of Rembrandt drawings at the Hermitage (1906b, 359–62, nos. 1518–35). The possiblity that the ex-Felix drawing, or a copy of it, formerly belonged to the Hermitage needs further investigation.

88 Cited from Hinterding et al. 2000, 253, no. 61 (entry by M. Royalton-Kisch). For a Dutch transcription of the reference and more about the letter's source, see ibid., 258, note 3; and Abbing 2006a, 54–55, no. NRD 38 [RD 1654/8A].

89 For additional data on what technical examinations and cleaning revealed about the double portrait, see Slive 1995, 332, note 26; and the pamphlet *Rembrandt in a New Light, Rijksmuseum*, no. 7, 1993.

90 Ferdinand Bol, *Erasmus Scharlaken and Anna van Erckel as Isaac and Rebecca*, Rijksdienst Beeldende Kunst, The Hague. See Blankert 1982, 23, 82, 84, and 151, no. 167; and de Jongh 1986, 319–21, no. 80.

91 Vignau-Willberg et al. 2001, 235, no. 64: "*Soo jachtich om Christus in zijn aantwoordt te verschalken konden schrifterlick aantw[oordt] niet afwachten.*"

92 Stuttgart's drawing *The Departure of Rebecca from Her Parents' Home* (Benesch no. 147). Benesch translates its inscription as: "*What matters here is that many neighbours are present to watch the departure of this beloved bride.*" Most probably it was inscribed by Rembrandt for the benefit of his students.

93 For Heyblocq and his album, see the faithful facsimile and its comprehensive accompanying volume *The Album Amicorum of Jacob Heyblocq: Introduction, Transcriptions, Paraphrases and Notes to the Facsimile*, ed. Kees Thomassen and J. A. Gruys (Zwolle, 1998).

94 See Bredius 1909. The Stockholm painting is Bredius no. 600.

95 For extensive analyses, which include a survey of earlier opinions, see Van de Wetering 1995; and Haverkamp-Begemann et al. 1999, 219–28, no. 70.

96 Of course, study of the source, meaning, and significance of the activities of asses and donkeys as school teachers or musicians in works of art, emblems, and proverbs can be rewarding; for example, see Gibson 2007–8.

97 Haverkamp-Begemann et al. 1999, 225, note 2, recognized that the artist's name is written by the same hand as that on a drawing in Berlin attributed to Govert Flinck, *Tobias Healing Tobit* (Sumowski 1979–, vol. 4, no. 980^{XX}). Like the Metropolitan's satire, it too was in Baron Vivant-Denon's (1747–1825) collection. Hence, the signature may have been written by or for Vivant-Denon.

98 Haverkamp-Begemann et al. 1999, 221.

99 The two sketches at the British Museum are Benesch nos. 70 and 1043. A word of caution about the former. It may very well be by Rembrandt's pupil Govert Flinck, who was strongly under his master's influence when he studied with him in the 1630s (see Royalton-Kisch 1992, 40–41, no. 7; Schatborn 1994, 21; Hautekeete 2005, 70–73, under no. 22).

100 Walsh 1986, 12–13.

101 Neumann 1918, 77f.

102 Sumowski 1979–, vol. 8, no. 1791^{X}. The drawing, which is on vellum, is at the Ashmolean Museum, Oxford. In my view, attribution of it to Maes is questionable.

103 Royalton-Kisch 1992, 114, no. 68.

104 When he visited the city in 1663, Christian Knorr von Rosenroth noted in his journal that he saw a *Sceleton hominus in Sceleto equi* in its *Theatrum Anatomicum*; see Fuchs and Breen 1916.

105 Van de Wetering 1997, 210.

BIBLIOGRAPHY

Bartsch See Bartsch 1797
Benesch See Benesch 1954–57
Bredius See Bredius 1969
Corpus See Bruyn et al.; Van de Wetering et al.
KRH *De Kroniek van het Rembrandthuis*
NKJ *Nederlands Kunsthistorisch Jaarboek*
OH *Oud Holland*

Abbing, M. R. 2006a. *Rembrandt 2006: New Rembrandt Documents*. London.

———, ed. 2006b. *Rembrandt 2006: Essays*. London.

———, and P. Tuynman. 2006. "Rembrandt's Drawings of the Elephant Hansken." In Abbing 2006b, 173–89.

Ackley, C. S., et al. 2003. *Rembrandt's Journey: Painter, Draftsman, Etcher*. Exh. cat., Museum of Fine Arts, Boston—The Art Institute of Chicago. Boston.

Andrews, K. 1985. *Catalogue of Netherlandish Drawings in the National Gallery of Scotland*. 2 vols. Edinburgh.

Bakker, B., M. van Berge-Gerbaud, E. Schmitz, and J. Peeters. 1998. *Landscapes of Rembrandt: His Favourite Walks*. Exh. cat., Amsterdam Municipal Archives—Institut Néerlandais, Paris. Bussum.

Bartsch, A. von. 1797. *Catalogue raisonné de toutes les estampes qui forment l'œuvre de Rembrandt, et ceux de ses principaux imitateurs*. 2 vols. Vienna.

Benesch, O. 1954–57. *The Drawings of Rembrandt: A Critical and Chronological Catalogue*. 6 vols. London. 2nd edn., enl. and ed. E. Benesch. 6 vols. London and New York, 1973.

———. 1960. *Rembrandt as a Draughtsman*. London.

van Berge-Gerbaud, M. 1997. *Rembrandt et son école: Dessins de la collection Frits Lugt*. Paris.

Bergström, I. 1966. "Rembrandt's Double Portrait of Himself and Saskia at the Dresden Gallery" *NKJ* 17:143–69.

Bevers, H. 2006. *Rembrandt: Die Zeichnungen im Berliner Kupferstichkabinett*. Exh. cat., Kupferstichkabinett, Berlin. Ostfildern.

———, P. Schatborn, and B. Welzel. 1991. *Rembrandt: The Master and His Workshop, Drawings and Etchings*. Exh. cat., Kupferstichkabinett, Berlin—Rijksmuseum, Amsterdam—The National Gallery, London. New Haven and London.

Bikker, J. 2005. *Willem Drost (1633–1659): A Rembrandt Pupil in Amsterdam and Venice*. New Haven and New York.

Bisanz-Prakken, M. 1995. *Drawings from the Albertina: Landscape in the Age of Rembrandt*. Exh. cat., Drawing Center, New York—Kimbell Art Museum, Fort Worth. Alexandria, Virginia.

———, et al. 1989–90. *Begegnungen/Ontmoetingen: Meisterwerke der Zeichnung und Druckgraphik aus dem Rijksprentenkabinet in Amsterdam und der Albertina in Wien*. Exh. cat., Albertina, Vienna—Rijksmuseum, Amsterdam. Vienna and Maarsen.

Blankert, A. 1982. *Ferdinand Bol (1616–1680): Rembrandt's Pupil*. Doornspijk.

———, et al. 1997. *Rembrandt: A Genius and His Impact*. Exh. cat., National Gallery of Victoria, Melbourne—National Gallery of Australia, Canberra. Zwolle.

van den Boogert, B., et al. 1999. *Rembrandt's Treasures*. Exh. cat., Museum het Rembrandthuis, Amsterdam. Zwolle.

Bredius, A. 1892. "De schilder Johannes van de Cappelle." *OH* 10:26–40.

———. 1909. "Uit Rembrandt's laatste levensjaar." *OH* 27:238–40.

———. 1969. *Rembrandt: The Complete Edition of the Paintings*. 3rd edn., rev. H. Gerson. London and New York.

Brenninkmeyer-de Rooij, B. 1984. "Theories of Art." In B. Haak, *The Golden Age: Dutch Painters of the Seventeenth Century*, 60–70. New York.

Broos, B. P. J. 1972. "Rembrandt en zijn eeuwige leermeester Lastman." *KRH* 26, no. 3:76–96.

———. 1981. *Oude tekeningen in het bezit van de Gemeentemusea van Amsterdam, waaronder de collectie Fodor*. Vol. 3, *Rembrandt en tekenaars uit zijn omgeving*. Amsterdam.

———. 2005. "Rembrandts eerste reis naar Friesland." *OH* 118, nos. 1–2:79–91.

Bruyn, J., B. Haak, S. Levie, P. J. J. van Thiel, and E. van de Wetering. *A Corpus of Rembrandt Paintings*. Vol. 1, 1982; vol. 2, 1986; vol. 3, 1989. The Hague, Boston, and London. Cited as *Corpus*. (For vol. 4, see Van de Wetering et al., *Corpus*, 2005.)

Cats, J. 1632. *Spiegel van den voorleden, en jegenwoordigen tijdt*. Part 3. The Hague.

Cavalli-Björkman, G., ed. 1993. *Rembrandt and His Pupils: Papers Given at a Symposium in Nationalmuseum Stockholm, 2–3 October 1992*. Stockholm.

———, et al. 1992. *Rembrandt och hans Tid / Rembrandt and His Age*. Entries on drawings by B. Magnussen. Exh. cat., Nationalmuseum, Stockholm. Stockholm.

Chapman, H. Perry. 1990. *Rembrandt's Self-Portraits: A Study in Seventeenth-Century Identity*. Princeton.

Cormack, M. 1966. *Rembrandt and His Circle: An Exhibition of Drawings from the Collection of the Fitzwilliam Museum, Cambridge*. Cambridge.

Dickey, S. S. 2004. *Rembrandt: Portraits in Print*. Amsterdam and Philadelphia.

Dittrich, C., T. Ketelsen, et al. 2004. *Rembrandt: Die Dresdener Zeichnungen 2004*. Exh. cat., Kupferstich-Kabinett, Dresden. Cologne.

Ducos, B., and B. Mottin. 2008. "An Icon of the Rembrandt Myth: Recent Discoveries on the Louvre's *Self-Portrait at the Easel*." In *Rembrandt: Three Faces of the Master*, ed. B. Leca, 72–92. Exh. cat., Cincinnati Art Museum. Cincinnati.

van Eeghen, I. H. 1956. "De kinderen van Rembrandt en Saskia." *Maandblad Amstelodamum* 43 (October):144–46.

———. 1969a. "Elsje Christiaens en de kunsthistorie." *Maandblad Amstelodamum* 56, no. 4:73–78.

———. 1969b. "Rembrandt aan de Amstel." In *Rembrandt aan de Amstel*, [unpaginated]. Amsterdam.

———. 1977. "Willem Jansz van der Pluym en Rembrandt." *Maandblad Amstelodamum* 64, no. 1:6–13.

Emmens, J. A. 1968. *Rembrandt en de regels van de kunst*. Utrecht. Reprint, Amsterdam, 1979.

Fuchs, ed. 1916 [cited as Fuchs and Breen 1916]. "Aus dem Itinerarium des Christian Knorr von Rosenroth." Introduction and Dutch trans. of the Latin text by J. C. Breen. *Jaarboek Amstelodamum* 14:201–7.

van Gelder, J. G. 1961. "The Drawings of Rembrandt" [review of Benesch 1954–57]. *The Burlington Magazine* 103:149–51.

Gersaint, E-F. 1751. *Catalogue raisonné de toutes les pièces qui forment l'œuvre de Rembrandt*. Pub. and ed. Helle and Glomy. Paris.

Gerson, H. 1961. *Seven Letters by Rembrandt*. Transcription by I. H. van Eeghen. The Hague.

Gibson, W. S. 2007–8. "*Asinus ad lyram*: From Boethius to Bruegel and beyond." *Simiolus* 33.1–2:33–42.

Giltaij, J. 1988. *The Drawings by Rembrandt and His School in the Museum Boymans-van Beuningen*. Rotterdam.

———. 1989. "The Function of Rembrandt Drawings." *Master Drawings* 27:111–17.

Goldner, G. R., et al. 1988. *European Drawings*. Vol. 1, *Catalogue of the Collections, The J. Paul Getty Museum*. Malibu, California.

Haak, B. 1974. *Rembrandt Zeichnungen*. Cologne.

Hautekeete, S. 2005. *Les Dessins de Rembrandt et ses élèves appartenant à la collection Jean de Grez*. Exh. cat., Musées Royaux des Beaux-Arts de Belgique, Brussels. With an essay by P. Schatborn.

Haverkamp-Begemann, E. 1961. *Kunstchronik* 14, nos. 1, 2, 3:10–28, 50–57, 85–91, respectively. [Review of Benesch 1954–57.]

———. 1973. "Eine unbekannte Vorzeichnung zum 'Claudius Civilis.'" In *Neue Beiträge zur Rembrandt-Forschung*, ed. O. von Simson and J. Kelch, 31–43. Berlin.

———. 1982. *Rembrandt: The Night Watch*. Princeton.

———. 1989. "Rembrandt as a Draughtsman: The Changing Image." *Master Drawings* 27:105–10.

———, et al. 1999. *The Robert Lehman Collection*. Vol. 7, *Fifteenth- to Eighteenth-Century European Drawings: Central Europe, The Netherlands, France, England*. Princeton.

Hinterding, E. 2006. *Rembrandt as an Etcher: The Practice of Production and Distribution*. 3 vols. Ouderkerk aan den IJssel.

———, et al. 2000. *Rembrandt the Printmaker*. Exh. cat., Rijksmuseum, Amsterdam—British Museum, London. London.

Hofstede de Groot, C. 1906a. *Die Urkunden über Rembrandt (1575–1721)*. The Hague.

———. 1906b. *Die Handzeichnungen Rembrandts*. Haarlem.

Jaffé, M. 2002. *The Devonshire Collection of Northern European Drawings*. 5 vols. Turin.

de Jongh, E. 1986. *Portretten van echt en trouw: Huwelijk en gezin in de Nederlandse kunst van de zeventiende eeuw*. Exh. cat., Frans Hals Museum, Haarlem. Zwolle and Haarlem.

Klessmann, R. 1973. "Zum Röntgen-Befund des Potiphar-Bild in Berlin." In *Neue Beiträge zur Rembrandt-Forschung*, ed. O. von Simson and J. Kelch, 44–47. Berlin.

Lange, C., and R. Diederen. 2007. *Das ewige Auge—von Rembrandt bis Picasso: Meisterwerke aus der Sammlungen Jan Krugier und Marie-Anne Krugier-Poniatowski*. Exh. cat., Kunsthalle München der Hypo-Kulturstiftung. Munich.

Lieure, J. 1924. *Jacques Callot: La Vie artistique: Catalogue de son oeuvre gravé*. Paris.

Lippmann, F., et al. 1888–1911. *Original Drawings by Rembrandt Harmensz van Rijn*. 4 vols. Berlin and The Hague.

Lugt, F. 1915. *Wandeling met Rembrandt in en om Amsterdam*. 1st edn., April 1915; 2nd enl. edn., September 1915.

———. 1920. *Mit Rembrandt in Amsterdam*. German trans. of 1915 Dutch edn. by E. Hancke, Berlin.

———. 1933. *Musée du Louvre: Inventaire général des dessins des écoles du Nord*. Vol. 3, *École hollandais (Rembrandt, ses élèves, ses imitateurs, ses copistes)*.

Lunsingh-Scheurleer, P. 1980. "Mogul miniaturen door Rembrandt nagetekend." *KRH* 32, no. 1:10–40.

van Mander, K. 1604. *Het Schilder-boeck*. Haarlem. 2nd edn., 1618, includes an anonymous biography of Van Mander. This voluminous handbook for artists and amateurs is divided into six sections. The one particularly pertinent to the present text is a gloss on Ovid: *"Metamorphoses": Wtlegghingh op den Metamorphosis Pub. Ouidij Nasonis*.

Mayer-Meintschel, A. 1970–71. "Rembrandt und Saskia im Gleichnis vom Verlorenen Sohn." *Jahrbuch, Staatliche Kunstsammlungen Dresden* 8:39–57. Reprinted in Neidhardt 2008, 146–59.

Mitsch, E. 1969. *Die Rembrandt-Zeichnungen der Albertina*. Exh. cat., Albertina, Vienna. Vienna.

du Mortier, B. M. 1989. "Costume in Frans Hals." In Slive et al. 1989, 45–60.

Müller-Hofstede, C. 1956. "HdG 409: Eine Nachlese zu den München Civilis Zeichnungen." *Konsthistorisk Tidskrift* 25:12–55.

Neidhardt, U., ed. 2008. *Festschrift zum 80. Geburtstag von Annaliese Mayer-Meintschel*. Dresden.

Neumann, C. 1918. *Aus der Werkstatt Rembrandts*. Heidelberg.

Pels, A. 1681. *Gebruik en misbruik des toneels*. Amsterdam.

Pijl, L., et al. 2005. *van Cuyp tot Rembrandt: De verzameling Cornelis Hofstede de Groot*. Exh. cat., Groninger Museum, Groningen. Ghent.

Plomp, M. C. 1997. *The Dutch Drawings in the Teyler Museum*. Vol. 2, *Artists Born between 1575 and 1630*. Haarlem, Ghent, and Doornspijk.

van Regteren Altena, I. Q. 1950. "Retouches aan ons Rembrandt-beeld. I: De zogenaamde voorstudie voor de Anatomische Les van Dr Deyman." *OH* 65:171–78.

———. 1954. "Retouches aan ons Rembrandt-beeld. II: Het landschap van den Goldweger." *OH* 69:1–17.

———. 1955. *OH* 70:118–20. [Review of Benesch vols. 1, 2.]

Renger, K., and A. Burmester, 1985–86. "The Munich Rembrandt Forgeries Reconsidered: A New Technical Approach to the Investigation of Drawings." *Master Drawings* 23–24:526–37.

Robinson, W. W. 1987. "Rembrandt's Sketches of Historical Subjects." In *Drawings Defined,* ed. W. Strauss and T. Felker, 241–58. New York.

———. 1998. "Five Black Chalk Figure Studies by Rembrandt." *Master Drawings* 36:36–45.

———. 2002. *Bruegel to Rembrandt: Dutch and Flemish Drawings from the Maida and George Abrams Collection*, with an essay by M. Royalton-Kisch. Exh. cat., British Museum, London—Institut Néerlandais, Paris—Fogg Art Museum, Cambridge, Massachusetts. New Haven and London.

Rosenberg, J. 1956–59. *The Art Bulletin* 38 (1956): 63–70 [vols. 1–2]; ibid., 41 (1959): 107–19 [vols. 3–6]. [Review of Benesch 1954–57.]

———. 1959. *Great Draughtsmen from Pisanello to Picasso.* Cambridge.
Rotermund, H.-M. 1963. *Rembrandts Handzeichnungen und Radierungen der Bibel.* Stuttgart.
Royalton-Kisch, M. 1989. "Rembrandt's Sketches for His Paintings." *Master Drawings* 27:128–45.
———. 1990. "Recent Publications on Rembrandt's Drawings." *The Burlington Magazine* 132:131–36.
———. 1992. *Drawings by Rembrandt and His Circle in the British Museum.* Exh. cat., British Museum, London. London.
———. 1993. "Rembrandt's Drawings for Prints: Some Observations." In Cavalli-Björkman 1993, 173–92.
———. 1998. *The Burlington Magazine* 140:668–69. [Review of Plomp 1997.]
———. 2000. "From Rembrandt to Van Renesse: Some Re-attributed Drawings." *The Burlington Magazine* 142:157–65.
Ruessink, H. 1989. "Hendrickje Stoffels, jonge dochter van Bredevoort." *KRH* 41:19–24.
Russell, M. 1975. *Jan van de Cappelle (1624/6–1679).* Leigh-on-Sea.
———. 1977. "The Iconography of Rembrandt's Rape of Ganymede." *Simiolus* 9:5–18.
Saxl, F. 1910. "Zur Herleitung der Kunst Rembrandts." *Mitteilungen der Gesellschaft für verveilfältigende Kunst, Beilage der "Graphischen Kunst,"* 41–48.
Schapelhouman, M. 2006. *Rembrandt and the Art of Drawing.* Zwolle and Amsterdam.
Schatborn, P. 1978. *OH* 92:132–36. [Review of W. Wegner, *Die Niederländischen Handzeichnungen des 15.–18. Jahrhunderts (Katalog der Staatlichen Graphischen Sammlung München,* vol. 1)].
———. 1981a. "Van Rembrandt tot Crozat: Vroege verzamelingen met tekeningen van Rembrandt." *NKJ* 32:1–54.
———. 1981b. "Kinderen door Rembrandt." *KRH* 33, nos. 1–2:1–32.
———. 1985a. *Catalogue of the Dutch and Flemish Drawings in the Rijksprentenkabinet, Rijksmuseum, Amsterdam.* Vol. 4, *Drawings by Rembrandt, His Anonymous Pupils and Followers.* The Hague.
———. 1985b. "Tekeningen van Rembrandts leerlingen." *Bulletin van het Rijksmuseum* 33, no. 2:93–109.
———. 1987. "Rembrandt's Late Drawings of Female Nudes." In *Drawings Defined*, ed. W. Strauss and T. Felker, 307–17. New York.
———. 1989. "Notes on Early Rembrandt Drawings." *Master Drawings* 27:118–27.
———. 1994. *OH* 108: 20–24. [Review of Royalton-Kisch 1992.]
———. 2006a. *Rembrandt.* Paris.
———. 2006b. "Drawings Attributed to Carel Fabritius." *OH* 119, nos. 2–3:130–38.
———, and M. de Winkel. 1996."Rembrandts portret van de acteur Willem Ruyter." *Bulletin van het Rijksmuseum* 44:382–93.
———, et al. 2006. *Rembrandt, dessinateur: Chefs-d'oeuvres des collections en France.* Exh. cat., Musée du Louvre, Paris. Paris.
Scheller, R. W. 1969. "Rembrandt en de encyclopedia verzameling." *OH* 84:81–147.
van Schendel, A. 1956. "De schimmen van de Staalmeesters: Een röntgenologisch onderzoek." *OH* 71:1–22.
Schneider, C. P., et al. 1990. *Rembrandt's Landscapes: Drawings and Prints.* Exh. cat., National Gallery of Art, Washington, D.C. Boston.
Schröder, K. A., M. Bisanz-Prakken, et al. 2004. *Rembrandt.* Exh. cat., Albertina, Vienna. Wolfratshausen.
Scrase, D., and T. Vignau-Wilberg. 1995. *The Golden Century: Dutch Master Drawings from the Fitzwilliam Museum Cambridge.* Exh. cat., Staatliche Graphische Sammlung, Munich—Kurpfälzisches Museum, Heidelberg—Herzog Anton Ulrich-Museum, Braunschweig—The Fitzwilliam Museum, Cambridge. Schirmer/Mosel.
Slatkes, L. J. 1980. "Rembrandt's Elephant." *Simiolus* 2:7–13.
Slive, S. 1953. *Rembrandt and His Critics: 1630–1730.* The Hague. Reprint, New York, 1988.
———. 1965. *Drawings of Rembrandt: With a Selection of Drawings by His Pupils and Followers: Based on the Facsimile Series Edited by F. Lippmann.* [see Lippmann et al. 1888–1911]. 2 vols. New York.
———. 1988. "The Manor Kostverloren: Vicissitudes of a Seventeenth-Century Dutch Landscape Motif." In *The Age of Rembrandt: Studies in Seventeenth-Century Dutch Painting*, ed. R. E. Fleischer and S. S. Munshower, 132–68.
———. 1995. *Dutch Painting: 1600–1800.* Pelican History of Art. New Haven and London.
———. 2001. *Jacob van Ruisdael: A Complete Catalogue of His Paintings, Etchings, and Drawings.* New Haven and London.
———. 2008. "Notes on Rembrandt Drawings: An Anthology." In Neihardt 2008, 34–37. (First publication, in a slightly different form, of the introduction to the present book.)
———, et al. 1989. *Frans Hals.* Exh. cat., National Gallery of Art, Washington—Royal Academy of Arts, London—Frans Hals Museum, Haarlem. London.
Sluijter, E. J. 1986. *De "Heydensche Fabulen" in den Noordnederlandse schilderkunst circa 1590–1670.* The Hague.
———. 2006. *Rembrandt and the Female Nude.* Amsterdam.
von Sonnenburg, H., W. Liedtke, et al. 1995. *Rembrandt / Not Rembrandt in the Metropolitan Museum of Art.* Vol. 1, H. von Sonnenburg. *Paintings, Problems and Issues*; vol. 2, W. Liedtke et al. *Paintings, Drawings and Prints.* Exh. cat., Metropolitan Museum of Art, New York. New York.
Starcky, E. J. 1988a. *Musée du Louvre: Inventaire général des Dessins des Écoles du Nord: Écoles allemande, des Anciens Pays-Bas, flamande, hollandaise et suisse xve–xviiie siècles: Supplément aux inventaires publiés par Frits Lugt et Louis Demonts.* Paris.
———. 1988b. *Rembrandt et son école: Dessins du Musée du Louvre.* Exh. cat., Musée du Louvre, Paris. Paris.
Strauss, W. L., and M. van der Meulen. 1979. *The Rembrandt Documents.* New York.
Sumowski, W. 1956–57. "Bemerkungen zu Otto Beneschs Corpus der Rembrandt-Zeichnungen, I." *Wissenschaftsliche Zeitschrift der Humboldt-Universität zu Berlin, Gesellschafts-und sprachwissenschaftliche Reihe* 6:255–81.
———. 1961. *Bemerkungen zu Otto Beneschs Corpus der Rembrandt-Zeichnungen, II.* Bad Pyrmont.
———. 1979–. *Drawings of the Rembrandt School.* 10 vols. New York. (In progress.)
———. 1983–94. *Gemälde der Rembrandt-Schüler.* 6 vols. Landau.

Turner, J. S., with contributions by F. Stampfle. 2006. *Dutch Drawings in The Pierpont Morgan Library: Seventeenth to Nineteenth Centuries*. 2 vols. New York.
Valentiner, W. R. 1905. *Rembrandt und seine Umgebung*. Strasbourg.
———. 1925–34. *Die Handzeichnungen Rembrandts* (*Klassiker der Kunst*). 2 vols. Stuttgart and New York.
Vignau-Wilberg, T., et al. 2001. *Rembrandt auf Papier: Werk und Wirkung. Rembrandt and His Followers: Drawings from Munich*. Exh. cat., Alte Pinakothek, Munich—Museum het Rembrandthuis, Amsterdam. Munich.
Visser, M. C. [= W. Martin]. 1906. *Die Urkunden über Rembrandt (1575–1721). Erstes Supplement*. The Hague.
Vogel-Köhn, D. 1981. *Rembrandts Kinderzeichnungen*. Cologne.
Vogelaar, C., et al. 2005. *Rembrandt's Mother: Myth and Reality*. Exh. cat., Stedelijk Museum, Lakenhal, Leiden. Zwolle.
Voute, J. R. 1990. "Rembrandts reis naar Bredevoort." *KRH* 42:40.
Walsh, J. 1986. "Rembrandt's *Christ in the Storm on the Sea of Galilee* Re-examined." *Fenway Court* (Isabella Stewart Gardner Museum):6–19.
van de Wetering, E. 1995. "Rembrandt's *Satire on Art Criticism* Reconsidered." In *Shop Talk: Studies in Honor of Seymour Slive*, ed. C. P. Schneider et al., 264–70. Cambridge, Massachusetts.
———. 1997. *Rembrandt: The Painter at Work*. Amsterdam.
———, et al. 2005. *A Corpus of Rembrandt's Paintings*. Vol. 4, *The Self-portraits*. Dordrecht.
White, C. 1968. "Rembrandt's Etching and Drawing of a Cottage with a White Paling." *The Burlington Magazine* 110:390–94.
———. 1975. "A Rembrandt Copy of a Titian Landscape." *Master Drawings* 13:375–79.
———. 1999. *Rembrandt as an Etcher: A Study of the Artist at Work*. 2nd edn. New Haven and London.
———, and K. G. Boon. 1969. *Rembrandt's Etchings: An Illustrated Catalogue*. 2 vols. Amsterdam, London, and New York.
Williams, J. L., et al. 2001. *Rembrandt's Women*. Exh. cat., National Gallery of Scotland, Edinburgh—Royal Academy of Arts, London. Edinburgh.
de Winkel, M. 2001. "Fashion or Fancy? Some Interpretations of the Dress of Rembrandt's Women Re-evaluated." In Williams et al. 2001, 55–63.
———. 2006. *Fashion and Fancy: Dress and Meaning in Rembrandt's Paintings*. Amsterdam.

INDEX OF COLLECTIONS OF ILLUSTRATED REMBRANDT DRAWINGS

CONCORDANCES

Concordance of figure numbers of Rembrandt drawings illustrated in the present volume with the catalogue numbers in Benesch 1954–57 and the enlarged edition of 1973.

NB: — = not in Benesch

Slive fig. no.	Benesch cat. no.
1.1	53
1.2	54
1.4	57
1.5	—
1.7	432
1.9	437 recto
1.11	1171
1.13	1177
2.1	440
2.2	360 recto
2.4	427
2.5	441
2.6	1184
2.7	56 recto
2.8	—
3.1	433
3.2	1178
3.3	1179
3.4	1180
3.7	1175
3.8	661
3.9	759
3.11	758
3.13	768
3.15	749 verso
3.16	767
3.18	762a
3.19	763
3.20	442
3.22	—
3.23	1181
4.2	219
4.3	340
4.4	341 recto
4.5	336
4.6	140
4.7	218
4.8	152
4.9	1005
5.1	7
5.3	12
5.5	20
5.8	87
5.9	295
5.10	1069
6.1	289
6.2	249
6.3	396
6.4	395
6.5	250
6.6	1099
6.7	1101
6.8	314
6.9	315
6.10	1103
6.11	1105
6.12	1106
7.1	246 recto
7.2	426
7.3	255
7.4	283
7.5	259
7.6	280a
7.7	421
7.8	706
7.9	313
7.10	401
7.11	1140
8.1	409
8.2	416
8.3	263
8.4	469
8.6	100 verso
8.7	529
8.9	400
8.10	659
8.11	736
8.12	1172
9.4	21
9.7	137
9.8	376 recto
9.9	423 recto
9.11	1161
9.12	1142
9.13	1122
10.1	457
10.2	775
10.3	1214
10.4	456
10.6	455
10.8	777
11.1	815
11.2	800
11.3	806
11.4	817
11.6	C 41
11.8	1333
11.9	—
11.10	1259
11.11	1239
11.12	1268
11.13	1265
11.14	1266
11.15	—
11.16	1232
11.17	845
11.18	1267
11.19	1351
12.1	341 verso
12.2	466 recto
12.3	796
12.4	462
12.5	826
12.6	1275
12.7	1278
12.8	1270
12.10	1309
12.12	1334
13.1	448
13.3	770
13.5	1207
13.7	1186
13.9	443
13.11	444
13.12	445
13.14	451
13.16	—
13.17	1190
13.18	1197
14.1	116
14.4	1210
14.6	521
14.7	540
14.8	92
14.11	961
14.12	913
14.14	1061
15.1	567
15.3	569
15.4	570
15.5	886
15.7	163
15.9	164
15.12	183
15.13	388
15.14	184
15.15	188
15.16	185
15.18	95
15.19	99
15.20	547
15.21	931
15.22	988
15.24	1047
15.27	1057
16.1	A 35a
16.4	468
16.5	969
16.7	756
16.8	728

Concordance of catalogue numbers in Benesch 1954–57 and the enlarged edition of 1973 with the figure numbers of Rembrandt drawings illustrated in the present volume.

Benesch cat. no.	Slive fig. no.
7	5.1
12	5.3
20	5.5
21	9.4
53	1.1
54	1.2
56 recto	2.7
57	1.4
87	5.8
92	14.8
95	15.18
99	15.19
100 verso	8.6
116	14.1
137	9.7
140	4.6
152	4.8
163	15.7
164	15.9
183	15.12
184	15.14
185	15.16
188	15.15
218	4.7
219	4.2
246 recto	7.1
249	6.2
250	6.5
255	7.3
259	7.5
263	8.3
280a	7.6
283	7.4
289	6.1
295	5.9
313	7.9
314	6.8
315	6.9
336	4.5
340	4.3
341 recto	4.4
341 verso	12.1
360 recto	2.2
376 recto	9.8
388	15.13
395	6.4
396	6.3
400	8.9
401	7.10
409	8.1
416	8.2
421	7.7
423 recto	9.9
426	7.2
427	2.4
432	1.7
433	3.1
437 recto	1.9
440	2.1
441	2.5
442	3.20
443	13.9
444	13.11
445	13.12
448	13.1
451	13.14
455	10.6
456	10.4
457	10.1
462	12.4
466 recto	12.2
468	16.4
469	8.4
521	14.6
529	8.7
540	14.7
547	15.20
567	15.1
569	15.3
570	15.4
659	8.10
661	3.8
706	7.8
728	16.8
736	8.11
749 verso	3.15
756	16.7
758	3.11
759	3.9
762a	3.18
763	3.19
767	3.16
768	3.13
770	13.3
775	10.2
777	10.8
796	12.3
800	11.2
806	11.3
815	11.1
817	11.4
826	12.5
845	11.17
886	15.5
913	14.12
931	15.21
961	14.11
969	16.5
988	15.22
1005	4.9
1047	15.24
1057	15.27
1061	14.14
1069	5.10
1099	6.6
1101	6.7
1103	6.10
1105	6.11
1106	6.12
1122	9.13
1140	7.11
1142	9.12
1161	9.11
1171	1.11
1172	8.12
1175	3.7
1177	1.13
1178	3.2
1179	3.3
1180	3.4
1181	3.23
1184	2.6
1186	13.7
1190	13.17
1197	13.18
1207	13.5
1210	14.4
1214	10.3
1232	11.16
1239	11.11
1259	11.10
1265	11.13
1266	11.14
1267	11.18
1268	11.12
1270	12.8
1275	12.6
1278	12.7
1309	12.10
1333	11.8
1334	12.12
1351	11.19
C 41	11.6
A 35a	16.1

INDEX

Note: Page references in **boldface** indicate illustrations and captions.